Cry For My Revolution, Iran

Cry For My Revolution, IRAN

MANOUCHER PARVIN

انتشارات مزدا
mazdā publishers

Library of Congress Catalog Card No.: 87-60041
ISBN: 0-939214-43-1

Set in Garamond by American Printing Center, Lexington, Kentucky 40508

Manufactured in the United States of America

Acknowledgments

This is a historical novel—a novel of fact. The improbable or incredible events recounted are invariably *factual* or else poetically *true.* The characters and the plot are fiction, but historical events and political figures are all real. The unknown men and women of the novel form the connecting links between the historical events, between stability and revolution—like agitated atoms that in a chain reaction create a nuclear explosion. This novel is dedicated to the unknown revolutionary who shouted in front of the firing squad, "I will come back, Iran." Until a memorial is constructed to honor the many unknown revolutionaries, these words could perhaps serve as a monument to their altruism.

Scores of friends and colleagues, some of whom I know to be ideologically antagonists, have been of longstanding help to me. Through them, I have become the recipient of underground publications and in effect an eyewitness to some events that had escaped my own eyes. Moreover, I have been offered religious, historical, psychological, and political counterpoints outside my own imagination. Virtually all of this and other forms of assistance have been rendered to me free—a labor of love for art, truth and justice. My memory has lost track of many who have helped me over the years, and a good number whom I do remember have preferred to remain unmentioned. So the following names given alphabetically are only a part of the whole team, like the novel itself which had to be reduced from nearly three times its final size. The first group is made up of individuals who were involved in the whole novel and the second group those who helped with certain parts or aspects.

My thanks to Ms. Christy Berndt for typing, editing, Xeroxing, and dealing with the word processor; Dr. Susan Chester for reading and literary criticism; Dr. Fleur Eshghi for helpful comments and critical analysis of Iranian women characters; Mr. Richard Fioravanti for typing, editing, and research of preliminary drafts; Dr. Reza Ghorashi for providing important, rare research materials; Professor Sheldon Liss for his constructive and creative suggestions related to historicity; Mrs. Madeline Parvin for her literary critique of the novel; my son, Ruzbeh Parvin, for some typing (while complaining of my illegible handwriting), and proofreading; Mrs. Becky Tompkins for creative editorial assistance and technical advice for the final draft.

Special thanks to the following for their specific assistance: Dr. Ahmad Ashraf, Professor Hans Bloomstein, Professor David Buchthal, Mrs. Linda

Case, Professor Mansur Farhang, Professor Emil Grunberg, Professor Ali Hajjafar, Professor Leo Hamalian (Editor of *Ararat*), Professor Marianne Hill, Professor Charles Issawi, Dr. Hassan Javadi, Professor Haider Ali Khan, Mrs. Taviishi Malhotra, Dr. Bizhan M. Nia, Mrs. Nahid Rachline (Author), Ms. Lynne C. Reinner (Editor), Professor Phillip H. Schmidt, Mrs. Susan Schmidt, Ms. Maurie Sommer, Dr. Beverly Wheeler.

None of these generous persons are in any way responsible for what is said or left unsaid or done in this work of fiction. In fact the only responsible party is history itself, which *we have* made collectively and which has prompted this work. So this book is merely a reflection of history of *my* consciousness—*my* version of events and *my* interpretation of the causes of a historical tragedy. If you note that some of the fictional characters correspond to actual persons you have known, you must know that it is a coincidence, even though an unavoidable one.

This book could have been written in Persian, the author's mother tongue. But it is not, because, among other motives, the author wished to show the ordinary American citizen how his taxes and unquestioning support of U.S. foreign policy can inflict devastating damage on victims whom he will never know. And to show the living victims who the responsible overseas culprits are, and how the U.S. citizens manage to tolerate injustice by distancing themselves from the victims of their government.

If in our technological and atomistic society the words love, justice, truth, and freedom still have operational significance, then this novel is written to celebrate their potential force in the salvation of man.

—M.P.
Bath, Ohio
Fall 1986

Contents

Cry For My Revolution, Iran

CHAPTER 1

Beginnings

In the beginning the world was full of beginnings. The sun ejected a ball of fire, the earth, into icy space. A hundred thousand years of continuous torrential rain flooded the young planet. Later on, animals and plants new and diverse emerged to cover the land. There was no history yet; no man, no cannibal, no slaveowner, no feudal landlord, no capitalist, no commissar fought over possessions, and no adjectives distinguished beauty from ugliness. Yet things were cooking, only without a cook or anyone to ask the obvious: What is cooking? Giant leafy trees, dinosaurs and wild vegetation sank into the earth and were squeezed and boiled until a jet black viscous syrup—petroleum—flowed underground.

Not until eons later did man evolve, but he quickly got busy and made machines that drank the petroleum from underground.

More time lingered under the clouds until, at the beginning of the twentieth century, a Mr. D'Arcy, a big golddigger in Australia, discovered petroleum around the shores of the Persian Gulf. Then on a fateful afternoon a Shah—of a dying dynasty—high on opium and wine, his left hand fondling the bosom of a concubine, hastened to sign with his idle hand a famous treaty giving away nearly a whole country's petroleum for just pennies.

To no one's surprise, the British bought the lease and proceeded to build the largest refinery in creation to siphon oil and energize the ships and all the motor vehicles they could make to run the British Empire. So it was nature's cooking, wine, bosoms and greed which were the ultimate causes of so much grief.

* * * * *

Professor Pirooz stopped musing as the subway screeched to a halt. The lights went out, the blackness of the tunnel invaded the cars, passengers cursed, and a woman screamed that she felt a hand on her crotch. Professor

1

Pirooz' thoughts abandoned him and ran to seek some light.

With the power restored, the train again hurtled beneath Manhattan, an island spinning and circling around a sun traveling inside the Milky Way, which took everything into the infinite unknown. Pirooz clenched the strap tightly for balance while the thought of going in so many directions made him dizzy. He wondered: If the Big Bang thrusts everything outward, like fireworks searing the sky, where did all this crisscrossing come from? How could anyone ever know where he is being taken at any one time?

The conductor's garbled words through the loudspeaker answered Pirooz' question. "One Hundred and Twenty-fifth Street, Harlem Station."

"Son of a bitch. I missed my stop."

The train, emerging from the tunnel, gradually climbed upward, stopping at the elevated platform high above the ground. The sun shone through the windows where the Professor had expected the sooty vaults of his own underground station. Though these misses were the rule of his life, he could not get used to them or overcome them.

The young professor stepped onto the platform, rubbed his eyes and scanned the trucks, buses and taxis scurrying around beneath him. As he descended to the street the staircase shook violently as if struck by a cannonball—a downtown train was arriving and the other was rumbling off to the Bronx. The world appeared a trifle steadier at ground level, but that, he knew, was only an illusion. The hardest pavement and the most solid building were composed of minute particles dancing furiously as though celebrating their existence in a spectacular party that would never end. Pirooz concentrated and imagined seeing the movement and hearing the cosmic music that compels the dance.

A beggar appeared before him, unshaven and with soot on his face, holding a bottle. Pirooz then saw a bag lady with a torn dress, feeding from a garbage can and rambling on to herself. "She was one of the thousands in New York City streets—the largest psychiatric open ward in the Universe," Pirooz thought. Close by, he winced, as a big boy beat up a smaller one. Crowds streamed indifferently in every direction. He sighed at the unhappiness around him and asked himself, "How can I help?" Pirooz was involved in various causes, but his frustrations had led him to conclude, "Nothing endures change except for human misery."

The Professor's thoughts turned to his unwritten book, which he would entitle Undelivered Lectures. In it he would express all the ideas that convention and self-preservation had required him to stifle. Nothing was yet on paper, but for months he had rewritten the introduction many times in his mind, and he did so again.

"My destiny is to profess at all costs, no matter what, when or how," he began his apologia. "With some patience, you, dear reader, will learn that professing was never just a job, but my true calling. For this belief I am in a minority and thus in trouble. I am a problem for the world and the world is a problem for me.

"I am from an old country, with all the afflictions and confusions of old folks trying to be born again. True, I have made plans, but I have learned that plans once born have their own minds. So I am a fatalist with an explanation. Man may create ideas, inventions, children, friends, businesses, governments, resolutions and revolutions, but he cannot control them. I make no claim to being the first to discover this principle. God must have noticed, just as He let the universe out of his fingertips, that it isn't easy to control His own creations. So He made heaven and hell to try to control man." Pirooz mumbled, "In the same way, a revolution may be pulled off but probably no one can control the darned thing. I wish, I just wish, that Ali knew this."

With that the Professor's thoughts froze in his mind. Last night's dishes had to be washed, nearly forgotten letters had to be answered, papers piled on his desk had to be graded, and the dead stereo had to be repaired. He hated details and chores, but he was condemned to face them every day. Pirooz fled from them all to continue composing his book.

"Oil is the original culprit. Remember! The British exploited the oilfields of Iran for half a century. Finally, early in the 1950's, Prime Minister Mossadegh said enough is enough, and nationalized the Anglo-Iranian Oil Company. The British and Americans, apprehensive that Mossadegh might set an example, attempted to overthrow him with an international boycott of Iran's oil. The nationalized oil is stolen property, the leaders of the Free World reasoned.

"But the people loved Mossadegh and he loved the people. Before the roof fell in, Mossadegh tried hard; he pledged that the British would be compensated fully. He won all his legal battles. Tears rolled down his face as he pleaded for understanding. He wept like a hurt boy in front of reporters, members of parliament, the International Court in the Hague, as he explained the injustice of British exploitation of the poor and the powerless of Iran. He cried all the way to the cover of *Time* Magazine as "Man of the Year." He even cried for President Eisenhower and Secretary of State John Foster Dulles, but to no avail. They had no sympathy for a weepy old prime minister. No one cared if even the whole nation cried. As they listened to him, they planned his downfall. In the interim, economic chaos ensued. The Shah, failing to force Mossadegh's resignation, fled the country. The British Navy roared close to the refinery, and the Iranian generals waited in the shadows for a coup.

"I was seventeen and green as spinach leaves when August 19, 1953, entered my life with a vengeance. On that day we marched through the streets of Teheran in support of Mossadegh, shouting, "Death to British

Imperialism.'' Never having witnessed dying, I did not know what "death" signified. I also did not know that "British Imperialism" was already dead; it was the U.S. variety we had to worry about. We shouted nonetheless. Arm in arm with my young friends, marching, chanting beneath banners proclaiming our just cause, we turned the corner toward Parliament Square. The shower of bullets that met us, piercing the space around us, shocked me out of my youthful dreams. Before my senses could recover, I was pulled to the ground by the falling weight of my two friends, whose arms were still linked to mine. Susan was dead instantly. Baback, his face ripped away like a mask, the blood soaking his body, lay in a pool of blood. Amid the dust and smoke, heads, arms, legs and bodies lay entangled, some smashed, some spurting bloody fountains, some dangling oddly. Blood ran into the gutters. The blast of bullets and the shrieks of marchers gave way to quivers and moans as the dying protested and the wounded tried to crawl away from the pain. The seconds lost momentum and dragged out the horror. My ear to the ground, I heard the sound of a thousand footsteps running, some hunting life, some fleeing death.

"Stunned, but otherwise unharmed, I lay in the street beside Baback. His faceless frame was seized by a horrid shudder; then he stopped dead like a tuning fork struck by fate and the vibrations ceased. I don't remember much else that day. For Baback and for thousands killed all over Iran, the suffering was over, but I would live with the hurting losses. The pain doesn't go away.

"The military coup, organized with the help of the CIA, crushed constitutional rule and put Mossadegh in jail, sent his foreign minister, Dr. Hussain Fatemi, to face a firing squad, and killed my beliefs in the efficacy of non-violent political action.

"Imperialism and murder were linked in my thoughts forever. Forgive me for being simple. Remember that I was only seventeen, trying to convince the British and Americans that Iran's oil belonged to Iranians, that others should keep their hands off. That was August 19, 1953. The civilian population was soon brought under control, thanks to American advice, technical help and weapons, as the Shah was to proclaim later, and thanks to direct CIA intervention, as it came to be known. The whole country was taken hostage, the protesters locked away in prisons, or banished, or killed. The gasoline, and the sweat and blood of Iranian oil workers, began to flow into the ever thirstier gullets of bigger and bigger cars that streaked the highways of the Western world. Consumers saw the dollars and gallons ringing up at the gas pump, but nothing else.

"In a few months that same oil propelled a noisy SAS aircraft, with me as a passenger, high above the clouds to the United States." Pirooz smiled as he remembered his grandmother's urgent words at the airport: "Hold on fast to the plane, lad, so you won't fall out!"

"Thousands of miles, years, and hard work went by. I became Americanized, lost my courage, but kept my follishness." Here the Professor had to interrupt his mental book. He turned, retraced his steps for half a block, and entered a Columbia University-owned apartment building.

He marched through the faded lobby to the row of mailboxes. His hand, a faithful ally which could get things done without disturbing his mind, turned the key, reached in, felt the sides and back, then emerged and pushed the door shut. The box was empty; it was Sunday, although he didn't know it. It might have been Tuesday or Thursday or Saturday, days when he also had no classes. He stepped into the elevator.

The Argentine woman, Helena, smiled at him, her body slender and firm, her eyes brown, her black hair hanging soft and shining to her waist, no bra, her bronzed skin tormenting the Professor. She wore a pair of worn-out jeans, so light and so tight they were her skin colored blue. All was concealed beneath, true, but tempting details bulged. Months later his trembling fingers would find that she wore no panties beneath those crushing jeans. Animal magnetism—the idea popped into his head. She was the magnet; he was the animal. Softly he said, "Hello"; she gently responded with a big smile.

He steadied himself against the brass handrail as the old elevator tossed around its shaft, throwing Helena's breasts up and down, and then jerked to a halt in a chorus of mechanical clicks. When she bent to pick up her laundry basket, his eyes locked on her round buttocks struggling to explode out of her jeans. She left with a twinkle in her eyes as he was carried to his floor.

He bent down to pick up the *Times* at his door. He got the first two sections; the rest spilled on the floor—all the news that's fit to surprise. Not Saturday but Sunday, the day of the week signalled by a heavy pile of newsprint at his feet. He entered his apartment with Helena still wiggling in his head. He took off his coat, threw it on the couch, and walked straight to the kitchen. He grabbed a spoon and a napkin, picked through the icebox, took a container of yoghurt and an apple. As he snacked on the apple, his eyes lit on the disorderly pile of dirty dishes in the sink. He waved goodbye to them with his spoon, whispering, "Never on Sunday."

He stopped at the mirror on the closet door, which reflected a six-foot, thirty-two-year-old body with soft, light brown skin, elongated brown eyes seeming half closed, long black hair parted in the middle, and a moustache drooping over the lip, all looking a bit like Peter Sellers. The reflection looked fit, Pirooz thought. He swam, jogged, played tennis and racquetball or did calisthenics. "I coerce my body in order to get a few hours' peace of mind," he declared to friends.

"But would Helena like me?" the Professor asked his image, which remained silent as expected. If Pirooz could have heard through the walls and if he had known Spanish, he would have known that Helena at that moment was saying to her friend, "Damn it, I like Pirooz, the whole package—mind and looks. I'd like to know what is inside the man. I'm afraid I'll have to take the first step. After all, he's a professor and I'm a student."

Pirooz winked at his image in the mirror before walking away. He kicked off his shoes in the living room, turned on the stereo, sat on the carpet and leaned against the couch, pushing it back against the wall with a jerk.

He breathed more easily, secure in his own nest at last. The music of a Persian tar caressed his eardrums.

Who fixed the stereo? he wondered. By pushing the couch against the wall he had pushed the loose plug into the socket, but he was unaware of this. Though Pirooz knew some physics, still, to him gadgets were mysteries made of the stuff dug out of the earth. The dead stereo with the music of a tar was a miracle.

The energized electrons raced through the stereo, as the exotic Persian notes flew across the room, vibrated against the windows and caught up with the seagulls in flight over the Hudson River. The music also energized the electrons in the Professor's nervous system. Suddenly he became hopeful, wishful. If the stereo could repair itself, perhaps the dishes would wash themselves. Tomorrow they would greet him neatly stacked and spotless, like the ones in the TV dish detergent ad.

His eyes scanned the headlines. People alive yesterday were dead today in Vietnam. A few with names, faces, homes and families were Americans. Their pictures would flash on his TV. The rest had no name, no face; they were yellow and dispossessed, all of them identified by a single number— today the body count was 235—and the TV would show their corpses face down. Those with names dropped bombs on those who were numbers.

The Professor switched to another headline. "Columbia University Bans Demonstrations; Two Students Arrested." He searched the article anxiously for names. Ali Keshavarz, a cousin and student of his, was a rebel leader of the Students for a Democratic Society—SDS—but he had not been arrested. The students had risen in rebellion to demand a voice in the University's governance. They threatened to strike, to shut down the school by force, and the administration countered with threats of expulsion and arrest. These were not rebels without a cause; they were just part of a cause without a chance, the Professor thought. He dipped into the yoghurt and bit on the apple. He was hungry. Injustices he could do nothing about made him nervous.

He continued to read, jotting down fragments of thoughts on a legal pad as he felt relaxed with the sound of the tar. He didn't budge when the phone rang; he was secretly striking against its authority. His friends would forgive him if they knew how he felt. Pirooz did not know that Helena was calling to ask for some sugar. The Professor would have given her all the sugar plantations in Hawaii if they belonged to him.

The other day he had seen Helena on the steps in front of Low Library, the sun's rays warming her as she gazed at the fountain. He wanted to rush to her, to kneel and hold her lovely hands, to tell her that she had become a fixed picture in his head, a flowing wine in his heart. He wanted to tell her that he had been told of her tribulations, of her father's disappearance in Argentina. He wanted to tell her that he knew she had fled for her life from the secret police. He wanted to tell her that he understood, that he fought for the same cause.

Tenderness streamed into his heart. He wished to prepare a pistachio-carrot rice dish for her, to take her to a Spanish guitar concert, to sit with her in front of a fireplace, to stroke her hair, to listen to her, to know her.

Then something hot rushed through Pirooz' mind and wrung his heart. He wanted to tell her more, something not easy to say. He wanted to tell her, "I die for your lips, and the smile that curves them; I die for your long neck and the soft, solid shoulders that support it; I die for your touch; Helena, I die for one hug."

The Professor got up and nervously circled the coffee table, like a horse turning a millstone. "What do you want, you confused dreamer, her politics or her body, and what about her as a person? I want everything about her, but I can only love a woman in revolt. What love?" he paused to reflect. "I haven't even talked to her yet. But maybe, ... who knows?"

Time went by, and another day was gone. Several hours later he lay in bed and thought. The world and I don't get along. Who is going to change? He drew the sheet over his head, hiding a level deeper from the real world. Pirooz smiled and asked once more the question of many other nights, the question of all time: "How have you, Sir, contributed to the mess in this world? Professor Pirooz, tell me your tale."

CHAPTER 2

Rebellion and Violence

On a beautiful morning, Ali Keshavarz sat behind Sara Patrick in Professor Pirooz' class at Columbia. Ali tried to concentrate, but instead stared at her hair and watched the glistening light dancing down the golden waves. He wanted to touch the hair, the light, the head, her neck. They were friends, but now Ali felt more and wanted more.

As the Professor's voice grew louder, Ali became more attentive.

"It is simple enough. Marketworthiness summarizes a great deal of American life today. Unconsciously and gradually Americans have internalized the creed of the salesman. Most people are busy improving their market price by embellishing their faces, words, clothing, homes—exterior."

"Education has become a quest for career skills, and scholarship is pursued for tenure and promotion. 'Decency' is projecting a good image; friendship has become winning people over, while compassion is formalized into giving unwanted things to the Salvation Army. Beauty is make-believe cosmetics, love is the number of orgasms"—nervous laughter from the students—"politics is public relations and effective media blitz, and religion is a silk dress and a colorful hat on Sundays. Money measures happiness. The market sets all prices; ethics is given a low price. The slogan is 'Nice guys finish last,' and no one will say otherwise."

Ali raised his hand. "Professor Pirooz, how does the student revolt on campus fit 'marketworthiness'?"

"The students are fighting the university authorities who are prodding and training them to become marketworthy, or worthy to serve the state which protects business interests. Business and government are Siamese twins. The radicals are crying 'No' to this demeaning fate."

"What is so demeaning about working for government or business?" a student inquired.

"In many situations it entails compromising one's humanity for profit or power."

8

Another student asked, "What other options does the individual have?"

Pirooz thought for a moment. "You really want to know?"

"Yes," the student replied.

"Well," Pirooz continued, "you can go along with the scheme and maybe become wealthy, powerful—"

Ali interrupted the Professor. "and corrupt."

Pirooz looked sharply at his cousin and continued, "or fight against the system and be crushed. There are few successful revolutionaries alive. The third option is to deny the luxuries that submission brings and avoid the pains that disobedience causes, by neither fighting against nor cooperating with the system, by going along a little, kicking a little, and just trying to survive." Pirooz knew that was what he was doing himself.

Pirooz left the classroom immediately after the lecture to have lunch alone. The world around him was in turmoil, and the faculty dining room was filled with arguments. Some supported the radicals cautiously, and some sided with the administration, but with qualifications. Pirooz was a revolutionary at heart, but not in practice. He would avoid violence at all costs.

Ali and Sara left Pirooz' class together. Sara asked, "Are you ready for the debate?" Her two friends, Ali Keshavarz and Eric Saunders, were to debate the student uprising on the radio program she hosted.

"I think so." He then demanded, "Whose side are you on, Sara?"

"I'm a reporter; I stay neutral."

"No one is ever neutral," Ali retorted.

"This reporter tries to be." Ali shook his head and let the matter go. He changed his tone. "Can I take you to dinner?" A few days ago, after Sara had typed his paper to meet a deadline, Ali had discovered that Sara was no longer serious about Eric. Eric had wanted a commitment from her but she wasn't ready.

Sara took a long look at Ali. Ali was tall, with broad shoulders, his fair skin contrasting with fierce brown eyes and curly black hair. He wore a white shirt and blue jeans. She was attracted to his forthrightness and the intensity flaring within him, like standing close to a torch in winter. Her eyes flirted with his, but she said, "Thanks, but I have a paper to finish. How about next week, okay?"

"Yes," Ali said. "Don't forget the SDS rally today."

"Of course not; I'm covering it." Then she turned and glided down the steps; her hair blew with the wind as she disappeared into the crowd.

Sara knew she was attractive. The eyes of strangers had followed her all her life. Pirooz had remarked to Ali, "God must have consulted Raphael on her proportions." Her deep blue eyes, her blonde hair, loose and easy with a touch of natural curl, her lips full, her brightness and the halo of confidence surrounding her—all brought joy to Ali.

Sara could play the guitar sensitively, ski downhill without fear, and ride a sailboat like a swan. She knew the right things to say, carried a smile wherever she went, and danced with charm. She was even-tempered and sensitive to the needs of others, and she avoided confrontations.

Her father was an executive in a Baltimore shipping company. It was her mother's plan to make her another Jacqueline Kennedy, but Sara was more than just another product of an expensive upbringing. She had already disappointed them by not going to Smith, her mother's alma mater. Sara had long ago stopped confiding in her parents, her values had diverged from theirs; to her they were as unbending as 500-year-old redwoods.

A lonely flame flickered deep inside her, urging her toward the unknown, but too many options made it difficult for Sara to choose. For one thing the potential conflict between a career and a family bothered her. She had majored in journalism at Barnard College and worked for the campus newspaper and radio station. She swore by reporters' neutrality, but she didn't want to reflect the world just like a mirror. Instead she took sides, as Ali advocated, but ever so cautiously.

Ali inflamed Sara's doubts every time they met. He was a threat to her beliefs, to her roots. Sara wanted to improve the world by reporting its faults and making people face them. Ali wanted to improve the world by turning it upside down.

After leaving Sara, Ali crossed the campus deep in thought. He passed Butler Library, whose bronze doors and massive rows of grey columns concealed mountains of ideas within; he pushed through a crowd of students—radicals and conservative hecklers—surrounding the Sundial, a campus landmark and the site of increasingly militant SDS rallies.

Born in Teheran, Ali had been brought up to be a scholar like his father, the theologian, Mehdi Keshavarz. He began studying Arabic at five years of age in order to read the Holy Koran, and English at seven to learn modern science. In a few years he took advanced English courses at the Iran-American Society, which the U.S. government funded. (Years later he would blow up the building's entrance to protest U.S. support for the Shah.) Ali's high school English teacher had been an Iranian trained at Oxford, so Ali had a slight British accent. Using his training in logic and science, he always tried to get to the heart of questions.

Ali loved and admired his elder brother, Abbas. It was Abbas who had taught him chess and soccer, had taken him to the movies, had read him poetry, had bought novels for him, and had talked to him about history and politics. On Ali's thirteenth birthday, Abbas had handed him the illegal and banned Communist Manifesto, while quoting the famous words of Marx, "Workers of the world, unite. You have nothing to lose but your chains." Ali hid it from his parents, concerned that it would upset them.

Just a year later, in June, 1963, Abbas was shot dead in a peaceful rally against the Shah. Hundreds of dead and injured lay beside Ali's brother. Ali never saw Abbas's corpse, just his suit with bloody holes in it, and whenever he remembered his brother, he imagined those bloody holes in the suit. From that day, the world would never be the same for him as his ideas crystallized into a commitment to socialist revolution. He had a temper when it came to politics, which he fought unsuccessfully. "Use your temper, don't let it use you," Pirooz had advised him.

His father and his first cousin, Pirooz, then conspired to encourage Ali to go to the U.S. to save him from his own expressed wish to join the underground, and from dangerous street demonstrations against the Shah. Pirooz had written him, "The revolution needs scientists, too! Even though the U.S. supports the Shah, you should know how it is done and how the U.S. operates."

Ali's mother, Fatema, was a traditional Muslim, full of love and caring for all the things around her, especially the poor and innocent. Ali had inherited his mother's compassion, his father's scholarly attitude, and his brother's political commitment, but the intellectual arrogance and revolutionary single-mindedness were all his own.

Ali read voraciously and listened to Shostakovich, Brahms and other western composers. He played for the school chess and soccer teams. Losing made him depressed. When Ali had confided in Pirooz, "I can't grow out of this problem," Pirooz had replied, "Why should you? What's wrong with a healthy depression after a loss?" Ali would talk politics with anyone who would listen. He was foolishly, impeccably honest. The Professor wrote in his diary, "Ali knows what he wants, but not how to get it." Ali was awkward at dancing and smalltalk. He found them useless, irrelevant, bourgeois. After a glass of beer at Pirooz' party, Ali had teased, "Until the world socialist revolution, parties cannot be that much fun!"

Ali was tempestuous, Sara calm, Ali an advocate, Sara a reporter, Ali ideological, Sara practical, Ali an energetic speaker, Sara a patient listener. Sara had the means but was uncertain about conflicting goals, while Ali's goals were crystal clear but his means were not at hand. It was impossible for Ali not to be drawn to her. All that intelligence, beauty and kindness just in her blue eyes. For Sara, Ali was tempting, so different from other young men she had met before.

Eric Saunders, one of those young men, looked out of the window of Professor Wharton's office at the traffic jam on Amsterdam Avenue. Cars blocked each other like people's goals at cross-purposes. Eric had just left the hecklers at the Sundial for an appointment which Professor Wharton had arranged that morning.

Eric, a bit taller than average, with hazel eyes and reddish blond hair cut neatly, wore a grey pin-stripe suit, white oxford shirt and red striped tie.

He had made his way in life under his own steam, valedictorian in high school, a B.A. *summa cum laude* in political science, and now only a few months away from a law degree at Columbia. He was enchanted with the Middle East, the birthplace of civilization and great prophets. He took courses about the region with an eye on a career as an international lawyer with an oil company.

His mother, a college teacher, had pushed her child to succeed. His father sold cars on commission, but Eric called him a sales manager, and by repeating it over time Eric believed it himself. Eric read the *Wall Street Journal* regularly and watched *Mission Impossible* occasionally. He liked the economics of Milton Friedman, the politics of Henry Kissinger.

Eric was a good Catholic and had a strong sense of civic duty. He had gone through the ranks of the Boy Scouts. He kept his promises and was never late for an appointment.

But Eric could not solve an annoying problem. His confessions and the priest's absolution could not cure him of claiming a close point if he had to win on the tennis court, or bending the truth on rare occasions off the court. His desire to win, to get ahead, to be in a position to do good sometime in the future, demanded uncomfortable compromises. How could anyone be perfect in an imperfect world? Eric would ask himself. To soothe his conscience, Eric sometimes doodled, "Nobody is perfect," and then underlined it several times. Nevertheless, every New Year, he would resolve to free himself of this nagging problem. Once the parish priest told him the saints had to struggle for a long time to rid themselves of temptation, a fact that assuaged Eric's troubled conscience. He was anxious to finish law school so he could get on with his career and life away from school.

Eric loved Sara for the obvious reasons, but also because she was so sympathetic to everyone and yet so steadfast with her women's lib views. She was a real Catholic even though she didn't attend Mass. Eric wished to have Sara for a wife, but Sara would not marry him at this time, since her studies, news reporting and feminist politics demanded her full attention. So the two agreed to be just friends and decide later if there was more to the relationship. Eric knew pressure would only drive Sara further away. He could not tell her how much he loved her, not yet.

But Eric felt jealous. He had seen Sara and Ali together on campus quite a few times, engrossed in conversation. And he had not liked seeing them giggling as Sara had tried to show Ali a new dance at Pirooz' party. Eric missed what he had with Sara, but he bore the pricking inside patiently. He was sure Sara would become disenchanted with Ali eventually. Sara was impressed with how maturely Eric had accepted the change in their relationship. It was Eric's nature to accept the world for what it could offer him or what he could achieve in it. He knew what he wanted and knew how to get it, Pirooz had commented.

As a leader of the Young Republicans and a Nixon campaigner, Eric found it natural to defend the conservative cause on the campus. It was for this reason that Professor Wharton wanted to meet with him today.

Head of the Institute for Defense Analysis, Professor Wharton controlled military research and development funding at Columbia. The staff of the Institute performed political risk analysis to predict revolutions for the CIA and for multinational corporations. Wharton also recruited promising graduate students for the CIA. Eric had studied with Wharton.

After a bit of small talk, Wharton came to the point. "Will you accept a couple of assignments which will help the Institute and save this great university?"

"Why, yes," Eric replied enthusiastically. This could be the break Eric had hoped for. Wharton knew government officials, international bankers, oil executives and star academics; he was a frequent consultant to the highest levels of government.

"Good," Wharton said. "Radicals may invade the Institute offices, so we are forced to protect our classified documents. I know you are an amateur photographer. We need clear photographs of troublemakers so campus security can identify them before they strike our offices. This must be secret, so I will give you credentials as a photographer for the alumni magazine. Will you do it?"

"Of course, Professor Wharton," Eric said. Before he left, Eric reminded Wharton that he had mentioned a couple of tasks.

"You're right," Wharton said. "Can you also organize conservative students to oppose the radicals? Call it the Majority Coalition. Set up an office, plan rallies and arrange press conferences, expose the troublemakers. No one should think communists have mass support. Also, with the help of a lawyer, prepare a suit against SDS if they disrupt classes. Don't worry about funds; I'll make arrangements for private contributions. It goes without saying that our conversation is confidential."

Eric said, "I understand, Professor Wharton." The two worked out the details as Eric, full of expectations about Wharton's confidence in him, listened and took notes.

Eric would have rejoiced even more if he had known that Professor Wharton had already mentioned his name to the Central Intelligence Agency as a possible recruit. Saunders could be a real asset to the Agency, Wharton thought. He may not possess the shrewdness to take him to the top, but with proper guidance he could be quite useful.

Wharton had his own silent crisis. Female students baring their bottoms on Broadway boosted Wharton's blood pressure. He deprecated the scene, yet he watched it with desire. The grapevine murmured that his own daughter at Barnard College had been mooning, too. The chaos and nudity mushrooming around him made Wharton wonder about the end of

Western civilization, and reminded him of his own failure as a father. He had had little time to be a father. His daughter should have been brought up with more discipline; the whole generation was undisciplined, he thought.

* * * * *

After his solitary lunch, Professor Pirooz strolled to the Sundial. Speakers representing the radicals and the reformist groups took turns. Issues appeared and disappeared. Pirooz heard words he knew in a thousand variations: ". . . the unjust and illegal war in Vietnam and racism at home must end . . . The school must stop being a slumlord in Manhattan and a recruiting ground for CIA agents . . . Students and faculty must participate in university governance. ..."

A couple of hundred students chanted, "Down with the Deans! Down with the ruling class! Down with Imperialism!' From other corners hecklers jeered at them, "Expel the commies! Throw them out!"

Thousands of students were drawn into school politics. But Pirooz found no program and no concerted action, only confusion and anger. He wondered if his students would recognize the connection between the political theories he taught and the actions they were now undertaking. But most students felt like the reporter Sara, who had confided to Pirooz that she disagreed both with Ali and the radicals, and with Eric and the anti-communists. Her political views were not yet a logical whole, like Ali's Marxism or Eric's conservatism. She did not have answers, as they did. Sara wanted some gradual, negotiated, peaceful reform.

Pirooz wanted to join the crowd, to help, to lead. But he stood by and watched, pulled back by pessimism and skepticism, by the odds against success, by the fear of violence. Pirooz had been a vegetarian since the age of five, when he had seen a lamb's head cut off on the Islamic Day of Sacrifices. Baback's face ripping away like a mask came back to him often. He had had his fill of violence. "Face it, Pirooz," he said to himself, "you're a bourgeois intellectual to Marxists and a closet Marxist to bourgeois intellectuals. You can't be much more without getting your hands dirty." A part of Pirooz wanted to get his hands dirty, to risk his job, freedom, or even life. Pirooz felt the ambivalence—the pest of the soul—and thought he was attacked, but not captured by it. He struggled against total submission, total paralysis.

After a week of fruitless discussions, a delegation of student leaders, including Ali, had begun to negotiate with the Dean in Hamilton Hall about school reform and reinstating their expelled comrades. Students at the Sundial across campus were awaiting the outcome before going on strike.

A radical leader announced, "The negotiations are about to end. I say let's go to the site of the action. On to Hamilton Hall!''

Sara, carrying her recording equipment, followed the marchers. The Professor followed, too. Demonstrations were banned. The march was illegal—a challenge.

Eric caught up with Sara in front of Hamilton Hall and kissed her on the cheek. Sara stood impassively. At one time Eric had fit Sara's plans. He had many good attributes and a splendid career ahead of him. She knew Eric wanted her, but there was no fire between them. Her smouldering now was for Ali.

"Don't we make a good team of newshounds?" Eric said to please her. Sara noticed his camera equipment, but Eric said nothing about Professor Wharton.

"Are you ready for the debate?" Sara asked.

"I'll survive it." Eric replied as he took pictures of students outside Hamilton Hall. He took the Professor's picture, too. Eric did not know what to think of Pirooz, who sounded sympathetic to socialism while enjoying the fruits of capitalism. To Eric, Pirooz seemed like a troublemaker, who actually caused no trouble. He was imaginative, witty and popular. Sara spoke highly of him. But like other idealists, Pirooz refused to see the world the way it was. Eric dismissed Pirooz from his mind and studied the marchers.

Most of the demonstrators were anxious to take over the school. Here were the Afro-American militants, the leftists in lumberjack shirts, Progressive Labor in white shirts and wingtips, hippies in army surplus, and anti-war liberals in casual sportswear, all waiting—some anxious, some just curious, some hoping for negotiations to fail. University security officers looked on.

Ali was first to emerge from the Dean's office. A flashbulb went off in his face. He recognized the photographer who had led hecklers the day before. Ali approached Eric, as everyone watched. "Why are you taking pictures?''

Eric calmly showed him his press badge. '

"We didn't issue your badge. Out!''

Eric hesitated. "Out, out,'' a couple of radical students shouted.

Eric resented being pushed from the building. He was legal and the demonstrators were illegal. But he didn't resist; he could not resist in any case. He had completed Wharton's assignment.

Ali led the negotiators out of the building and stood at the top of the steps in front of a couple of hundred students. One student shouted, "Ali, what happened in the Dean's office?''

Ali waved his hand. "Fellow students and comrades, the Dean has refused to act on our legitimate demands for university reform. I say we liberate Hamilton Hall!''

"Do it!" one student shouted, and the chant went up, "Do it! Shut the school down!" Ali motioned for silence. "Do it!" the chanting continued. Ali waited until the crowd settled down.

"Columbia University is run by trustees most of whom are corporate presidents. The school of business turns out executives of multinational companies that exploit the poor of the world; the law school produces corporate lawyers, who defend the exploiters, ROTC trains navy officers to be gunboat diplomats, and the university recruits agents for the CIA. Many leaders of poor countries receive training here to serve U.S. interests and not those of their own people. The Institute for Defense Analysis serves the U.S. government in research for chemical warfare. The Manhattan Project, which produced the first atom bomb, started in Pupin Hall right on this campus. This university is a partner of Imperialism; it is Imperialism.

"The portrait of President Eisenhower in Butler Library reminds us of his elevation from the Columbia presidency to the U.S. presidency. He ordered the CIA-inspired coup in Iran, enslaving an entire nation, and did the same in Guatemala in 1954. Both of these CIA actions resulted in thousands of innocent people being exiled, imprisoned, tortured and killed over the years." Ali paused, then he concluded, "Columbia should not be involved in any way in such exploitations.

"But the University has turned a deaf ear to our legitimate demands. So now we must deny its legitimacy and turn a deaf ear to its authority. We must shut down this University and create a school to serve the people, not the capitalists. As a start, we declare Hamilton a liberated Hall!"

Radical students poured into the building and occupied it. From then on, no teaching or research were permitted in Hamilton.

The rebels knew they would soon have to face the forces of law and order. So barricades went up and Ali joined comrades in gathering paper towels from the bathrooms and pouring water in wastebaskets, to neutralize an expected teargas assault.

Pirooz did not wait for the demonstration to become a siege. He left for his apartment deep in thought. He felt there were other ways to fight. Let the students do their thing; he would do his. The radicals did not know that nothing is liberated by occupying a few buildings for a few days. But more than that, he was fearful of what would become of his impetuous cousin, Ali, and his comrades.

Eric left the demonstration to call a press conference announcing the formation of the Majority Coalition opposing the uprising. He thought of students to telephone as he rushed home.

Sara raced to the radio studio to edit her tapes and write a newsfeed.

Ali was up all night in Hamilton Hall, thinking, talking, organizing, planning. By midnight the various revolutionary groups had been reinforced and reorganized. SDS wanted the reinstatement of the expelled comrades, while Blacks and foreign students demanded proportional enrollment of all races. Ali criticized their factionalism and asked, "Do you expect the administration to unite us and hand us a voice in university government?" Before dawn, Ali led the SDS faction from Hamilton Hall and seized Mathematics Hall. A coordinating committee was elected to preserve the appearance of unity.

* * * * *

Days went by. The rebels, buoyed by their initial success, liberated more buildings with each passing day, extending their control over the campus and bringing academic activities at Columbia to a standstill. Nothing quite like this had ever happened in the history of the United States.

Food was delivered to the young rebels, and revolutionaries took turns leaving for "time off," including going to the West End Bar.

Ensuing negotiations with university officials did not resolve the conflict. Meanwhile the administration and the city police plotted a "bust." Threats and counterthreats filled the city of New York. Ali reminded his comrades that talking does not make rulers change their minds or fade away.

* * * * *

The next Wednesday morning, the telephone's furious ringing drew the Professor out of bed and out of his bedroom.

"Hello," the Professor said before he remembered. My telephone strike! I am licked by this black gadget, damn it.

"Good morning." A woman's barely audible voice softened him. "This is Sara Patrick, Professor Pirooz. I called just to remind you that Ali will be on WKCR at ten to debate Eric about the revolution."

"A riot, not a revolution," the Professor corrected Sara. "And who's Eric?"

"Eric Saunders. He took your Middle East course last year."

"Oh, yes, him!"

Sara asked, "What do you think of an unstructured debate?"

"Just like a boxing match," the Professor replied. "Tell them that even boxing has rules. Thank you for the reminder."

The Professor hung up and went to the kitchen to start his espresso. He rushed back and turned on the radio.

The telephone rang again. Damn it! It's a conspiracy. He answered, "Who is it?"

A pause, and then "Is Mrs. Pirooz at home?"

"Why?"

"We're offering our spring family picture at a discount. An eight-by-ten color portrait for only—"

"Stop, lady. There is no Mrs. Pirooz. What right do you have to disturb me?"

"Then get an unlisted number, you alien," the voice said and slammed the phone. The slamming and the word "alien" echoed in his mind like the sound of a cannon trapped in a canyon.

Pirooz heard the espresso bubbling, so he raced back to the kitchen, where the fountain of the Italian gadget was spurting the last drops of coffee into the steel container. He filled a small cup with hot water to warm it up, then emptied it and poured in the espresso.

He carried a bag of garbage to the front door and exchanged it for the *New York Times,* going to sit in his usual spot against the couch, taking another sip of coffee. The coffee tasted awful. He knew why and hurried to the bathroom and brushed his teeth.

The telephone rang. The Professor rolled his eyes to the ceiling, then picked up the phone once more. "Yes?" His countenance lightened as he recognized the voice. "How are you, Ali?"

"Fine."

The Professor listened attentively. "Yes, the debate. Good luck, Ali. Give that capitalist agent a hard time."

"Agent?" Ali asked.

"They're all agents."

"I see, just the same as calling me a communist agent."

"Yes, that's it. I've seen him in and out of Wharton's office, and Wharton is up to no good." The Professor warned, "Ali, be careful."

"Don't worry, I'll take care of Saunders."

"Him, too, but I'm worried about a police 'bust' and bloodshed. Get out of their way. It doesn't necessarily help the revolution to get your head smashed."

"I will do my best. Goodbye."

"Goodbye."

A few minutes later, Pirooz heard the radio. "Good morning, this is Sara Patrick, the host of WKCR's public affairs program, 'Issues.'"

Pirooz listened intently, and soon Ali was finishing his opening remarks. "Along with the city housing authority and the Catholic Church, Columbia is one of the largest slumlords in New York. Poor and old tenants are thrown into the streets under the pretext of renovation. In addition, the University supports the war in Vietnam and the enslavement of non-whites by investing its endowment in South Africa.

"These actions defeat the real purpose of a university to create and disseminate knowledge which benefits man. Faculty, students and the community must return Columbia to its true mission."

The Professor nodded his approval as Sara introduced Eric.

Eric began, "First, we must find jobs for the poor but avoid handouts. Our humanity is not diminished by demanding that anyone able to should carry his own weight. Second, through diplomacy with our ally, the Republic of South Africa, we can influence them to modify apartheid. It has taken a long time for that problem to grow to such severity; it will take a long time to resolve it without infringing on anyone's rights."

Ali whispered loudly, "Just modify?"

"Yes, improve the condition of Blacks and make sure the country is safe from subversion. If South Africa falls into the wrong hands, the Soviets will have a virtual monopoly on chromium, a vital strategic metal for industry and the military. We must not undermine our national security and the stability of the Free World." Eric continued, "Third, the tragedy in Vietnam is deplorable, but responsibility lies solely with the communist aggressors. The US is responsible to our Southeast Asian allies, and we cannot shirk our responsibility by avoiding the extreme action forced on us.

"Finally, none of Mr. Keshavarz' accusations implies that Columbia University acted illegally. There is no legal basis for his complaint. I believe the issue is not alleged student grievances, but the illegal obstruction of teaching and research at Columbia. Mr. Keshavarz, you and your friends are destroying a great university, and you must suffer the legal consequences."

Ali exploded as soon as Eric finished. "Look at the evidence, Mr. Saunders! If everything is democratic and legal in the U.S., then why must millions struggle for civil rights? Why is a great percentage of prison inmates in the U.S. Black? I suggest that you use your legal expertise to make the University, the U.S. and the Free World just and democratic."

Cold anger boiled within Eric. "I prefer that my opponent refrain from personal advice. The forcible occupation of the campus is trespassing, pure and simple. It makes no difference if a Soviet army or their agents invade our campus—it is still breaking the law."

Ali interrupted. "You talk about laws, Mr. Saunders. Do your laws guarantee a job, minimum shelter, food, health care or dignity to citizens? Aren't these the most important of all needs?"

Irritated, Eric answered, "The United States is not a charity institution. Public and private agencies exist to relieve the burden of the poor. We have no law to seize property and redistribute earned wealth, as you suggest. For that kind of law you must look to the communists."

Ali quickly replied, "Good! So only communists have laws that guarantee jobs, shelter, food and health care?" When Eric said nothing for a moment, Ali continued, "I appreciate your silence."

Eric kept his composure. "Our laws provide fair and equal treatment for all people. Why do you think the United States is the mecca of immigrants, Mr. Keshavarz? You ought to know!"

Ali shot back, "Equal treatment? Is it equal treatment to let the Ku Klux Klan kill civil rights workers? Do rich and poor get the same justice?"

"Mr. Keshavarz, stop being an idealist,"Eric replied pedantically. "Laws cannot produce a perfect government, perfect business, perfect citizens or a perfect society. The radicals think they can create one, and look at what their idols have done in Russia and its satellites."

Ali insisted, "No faults of the Soviet Union can absolve the U.S. of its wrongdoings. For years, many white folks, local governments and also the U.S. tolerated lynchings. The fear of lynching has terrorized and silenced millions of exploited blacks for centuries. Is toleration of lynching in the past and oppression even today a necessary imperfection of the system? Is this the 'American Dream' for the black man? Mr. Saunders, compared to the European monarchs the Founding Fathers had a vision but quite a few of them were slaveowners, and it is said they wrote the Constitution to protect their property and their slaves. Read the Constitution! Unfortunately, the Bible like the Koran has not condemned slavery as a sin. I imagine at the time the Founding Fathers found an idealogical heaven in the Holy book!"

Eric replied angrily, "There is no slavery in America today; the issue was resolved long ago. In any event, the Holy Bible and history of the United States are not on trial here, and I need not respond to anti-American propaganda. Tell me, Mr. Keshavarz, do you mean this riot is by poor and oppressed Ivy League students?" Eric pressed on. "If you're for the poor, why don't you give your food and shelter to them?"

Ali replied, "Mr. Saunders, if I give my food away, I will become hungry myself. Exchanging hunger doesn't combat hunger, does it?" Ali lowered his voice. "Why do you reduce this debate to a personal attack, Mr. Saunders?"

Pirooz nodded his head at the radio in approval. Eric ignored Ali's tactic. "I believe it is my turn to ask you a couple of questions which I am sure are of public interest. If Columbia University is so dreadful and the United States so unjust, why did you come here all the way from Iran? Were you dragged here, Mr. Keshavarz?"

"It was worse than being dragged, in effect I was pushed here!" Ali shot back. "More than ten thousand U.S. military advisors, police and secret police instructors, and propaganda experts support the Shah's coercive rule. I could not live under such a regime or fight it. I came here to find out how to stop U.S. aggression and to study chemistry to make explosives!" As soon as Ali said it, he knew he had made a mistake; his anger had gotten the best of him.

Eric exclaimed triumphantly, "Chemistry for explosives! Terrorism!"

"Yes," Ali said, regaining his composure. "Chemistry is the same science used to make Agent Orange to destroy food and napalm bombs to burn people in Vietnam. Isn't that so, Mr. Saunders?"

Eric changed the subject and retorted. "This riot is illegal. I want to finish my studies. Do you understand?"

Ali shouted back, "Worry instead about the masses of illiterates and hungry in this world."

"I'm not responsible for their illiteracy or their hunger."

"You are—your country has a hand in it! The U.S. exploits Black people here and brown people in Latin America." Ali became angry. "Tell me, Mr. Saunders, who killed my brother, whose only crime was to shout 'Ballots, not bullets'? Was it the soldiers who shot him dead, the Shah who ordered the shooting, the CIA who installed the Shah and trained his army, or the U.S. who provided the arms? Remember the Nuremberg Trials, Mr. Saunders. You don't have to pull the trigger to be guilty of murder."

Eric's anger pushed him to express his pent-up feelings. "No amount of exaggeration and distortion can make the U.S. look like Nazi Germany. You should be extradited for breaking U.S. laws and attacking the Constitution!"

Sara interjected in vain, "Gentlemen, please—."

Ali raised his voice. "When the CIA agents who have broken the laws of my country are deported, Mr. Saunders, then I will gladly extradite myself from your country."

The Professor said aloud, "Children, children with large bones. Ali is an uncompromising idealist and Eric a heartless lawbook."

He heard the last words of the debate as he strode to the window and looked down ten floors to Riverside Drive and the park sloping to the highway and the Hudson River. The cars and sailboats looked like toys.

Pirooz stuck his head out the window, careful not to touch the sooty ledge. "Attention, everyone!" he shouted, certain that the dead fish riding atop the polluted water, the squirrels in flight on treetops, the stray dogs in the park and the toy-like people would not contradict him. "People of the world, listen to one another, listen patiently! You may understand each other. You may stop maiming bodies, personalities, humanity."

Pirooz paused and looked at the vendors, the volleyball players, the runners, the picnickers, the children in uniform, the beggars. He heard white noise, the black noise and the machine noise, a whole scale of different noises all mixed together and felt he had nothing else to say to the world, to the sounds, to himself.

Instead, he dreamed of something easy, something relaxing, a world restructured according to his wishes: weapons destroyed, violence ended, laws rendered more just, jails opened, creative work and play diffused to all and love blossoming in every heart. No debates, no undelivered lectures. No wars! Helena not leaving the elevator but holding his arm tightly, coming to his place for the wine, fruit and cheese on his coffee table.

The telephone interrupted him. It was Sara. "What did you think of the debate?''

"You mean the mud slinging."

Sara said, "I turned off the microphones before we got into trouble with the FCC. At the end Eric called Ali a communist, and Ali shouted as he left, 'I am mad and I will stay mad until all CIA agents are buried in one big grave of history."

"What did you expect, Sara?" said the Professor. "We have several kinds of rioting going on, and no one is listening to anyone else. The University is becoming like the real world. Anyway, you did your best. I'll see you."

"Goodbye, Professor."

Pirooz hung up without hearing Sara's last words. In the next brownout, Helena and I may get stuck in the elevator, he thought. He continued talking to himself. "God, why did you throw me this obsession?" The Professor had a habit of blaming God, who he believed did not exist and thus could not be offended.

* * * * *

A couple of hours after the debate, Ali joined Sara in the Hungarian pastry shop. They looked at each other, drank their coffee and kept silent. Shocked by Ali's having gotten carried away in the debate, Sara remembered an incident a few weeks ago.

A snowstorm had filled the world with white flakes. Sara and Ali were coming out of class and were about to cross Broadway. Traffic over the packed, slippery snow was bumper to bumper. Cars moved slowly and splashed slush as students rushed dangerously between them to reach the subway station in the middle of Broadway. Two huge female statues holding the symbols of the Arts and the Sciences guarded the entrance to College Walk and witnessed the busy activity.

A tiny old couple stood hopeless at the slushy curb, looking like two ants wanting to cross a river. Suddenly Ali bent and whispered something into the old woman's ear and then asked Sara to stop the traffic. Sara stepped into the street and raised her hand while Ali picked up the lady like a baby and dashed across Broadway. Passersby stopped and stared in disbelief. The halted cars did not blow their horns. Ali rushed back and helped the old man across too. The old lady then held Ali's neck, brought him close and kissed his cheek. Ali kissed her in return. Some students clapped, and the old lady flushed behind her wrinkles. Sara never forgot that scene.

A few months after the radio debate in the summer of 1968, when Sara rested in Ali's arm with nothing separating them but their skins, she teased him, contrasting the event on Broadway and the debate. "Tell me, Mr.

Obnoxious, how could you be so caring one minute and so rude the next?"
Ali kissed her and retaliated. "Well, Ms. Public Relations, I don't
know. My politics are what they ought to be, but they appear obnoxious to
you. I can't expose injustice with a smile. I wish words would not hurt."

But now in the coffee shop Ali and Sara remained as silent as the
wooden table between them. Sara had not seen this side of Ali exhibited in
the debate and did not know what to say. Ali was still boiling within. Finally
they chatted about the uprising. Sara knew criticism of Ali would not do any
good. Nevertheless she said, "You can't attack the U.S. Constitution, Ali,
and expect sympathy for your legitimate grievances." She became angry
when Ali wouldn't even consider her sharing or paying the bill.

Then just as they said goodbye, Ali held a strand of Sara's hair and
said, "May I?" He kissed it. Sara smiled as he continued, "I'm not sorry for
my intransigence in the debate, but I am sorry it happened on your show."

Sara asked, "Where are you heading?"

Ali answered, "I'm going to stay in the Mathematics building
tonight."

"Be careful," Sara admonished him. "There's talk of a police bust."

"Use your camera if there is a bust," Ali suggested.

"See you later, Ali." Sara turned onto 110th Street and headed toward
Broadway.

Sara's head was full of Ali as she walked to her apartment. Ali and Sara
were being pulled toward each other as the world around them was pulling
apart. His politics were too radical, yet she wanted to know more; his future
was uncertain, yet she was drawn to him. Fear and curiosity struggled in the
core of her interest in Ali. His sincerity was infectious, no doubt about it,
but his ideas were alien. Eric sounded more familiar, more reasonable.

Late that Wednesday night, Sara in bed thought about Ali sleeping in a
classroom. "But, is he wrong?" Sara asked herself once more as she
remembered Ali's words. "In the good and rich U.S.A., hunger must be
outlawed, homelessness must be outlawed, uncared-for ailments must be
outlawed, poverty must be outlawed, and no less capitalism must be outlawed." Sara admitted to herself, "I never thought about it that way. Is it
possible to have such laws? Is Ali crazy, a prophet or just an idealist?" Sara
wanted to be with Ali, to ask him a thousand questions, argue with him and
tell him that he was just another "male chauvinist pig" for not letting her
pay for her coffee. But Sara realized she could learn something from Ali and
Pirooz. The two Iranians were like windows to a different world: Ali a bright
pane through which one could see a new light and Pirooz a stained glass
diffusing the light to many colors. They induced Sara to question her own
comfortable values and beliefs.

Ali thought of Sara on his way back to his post at the Mathematics
building. She wants to report. A good start, a good intention. Maybe she

will soon report the reality behind the reports. She will learn.

* * * * *

Thursday came and was gone quickly, as tensions grew. The police spread onto the campus like weeds. Rumors of a possible police assault flowed from mouth to mouth, from building to building. The administrators were under pressure to use the police, but they hesitated. They were worried that casualties would hurt the school's image and ruin their own careers.

Newspapers and TV networks were filled with demands to clear the buildings. They favored the administration. What else could be expected? Ali pointed out. The capitalists have the media, the lawyers, and the Board of Trustees in their pockets.

People on campus wore armbands of different colors to distinguish their siding with different political groups. Surrounding Mathematics Hall and standing behind the police, the Majority Coalition, led by Eric Saunders, were wearing blue armbands and chanting, "Out, out, kick the communists out!" They cheered the police, they threw eggs which shattered against the windows, oozing yellow. Eric was alert to get away in case shooting broke out.

Eric envied the demonstrators even as he hated them. The rebels were full of vitality, he thought, but they were wrong, misguided and stupid, their courage wasted. Eric wistfully dismissed what he perceived as the rebels' adventurous appeal. He had a job, a future to build; he would continue to bask in Professor Wharton's approval. He had to lead the Majority Coalition, to rescue Columbia University from chaos, to rescue "America" on Morningside Heights.

He thought about Sara, but that was painful. Why wouldn't she accept his offer of marriage? A lot of women would fall over themselves, all over him. He had seen her often lately with that Ali Keshavarz. What did she find in Ali, a foreigner, just a junior, a communist, an outlaw?

"I know what to do," Eric smiled as an idea came to him. "I can help my country and myself. Why didn't I think of it before?" Eric suddenly felt great satisfaction.

The campus was in a state of siege. Pirooz and a number of colleagues wore white armbands. They had organized a group called the Concerned Faculty, hoping for a peaceful resolution of the conflict, and with arms linked they shielded the rebels in Mathematics Hall from the police. Pirooz wanted to support the rebels, but also he wished to be close to Ali. Pirooz was merely a rebel in theory, while Ali put his theory into practice, "standing up to the motherfuckers," as SDS put it. Pirooz was skeptical, but stayed put. He sensed police frustration turning to anger.

Ali meanwhile was inside Mathematics Hall, barricaded, worried, and fortified by an untested will. The besieged rebels wore red armbands, with vaseline smeared on their faces and cigarette filters stuck in their nostrils, prepared for teargas. Piles of furniture blocked the entrances—a token shield, Ali thought. He knew the cops could enter through underground passages and softly protected doors and unprotected windows. The resistance was merely symbolic; defeat was certain. Yet the students continued to fight for symbols, since ideological resistance was sure to make the nightly news, and awaken people to the state of liberty in the U.S.

Outside, Sara was wearing no armband. The eyes of students and police followed her as she carried electronic equipment from group to group. She was concerned about her newsfeed. She wanted to get the facts, to explain the tensions, to be exact, thorough and impartial. Sara was deadly serious and did not notice the attention. She ran like a carrier pigeon with war messages strapped to her leg, now in flight and now in danger of being shot down by the enemy. Although she was worried about Ali, she held her concentration.

Other groups clustered around, their attentions absorbed in the coming battle for control of their university. Every rumor was eagerly seized, for no one had any experience with a student rebellion.

Late evening and early morning were inseparable. Thursday and Friday were still joined. Cops in blue, badges on their chests but nameplates removed, nightsticks squeezed in their fists, guns strapped to their sides, anger in their faces, stood impatiently, tense and ready. The rebels had called them pigs, day after day. Threats of force and counter-threats rode the radio waves and filled the air blurted from bullhorns. For days now the students had defied the order to vacate the buildings. Tension seemed to stretch the time and to stretch nerves beyond the anatomies of individuals, linking them together.

But most people in Manhattan were asleep, unaware of the rising tensions on the campus. Yet as stars piercing the pall of chemicals and dust that hung over the city joined streetlamps to light the arena, fields of diverse emotions flowed from opposing groups at the campus, curled and mingled in the intervening space. Policemen, held together by the glue of indoctrination, sought specific objects on which to release their anger at the disrespectful treatment from the rebels.

Hours before dawn, the police burst into Hamilton Hall and dragged out the foreign and Black students, who resisted passively by their weight. These once-bold rebels were put into the waiting police wagons, their noisy struggle ending in a whisper. In a few hours they would be released. The authorities sighed with relief, for they didn't want trouble with Blacks; they were afraid of Harlem going up in flames.

Pirooz looked at his watch. It was past midnight and the moon paled his face. He tried to ease the tension and turned to a policeman standing behind him. "I wish we could all go home, officer."

"Fuck off," sneered the officer from the corner of his mouth.

Aha! The lines of communication were open, a frank discussion of the issues, Pirooz told himself. "Keep cool, listen to him, Pirooz. You may learn the deeper meaning of 'Fuck off.' "

Mathematics Hall was still in the hands of striking students, a fortress of idealists in the belly of the beast. A police bullhorn blared the decision of authority. "On behalf of the trustees of Columbia University . . . " Those in white armbands, determined to keep the cops away from the rebels, tightened their grip. Fear penetrated everyone, illuminating the tensions within like a huge x-ray device. The fear of one another divided the groups.

A blue mass of policemen edged toward those with white armbands, smashing into the chain of which Pirooz was one link, and snapped the chain to pieces.

Suddenly the Professor was hurled to the ground with a kick from a man holding his wrist—a plainclothesman with a white armband, pretending to be a colleague. A nightstick appearing from nowhere came within inches of his head, struck his left shoulder blade seemingly with the force of a sledgehammer, collapsing him onto the grass. A surge of pain pulsed through him, briefly eclipsing the dominion of fear, a moment of dark unconsciousness, and then the triumphant return of fear. The Professor staggered to his feet, oblivious to the pandemonium, his throbbing shoulder, the whole world. He ran instinctively toward the Broadway gate. Human bodies eddied past him, emotions of opposite charges and intentions clashing on either side. Amid the sparks and screams of accidental or deliberate collision, he ran off the scene.

The police attacked Eric, too. Like a sudden storm, disbelief overcame the Majority Coalition in blue armbands. They were for the police, they protested in vain, but the police didn't care; they couldn't tell one student from another, one armband from another. Everyone was now the enemy. The blue armbands dispersed and fled, disappearing around corners, through bushes, into unoccupied buildings, wherever their fears carried them. Eric ran toward Broadway, pale, his hair erect like a cornered cat's. A policeman caught up with him and confiscated his camera. The agents of law enforcement hate adverse evidence.

The police came at Sara, too. She bravely waved her press credentials, but the cops hate the press, too. One of the policemen yanked her tape recorder from her shoulder, throwing it to the ground. Sara protested, but they dragged her away.

On the campus, blood flowed. Some symbols died as others were being born. White armbands turned red, blue ones purple. The old campus became a battleground with no rules. The birthplace of ideas began to turn into a graveyard of ideals.

The protective circle of white armbands was broken and gone. The besieged in Mathematics Hall heard the screams, saw the turmoil below. The windows were pictures of violence. Ali looked at the campus and saw Picasso's *Guernica* in New York, a scene of brutal violence unleashed on unsuspecting man and beast. The rebels inside felt the tension, sharp as pain, shooting down their spines. They stood behind barricaded doors, some challenging death, some fearing injury, some resigned to whatever would come next, some ready to surrender and renounce their beliefs and regret their actions.

The blue-clad Tactical Police Force, boiling, impatient, loose and in motion, were oblivious to these individual differences. The rebels had taunted them for days, the braless girls had tempted them, the professors had looked down on them. They rushed to beat, to crush, to drag, to arrest, to get even. But their guns would remain silent. Orders were orders.

Shoulder to shoulder, the rebels stood fast. For the first time in their lives they felt their fates touching. For some, the spark of revolutionary unity would survive this initial failure.

With a military charge the police stormed the doors, billyclubs raised. There was no talk, no offer of peaceful surrender, as in Hamilton Hall. The SDS were communists. They deserved what they got. Clubs descended with the force of hate. Boots swung wide and struck bodies on the floor. Dust and moans mixed, and brutality filled the halls of learning.

Ali fell with a blow to the head. His world went black. His friends fell around him. They were kicked, stomped on, dragged away.

The violence continued its zigzag course, through building after building and around the campus well into the day. When the sun rose the radio screamed the world awake and newspapers printed, "Columbia Busted. 720 Students Arrested, 148 Injured."

Professor Pirooz could not remember how he traversed the two hundred yards from Broadway. The door to his apartment opened and shut in one motion. He had not cried since his father's death in the winter of 1960, but today he fell and sobbed silently. His mutilated emotions tormented him as much as did his shoulder injury, which by now was throbbing mercilessly. Henceforth, whenever the weather was humid, his left shoulder would ache.

Sara, dragged to the police station, had known about the repression of women, but while arrested she understood Pirooz' statement in a new light: "Law is made by the ruling circles, and others must obey it or be punished by it."

Eric, too, learned an important lesson. The power of the police to smash the strike impressed him deeply, even though he was hurt and angry. They should have moved on the first day of the strike to establish law and order on campus, but why hadn't they? Because of the successful police bust at Columbia, Eric made decisions years later which would affect many lives.

Coming out of a coma, Ali became more convinced that he had been right all along—revolution was the only answer to imperialism. There was no peaceful way to stop the oppression.

The Professor had horrible nightmares, the memory of the bloody events of 1953 in Teheran mingling with those in New York. He was awakened many times, a cold sweat over his body. He called to Ali in his dream, but the result was the same. He could not sleep, remembering March 1953 and Baback's face ripped away like a mask. Then it was June 1963, and Ali's brother Abbas, Pirooz' cousin, was killed. He called Ali's apartment, but there was no answer. He phoned Sara and heard only a cold ringing.

He worried about Ali, Sara, his colleagues, even the conservative Eric. Pressed by his solitude, his fears and frustrations, he sat on the corner of his bed, bearing the pain of loneliness alone. He refused to go to the window and look at the Hudson to soothe his nerves, as he occasionally did. He was afraid of seeing a river full of blood. He asked himself repeatedly, "Why did I run away? Why didn't I join Ali?"

Thoughts and doubts besieged Pirooz, and he gave up trying to sleep. One moment he wanted to become a revolutionary, to risk everything, and then the next he became hopeless, felt helpless. How could he do it? He got up and wrote a note, "I don't know what I want or how to get it. I am behind Ali, Sara and even Eric." He whispered to himself, "I will find Ali the first thing tomorrow. The police wouldn't dare to slaughter students in Manhattan like in Teheran."

CHAPTER 3

Hospital

Later that day, the Professor lay on the couch, his shoulder aching, and imagined a monk aflame in Saigon. Today was May Day, but Pirooz felt no solidarity, only fear and pain.

The telephone rang and as he meekly answered it, a wave of pain rippled over his face. He dropped the receiver, damned his self-pity, dressed and rushed out toward St. Luke's Hospital. As he crossed Broadway, he heard someone calling him, but he didn't respond. Sara caught up to him. "Oh, my God! Ali is hurt. I was arrested. Are you going to see Ali?"

Pirooz said, "Yes,"and quickened his stride, as Sara raced behind. He was rushing to see Ali, who had acted out Pirooz' own youthful dreams.

At the hospital, Ali's lip cautiously approached the edge of a styrofoam cup of coffee. Bandages covered his head and forehead in a turban of white gauze. The tensions of the recent event had dissolved. Calm and reflective, Ali looked like a holy man. The cup hung in midair as the door was flung open and Pirooz burst in. "Ali!"

"Pirooz! Salaam!" Ali placed the cup on the tray. "Hello, Sara. It's nice to see you all," Ali said.

Sara exclaimed, "Does it hurt?"

"I'm drugged now, but last night it felt like someone was stomping grapes inside my head."

Sara and Pirooz exchanged glances. "Is it serious?" Pirooz asked.

Ali brushed aside their concern. "It's not that bad. The judge and the dean are going to be the real pain."

"How is that?" Sara inquired.

"I heard that the University is going to sue us."

"Sue you? After breaking your head?" the Professor protested.

"Right!" Ali replied. "We didn't raise a finger, yet the police beat us to the ground and then beat us on the ground, while all along they called us outlaws. We were fools to expect peaceful arrests; we should have run away or have fought back." He stopped. "What happened to you, Sara?"

29

"The police took my press pass, smashed my equipment and put me in a cell with other students," she said. "They freed us at three in the morning without a charge. When I reminded the captain of press freedom he ..." Sara stopped, embarrassed, unwilling to repeat the cop's gesture.

Ali interrupted, "If this had happened in Havana, the U.S. press would scream, 'Socialism is a failure; students have risen against Castro the dictator!' But now they won't even whisper that capitalism has failed when its brightest students are clubbed for opposing it."

"Wait, Ali," Sara protested. "Even Eric said that though he disliked the strike, he hated the unlawful and unnecessary police action. He asked me to tell you he felt very bad you were hurt."

While Pirooz told them what had happened to him, Sara listened as she stared at Ali. His dark, searching eyes, his compelling voice, the articulate gestures of his hands, all suggested a power that Sara found exciting. She knew Ali was committed to ideas she could not quite understand or accept, but still, listening to him was always interesting, no matter how much she disagreed.

Her eyes wandered over his eyes, his thick moustache, long face, solid shoulders and black hair hanging below the bandages. A growing desire stirred in her to reach and touch Ali. She paused before walking to Ali. She placed her right hand on his left, squeezing gently. "I have to go, Ali. When will they let you out?"

"Tomorrow afternoon, I think."

"I hope so," Sara said. "Please call if I can be of any help, okay?"

Ali smiled. "Are you sure?"

Sara replied, "Absolutely! See you tomorrow, Ali. Goodbye, Professor Pirooz." Her fingertips lost contact with Ali's and a feeling of emptiness replaced her brief excitement. Her sudden movement, her words and motions, disrupted the equilibrium of the room. Ali, still feeling the softness and electricity of her touch, followed her departure with his eyes.

The week of rebellion had temporarily buried Ali's attraction to Sara. But this morning was different, and he was free to feel the force of his instincts. All of a sudden the little things Sara had done for him took on new meaning. He remembered her hauling books from the library when he was sick, lending him class notes, typing his term paper, bringing coffee when he manned the revolutionary literature table on campus, and all those long, unguarded gazes. If Sara would return now, he would tell her she was on his mind a lot.

But Sara already knew that. She had sensed something, too. As she entered the elevator she had already in her mind purchased roses for Ali. Why should only men be the givers of beautiful roses? Sara thought. She would invite Ali for dinner. After all, where else could Ali get a homemade American meal? Eric was far from her thoughts, as he would soon be far away from her in Washington. She knew Eric would pursue his career as Ali struggled for revolution. They were different. Eric had hazel eyes and blond hair, was rational, accommodating, indirect, controlled, reliable, and believed in God and free enterprise. Ali had brown eyes and black hair, was exotic, uncompromising, direct, spontaneous, and believed in socialism and revolution. Eric had realistic goals; Ali's seemed impossible. For Sara, Ali was a revolution as well as a revolutionary. But despite their differences, or maybe because of them, he dominated her present. The thought of his touch quickened her steps until she found herself in front of the florist on Broadway. At this moment there was nothing on Sara's mind but Ali and roses.

In the hospital, the Professor, Ali's cousin only a dozen years older, turned into an uncle and began to lecture Ali in Farsi. "Ali, listen. Your father has my word on your safety. Please do your best to keep your skull in one piece."

"I will," said Ali. "Please don't write a word about this to my parents. I will write myself. They have enough worries with my sister, Zaman, revolting against all their traditions." After a pause, Ali continued, "But self-survival isn't everything, you know. Sacrifices by individuals are necessary to push history forward."

Pirooz' voice changed. "I must admit, Ali, with campus experience you've become damned good at these little speeches."

Ali smiled widely. "You never stop teasing me."

But Pirooz was serious. "Politics is a jackass on a mountainside. Ride it cautiously, make sure it doesn't buck you off. Look at your head: stitches, bandages, pain. Remember, you're here to study science, not to topple good old Uncle Sam."

"Believe me, Pirooz, I don't enjoy a broken head." Ali raised his hand in a mock oath. "I promise to keep it intact for you."

"That's my boy! Now get some rest. Call me any time; my present mood will glue me to my apartment. And where can I take my despair anyhow?" The Professor stopped his self-pity; it was Ali who needed care. "I'll order you some fruit this afternoon. You shouldn't have to recover on hospital food." He stood up. "Incidentally, how do you feel about Sara?"

Ali grinned. "She sort of turns me on."

"You're not the only one." Pirooz smiled broadly and left, his mood passing from sadness to modest wellbeing.

The next morning, Pirooz left for the hospital more relaxed after a breakfast of feta cheese, pita bread and honeydew melon. He passed a drycleaner, a florist, a restaurant, a grocery, a copy shop and an Indian clothing shop on Broadway. His olfactory sense was sharp and he could tell blindfolded which shop he was passing. But today he didn't notice the smells or the colors; he was worried about Ali's dangerous zeal which impelled him to confront authority, from God down to the landlord and university administrators. But the Professor's deep affection for Ali went beyond that of a relative, a teacher, even a good friend. Their bonds were cemented by a shared ideology; his hopes were tied to Ali's. Still Pirooz wasn't clear how Ali could create a revolution, nor why he would jeopardize his studies. But he knew that while Abbas's death may have lit the candle to show Ali the way, it was the slow death of the nation under the Shah that compelled Ali forward now.

At the hospital, Pirooz brusquely pushed open the door to Ali's room. His entrance caught two young men unaware, but Ali was not to be found. Without a word of apology to the startled patients, Pirooz turned back into the hall and rushed to the first white uniform in sight.

"Where is Ali?" he demanded.

The white man in a white uniform didn't turn to face him, saying only, "Check with the receptionist."

Pirooz tried the next white uniform. "What has happened to Ali?"

A small, grandmotherly figure turned to him. "And who is Ali?"

Impatiently, Pirooz responded, "I mean Mr. Keshavarz, the man with the fractured head in that room."

"It's not fractured, just lacerations and contusions," replied the nurse. "He's in the other wing. Turn left at the end of this hall and ask one of the nurses."

"Why was Mr. Keshavarz moved?" Pirooz demanded loudly. But without waiting for an answer, he turned on his heel and left the nurse behind. The Professor had what he called an authority complex. To him even a reasonable suggestion from an authority was hard to accept. Ali, he thought, had a similar problem, except that the young man resolved it by confrontation and not by withdrawal as Pirooz did.

When Pirooz reached Ali's bed, he was fuming at the rearrangement. "Why did you let them do that?"

"Do what?"

"Bounce you around."

"Calm down, Professor," Ali said. "It's the money, nothing else. The University refused to cover injuries in the bust, so I'm here. Look, there is less traffic noise here and I have a chance to observe a big hospital ward."

"You could have gotten hurt," Pirooz protested.

Ali tried to calm Pirooz down. "Listen to this. Because of the street noise, I asked to be moved, but they said no until it suited them. They tested me and filled me with chemicals, but they told me nothing, as though I were a disease, not a patient."

"A disease taking a person to the hospital," Pirooz remarked.

"And just look around! See the impact of historical discrimination in a supposedly free society at first hand. The cleaning person is a Black woman, the janitors and guards are Black or Puerto Rican men, and the nurses' aides are women. The nurses are white and the doctors and administrators are all white men—the U.S. class structure in miniature."

Pirooz interrupted Ali, "Yes, the hospital is sicker than the sickest person in this ward. The doctors' income is much more than the nurses' who make more than the lab technicians, the nurses' aides, the janitors, right down the line. At the top sit the very rich, and at the bottom the very poor. Many doctors worry more about their investments than about their patients."

Ali said, "In this hospital the personnel is stratified and the relationship is hierarchical like the army and Indian caste system combined. Every duty, every task of each individual is specified to the last detail. Fear of libel suit keeps every one in check and impedes expression of compassion and promotes mountains of paper work. So the physician-patient relationship is turning into an adversary one much like that of the employer and employee, police and citizen."

Ali then concluded, "So hospitals are no different than government, business or the university or other institutions."

The Professor almost shouted, "Exactly! The physicians have monopoly power. In effect the patient is told what medicine or care to buy and at what price. More funds go to cure disease than to prevent it. Children are vaccinated only because if they die now they won't get sick later."

"An interesting conclusion," Ali interjected. "Dead people never get sick! But don't you think that is going a bit overboard?"

"Exactly!" In his tirade Pirooz did not notice Ali's facetiousness. "They keep a rich terminal patient alive, but let the rescuable poor die. Profit is God; it tells who dies now and who dies later. Doctors should be paid to maintain health, not just to cure disease." Pirooz raised his voice as if in class. "Goddamn it! Profit dominates everything."He stopped abruptly. "I'm so upset I forgot about you, everything."

"No, you didn't forget everything, you remembered all the patients in the capitalist world except me!"

Pirooz didn't answer. Instead he pointed to the table. "Red and white roses?"

"From Sara. They're nice, yes?"

"Nice is understating it. Ali, wake up. Has she been here again?"

"No! These roses came in with the wind."

"Is your relationship going anywhere?"

"I don't know. She's very attractive, but I'm not sure if I have the time now."

"Only a fool has no time for love, and you're not a fool, Ali."

"No," Ali declared. "I can be a fool. Didn't you tell me yesterday that politics is riding the back of a jackass?"

Pirooz ignored Ali. "Now, if I understand American courting customs, you have to make the next move."

"I'll consider it. I wish I knew whether she was still interested in Eric. He and I are opposite poles for Sara. Eric guarantees her return to her suburban origins, and I draw her to the unknown. What chance do I have?"

"An excellent chance. Saunders is headed to Washington. The field is yours."

"How do you know that?"

"He asked me to write a recommendation, but I forgot to do it. Yesterday he sent me a card thanking me for the good recommendation, which I never wrote. Wharton's recommendation must have worked."

"I'm just curious. What kind of job is it?"

The professor answered, "We live in America. In the bourgeois ethic, that will remain a secret."

Ali didn't get what he wanted. "It is helpful to have a professor for a cousin. He keeps you perfectly half-informed."

"I can't figure Saunders," Pirooz mumbled to himself. "In the Middle East final exam he repeated my lectures verbatim. I had to give myself and him an 'A'! A conservative writes a Marxist analysis of the oil industry, and I have to ignore his real convictions, just as he pretends to agree with me. How can this be?"

Ali explained, "Simple! What if Saunders says, 'Professor Pirooz, as a Marxist, what are you doing at Columbia, a capitalist-dominated institution?"

Pirooz frowned and became sullen. Ali knew he had touched a soft spot. "Well—" Ali began.

Pirooz interrupted, "This conflict in my life must be exposed. I won't carry a gun, but I feel very frustrated at times. The best I can do is to inform the world." As an afterthought he mumbled, "I have become like them."

Ali asked, "Like whom?"

"Like those Americans we criticize: half their words are spoken to pretend that things are what they're not. In any case, don't belittle Saunders. He's a principled fellow in his own way."

"Just a lost soul."

"To him, you're the one who is lost."

"And to you?" Ali inquired.

"We are all lost," Pirooz said melancholically.

Ali tried to cheer him up. "How are you doing in the courting business, Pirooz?" The two men looked at each other, a bit surprised. Ali had never been so critical of Pirooz' work or talked so freely about his private life.

Pirooz didn't mind the change in their relationship. "Actually, I have a date tonight with a beautiful woman with whom I am in love and whom I hardly know. We see each other in the elevator, but we've spoken only on the telephone. She called my office the other day, left a message that she had tickets for a guitar recital and asked me to join her. The secretary must have smelled something. She looked at me in a funny way all day."

"It must be a shock to be asked out by a woman, isn't it?"

"I'm not shocked, Ali. Actually, I am relieved she made the first move. In any case, I'm a socialist, not a male chauvinist."

Ali could not help laughing so hard his stitches hurt. "Let's face it, Pirooz. Everyone has a little male chauvinist pig hidden within. Even some women do!"

"Women?"

"Yes, see how the professional women look down on the housewives!"

"That's class consciousness, not chauvinism."

"Oh, yes." Ali understood. "What's her name?"

"Helena Orsini. She's a graduate student in Spanish literature."

"Helena Orsini," Ali said. "I know her. We worked together in a human rights organization which accomplished next to nothing. We petitioned the UN and wrote letters to newspapers and U.S. government officials. When things got silly Helena and I sang revolutionary songs in Farsi and Spanish in the back of the room. Her father disappeared in Buenos Aires." Ali thought of Abbas. "Just imagine how many political victims we know."

Pirooz changed the subject, "What are your plans when you get out?"

"Well," Ali replied, "if they don't arrest me, I'll have to expose the police brutality and unlawful arrests. I must also attend a meeting of the Iranian Students Association."

"What is happening there?" Pirooz waited for Ali's response, but instead Ali was sitting upright, looking intently past him. Pirooz turned around. It was Sara, picking her way down the aisle towards Ali's bed. Her hair was caught in a ponytail with a red ribbon, and Ali smiled to recognize the radicals' armband.

The Professor remembered the bouquet of roses. "You return?"

"Unfortunately, yes," Sara said.

"Unfortunately?"

"Yes. I wish I hadn't left Ali in the first place." Sara's admission filled Ali with joy, and she surprised herself a little. Sara swept up to Ali. "How are you?"

"I'm okay." Sara had all the fresh news from the campus, and Ali encouraged her to tell him about it. Ali wished he was involved, too.

When Sara finished she turned to the Professor and said, "Please excuse me for breaking in. Do go on with your conversation."

"We were just talking about the Iranian Student Association," Ali said.

Sara said, "I've seen their press releases and posters. They're against the Shah, aren't they?''

"That's right," said Ali. "The organization is a mix of groups who oppose the Shah for various reasons. Leftists of various persuasions want his ouster, while the National Front students demand a return to constitutional monarchy. The Front is the legacy of Dr. Mossadegh and is now an umbrella for groups demanding that the Shah reign, not rule. Moderate Muslim groups want the same, but the militant ones following Ayatollah Khomeini's line have no use for the Shah at all. It's ironic. The Allies ousted the Shah's father because he sided with Hitler, and now the Iranians want to oust the Shah because he sides with the U.S. and others, but not his own people.''

Sara protested, "You mean the U.S. president is the main culprit?''

"I mean all the U.S. presidents.''

Ever since she had come to New York and especially in Pirooz' course, Sara had heard that the U.S. had done some shameful things overseas, but she still believed, as most Americans do, that in general the U.S. stood on the side of the good. "I don't agree with you, but I don't want to argue now.''

Pirooz was a fence-mender. "That's fair, Ali.'' Ali nodded.

"I want to know about the religious angle in politics, since I'm writing a report on South American radical priests," Sara said. "What do the Islamic clergy say about the Shah?''

Ali responded, "By confiscating religious land, by curbing the clergy's legal privileges and by tolerating nudity in the movies in the name of modernity, the Shah has shrunk the mullahs' pocketbooks, sawed their privileges in half and injured their faith, Islam. So the clergy have been up in arms. Right now, Dr. Yazdi is the leader of the moderate Islamic students in the U.S. He claims Islam has all the answers, but he can never explain why it has failed to solve the problems we inherited from the past.''

Pirooz interrupted. "Let me tell you the strange way the Iranian Student Association got started in America. Early in the 1960's, a few students got together and debated whether to get involved in politics. Ardeshir Zahedi, whose father was the general that led the 1953 coup, tried to convince us otherwise, but the students paid no attention to him and organized anyway.

"The Shah's debt to his father and Ardeshir's loyalty made him a favorite of the Shah, so later on he was appointed ambassador to the United States. The recent graduate of an agricultural school in Utah was an overnight diplomat who married the Shah's daughter and became an influential voice in the regime. It is widely known that his main task now is throwing lavish parties and offering gifts of caviar, silk rugs, women and cash to VIP's and the press. Iranian students in the U.S. have been denouncing this profligacy and the Shah, while U.S. presidents have been praising the Shah and universities here have been showering His Majesty with honorary degrees."

"It's amazing how different your opinion of the Shah is from that of most Americans," Sara said.

Ali replied, "Not amazing; the tragic result of brainwashing."

"But I've read some criticism of the Shah in the press."

"There are exceptions," Pirooz explained, "but the general impression of the Shah in the U.S. is positive. He has been sold to the public as a good leader and a modernizer of a backward country."

Ali said, "Such opposite images of the Shah are easy to explain, because he's good to American business and government, but not to the people of Iran. Soon a revolution in Iran and a demand for 'Yankee go home' will shake up the President, the CIA and quite a few Americans. Now, Sara, you can see what caviar does as it moves from the Iranian embassy to the press: it produces not more sturgeon but more misinformed American citizens."

Sara and Pirooz smiled and shook their heads, while Ali, satisfied with his comment, grinned.

Pirooz turned to Ali. "What is it like in the student association these days?"

"The Shah is coming to the U.S. to accept an honorary degree from NYU, and we'll be planning a demonstration at our next meeting. I hope it will be the biggest one we've ever organized. Ghotbzadeh is coming up from the Washington chapter for this meeting, and Dr. Chameron is coming, too."

"Ghotbzadeh," Pirooz remarked, his eyes flashing. "He flunked out of some small college in Maryland, and now the immigration office is after him for political reasons which they have disguised as his academic problems.

"I must tell you this. A couple of years ago we were on a hunger strike sitting across from the White House. When Ghotbzadeh went away to call reporters, a student saw him at a lunch counter, drinking a big milkshake. That son of a bitch was the one who proposed the hunger strike in the first place! Excuse me, Sara. Professors also swear and do everything that everybody else does, in case you didn't know." The three laughed. Pirooz asked, "What else is happening, Ali?"

"The student organization has grown a great deal in recent years. We are five thousand strong. Even though opposition to the Shah keeps us united, still ideological and personal conflicts are brewing. The National Front opportunists and Islamic fanatics may yet destroy the student movement in America, but so far Rookney manages to keep everybody in line."

Pirooz shook his head in resignation. "Things don't seem to have changed since I was a student and active in the association. But you must do your best to stay united, Ali."

"Why spend so much effort here?" Sara asked. "You can't change things in Iran from New York."

"First," Ali said, "because it's the only organization which openly opposes the Shah. And because we can recruit students to form a political vanguard in Iran."

A grin rippled across Pirooz' face. "Espionage."

"Why not? It's for a good cause."

Sara was now feeling the exhaustion of the day's events. "I see my contribution to this conversation is limited. I have to go, anyhow."

Pirooz, seeing the look in the eyes of Ali and Sara said, "I must leave, too." He bade a quick farewell and walked to the bank of elevators thinking of Ali and Sara together, as he thought also of his upcoming evening with Helena.

Sara drew her chair to Ali's bedside and let Ali surround her hands in his. Their eyes were free and their words struggled to become freer. "I'm very happy you're all right," she said.

"I am, too, but . . ."

"But what?"

"What can I tell you?" Ali said gently.

"Everything!"

"Now?"

"No, not now. Will you come to dinner at my apartment?"

"I've been waiting for your invitation all my life." Ali smiled.

Sara smiled back and said, "Your patience has paid off. And now, can I ask you a personal question, Ali?"

"Whatever you want."

"Whatever? Are you sure?"

"Yes!"

"Why do you always contradict and belittle everything? Don't you see anything good in America?"

"Yes, plenty, but I never talk about it, because for me imperialism's evil dominates whatever is good in America."

"Is it because of your brother Abbas?"

"No, I'm beyond that. It's because of other people's brothers," Ali said thoughtfully.

"But what about happiness, Ali, your happiness? You can't live in the trenches a whole lifetime." When Ali remained silent she insisted gently, "I'm talking about happiness, Ali."

"Yes, you have a point, but I am more unhappy now because I'm reminded that I don't know what happiness is!"

"Do you have to make things so complicated?"

"I don't make them—they just are complicated," Ali retorted.

"Well, I disagree. I can tell you a couple of things to make you happy, one in a small way and one in a big way."

"What?" Ali asked curiously.

"Because of your prompting, I have been studying Marx and Lenin on women's emancipation, something feminists in the U.S. don't often do."

Ali was excited. "Really? Really, Sara, you did that? I must read it myself," Ali added.

"Yes, you and Pirooz and other male chauvinists must read the stuff." The couple laughed. Sara continued, "But tell me, aren't you a little happier now?"

Ali said impatiently, "Yes, yes, but what's the big one?"

"If you eventually pull off a revolution in Iran, won't you be very happy then?"

"Yes, the happiest."

"Then you already know two things that make you less unhappy, and if you look around you will find more. Life is not all repression and suffering."

Ali smiled. "I surrender."

"You'd better." Sara brought her lips to his and they kissed gently. "I have to go."

"First you set fire to my expectations, and then you pour ice water over me."

"That's a liberated woman for you. I'll call you tonight." Sara left the room, and Ali felt as if a light had been switched off.

CHAPTER 4

The Future
Leaders Roar

The New York chapter of the Iranian Student Association was on the ground floor of a hotel on 104th Street west of Broadway. The hotel was a murky place, one of many catering to welfare recipients, for whom the city paid high rents. The degrading conditions were excused as "temporary," although people were born and grew up in them. Mixed with the elderly on Social Security and the poor, the hotel housed thieves, drug dealers and addicts, and prostitutes of all colors, who hung out with their pimps close to the entrance. Occasionally young male prostitutes competed with the women over their turf. A bag lady gave lectures, mixing topics, but few passersby listened.

Ali climbed the worn granite steps past a hooker loitering in the door-way, entered the grimy and smelly lobby, turned right, and opened the door to the Iranian Students Association.

The large room had newspapers and leaflets left here and there, posters covering the walls, and styrofoam cups and crumpled papers beside chairs in intimate groups, vestiges of unresolved debates. A locked door at the back led to a small office, with a mimeograph and shelves piled with newspapers and books. A black telephone lay on a discolored desk hugging an old chair. A large poster of Dr. Mossadegh hung behind the chair. Only Hassan Rookney, the chairman of the New York chapter and former president of the Iranian Students Association in the U.S., held the key to the locked room.

The Iranian students were mostly from middle class families, with a few rich and a few poor. Students whose parents could not support them had to hold jobs on the side, which were in violation of U.S. regulations on student visas.

Ali was early, but a number of students, young and old, from various colleges, were already in the room. Eyes turned to the door as Ali walked in. The leftists greeted him warmly; their ideological unity proved a strong emotional link. Others acknowledged Ali with a nod. Soon the room was nearly full, about forty people, and Rookney appeared from the back room. Hassan Rookney was tall, thick-set and fair. He had the healthy complexion of an athlete, though he seldom exercised. He wore a tweed suit, white shirt and solid yellow tie. His father, a hard-driven landlord in Iran, had transmitted his ambition to his son. But Rookney tilled the soil of politics; he hoped to harvest power. His uncles were politicians and prominent members of the National Front. Ali didn't trust him; he was aware that Rookney could smile as he frowned on the inside, could agree, knowing he would not keep his promise. Rookney spotted Ali with his comrades. He did not like admirers around anyone but himself.

"Look at those bandages," he said affably. "Ali, for God's sake, stick to one woman."

"I am searching for *the woman,* the only one," Ali reacted.

Rookney laughed. His followers laughed too. Ali knew that Rookney did not put much stock in ideas. Political action must have concrete rewards, and therefore Ali should not have participated in the Columbia uprising; such was Rookney's political logic. Even so, Ali admitted, he could learn from Rookney political techniques and tactics for dealing with students.

Rookney placed his notes on a shortlegged wooden desk and the students turned to face him. Announcements would be made, policies debated, plans drawn up, and a lecture would conclude the meeting, all in Farsi.

The Islamic group gathered in the front rows around Dr. Yazdi and Dr. Chameron. Sadegh Ghotbzadeh sat next to them. The leftists formed a tight group at the back. The National Front students were scattered, Ali thought, just as they lacked a tight ideology. They just loved Mossadegh and followed his path of nationalism, constitutional monarchy, negative neutrality between superpowers and trade with both the socialist and capitalist blocs. By negative neutrality they meant Iran granting no favors to either the U.S.S.R or U.S.

Rookney banged on the table. "Dear friends, I am pleased to welcome Mr. Ghotbzadeh and Dr. Chameron to our chapter."

Before Rookney could say another word, Ghotbzadeh leapt to his feet. "My brothers, I bring you the good wishes of students in Washington, D.C. . . ." A tailormade blue suit and white silk shirt covered Ghotbzadeh's well-proportioned, tall frame. His face, with a strong jawline, exhibited fair, healthy skin. A wisp of soft, black hair drifted casually over his forehead.

His father was a successful merchant, and his mother a strict Muslim. Ghotbzadeh prayed regularly, but he also drank and ate pork. Decent women wore the veil, he believed, but he enjoyed the company of blondes in bikinis. The students tolerated Ghotbzadeh's flamboyance because his motives seemed obvious, and somewhat genuine.

Ghotbzadeh finally finished, smiled broadly and sat down. Rookney thanked him and changed the subject. "I am also glad Ali is with us in one piece. Let me say that we have no business tangling with the local police. We have no quarrel with Americans."

Ali wanted to challenge Rookney's comment in spite of Pirooz' advice on unity, but he held his tongue.

"In any case," Rookney resumed, "we have a lot of business. The Shah is coming and we must organize demonstrations against him. Also, the next issue of *Iran Letter* is overdue. Ali has promised to write the editorial. I wonder if—"

Ali cut in, "I have it here."

Surprised, Rookney said, "Good. Thank you." Ali knew Rookney disliked relying on leftists for most of the writing, because the paper became more radical than he wished.

"Please hand in your articles. The paper is important. Also, we must start contacting every new Iranian student entering the U.S." He looked at his notes. "A committee must prepare a position paper for the upcoming confederation meeting in Europe, or else Mr. Bani Sadr will stamp his Islamic economics and sociology on the student platform."

Some students grinned, but Dr. Yazdi protested, "What is wrong with Islam?"

Rookney replied curtly, "Nothing! I just want there to be a genuine debate on every issue. Let's stay on the track."

Rookney succeeded in preventing Bani Sadr from stamping his Islamic ideas on the student convention platform, but just a dozen years later the same Bani Sadr would become the first president of the Islamic Republic of Iran and try to stamp his Islamic ideas on the whole country. However, not being Islamic enough for the fundamentalist Khomeini, President Bani Sadr would have to run to Paris for his life before his term was to have been up.

The discussion this afternoon turned to the tactics of the planned demonstrations against the Shah, the publicity to be used, and contributions to cover expenses. Soon a frustrated leftist took the floor. "Our demonstrations are like picnics. The cause of workers and peasants in Iran calls for greater militancy. We must unite and work for a revolution."

Rookney answered, "Revolution is out of order. We must make the Shah reign, not rule. The return to constitutional monarchy was Dr. Mossadegh's program and should be ours."

Ali whispered to his comrade, "We'll take it from there."

Another Marxist piped up. "Why are unity and revolution out of order, Mr. Rookney? Mossadegh is gone and his methods have failed. There is no use pleading with the Shah; he is the one who has stolen our freedom. Do you think he will suddenly give it back? Anyway, we can't compete with ABC, NBC and CBS, who promote the Shah in the U.S. Look! Huge demonstrations can't stop the noisy and well-documented massacres in Vietnam, so how do you expect our tiny demonstrations in New York to stop the Shah's silent killings in Iran?''

Rookney saw Yazdi struggling for recognition. "The Shah is the enemy of Islam," Yazdi said. "We can unite the seven thousand Iranian students in the U.S. on that basis." Then he fell stone silent.

Dr. Ebrahim Yazdi was a soft-spoken man of medium height. He wore a slightly rumpled, light green suit, white cotton shirt, no tie, and well-worn shoes. A pharmacologist, Yazdi could not afford Ghotbzadeh's ostentation even if he cared for it; he had to feed a growing family. He weighed his words as carefully as he weighed ingredients in his lab. He was quiet but firm, believing in "evolution, not revolution," and "the power of persuasion over that of confrontation," as he said.

Yazdi was a true Muslim who never missed a prayer or a day of fasting and did not touch alcohol. To him, Islam was a powerful spiritual force in the nation which could be harnessed to restore the constitution and, tempered with practical considerations, to govern the country.

A leftist shouted, "Can't we leave religion out of politics?"

Rookney rapped on the table. "Some of our leftist friends are full of ideological strictures. They are just as rigid as the reactionaries. Gentlemen, I beg of you. Left or right, we are all against tyranny in Iran. Let's stop quarrelling."

Ghotbzadeh leapt to his feet. "I object! Dr. Yazdi and I are Muslims, not right."

Smiling broadly, Rookney said, "I agree." Over the laughter, Ghotbzadeh protested, "Mr. Rookney, Islam is no joke."

Rookney replied respectfully, "I have nothing against Islam. I am myself a *Sayyed*, you know.' Rookney meant he was a descendant of the Prophet Muhammad and Imam Ali.

"Mr. Chairman, may I?" Yazdi requested.

"Please be brief."

"There is no room for decadent Western culture or alien atheist Marxism in Iran or in our hearts—"

Ali lost his patience and stood. "Mr. Chairman."

"Yes."

"Alien! What happened to history? Are we expected to be afflicted with amnesia now?" Ali proceeded after a pause, "Islam came from Arabia to replace Zoroastrianism in Persia. Marxism is from Germany. Pick your alien ideology and location, Dr. Yazdi." Ali then calmly said, "We want political freedom and economic justice, just as you do. We must get weapons and ideas from anywhere we can and revolt. The Shah is the only alien!"

Rookney motioned for quiet as Ghotbzadeh shouted back, "Islam will prevail!" An uproar arose from the front of the room, everyone shouting at once.

When order was restored, Dr. Chameron, a calm, gentle, scholarly-looking Berkeley electronics scientist with a receding hairline, stood up. "We need mutual respect and unity among ourselves to fight injustice in Iran."

Rookney responded. "Thank you, Dr. Chameron. We can't waste our time trying to convert each other. Let's set aside our factional squabbles for just one minute and—"

Ali interrupted, "We better convert each other to some degree or else with such deep and basic divisions among ourselves we will not be able to govern the country, even if we win the revolution. Then we will surely fall prey to a counterrevolution."

A shotgun reverberating in the hotel lobby abruptly finished the debate. Faces paled at the report of the gun. Screams and curses reached the room from outside. A drug bust, some students whispered. It had happened before.

Suddenly, the door slammed open. Two policemen burst into the meeting, holding guns in their trembling hands. "Keep still! This is a raid," one shouted.

Fear rushed into the room like an arctic wind slapping faces. The students fell silent. The open door framed policemen pushing handcuffed men, while a half-naked woman trailed behind. Sirens filled the neighborhood, the world, it seemed.

Rookney turned to the officers. "You have no right to—"

"Shut up!" the big cop shouted, gripping the gun in both hands and aiming into the center of the room.

"We have a search warrant," the smaller cop said matter-of-factly.

Rookney insisted, "We are Iranian students."

The big cop pointed his gun at Rookney. "I said shut up, you Eye-ranian! Now get your ass on the floor. Move it!"

Rookney was shocked. He hesitated, afraid to defy the police but also embarrassed to submit to his demand. Ali, in an unusually conciliatory voice, said, "Officer, you are jeopardizing your job. Don't commit an un-provoked error. We're not armed. Look, this room is full of witnesses. This is no pusher's rendezvous."

The officer, startled by Ali's word "job," hesitated, giving Ali a chance. Ali rose slowly. "Don't aggravate the situation. Put down your gun, please!"

The American wife of one of the students said, "He's right, Captain. Please be careful."

The posters with strange faces and writing and the polite demeanor of the students convinced the officers; they lowered their guns. The big one broke the tension. "Okay, but stay put until the lieutenant comes." As everyone relaxed a bit, Ali said, "Mr. Rookney, you don't need to lie on the floor."

The students waited, edgy and silent as though frozen in a photograph. At last the lieutenant showed up and announced, "Okay, men, these are Eye-ranians; it's all over. Let's go." He then looked at the students. "Carry on, fellows," and the policemen left.

In the lobby the smaller patrolman asked, "What the hell are Eye-ranian students doing in this dump?"

The lieutenant shook his head. "Who knows? They may not know any better, or else they're used to it in Eye-ran."

"Yeah, you're right, Lieutenant. This is America, not some Arab desert country." Ali's turban-like bandage was still in his mind.

Back in the room, Rookney was shaken and embarrassed. Ali came to his rescue. "I move we adjourn and reconvene on Saturday."

Rookney managed to mumble, "Will anyone second the motion?"

It was done and the meeting came to an end. Most filed out while a few lingered on, talking quietly. Ali went up to Rookney. "Don't let it bother you. My head bears the same injury as your pride."

Rookney nodded, appreciating Ali's sympathy, and said warmly, "You surprised me with your coolness."

Ali smiled. "Frankly, I surprised myself. Admit it, Rookney, my broken head is a good experience."

Rookney smiled, too. "Will you be just as cool in our meetings from now on?"

Ali reacted. "Never! Not with those invisible turbans around."

"Invisible turbans?"

"Yazdi is a disguised mullah."

"Oh." Both men laughed, never guessing what was to happen in the future when thousands of invisible turbans became visible after the revolution and began to control every aspect of life in Iran.

Dr. Yazdi, Dr. Chameron and Ghotbzadeh joined them. Yazdi said in a friendly tone, "I wish you had more faith in Islam," as they all shook hands and said goodbye. The police bust had been a painful reminder of the torture and murder at home, perpetrated by similar officers of the law, which had brought these struggling young Iranians together.

Ghotbzadeh saw the lieutenant in the lobby and said, "You owe us an apology."

The lieutenant frowned. "You must be kidding. You're lucky I haven't arrested you, big boy."

Dr. Chameron said, "Mr. Ghotbzadeh, please! Don't insist."

"That's better," said the lieutenant. To scare Ghotbzadeh he took out a pad. "What is your name?"

"Ghotbzadeh."

"What?"

"Ghotbzadeh."

"Spell it."

A dozen years later on Thanksgiving Day, when the lieutenant was full of turkey, cranberry sauce and Budweiser, relaxing and watching the news, he was suddenly shocked as if hit with a charge of police brutality. The strange name he would always remember appeared on the screen and in the newscaster's voice. Ghotbzadeh! The lieutenant sat up and became attentive.

Ghotbzadeh's face, having become a bit fuller over the years, covered the Sony picture tube in full color. That's him, all right, the lieutenant said to himself. A number of microphones competed for Ghotbzadeh's words. "Mr. Foreign Minister, what is next for the American hostages?"

Ghotbzadeh frowned. "I will not respond directly, but trial for espionage is not out of the picture."

"Trial, shit!" the lieutenant shouted, banging his beer can against the armchair. Beer splashed onto the carpet and the chair. "I could have arrested that son of a bitch. Now he shoves it to our men overseas, to our President, and to the whole nation. I'll be damned," the lieutenant mumbled to himself.

His wife, angry at the spill, said, "Come on, George. Stop that. He's a foreign minister, ain't he?"

"Yeah, so what?"

"Well, dear, not everyone stays a lieutenant for thirty years."

The lieutenant threw his wife a dirty look. The football game was about to come on. There was no use arguing with her, she always had something to say.

Ghotbzadeh watched his own interviews on T.V. seeing his dreams coming true. Day after day, he basked in the greatest television exposure in history. He was on CBS, NBC, ABC, public TV, his voice carrying around the world. And day after day, the lieutenant watched Ghotbzadeh on the news and repeated, "I could have arrested that hostage-taker. I could have locked up the son of a bitch myself!"

* * * * *

The young rebels at the Iranian Students meeting that day would later become revolutionary leaders in Iran.

In the 1970's Yazdi and Ghotbzadeh would join the exiled Ayatollah Ruhollah Khomeini, who was then busy writing a book arguing the legitimacy of political, spiritual and juridical authority being vested in one person. Of course, Yazdi and Ghotbzadeh still believed that power was best left in the hands of experts like themselves. Unfortunately at the time, no one took Khomeini's governmental theories seriously.

In 1979, Yazdi would become vice premier for revolutionary affairs and interrogate the Shah's generals and ministers, sending most of them to the revolutionary court and often to the firing squad as corruption on earth. Dr. Chameron was to become the head of the secret police of the Islamic Republic. He did not like the job but could not refuse Khomeini's command.

* * * * *

Rookney, however, in a few years from the date of the New York meeting became the Shah's right hand man in the United States, even though the Shah had executed Rookney's uncle. Rookney felt that there was no other way to be politically effective but to join the Shah and try to reform the regime from within. And to his credit, Rookney refused a ministerial portfolio from the Shah. "Not until constitutional monarchy is restored," he confided to friends, meanwhile serving His Majesty in many unofficial and questionable capacities. For example, he paid hundreds of students to greet the Shah and wave flags whenever His Majesty visited places in the United States.

* * * * *

The evening of the student meeting, in front of the building, Ali watched as the police took away one last man, shackled and bleeding profusely from his forehead. The storm had died as suddenly as it had crashed into the hotel. The undesirables, like dry leaves, had fallen and been swept up into police wagons. Soon the pushers would make bail, and the confiscated dope would return to the streets under new management.

Ali saw the addicts and prostitutes returning, noting angrily that the women wore a great deal of makeup and little else. Prostitution was illegal, yet it was run as openly as Saks Fifth Avenue. The prostitutes were walking, talking and thinking merchandise, exploited by pimps, landlords, gynecologists, banks and police, all profiting from them in one way or another. No one bothered to ask where they came from or why they remained prostitutes. "Most citizens were led to believe that it was the prostitutes' own failure as individuals and no one else's," Pirooz had once lectured.

Ali walked north on Broadway. It was relatively safe to walk there in daylight, if one didn't mind the panhandlers who sat lonely over a cup of coffee on vandalized wooden benches in the small sliver of public concrete at 108th Street. Ali was careful to keep his distance; some beggars were threatening, and pedestrians often spared the change not out of pity but out of fear. A Columbia professor had recently been knifed in this vicinity for a dime.

Pirooz had remarked in class that there was more crime in New York than in the whole of England. He argued that the cause of crime is absolute and relative deprivation. His statistical work indicated that even rape is no exception. It isn't only sex but economics, too. As Marx did with Hegel, Pirooz stood Sigmund Freud on his head: If art and science are sublimated sexual desires, rape is the sublimation of unfulfilled economic and social drives. "Look," the Professor said, "in many cases, rape and robbery are perpetrated together."

Several weeks earlier, Professor Pirooz had lectured his students in a rage over a tragic news item about someone he knew. "Every social process has an ideological implication. An old lady was raped, her Social Security check was stolen, and she was left for dead by a heroin addict. The Daily News is filled with such stories. Who is responsible for this crime? Where did the heroin come from? Who stood to gain from its manufacture, its transport and distribution? Whose pockets did the old lady's money finally fill?" Pirooz asked angrily.

A student suggested, "Organized crime."

"Yes, but who is organized crime?"

"The cultivator, the processor, the pusher," a student replied.

"Strangely enough, they get a very small cut from the multibillion-dollar drug trade," the Professor countered. "The opium poppy is cultivated in a number of countries—Iran, Turkey, Thailand and so on—whose politics and economy are intimately tied to the United States. The flower is shining red and the poppy field looks as if it were on fire. It can't be hidden from a helicopter, or along the roads. But the peasant growers never see the real money. The landlords, who pay the government officials, smuggle the opium to a few processing centers in Hong Kong, Marseilles or Mexico City.

"The CIA, which can detect fish swimming upstream, fails to detect this big operation, even from its privileged position as advisor to the same governments through which the heroin traffic flows. In fact, the CIA in Laos and other places trains the police, while the countries' leaders are major suppliers of heroin on the world market. A UN report has implicated the Shah's family too, as a worldwide drug gang. The same is true with our allies, General Ky in Vietnam and Stroessner in Paraguay. The list is long.

"But then the heroin must get into the U.S. The FBI, which knows and notes every un-American thought in people's heads, is curiously blind to the drug traffic. At every step the smuggling is protected by those entrusted to stop it. The government is better organized to promote drug abuse than organized crime is. But the conspiracy spreads beyond government to legitimate businesses who then launder the profits.

"So, is it really hard to see how the old lady's cash was divided by the ruling classes here and abroad, cooperating in stealing her money?"

A shocked student waved for attention. "All of this set up, Professor Pirooz, for a hundred dollars from an old lady?"

"No," said the Professor. "There are millions of victims across the country, throughout the world, whose houses, apartments and bodies are assaulted by addicts who must steal to buy the heroin. Crime in general, including, of course, white collar crime, is the first or second largest industry in America today. It pays! Since Americans are not genetically more prone to crime than the British, then something else must be pushing people into crime."

Pirooz concluded, "Look out the windows of our classroom right in the heart of the capitalist world. There are over thirty thousand millionaires and over thirty thousand homeless in New York. There are people here as desperate as the poorest in India, but they freeze to death in New York, not in Calcutta. The rest of the world observes this mess and asks embarrassing questions. They will refuse to accept capitalism no matter how many bombs we drop on them, like in Vietnam, or how much foreign or military aid we ship them."

As Ali traversed Broadway deep in his reverie about Pirooz' lecture on crime, he saw Broadway filled with trucks unloading their boxes into the basements of the family-owned groceries and restaurants lining the street. A beer truck was unloading through the metal-covered hole in front of a bar. Between curb and building was a portable assembly of metal conveyors, the numerous little wheels minimizing friction and work—work, Ali mused, in both its thermodynamic and Marxist senses. A few wheels were sufficient to solve the friction of full cartons, but history has gone on and people have yet to invent something to diminish friction among themselves and within man himself.

As Ali turned right onto 111th Street, the bag lady he recognized hanging out in front of the hotel confronted him. "Young man," she shouted, "avoid the devil and your head shall be healed." Ali quickened his steps and pretended not to notice. "Young man, I'm talking to you. Ignore the devil whom God created to please God. Do you hear? Stop and pay attention. Do not listen to him, though God gave him a sweet tongue, or else you will be cast into the eternal fires of hell. Praise the Lord!" Ali barely heard the last words as he disappeared into the lobby of his apartment building.

* * * * *

Having planned the demostration well and obtained a New York police permit for it, several hundred Iranian students, including Rookney, Dr. Yazdi, Ghotbzadeh, Dr. Chameron and Ali, with Pirooz on the sidelines, embarrassed the Shah in his moment of triumph as he received an honorary Doctorate of Humane Letters from New York University. Waving signs, the students chanted, "Give him a degree in butchery!"

CHAPTER 5

Ali And Sara In Love

Like a memory from a remote past, the thought of Sara, the feel of her skin and the sound of her voice quickened Ali's steps. Sweating a little, he noticed his sudden acceleration and realized it was not wholly due to the steep descent from Broadway toward the low-lying river. He turned sharply into the lobby of Sara's building on Riverside Drive.

Riverside Drive had once seen the country estates of New York merchant capitalists, a day's trip up the island from Wall Street. Suburban villas, culturally and physically looted from Europe, eventually replaced the estates and were in turn scrapped for brick and limestone apartment houses with servant's quarters. When hard times fell, the suites were divided into smaller flats for the influx of professionals. Sara's building looked solid enough to last forever, frowning on the Hudson River below. The soot of years covered the facade as it covered all changes of the past. But though the structure could endure nature's harshness, its air of permanence was an illusion since man's greed could tear it down as it had the building's predecessors.

A doorman, old, weary, dark and small, stood by the elevators. He inspected Ali casually and asked no questions. His presence satisfied the tenants that their possessions were safe, but in fact the old man guarded nothing but the landlord's contractual obligation. He polished the brass fittings in the lobby while dreaming of his childhood and the warm breezes of Puerto Rico. The obstacles in his life, like the cushions of a pinball machine, had banged him around to this lobby on Riverside Drive. The old man accepted his low wages and the waste of his remaining days as his fate. He dreamed of the past, of the things he longed for but could not have and did not know why he did not dare to demand them. The doorman never thought of his future, which had been lost somewhere in the past. He might have wondered why a man should be paid to daydream and yet never asked to tell about it; but he didn't. He knew he could never afford to live in a building like the one he guarded and dreamt in.

51

Ali scanned the elevator for muggers before entering. When he rang the bell to the apartment, he was greeted by a visual and a voice check, and then the New York ritual of opening locks and safety chains. Ali's joyful anticipation of seeing Sara was displaced by a vision of New York as the center of a fearful world with every apartment a fortress.

Sara's impatience cut through his thoughts. "Ali, come in. What are you waiting for?" Awakened by a tender shock, Ali felt Sara take his hand in hers and draw him through a small foyer into the living room. Reality became Sara's touch.

Sara sensed Ali's excitement. She dropped his hand gently and stepped back to let Ali admire her. "I have wine and beer," she said, "and I think there's some Scotch." Ali, wrapped up in her display, could not respond.

"Oh, I'm sorry. Do you drink at all, Ali?" There were so many things she didn't know about him.

"Yes," he said, "I'll have a beer."

"Good. Sit down, please, and I'll be right back." As Sara turned to the kitchen, she saw in the window a reflection of Ali watching her. The telephone rang. "That's probably my mother. Excuse me," Sara said and left the room.

Ali walked to the large window and gazed over the treetops of Riverside Drive at the park and the quiet waters of the Hudson. To him it seemed a vast painting filled with life and motion, the work of a perfectionist who tirelessly retouched it with new colors and shapes, one day adding clouds to hide the sun, the next night dispersing them to reveal the moon, or else pairing passing boats with seagulls gliding above, changing rain to snow, swirling colorful industrial fumes: a new pattern all the time, no two compositions ever the same. Ali thought, the painter is man, nature, history and the cosmos all wrapped up in one brush.

Ali's eyes scanned the painting and saw a little boy crossing the bike path after his balloon, his mother waving her hand, a boat full of sightseers, a bus struggling downtown, uniformed schoolchildren from St. Hilda's-St. Hugh's lining up to cross from the park, and trees bending in the wind— like most people under pressure in their lives. Ali blinked. In this great art gallery the paintings passed by and the viewer stood still. Now the bus was gone, the schoolchildren had disappeared, the boat was farther downstream. Evening joggers in colorful running suits made their way through the park. Suddenly the streetlights came on to mingle with the distant stars, and the tree branches swung in celebration of a new wind. Though Ali couldn't see, he knew the Hudson was now a different river.

Sara drew his attention back as she glided across the room and handed him a glass foaming with beer.

Ali said, "You have a nice apartment."

"I'm looking after it for an associate of my father's who's out of town for the year," Sara said.

Ali sat on the large, comfortable sofa, and Sara sank into a soft leather armchair. She sipped some white wine and smiled at Ali. He cleared his throat and tried not to stare at Sara. "I wish my mother could call me."

"No, you don't."

"Why not?"

"Because every time my mother has nothing to do she calls me long distance, or my sister in Los Angeles or my brother in Washington, but mostly me, because I'm a better listener."

"What does she tell you?"

"First, the weather, second, the family's aches and pains, then her shopping and moving the furniture around, and, worst of all, which of the girls I know got engaged or married. This is to make me feel guilty about not finding someone." Ali had never heard Sara complain before.

"You don't want the calls?"

"Especially the reruns."

"What reruns?"

"For example, the dangers of New York City and people like you snatching me unguarded."

Ali grinned. "In that case, my mother should be worried, not yours."

Sara laughed. "Well, since we are into mother talk, what about yours?"

"First tell me about your family."

"There is not much to say. My brother is an architect and my sister is a bourgeois housewife, as you would say. We aren't that close. My father always said he'd support us through college, and beyond that we're on our own. Now, what about your mother?"

"I don't get calls, just letters. I write her every Sunday, just about."

"Are you pulling my leg?"

"No. My mother needs my letters more than I need the time. Besides, I'm greedy."

"She pays you?" Sara teased.

"In kind. She sends me all sorts of goodies and I must at least acknowledge I've received them." Ali interrupted himself and handed Sara a giftwrapped box. "I almost forgot. This is for you, all the way from Teheran by Pan American."

"What is it?"

"Open it."

Sara opened a box of big pistachios with the shells half open, smiling at her. "I see what you mean, Ali."

As they ate the nuts, Ali watched Sara sitting across from him. Her silky blouse, the same light blue color of her eyes, revealed her breasts. The beige skirt, which ended above her knees, exposed the curves of her crossed thighs disappearing into the soft leather of the chair. Conscious of the attention,

Sara shifted her legs.

Ali felt awkward. He wished to know Sara better, but he wanted to touch her more. He saw her as outgoing and relaxed, while he was tense, uneasy and in need. He knew she was broadminded and sensitive, without Eric's moral arrogance, and she would listen to new ideas openmindedly. Ali thought to himself, "What the hell am I doing analyzing Sara?"

"Sara," he said, "may I have another beer?"

"Yes, sir." Sara returned with the beer and pressed Ali to tell her of his family.

"You're asking for a long story," he said, "so brace yourself."

"Our house is in an old neighborhood of narrow streets not far from Parliament. My father is a theology professor. He is writing a book on the dangers of unifying religious and state authority. My mother prays, cares for father, waters the roses and feeds the canaries, and she helps in an orphanage. An old servant, Maryam, helps her around the house.

"My younger sister Zaman studies physics, a rare field for a woman in Iran. She is in love with an Armenian, a non-Muslim—and this is a secret to all but you and me! Her religious beliefs are not what they used to be. She is a feminist and is turning to radical politics. All of this in Teheran means trouble for Zaman.

"My brother Hussain is enchanted by Ayatollah Khomeini. He wants to become a mullah, a Muslim clergyman. In some ways we are alike, but when it comes to politics and faith we are worlds apart. We are all puzzled how the same family produced such different political views.

"My brother Abbas's daughter, Parvine, lives with us. Soon after Abbas was murdered—remember I mentioned it in the radio debate—his wife committed suicide." Ali saw a suit with bloody holes, and the words died on his lips as he mourned for a moment in silence.

"Our lives and dreams are different from yours in America, even though we have the same basic needs. Iran has a long history, and we are less impatient with the present and less anxious about the future than Americans. Persians are done with dominating other nations, but Americans are doing it now, though without knowing who they dominate and why. For Americans know-how is the essence, while the goals are secondary. Your problem is to stop exploiting; ours is now to stop being exploited."

Sara protested, "Ali, please don't lecture me! I ask about your family but I get politics. I promise you another slot on the radio, but let's have a moratorium on politics tonight."

Ali smiled to reassure her. "You're right. No more politics tonight. But you know Sara, sometimes I just have trouble forgetting the problems of my people."

"Let's drink to individuals, to our friendship, and to the meeting of East and West," Sara said. "By the way, how's your head?"

"Much better, thank you."

"I must confess I was surprised to discover how worried I was about you in the hospital."

"You were?"

"Are you fishing for compliments? I was interested in your head, cracked or healed."

"Do you want to feel your favorite skull?" A devilish smile spread over Ali's face.

"Yes," Sara sat beside him and put her hand gently on his forehead.

"It never felt so good until you touched it," Ali said.

They drank more and talked about movies, books, the summer, a new nude beach on Fire Island, her dreams, his plans, the fact that Sara and Zaman sought women's emancipation in two different worlds. The unity of things, the diversity of life, the sweetness of the persimmons and figs on the trees in Ali's home, the joy in Iranian children's eyes on the first day of spring, the New Year. They had much to say, much to hear, much to look at in each other, much to trust. They had to cross cultural gorges and oceans of misconceptions.

Sara was learning that there were two sides to Ali: the outward, hard, bitterly antagonistic revolutionary often at odds with the inward, sensitive, even soft, tender idealist. Sara admitted to Ali that she had liked him the first time she had seen him, but then Ali's harsh tongue had turned her off. "It was a struggle for me to take your arrogance," she said, "but I wanted to know you anyhow."

"My arrogance?" Ali inquired half-seriously.

"Yes, yours. You can be quite proud and unbending at times." Sara continued, "But now finally, veal scallopini with almonds has brought us together." They laughed, the two acquaintances becoming good friends.

After dinner they returned to the living room and talked more about themselves. Ali confessed he had been jealous of Eric.

"How unmarxist," Sara raised her voice in imitation of Ali.

Ali could not help but laugh. He said, "I wish I could free myself from jealousy."

"Don't do it—you'll be boring."

"How does Eric feel about your seeing me?" Ali inquired.

"He is handling it very maturely. Eric is realistic, and maybe he thinks this will pass."

"Maybe he's wrong," Ali said hopefully.

The food, the alcohol, the words and Sara's eyes changed Ali's mood to the happiest since he had left home. He relaxed and sank deep into the couch, closer to Sara—the most beautiful woman he had ever seen. He finished a brandy, and leaning forward to put the glass on the coffee table, his eyes fell on Sara's hand resting softly in her lap. Her silk skirt followed the contours of her legs. With a strong desire to trace that curve with his fingers, Ali put one hand over hers and swung the other around her shoulder, pulling her close while their knees struggled to occupy the same space.

A little surprised, Sara resisted, but not enough to discourage him. She lifted his hand, but Ali moved it gently to her breast. Sara trembled and cursed her inhibitions, while his hungry lips surrounded hers and their hearts pounded against one another like hunted deer.

It was late the next morning before Ali left Sara's apartment. He hadn't told her he loved her, though the intensity of his feelings kept him lightheaded for hours.

* * * * *

All classes at Columbia were suspended now, so he had nowhere he had to go; time was like a crane taking off from a marsh—slow, uncertain, halting and heavy. He headed to the library, a nest he returned to to lose himself in the ideas of others. But that did not work today. Eric intruded into his blissful thoughts of Sara. Sara had told Ali of Eric's persistent telephone calls, although she had maintained she was not interested in Eric. Ali tried to get his mind off Sara and Eric, but in vain. Every word of every book turned to "Sara." He saw her face in the giant windows. Finally he went to a telephone booth.

"Is that you, Sara?" Ali asked.

"Yes, Ali, nothing but me."

"I love you, Sara."

"Good! Tell me, how much reading and thinking brought you to that conclusion?"

"As a matter of fact I am in the library, but because of you I can't read or think."

"Good, again. Start feeling."

"You sound tough, like a conqueror."

"I am. I am also conquered, but I feel strong and good. I'm in love with you, whoever you are, Ali."

"Whoever I am, you deserve me. But I must see you now."

"Okay. The Hungarian coffee shop—it's on me."

"Okay," Ali said meekly, sensing that Sara had a point to make. He had paid the last time they were there together.

At the coffee shop, Ali asked pointblank, "Are you still seeing Eric?"

"Ali, dear," Sara said, "I'm not dating Eric. He has no claim on me; I'm my own woman. You already know all of this."

Ali was free of one worry, but new worries rushed at him later that night. Sara didn't say she was through with Eric forever, he worried with a new lover's insecurity. He thought of home, of his commitment to the revolution, and of his love for Sara. How could an ardent revolutionary fall in love with an American girl? The reality of the situation oppressed him. Could Sara go to Iran with him? Would she become sympathetic to his political plans? I must soon talk to her about my worries, Ali decided. Then he criticized himself. Should I consider politics the main thing in everything I do? Sara is right. I can be a revolutionary without trying to convince the world. Not everyone feels about Abbas the way I do. Why can't I accept Sara as she is? Ali did not know that Sara was ahead of him and had already accepted him for what he was.

For a while he lessened his political activities, and Sara limited her commitments to the radio and her time with her feminist friends. Both contrived to spend every available minute together.

The spring of 1968 was growing old and warm. But even in their most idyllic moments, Ali could not shake his fear that their joy would be short-lived, like a rainstorm over the desert sands. Ali's melancholy infected Sara as well, who struggled against it.

As they fed one another grapes and cherries one sunny day in Riverside Park, he tried to talk about his anxiety. But Sara said, "Oh, Ali, you're everything I want, but you're also a pessimist and a fatalist, which I don't want. Let's enjoy the moment today and not worry about tomorrow."

Smiling up at her as he lay in the lush grass, his head at her knees, he said, "How can I be a pessimist? Here we are eating grapes from Chile out of a wicker basket from the Philippines watching a ship delivering Hawaiian sugarcane to Yonkers, listening to the music of the British Beatles on a Japanese radio, and on top of that, being with you. And you say I'm not optimistic, seeing what man has done? Would your grandparents have believed the occasion that brings me and the grapes from the ends of the earth just for your pleasure, Sara? I call it a miracle!"

"My grandfather would scowl at the idea of you and me together! In any case, since when is international trade a miracle?" Sara laughed at her companion. "Is that Professor Pirooz' new theory?"

"What about your grandmother, what would *she* do?"

"Same as I, I suppose she would have loved you—she had my romantic weakness—but only if she didn't know you were a damned atheist." As Ali laughed, Sara put her arms around his neck, playfully punctuating her taunts with kisses, and not letting Ali speak. She said, "I don't have sleepless nights about the future of mankind, but about our future. I admit it. Last night I thought, What would it be like to live with you, to have your children? We have been going out for only a few months, and yet I feel I want to stay with you forever." Sara paused and put her palm against his cheek. "I've never felt this way before, Ali. I love you. I don't ever want to lose what we have. We can make it last, can't we, Ali?" Her eyes pleaded.

Ali drew her to him. With her face resting on his chest and her eyes closed, he kissed her eyelids and smiled as he gently pushed a cherry through her lips.

Sara opened her eyes. They were decisive. "If you have had your fill of that roach-infested apartment of yours, you are welcome to move into my place."

"Do you mean that?"

"Yes. All the way."

"What do I do with all the money I'll save?"

"I'll let you take me to my favorite operas at the Met."

The days grew warmer still, turning the spring into summer as their love grew stronger. On the third Sunday in June, Ali and Sara rowed aimlessly around the lake in Central Park and drifted with the rhythm of wind and waves. Sara reclined in the prow and enjoyed the sun on her bare shoulders. Ali sprawled facing her, but looked into the distance.

"Doesn't the sun feel good? Some say the sun is an aphrodisiac. What do you think?" Getting no response, she opened her eyes to see Ali's pensive gaze.

"What's wrong?" she asked. "For the past few days you've been acting as if you expect a disaster. Come on," she pleaded, "school is over and the pressure is off, at least for a while. Let's enjoy it."

"I'm sorry, Sara," Ali answered quietly. "It's not school or the usual things that worry me. It's Mr. Dixon." He began to twirl one of the oars under his palm.

"Who's Dixon?"

"An Immigration officer. He says he's going to deport me."

Sara sat upright at once. "Deport you? Why?"

"For holding a job without a work permit," Ali answered.

"Did you?"

"Yes. The foreign student advisor recommended the job, and I took it thinking they would inform Immigration. I had to help pay my tuition. Besides, I told the employer right away I was a foreign student. I certainly didn't hide anything."

Clouds moving across the sky covered the sun. The breeze picked up, and Sara felt the chill. She waited to hear more, but Ali fell silent. "That can't be all. Come on, Ali, a lot of foreign students do that. I know five or six guys who wait on tables or work as clerks. Nobody cares about that."

"Evidently someone cares about this case."

"But why pick on you?" As soon as she asked she knew Ali's response. "Is it your politics?"

"I think so. In your democracy the laws are applied selectively. When it suits them, officials use legal technicalities to conceal political motives."

"Why do you call it my democracy, Ali? I'm not doing this to you."

Sara came closer to Ali and took his hand. "Let's not debate. You're going to fight it, aren't you?"

Ali spoke softly. "Sara, I don't know yet what I have to do. I just know I have to see Dixon on Monday. Pirooz is coming with me." For a few moments neither of them spoke of their fears, contemplating Ali's few options.

Ali dreaded having to compromise himself to get out of the jam. He didn't want to leave America now with his studies unfinished and with his love for Sara growing. But his stomach knotted up whenever he anticipated the interview with Dixon. Ali's beliefs and the policies of the U.S. government intersected only on the battlefield, not on the calm shores of compliance. Ali was extremely critical of U.S. treatment of immigrant workers, for one thing. He was frustrated that he must comply with the ruling concerning his own future.

Sara whispered, "Come on, Ali, we'll figure out what to do. I know you don't believe it, but you can fight for your rights in this system."

"Yes," Ali said sarcastically, imagining Dixon trying to hammer him into submission. "I have lots of rights, you have lots of rights. The poor here have the right to live with roaches, to freeze, to ride dangerous subways, to be victimized by criminals, landlords, loansharks, bosses, doctors, mechanics, plumbers, politicians, policemen, dentists, bankers, lawyers and Dixons."

"Thanks for not including me," Sara mumbled to herself.

"What?"

"I said, 'Thanks for not including me,'" Sara repeated, raising her voice impatiently. Then she added calmly, "There you go again Ali, criticizing the U.S. and lecturing me!"

"Make fun, Sara, but you know I'm right. People can't change their situation."

"Stop it, Ali, please," Sara implored. "I've listened to this so many times. What do you expect me to do? I'm worried about you. Tell all this to the world, but just tell me what I can do for you. Let us be realistic, Ali. This could be a simple problem and may not require the overthrow of imperialism to fix it." The lovers smiled sadly at each other.

The sky had grown dark and threatening in the west, and thunder rumbled in the distance. Sara wanted to change the subject to get Ali off his gloomy thoughts. "We'd better start rowing to shore; it looks like rain. Did you hear today's forecast?"

"Goddamn it!" Ali, in his worst mood, exploded. "Why should I waste my time worrying about the forecast? I don't care if we get wet. Think about politics, not weather. Nature isn't the enemy, it's this wretched system."

Sara just looked at him calmly and uttered no word; like a giant oak she let the wind pass by. Despite his outburst, Ali grabbed the oars and began rowing in earnest, as big, heavy drops started splashing into the boat. Damn it, he thought, why do I argue with Sara? It isn't her fault. And it wasn't the first time he had disputed her logic while following her advice. Sara knew this fault and Ali knew also that she was more realistic and he valued her practicality. Sara had brought him down to earth and let him see things as he suspected others saw them. He had learned a lot from Sara about human beings and had acknowledged it to her and the Professor. People don't want to get wet; they have the right to communicate that feeling; Ali thought to himself. Ali stretched his hand touching Sara's knee, gently apologizing without words.

Sara, in turn, understood and forgave her impetuous lover for his explosion of anger. That Ali would accept nothing without a fight and his deep sincerity in everything he did had first attracted her. Sara had even heard herself repeating his ideas as her own in some of the feminist meetings.

The two lovers arrived home soaking wet. They held hands as they watched the angry, roaring storm through Sara's window, saw the snarl of lightning on the face of the sky, and felt the thunderbolt slamming the building. Trees were battered in unison and violently shed tears in big drops. The Hudson looked full of cold anger, the park threw people out. Every drop of rain, as if resisting gravity and its death, floated sideways with the whirling of the wind, only to fall and be smashed on the concrete pavement awaiting each rain drop as coldly as the next.

"That goddamn Dixon may force me to choose between you and home sooner than I want."

"Why not me and home together?"

"A revolutionary raising a family? That's impossible. And you know I have to fight the Shah."

Sara looked at Ali, kept silent, felt a chill. A tear drop mixing with a drop of rain from her wet hair rolled down across Sara's face. She knew something was wrong; this was a serious problem.

The lovers didn't lose sight of each other for days to come, hanging on to each other as though out in the storm.

Years later in solitary confinement, Ali would discover the full meaning of Sara's silences and little protests. It was hard enough for her to listen to her mother's complaints and subtle commands, but she had to bear the same burden with Ali so that he could get worries off his chest. Not until he was in prison did Ali come to fully appreciate Sara and how much he needed her. And in prison, he fell more and more in love with her, long after he had admitted he loved her.

CHAPTER 6

Immigration

In the Monday morning rush hour, Ali and Pirooz walked downstairs to the subway platform for an appointment with Mr. Dixon at the immigration office. As the echo of an approaching train ricocheted up the stairs, commuters desperate to catch it pressed the two Iranians downward. For those who had to punch time-cards, every minute of delay was a pair of scissors cutting off part of their paychecks.

The antique subway cars lurched from the station with a violent screech. Odors of last night's urine and vomit mingled with those of garlic, perfume and sweat to overwhelm Pirooz. It stank like a garbage dump near Teheran, except that here the smells sped from one end of town to the other. The hot air, the racket of the cars bouncing on an old trackbed, the tunnel wall punctuated by lightbulbs running past the windows, and the bored faces in the passing trains gave the impression of a horrid merry-go-round. The packed riders hung onto straps, swaying and jerking like the damned copulating in hell.

At a stop the noise lessened for a moment, and Pirooz said, "No matter how many times I ride the darned thing, I still don't believe it is real."

"I can't believe people put up with it," Ali answered.

"They say you can't fight City Hall," Pirooz replied. Everyone seemed resigned to the ordeal, he thought; neither private enterprise nor the government could provide a dignified or safe means of transportation. Pirooz would love to have one minute on CBS to announce as the top news item: "Millions of innocent citizens were mistreated today, and will be in the future as long as the New York subways remain the same."

The speeding train pierced the darkness of the tunnels, blasting apart congregations of metallic dust particles which hung in mid-air, replacing them with others in its wake. The *New York Times* had finally broken the news one day that the mayor had suppressed findings that these particles caused lung cancer.

The Professor and Ali stood all the way downtown and then walked to

61

the Federal Building on Church Street, office of the United States Immigration and Naturalization Service. There, thousands with drawn, confused faces, speaking in many tongues, entered, stood in lines, sat on benches, waited and prayed. It looked like a United Nations of the desperate.

Mr. Dixon's office was on the seventh floor, one of many cubicles separated by translucent panels which touched neither ceiling nor floor but stood on short, pig-like legs at the corners. Each office had two chairs, one desk and one picture of President Johnson. Opposite the cubicle, a plastic-cushioned bench held immigrants by day and napping janitors by night. Ali and Pirooz sat there and Pirooz said, "Be cool, Ali. Please don't question the regulations or Dixon's authority."

Dixon was on the telephone, and his bulky profile seen through the partition projected power. At last he appeared in the door and called Ali's name. When Ali and Pirooz stood up, Dixon scrutinized them over the top of his glasses.

Ali said, "Professor Pirooz has come to vouch for me."

Dixon looked at Ali. "Do you need an interpreter?"

"No."

"Then the professor didn't need to come." Dixon then addressed Pirooz. "You can wait here, if you wish." Dixon stepped into his office, and, with a raised eyebrow, Ali followed.

Pirooz sat down again with a sense of foreboding. He remembered his own numerous trips to the Immigration Office to get his green card; he remembered visits to the IRS, which resulted not in extra taxes but in an official explanation of why the audit was necessary; and he remembered two FBI agents dropping in on his apartment because he subscribed to the *Daily Worker,* which violated no laws.

I'm an outlaw within the law, Pirooz thought. I object to the way I am treated and the disadvantaged are treated, but my objection is tempered, my rebellion is contained. I want to survive and enjoy life in America, even as I suffer from it. I am not strong enough to risk everything to fight the system. Ali wants to destroy the reality he despises or be destroyed by it; he is the kind who causes change—a revolutionary, an artist, a scientist, a saint. Ali is more primitive and yet somehow more civilized than us conformists. He will be punished for trying to change reality. Artists do suffer and saints get killed.

Dixon meanwhile asked Ali to be seated as he fell into his own chair. He looked at Ali's long hair and heavy moustache and saw a troublemaker. Without ado, Dixon took out a form and read the questions to Ali. At length Dixon reached the heart of the matter. "Have you ever been a member of the Communist Party?"

"No." Only a fool would admit it, Ali thought.

"Have you ever belonged to any organization which seeks to overthrow the government of the United States?"

"No."

Dixon stared into Ali's eyes. "Are you a homosexual?"

"Excuse me?" The transition from subversion to homosexuality caught Ali by surprise.

Dixon thought Ali didn't know the word. "Have you slept with another man?"

Ali stared at the immigration officer, but Dixon's eyes retreated to his desk. "No."

Dixon opened Ali's file. It was thick, Ali observed. Internal memoranda, transmittal forms, endorsements, endorsements of the endorsements, and copies of documents made up the bulk of the file. The police report on Ali's admission to St. Luke's and a list of names from the Iranian and the Columbia student newspapers slipped through Dixon's hands.

A letter with a photograph of Ali, his fist raised, giving a speech, lay on top of a wad of papers held by a paperclip.

"To the Director of the Immigration Service," the letter read. "Your attention is directed to remarks made by Mr. Ali Keshavarz on radio station WKCR at or after 11:00 a.m., Wednesday, April 29, 1968, in which he questioned the constitutional authority of our country and stated that he studies chemistry to make explosives. As a leader of the communist SDS, he had a major responsibility for the illegal and forced closing of Columbia University. He is currently employed in the campus bookstore, which violates the U.S. work rule regulations. In my judgement, Mr. Keshavarz has violated the civil and criminal laws of the United States and should be expelled from our country."

The letter was signed, "Eric Saunders, President of the Majority Coalition." Attached were a flurry of correspondence and memoranda, and Dixon's assignment as case officer.

Dixon looked up. "You've left us no choice. I must issue an extradition order due to your violation of the work rule. However, I can adjust your departure date to give you time to settle your affairs."

Ali strove to remain calm. "I thought that the purpose of this meeting was to review my case. You have questioned me extensively, but I have not had a chance to respond to the charge. I had no intention of violating the work rule—"

Dixon interrupted, "Mr. Keshavarz, the regulations are concerned with actions, not intentions."

"I took the job with the assistance of the school placement office and the approval of the bookstore management. Don't you agree that the dean and the employer should know and follow the regulations? To me they represented legitimate authority."

Dixon smiled, thinking that, to a communist neither the dean nor the employer was legitimate, but to Ali it appeared natural to deny authority or appeal to it, as it suited his purposes.

"Mr. Keshavarz, your lack of knowledge does not absolve you of responsibility. Illiterate alien farmhands who work illegally are still responsible. Regulations are regulations; I don't make them, I just follow them." Dixon glanced at his watch.

Ali fought to control his temper. "But employers who hire cheap alien labor do conspire to break the law, don't they?"

Frustrated, Dixon said, "Yup!" He stared at the young Iranian who dared to attack the laws and law enforcement of the United States. At last Dixon said, "Mr. Keshavarz, you may appeal the decision and be represented by an attorney."

Ali protested mildly, "This is a Catch-22 situation. The dean finds me a job so I can pay my tuition, and now you advise me to hire a lawyer to stay in the U.S. But how can I pay a lawyer if I'm not allowed to work?"

Dixon pushed down on the chair arms to lift himself up. "I can say no more. My son is your age; he's a student, too. Mind you, your case isn't hopeless. I hear Joe, the guard downstairs, has a list of lawyers specializing in immigration cases." Then, his voice turning formal, Dixon held his hand out. "Mr. Keshavarz, you will soon receive formal notice of my decision." Ali shook hands hesitantly and fled from the office and his own pretensions. Ali knew he had much more to protest to Mr. Dixon, but he had promised Sara and Pirooz to behave very diplomatically. And so he pretended.

As Ali and the Professor walked to the elevators, Pirooz asked, "How did it go?"

"It looks bad. I have to go to court. It's strange. Dixon wouldn't listen to me, yet he told me indirectly where to get a lawyer. It sounds like an extortion scheme."

Pirooz said, "Possibly, but so what? To get a green card you need two citizens who have known you for five years to testify on your behalf, but the lobby is full of witnesses for hire. The officials know this, and some of them get kickbacks. Relax, Ali. Your problem may be solved without a big fuss. First, let's get hold of Dixon's lawyer. What's his name?"

"The guard downstairs knows," Ali replied. "You know, it wasn't easy, but I didn't tell Dixon what I think of him. I feel I've walked out of a sewer."

"Bravo! You'd better get used to it."

"Used to what?"

"A revolutionary must outwit the police and state. He must lie and plot better than they do, or else he's finished."

"Is it that simple?" Ali asked, a bit puzzled.

"No. He may even have to keep the truth from his family for their own sake and for the safety of the revolutionary party."

"Never," Ali responded.

"Then your ultimate goal is not revolution, and revolution is not for you. Listen, for a revolutionary, truth and lies, lawfulness and lawlessness are just the means. If truth works, then truth is good; if a lie works, then the lie is better. And if the law works then he follows the law and if the lawlessness works then he must become an outlaw. A revolutionary must be absolutely truthful to himself, to his comrades, to the revolutionary cause and above all to the ultimate interest of the masses." Pirooz was the perfect revolutionary in theory, if not in practice. He could not himself pull off as much as a white lie.

"What is the difference between a revolutionary and the Shah or Nixon, then?" Ali asked.

"A big difference. The revolutionary is for the common people, and the Shah and Nixon are for themselves and the ruling classes. So their truth and their lies are to further the interests which are not of the people neccessarily."

Ali felt a knot in his brain, realizing he had taken the first deceptive steps, but he couldn't know how far he would have to go. Ali insisted, "Doesn't this advice turn me into an opportunist?"

Pirooz answered impatiently and pedantically, "Read Lenin's *Left-wing Communism—An Infantile Disorder.*" The Professor then dashed into the first elevator that opened its doors, and Ali followed. The sensation of extra weight informed them the elevator was going up. Finally they reached the ground floor and set about finding Joe.

The guard was a prosperous-looking man of about fifty, with short, neatly combed silver hair and a well-tailored uniform. With a half smile, Joe asked the Professor about Ali's problem, as well as the name of the case officer. He listened like a physician diagnosing a disease. Then Joe recommended a Jacob Goldberg, writing down his telephone number. Pirooz handed Joe a five-dollar bill and thanked him. Ali observed from a distance, like a football coach continuing a game under protest. The scene reminded him of the passport office in Teheran, where cash changed hands and handshakes followed the bribe, where officials broke the law in broad daylight. His passport application had been stranded for months when he had refused to pay the bribe.

Ali and Pirooz went out into the downtown summer heat. "What are you going to do?" Pirooz asked.

"I want to expose Dixon."

"Why?"

"He's a crook."

"You've already convicted him?"

"Yup." Ali imitated Dixon.

Pirooz counselled Ali, "Dixon isn't worth a fight. Paying him off won't make the world worse and won't compromise you, it will just corrupt the system, which makes it easier to uproot it. Think of Cuba. It used to be Battista's gambling and prostitution joint and U.S. corporations' sugar and tobacco land. Corruption made it easier for Castro to rally the people, and throw out the regime and the U.S.''

Pirooz continued, "Look, if you pay, you will stay with Sara and finish your studies; if you don't—Well, you can't conduct a revolution in the Shah's prison.''

"I will get to Iran secretly. Tell me, why would Dixon want to send me to prison?''

"Come on, Ali," Pirooz said impatiently, "He's just sending you to the Chemical Bank. Maybe he thinks you have oil money.''

"But he knows I have to work to pay the tuition.''

Pirooz responded, "Just call the lawyer and find out what his fee is.''

"That's fine," Ali protested. "You state the options and then you make the choice for me.''

The two men fell silent. Pirooz hoped Ali would soon be in a better mood and change his mind.

That evening Ali, Sara and Helena met at Pirooz' to discuss Ali's problem. The four had become close friends in the recent months. For supper, Pirooz surprised them with a magnificent dinner of chicken breasts with Persian sweet rice flavored with pistachio nuts, slivers of orange peel, and carrots. After dinner, Ali called Goldberg's number. There had been no answer all afternoon. "Just once more," Ali mumbled.

In an apartment on West 25th Street, the telephone rang. Goldberg muttered, "Who the hell could that be?''

The man on the sofa, sipping a bourbon, motioned Goldberg toward the phone and whispered, "Maybe that cocksure Eye-ranian is rising to the bait." Goldberg had invited Dixon for steak and baked potatoes.

"May I speak to Mr. Goldberg?" the telephone voice said. "My name is Ali Keshavarz.''

Goldberg winked at Dixon. "This is Mr. Goldberg.''

Ali explained his case until Goldberg interrupted. "Who is the case officer?''

"Dixon.''

"I don't know him," Goldberg said, "but you should know that immigration is cracking down on students. No case is easy anymore.'' Goldberg paused to let his warning sink in. "But your case is not impossible.''

"How much will it cost?''

"I can't tell you on the phone. You'll have to come to my office.''

"To save time, how about a rough estimate?''

"Well now," Goldberg started, "I recommend a five hundred dollar deposit to be credited toward compensation at fifty dollars an hour.''

"For how many hours?" Ali insisted.

"Without the facts I have no idea."

"Thank you, Mr. Goldberg. I will think it over and call you."

"I shouldn't advise you at this point," Goldberg hurried to say, "but time is of the essence. Legal problems become incurable if left unattended." Ali's temper flared. "Don't threaten me. I'll expose your extortion." He hung up at once and moved away from the telephone as if from a scorpion.

Goldberg's expectations had bounced like a racquetball and smashed back into his face. He turned to Dixon. "That son of a bitch is cocky." Goldberg retrieved his drink and slumped into an armchair, disappointed at letting Ali slip away, and startled by the unexpected threat.

Dixon said, "I should have warned you. He's not easily frightened or coaxed."

Goldberg said in relief, "I'm glad he's off my back."

"Wait till I apply the screws. It's not just the work permit; he's up to his neck in the rampage at Columbia. If he's deported, he'll be put into a dungeon with other commies. He'll knuckle under, you'll see."

"I don't think you got the point, Dixon. He hung up on me."

" He did?" Dixon said unbelievingly.

"Goddamn intellectuals," Goldberg continued. "If you push them around like the regular immigrants, they'll cause trouble. We can't put this fellow on a job and keep him there to pay the legal fees as we do with the others."

Dixon grinned and said, "As far as Ali Keshavarz is concerned, we will just sit on his case. If he calls back, so much the better. If not, I'll make an example of him." Goldberg felt reassured.

"Well, Jake," Dixon said affectionately as he pulled himself up from the sofa, "it's getting late. Thanks for dinner. Remember, call me if you hear from Keshavarz again, and for God's sake use my home number."

When Dixon was gone, Goldberg turned on the TV, lit a cigarette, took a swallow of bourbon and slumped down in his chair. Ali's word "extortion" ate into him. The Dixon deal could lead to trouble, he thought. There must be some clean place in the legal profession for me. Several hundred thousand lawyers could get rich from people in trouble in the U.S., but he was on the bottom of the totem pole.

Goldberg, separated from his wife, wondered idly why Dixon had never married. His question would be answered years later by witnesses in court when the extortion scheme became an open sewer. Dixon, a closet homosexual, had accepted sexual favors from a few immigrants who could not have paid cash. Eventually, Dixon lost his job and Goldberg was disbarred; both were put in a minimum security prison briefly, but the Immigration Office continued to operate as before.

Uptown, Sara insisted, "What did Goldberg say?" When Ali kept silent, Pirooz tried. "You're caught in an ambush, Ali. Pay Goldberg or go to Iran."

"Repetition won't convince me," Ali replied sullenly.

"For God's sake, what did the man say?" Sara demanded.

"He wants fifty dollars an hour and won't tell me how many hours. That's fifty times what we don't know, and what do you get?"

"Fort Knox," said the Professor. "But be realistic. You've got to go along with him. What choice do you have?"

"I hung up on him. I'd have to borrow money for a legal battle and I'm not sure I could swallow all that's necessary in order to win."

"Such as what?" Sara demanded.

"Such as pretending I respect due process and behaving as though I believe it really works."

"Ali," Pirooz said, "listen to me. No matter how much you've learned about imperialism, it isn't going to help you start a revolution back home. Conditions aren't ripe yet. Your staying here or leaving will make no difference, except to yourself. So what if you call Goldberg back or get a lawyer and take a chance with an appeal?"

Sara added, "If you want to stay with us, do as Pirooz says."

Ali said, "Okay, but I wonder how 'equal protection under the law' can get me into the mess I'm in or make the lives of a million immigrant workers a tragedy."

"Come on, Ali," said Pirooz, "get to the point. It's your case now, not capitalism. Hell, there are thieves and bureaucrats all over the world. Iran is full of them. You can't fight each corrupt official personally. Let the revolution sweep them away. Work for the revolution. That means saving your own skin and others later."

"Okay, okay, Pirooz," Ali conceded. "I'll try, but I'm going back home, and whether I go in two weeks or after I've finished at Columbia isn't going to make much difference. If anything, life in New York is pushing me toward the revolution. I don't understand why the city doesn't turn out more revolutionaries."

Pirooz said, "You're saying New York should be the womb of revolutionaries?"

"Yes. New York has taught me that the colonial masses are not the only exploited and suffering people."

"Can you say one damned good thing about New York, Ali?" Sara realized she had asked him a similar question before, but his frequent criticisms of America were beginning to sound like a broken record.

Ali whispered, "I can name a thousand and one. I loved sitting beside you at the opera to hear *Turandot,* and all the wonderful Broadway and off-Broadway plays and the foreign movies. And just don't tell me of the New

York Philharmonic. I could live there if I could afford the rent.

"I don't want to admit it, but I loved the roller coaster at Coney Island, too. Remember, Sara, how you clung tight to me?" Sara smiled and held Ali's hand. "I like all the dancing and music in Central Park on Sundays. And then this wonderful cultural quilt of Jews, Italians, Blacks, Polish, Chinese, Puerto Ricans. Where else in the world do you find such a mixture?"

Pirooz' eyes glowed. Ali can be saved, he thought.

Then Ali became more somber. "More than anything else I like the fact that I can just borrow the books of Marx and Lenin and others and not have to hide them like back home, and I like the fact that the *New York Times* published my letter about torture in Iran."

"What is wrong with staying, then?" Sara asked.

Ali talked as though to himself. "I love New York, but it is still the injustice, the poverty and suffering of so many in the midst of affluence that I see most. I can't help it, it hammers on my soul every day." Ali reflected a moment, then said quietly, "You must cut out a part of your flesh if it is diseased. Anyhow, to stay with Sara I will fight in court, but I won't compromise my principles." He drew Sara close.

Pirooz said, "All right then, what are we going to do?"

Helena cut in. "This immigration harrassment could be a political attack on you, Ali. I think you should get a civil rights lawyer."

Pirooz argued, "It's impossible to prove a political motive, so you'll have to defend the case as a work rule violation. I will consult a law professor, and Ali, you find out how Ghotbzadeh got out of his recent immigration jam."

Sara offered to ask her father to seek help from his friend, Spiro Agnew, the Governor of Maryland. Also, she would inquire about the Legal Aid Society. Sara thought of getting Eric's advice, too, but she kept it to herself, guessing that Ali wouldn't approve. As speculation piled on speculation as to why Ali had been singled out by the Immigration Office, Sara could never have imagined that Eric's jealousy and zealousness were the cause.

Ali sat uncharacteristically quiet. He listened and thought. Deep down he agreed with Pirooz that there was no use struggling with Dixon, but it was difficult to let himself be exploited knowingly. He wanted to stay, but he left his options open.

"Professor," Ali interjected, "what do you think about Legal Aid?"

"It's a possibility," Pirooz said. "But you'll get a lawyer who prepares your case to gain experience, like medical interns who perfect their skills operating on the poor."

Sara held Ali's hand. Helena went to the television and turned on the late news. The report was of Vietnamese killed, property destroyed, land defoliated. It was the summer of the bombing halt, yet the bombs continued to drop; it was the summer of the campaign for peace, yet the war continued. The inability of Ali and Pirooz to rebel against brutality and injustice produced in them a sullen anger tinged with despair. They identified with the powerless, even with the dead.

Leaving Helena with Pirooz, Ali and Sara returned to their apartment. Later that night in bed, Ali whispered, "I've been in an awful mood, worse than my worst. Will you forgive me?" Sara, still angry with him, said nothing, so Ali continued, "I am pushed and pulled by opposite forces and desires I don't know how to handle. I love you, Sara. Even my bones crack for you!" Ali kissed Sara's nose, then her chin, her elbow, her knees and her ankle.

Sara tingled and pushed Ali away. "Why are you after the bony parts of me tonight?"

Ali sounded happier. "Just so they won't feel neglected. Also, I'm finding your hard bones and tough character as lovable as everything else."

"You are crazy Ali."

"Yes, I am crazy about . . ." Ali then stopped.

"You're after something," Sara said.

"I'm after everything—forgiveness, peace, love forever."

Sara melted in Ali's arms and Ali was lost in her love. That night stood luminous in the memories of the lovers.

CHAPTER 7

The Trials

Sara and Ali went downtown to the Legal Aid Society, where they spent the morning standing in line to fill out applications and be interviewed by a case worker. The waiting was as annoying as in the school Registrar's and the Immigration Office. But with the extradition menacing Ali, Legal Aid seemed the only reasonable and affordable choice. Sara's father wouldn't help, and Ali refused Eric's offer of assistance. Even though Sara's father knew how she felt about Ali, he had advised her, "Keep out of trouble, Sara, and concentrate on your work." She knew the phrase so well—"keep out of trouble and concentrate." She had had to listen to it politely from as far back as she could remember.

Ali's frustration brought last winter's rent strike into his thoughts. Left without heat, the tenants in Ali's building stopped paying rent and chose Ali as their leader. Ali's bronchitis flared up in the cold, sapping his energy. When the landlord filed suit, the court ordered the tenants to pay the back rent and the owner to repair the boiler. An absurd ruling, Ali thought, since thousands of boilers broke down that winter, the newspapers reported. More than a million tenants suffered part of the winter without heat, and the landlords saved on fuel. Tenants knew breakdowns and delayed fuel deliveries were deliberate, but only years later did the courts put the rent of unheated apartments in escrow unless repairs were made immediately.

Ali looked at the people in the Legal Aid office. A Black woman with hair uncombed and eyes without hope sat clutching an envelope as her two boys played at her feet. An old man raised his voice to the clerk to protest a delay. "We need our welfare check. My wife isn't dead, she's an invalid and I have to get back to her." The clerk replied, "We're doing our best, free of charge. Remember!"

Ali was angry that the poor had to beg for justice. Sara looked depressed. Ali whispered, "Injustice and exploitation are integral parts of capitalism."

Sara wouldn't concede that; she claimed it was only some judges who failed to uphold justice. Without turning her head, she whispered back,

"Then why are we wasting our time here?" a question to which Ali had no reply. Then she quickly added, "And surely there is injustice in the third world or socialist block countries." Ali remained silent.

Ali and Sara left after an interview. John Chamberlain, Jr., who would not meet them until the court appearance, was to be Ali's lawyer, free of charge.

When Sara told Eric about Ali's legal problems, Eric felt more turmoil than joy. He had succeeded in bringing Ali to justice, yet in his own eyes he had failed to be just. Eric felt guilty for withholding the truth from Sara, who had always been truthful to him. Also, he now knew Ali, who had not resisted the police, could be of no threat to national security or the Constitution. Ali talked big but he walked scared, Eric concluded. Ali's only real fault was his success with Sara, he had to confess to himself before he confessed it to the priest. Eric, the good citizen who gave blood to the Red Cross and considered himself a devout Catholic, was not quite satisfied with himself. The priest, hearing the whole story, assured him, "My son, you have committed no sin in reporting the truth to the authorities." When Eric suggested that he wished to help Ali now, the priest had said, "Let your compassion be your guide." But the Ali affair was no tennis game; Eric knew there was more at stake. If extradited, Ali's career would be in ruins; he could be imprisoned in Iran, even killed. Eric didn't want that on his conscience, or that sinful story in God's file on him. So with mixed emotions he called Sara to offer his legal assistance. Eric had access to some influential officials in Washington, he insisted. He felt relieved and satisfied, especially when Sara appreciated his offer more than he had expected. Eric was sincere, of course, but he felt ambivalent toward the outcome; if Ali won and succeeded in staying, he could lose Sara for good.

Back in Sara's apartment, Ali brooded the rest of the day, but Sara's smile, reassurances and loving attention gently soothed away his restlessness. Late at night, as he lay beside the sleeping Sara, questions continued to rush into his mind. Why am I undecided whether to go or stay in America? He had no answers.

Ali had embarked on the path toward understanding long ago. He had always been a questioner, a doubter. When he was not quite eight he had asked about the existence of God. Even his father, who always had answers for him, failed to convince him that God existed. But God was not the only object of his curiosity. Answers always created new questions. Ali was certain of the little he knew and the vast terrain he didn't know, but not knowing what he didn't know augmented his wondering. He called it the abyss of uncertainty and unknowingness. In his mind he climbed a mountain of questions, with the answers on the crest. But once on top of the ridge, the mountain rolled further uphill, new questions piling up to new crests, leaving many peaks unconquered.

Ali despised anyone, like Eric, who was certain about everything from the creation of the universe to the best brand of soup. But Ali was ironically not conscious of his own dogmatism in politics. "Ali is absolutely sure capitalism is all darkness and socialism is all light," Pirooz had told Sara. "If you want to understand him at this point in his life, you must understand this." Pirooz had also counselled Ali, "Don't forget, Sara hasn't had your experiences. Give her time to grow out of her upbringing and learn more of the world."

But if not politically, Ali was scientifically flexible and aware of his shortcomings. Except for trivial arithmetic principles or obvious facts, he admitted he would not know the truth even if he held it in his own hands. Tonight his uncertain future hung in his head demanding clarity. Ali considered himself unfixed, unfinished and unpolished, and he doubted that anything would ever become fixed or finished or polished about him. He did not want to be homogenized into the Islamic world he was born in or assimilated into the Christian world to which Pan Am had flown him.

Ali looked at the sleeping Sara for an answer, but saw only a glow in her cheeks. Her golden hair spread over the pillow, some strands thinly covering her face and trailing across his arm. A breeze cooled by the Hudson River blew through the window, and the strands lying on his hand billowed. Her breath, in harmony with the wind, caused her hair on the pillow to join the dance.

The question of his extradition showed its unfeeling face again. What did he want to do? Called from afar and sensing a call from within, Ali felt he must go back to Iran eventually. The man of action felt frustrated by his forced inactivity, by these American legal fetters. As he stared at Sara a sudden insight cleared away all his ambiguous motivations, like a lightning bolt illuminating a field. He was, he realized, using the extradition to convince himself, Sara, Pirooz and his comrades that he was determined to stay, when all the while he wanted to go. Ali strove to avoid wishful thinking, illusions and deception. The solution to any problem must agree with his intuition. He smiled, remembering the Professor's commandment, "Create a good working relationship between your conscious and subconscious and then watch wisdom beaming at you." His future began to become clearer, like a view from a glass window wiped of heavy dust.

Ali wanted to change the world, and in America all he could do was change himself. Everything in the U.S. conspired to focus his attention on comfort, security and success. Here he was only a pawn moved by other people, even by Pirooz, even by Sara. And Ali needed to—had to—be in command of his own life, even if he would make mistakes.

He looked at Sara again. He held a lock of Sara's hair to his lips and kissed it. He kissed it again and again.

He would have to leave her, even though he was in love with that golden woman. He would have to abandon school, his comrades, Pirooz, the revolutionary books he had not yet read, and his emotional attachments, strip himself naked and offer himself to the revolution. But Ali could not see yet that the price he had to pay was not just his own life, but more.

Why couldn't he be like everyone else? What was wrong with having his children nourished in Sara's womb? How could he say that happiness with Sara was not enough for him? Ali asked himself once more if he really wanted to leave.

Pirooz' advice became more meaningful as he gazed at Sara. He vowed to tell her that he would fight to stay until he finished school. He knew that Pirooz was right, that bribery in this case was not necessarily a compromise. If the revolution was the ultimate goal, then illegality was of no consequence. Ali thought of the rebels who robbed banks, not for personal gain but for the revolution; he could not imagine how close he was to becoming a bank robber himself.

Ali's life at this point could be portrayed in a still picture. The images of revolution and Sara's love were superimposed. Then his court appointment tomorrow flashed in his head, and he felt time carrying him there. He wished to stop time; if he could he would stop it forever with Sara at his side. Then, in the next moment, he wished the night would pass in an instant, the earth making a quick turn, like a globe jerked by a child wishing to see both sides at once.

Fate, time and space mingled in his mind. Ali's sense of time and its measurement by quartz crystals were worlds apart. His throbbing pain at the hospital slowed time, while his joyful picnic with Sara shrank it to a moment. But no matter how fast time travelled in different minds, everyone reached the same cosmic destination at once.

So, on Riverside Drive, the same dawn emerged, the same sunlight glittered from the treetops; for the lonely and for lovers, for the homeless and the rich, for prisoners and the free, the sun rose and lit the city all at once.

The breeze removed the hair from Sara's face and set it on the pillow, and Ali's thoughts left him to look at Sara. One breast, white, solid and conic, its peak tinged with pink, emerged from under the sheet. It had taken billions of years for that living sculpture to be chiseled, to emerge from other shapes as Sara's gift to him. The beautiful outline, and Ali's attraction to it, were nature's work. How fortunate he was! He could bend and kiss Sara's lips, breast and hair, and he did, softly, lest she wake up. Sara slept deeply, never having been loved so tenderly. His wakefulness and Sara's sleep maintained an equilibrium of two extreme states of being. Sara, too, had had her nights of wakefulness. But, tonight the physiological necessity of survival had forced her mind to resign, to shut down, to rest, to sleep. For the last few days she had cried in secret; Ali knew little of her torment. Sara had been taught not to speak of her joy or pains freely. And while she thought she had become free of her upbringing, she was not.

Ali's heart was like an expanding balloon filling with love for Sara. It was a long night for Ali, a short night for Sara, Ali deep in thought, Sara lost in dreams. Yet the two arrived together at the same sunrise, in the same bed, where they kissed furiously, as though reunited after a voyage across lightyears.

* * * * *

John Chamberlain, Jr., young, rather short, fair-skinned with a touch of red in his hair, sat on a bench outside the courtroom between the Professor and Ali. Sara was on Ali's right, quietly masking her fears. Pirooz and Helena were thoughtful, and Ali kept to himself.

Chamberlain had a Yale law degree, like his father. His grandfather had founded a prestigious Wall Street law firm, whose partners became corporate directors and Cabinet secretaries and ambassadors. In 1962, Richard Nixon had almost joined the firm, before going to his friends at Cadwallader, Smith. Young Chamberlain was a liberal, much to his father's dismay. So the partnership Chamberlain was entitled to by blood and training looked doubtful, "unless John gets smart," as his father put it. In the meantime, he was assigned to Legal Aid, to work his liberalism out of his system, to get tough in court and to get good publicity for the firm. Defending the poor was more to Chamberlain's taste than fighting corporate wars, but the Legal Aid workload was full of cases and empty of logistical support. To get landlords off the backs of the poor, to defend them from police brutality, to get compensation for defective merchandise they had been fooled into buying, to make insurance companies pay what they promised, and to right other petty injustices required an unceasing war, he felt. If his clients broke the law they went to jail; if the landlord, businessman, police captain or government agent broke it, a lawyer's visit to the judge's chambers, a politician or the bank could repair the damage. A legal aid lawyer without a fee appeared to be a bargain, but such lawyers had little influence, and the poor often understood the real cost only when it was too late.

* * * * *

Chamberlain leaned to face Ali. "Mr. Keshavarz, the government lawyer may try to provoke you. Please speak only when spoken to and stick to the point." Ali nodded.

Sara asked, "Won't he get to tell his side of the story?"

Chamberlain answered, "Perhaps, but our strategy is to set aside the extradition order, this being a first offense."

"That assumes he's guilty," the Professor protested.

Before Chamberlain could respond the imposing doors opened, and everyone followed Chamberlain into a large panelled courtroom. The room was empty except for a lawyer surrounded by a Latino family. Dixon, the Immigration Officer, and a government attorney came in and sat to Ali's left and one row back. Whispers broke the silence, but no words could be understood.

Pirooz noticed a large fly hovering overhead, as if to observe whether humans treated their own kind better than they treated flies. It buzzed around each person in turn, then repeated its tour. When the judge entered, everyone rose at the clerk's command, and the fly soared higher. Ali stood reluctantly, Chamberlain dutifully. The judge looked dignified in his robes. An American flag loomed behind his bench. The clerk made some preliminary remarks while the judge read legal papers. The fly buzzed disrespectfully over the head of the judge, who tried to shoo it away, but the judge's power made no impression on the fly, Pirooz thought.

When the clerk called Ali's case, Ali, Chamberlain and the government lawyer went up before the judge. The judge said, "Mr. Chamberlain, will you show cause why the petitioner should not leave the United States as instructed by the Immigration and Naturalization Service?"

Chamberlain glanced at Ali. "Your Honor, Mr. Keshavarz is a foreign student at Columbia University. The documents demonstrate his excellent scholastic record. My client made no false statements to his employer, and his job was recommended by the school placement office."

The judge looked at Ali and then at the government lawyer, Leeds, who took the cue to respond. "Your Honor, Mr. Keshavarz' employment violates the terms of his student visa. With over a hundred thousand foreign students, this country cannot allow them to take the law into their own hands."

"Mr. Leeds, have you any objection to the documents provided by the petitioner?"

"No, Your Honor. Just that they are irrelevant to this case."

The judge said, "I will be the judge of that."

"Yes, Your Honor."

The judge turned to Ali. "Mr. Keshavarz, what do you have to say for yourself?"

Ali stood, calm but unyielding. "Mr. Dixon has refused to look at the evidence. I am not the party who should be here, but the dean and the employer."

The judge interrupted. "Mr. Keshavarz, please come to the point."

Ali said, "That was the point!"

The judge was impatient to finish the case in order to prepare for a meeting with Senator Javits, whose support he needed to be promoted to the Circuit Court. Ignoring Ali's comment, he looked to Chamberlain. "Does counsel have any more to add?"

"Yes, Your Honor," Chamberlain said. "Deportation is a severe punishment for an unintentional first offense."

The judge asked, "Mr. Leeds, what's the usual procedure on this?"

"Your Honor, the immigration service is a compassionate institution. Even though enforcement is mandated by law, there are circumstances under which it may be relaxed. The present case does not warrant such a consideration."

The judge demanded, "Why not?"

"Your Honor," Leeds responded, "may we approach the bench?"

The two lawyers stood before the judge and Leeds whispered, "Your Honor, the petitioner was arrested during the rioting at Columbia. That constitutes the first offense."

Suddenly the judge grew interested in Ali's case. Political cases could be used for his own advancement. He turned to Ali and saw the bandage on his temple. Chamberlain asked to speak to Ali.

"What is this, now?" he exclaimed. "There's nothing to show you were arrested."

Ali said, "The police lost me in the hospital. The caseworker at your office decided that no arrest meant no arrest."

"Is it true you were with SDS and all that?" Chamberlain asked.

"Yes, all that."

Chamberlain said, "If you want the judge to withdraw the deportation order, please don't say anything political."

Ali smiled. "I must practice self-censorship?"

Chamberlain looked cross and stepped back to the bench. "Your Honor, if there has been an arrest, then let us see the record."

"Your Honor," Leeds replied, "more than seven hundred troublemakers were arrested that day. Mr. Keshavarz resisted and wound up in the hospital. The police were undermanned, and the paperwork just didn't get done correctly."

The judge scrutinized the arrest report. It was a legal travesty, he thought. The arresting officer's signature had been crossed out and another put in its place; the space for the charges was blank. The judge spoke to Leeds. "You realize, Mr. Leeds, I cannot sustain your order based on this." He spoke to Ali. "Did you participate in the uprising at Columbia, Mr. Keshavarz?"

Before Ali could answer, Chamberlain said, "Your Honor, that is self-incrimination."

The judge said, "You're right, but I'll waive the rules if the petitioner wishes to expedite the case.'"

Ali responded willingly, "Columbia ignored the legitimate demands of its students, faculty, tenants and workers for participation in its governance. We exercised our rights to strike.''

"That will be enough of that,'' the judge said irritably. "We're not deporting Columbia.'' Chamberlain frowned at Ali. Dixon looked pleased, Helena looked proud. Sara bit her tongue; Pirooz was concerned. The judge asked Ali, "Are you a member of SDS?''

"Yes. In addition I'm a member of the Iranian Students Association. Both are legal organizations.''

The judge asked, "Were you arrested?''

Ali said, "I was beaten without provocation. By failing to do the paper-work, the police failed to make an illegal arrest look legal.''

"Your Honor,'' Leeds protested, "Mr. Keshavarz' intransigence shows his disregard for our laws. It only confirms the appropriateness of the depor-tation order.''

The judge said, 'That is sufficient, Counsellor. We'll take a recess, and counsel will join me in chambers.''

As the judge vanished, Chamberlain whispered to Ali, "It doesn't look too bad.''

Chamberlain and Leeds joined the judge in the back room. Helena squeezed Ali's hand and whispered, "Bravo.'' Pirooz asked, "How can due process work with so much huddling behind the scenes?'' Ali and Sara waited silently.

A large desk, flags, books, photographs of his wife and two children, another photo of him shaking hands with Senator Javits, a collection of engraved gavels, and the two lawyers surrounded the judge. He said to Chamberlain, "For the good of the defendant and for the good of this coun-try I will ask the government to withdraw their deportation order, provided that your client guarantee to cease and desist from actions which caused his undocumented arrest.''

Chamberlain said, "The issue is the work permit violation, not the political conduct of my client.''

The judge said, "This is the best I can do for Mr. Keshavarz. Take it or leave it, Counsellor.'' Chamberlain agreed, and the judge concluded, "Gentlemen, let's go and I'll announce my decision.''

The judge returned to the bench and said, "Mr. Keshavarz, the government agrees to withdraw the deportation order. I will grant your peti-tion to stay if you agree to refrain from inciting riots, trespassing, resisting arrest and other illegal behavior.''

A chill ran through Ali. He was resolved not to be intimidated or com-promise his principles. He stood, his eyes emanating anger, waved his hand and said, "May I?'' but did not wait for the judge's response.

"The law says that aliens can't hold a job, but no law prohibits businesses from hiring them in sweatshops and on farms. One law says aliens have constitutional rights, but another excludes their children from public schools. One law taxes them, but another denies them social benefits. Thus immigrant workers are kept in slums, in temporary shacks, in flatbed trucks on the move, in the dark and in debt. They can't organize because they're aliens. I speak for myself, but also for workers who cannot defend themselves in English. Nothing can bend me to submit to this double standard. If I stay I will express my human rights."

The Latino boy stood to face Ali and clapped his hands as hard as he could, shouting, "Bravo! Bravo!" as his parents pulled him down.

Ali smiled at the boy and turned back to demand, "Where is the owner of the store who hired me, who also broke the work rule? Where is the dean who instructed me to get an illegal job? Where is the policeman who bashed my head in? Where is Mr. Goldberg, Mr. Dixon's extortion partner? Where are the authorities of Columbia, who have violated the charter of the university? Where are the Presidents who have caused death and destruction in Vietnam and Iran? Where are all these guilty parties?"

Dixon went white as a sheet and his hands grabbed the table. He stood up and blurted out, "Your Honor, I deny this accusation categorically. I don't recognize the name Goldberg." Then he flushed and felt the roof falling in on his head. Leeds pulled him back down to his seat, whispering, "Shut up, you asshole."

Ali pointed a finger at Dixon. "Look how the truth makes him squirm! I am punished for exercising freedom of speech to stop these wrongs that the justice system has failed to stop. I consider myself the real officer of the law today. I accuse this court of suppressing evidence and compromising my rights."

The judge had had enough. "Mr. Keshavarz, our patience has a limit. My court has no place for radical rhetoric."

Ali said, "What I have said is relevant and true, but if relevance and truth have no place in this court, then neither do I."

"Mr. Keshavarz," the judge said icily and impatiently, "you have a lot to learn, but it won't be in this country. Since you refuse to accept my decision, I rule that the deportation order stands. This hearing is adjourned."

Ali raised his voice. "You need not look overseas to find cases of human rights violations. Look at me and look at millions of immigrant workers."

The judge said, "One more word and I'll find you in contempt of court."

Ali stormed out and Sara ran after him. Pirooz scowled at Dixon and the judge, and then followed Ali as Helena held his arm. Chamberlain said, "Thank you, Your Honor," and tried to catch up with them all.

Ali was an inactive volcano covered by an ice storm. He shook his head in disbelief and whispered to Sara, "Justice is now legally dead in New York. The unsuccessful rent strike, the wounds of the bust, the deportation without cause are the limbs of its corpse. I'm sorry for us, but I had to do it,

Sara.''

When Chamberlain joined them he said, "Mr. Keshavarz, I had no right to negotiate on your behalf without your consent. I wanted to save the case.''

Ali replied, "I know you were trying to help, but I will no longer give in to the Dean, the landlord, the cops, Dixon and Goldberg, the judge, or bastards like them.''

Chamberlain offered to take them to a coffee shop to discuss the next step, and Pirooz said, "Lead on, Mr. Chamberlain.'' Sara followed in shock and Helena looked at Ali with admiration.

They sat at a booth. It was midmorning and the coffee shop was empty. At once a waitress appeared, a pyrex coffeepot in one hand and menus in the other. "Would you like some coffee, dear?'' she asked Sara, then looked at the others, waiting for their word. She had aged unevenly. Her smile was constant and sad, like the queen of hearts in a worn-out deck of cards. She wore a miniskirt; she had to to hold the job. After she had taken their order, a menu left on the next table fell. She bent down to pick it up and revealed a purple vein running down her left leg. Her buttocks showed.

"She must be a grandmother,'' Pirooz whispered loud enough for everyone to hear.

Ali and Sara exchanged uneasy glances. Helena kept her eyes where the menu had fallen. "I wish the waitresses would organize against nudity in restaurants.''

"Who is responsible?'' Sara asked.

"Everyone,'' Pirooz said. "The owner, the customers, even the waitress herself.''

"And capitalism,'' Ali added.

Chamberlain changed the subject and asked Ali, "By the way, what was that outburst about Goldberg?'' When Ali explained, Chamberlain raised his eyebrows. "So Dixon is a crook. I thought the deportation order could be harrassment on account of the uprising.''

"Maybe both,'' Ali said.

Helena looked at the lawyer. "The bookstore is non-union. Ali couldn't organize or join a union without risking his visa. No matter what started this, it's political.''

Pirooz asked, "John, couldn't Dixon's extortion scheme be used for an appeal?''

"Theoretically, yes,'' Chamberlain responded. "But it's Ali's case, not Dixon's.'' He asked Ali, "Why didn't the university defend you?''

"How could I ask? I'm a black sheep.'' They didn't know that Leeds had talked to the dean, who had assured him the university would not intervene.

Pirooz turned to Chamberlain. "Has the judiciary any independence, or are politics and law two sides of the same coin?''

Chamberlain answered, "In small cases where there's no public attention, anything can happen."

Helena asked, "How about organizing to publicize Ali's case, then?"

"Do what?" Sara asked.

"Demonstrate in front of the Immigration Office. Write to the newspapers," Helena replied.

Chamberlain said, "That could cause a backlash and help the extradition."

"John, what's our next move?" Pirooz interrupted.

"We could appeal, but it must be disciplined, not political. I sympathize with Ali's frustration, but he was close to being cited for contempt. It's possible to be victimized while seeking justice."

"Like going to the hospital and catching a new disease," Ali said.

Sara said, "Please, Ali! We must stop the Establishment from deporting you, not seek an indictment of the Establishment."

John Chamberlain said, "I have an appointment. I must leave." He picked up the check and gave Ali his card. "If you want to appeal, Legal Aid and I will be on your side. But it must be without politics." Pirooz and Helena left with the lawyer, and Ali and Sara were alone.

Ali's point of view had infected Sara. The turmoil at Columbia and the killing in Vietnam had made the government seem to her an out-of-control monster, and the university, the best hope, was also smashed, like Ali's head. Society as a whole had become a living person for her, and she worried about its ailments. Ali had learned from Sara, too. He was trying to soften his intellectual criticism. He understood people's motives a little better now. The individual was resurrected for Ali as society sprang alive for Sara. Their relationship, energized by love, allowed them to communicate more humanely than Ali's Marxism and more realistically than Sara's politeness and compassion, and created a new closeness. They understood each other even when they disagreed.

But Sara's worries had evolved over the past week into anger. She now doubted Ali's love for her and thought he had acted irresponsibly. "Well, you did it," she blurted out. Before Ali could respond, Sara put her index finger to her lips commanding Ali to be silent. Her eyebrows knitted, a frown overtook her understanding disposition, cold anger emanated from her eyes and her voice trembled. "You think you've punished the Establishment, eh? You have only punished me, us, even your revolution. You could have nodded 'yes' to the judge and walked out of court in charge of your life."

"I couldn't lie," Ali interjected.

Sara said, "You tell me the justice system in the U.S. is a farce, a tool of the ruling class. Then, for God's sake, why must you be honest with them?''

Ali tried to respond but Sara continued, "I'm not done, and don't start your usual lecturing again. I'm tired of hearing of U.S. responsibility in Iran, and tortures and death. There is more to life than—''

Ali rushed in. "All facts, whether you like it or not. My brother's muder is a fact.''

"Yes, they're facts, all right,'' Sara said, "but listen to me, for once!'' Ali was shocked. He had not seen this side of Sara before.

"Tell me, who is doing the actual torturing and killing in Iran, the CIA agents or Iranians?'' Sara inquired.

"The Shah is part of the CIA.''

"Come on, Ali! There has been torture in Iran for thousands of years, Pirooz tells me.''

"The feudal lords and the Shahs were the ruling class, not the people.''

"But that's normal in any culture.'' Before Ali could answer, Sara continued, "Women are brutalized in Iran. Aren't their husbands part of the 'people'?''

"Men in Iran don't drop napalm bombs on women,'' Ali rushed to answer.

"Listen, Ali, that's not the point. You haven't beaten up women and I haven't dropped any bombs.''

"What are you getting at, anyhow?'' Ali asked impatiently, taken aback and surprised by Sara's knowledge and persistence.

Sara responded, "First, Iranians, even the victims, must accept some responsibility for the coup, for atrocities and murders. If they don't they will never unshackle themselves. Second, you should not have used my love for you and then flushed it down the toilet.'' She raised her voice and banged the table. "Damn it, you tell me you love me, but you're more interested in the dead. Look at me, Ali. I'm alive, but I'm wounded inside.''

The lovers exchanged sharp glances. Ali felt on trial again and about to be judged guilty. Sara's voice rose. "You didn't have to raise my hopes, troubling with a Legal Aid lawyer and all. You never did intend to keep silent and win the case, did you? I know you aren't deceptive, so your mood in the court must have dictated your intransigence with the judge. I don't think anyone with a temper like yours is suited for revolution.''

Sara's icy words poured over Ali, surrounded him, squeezed cold into his bones. He felt a pang in his heart. Her determination cut his own determination like a knife through water. Ali said meekly, "Sara, we're in a restaurant.''

"So what? Just a bourgeois spot, eh.'' Sara retorted.

"I understand you, but can we talk at home?'' Ali begged.

The waitress returned to the table as the lunch crowds began to pour in. "Can I get you anything else?'' she asked, clearing away the cups and napkins and wiping the table. Sara said, "Let's go, then." Ali placed a couple of dollars on the table, and the lovers rushed out, as though fleeing their future.

On the subway uptown, Sara thought of the night Ali had gone to a Persian poetry recital at Columbia and a little party afterwards. When he got back, Sara was upset and asked, "Why are you so late?"

Ali replied, "I volunteered to clean up the mess."

"Volunteered?"

"Yes. There were janitors, but I wanted them to go home early."

"Did they go?"

"No. They had cake and coffee and then joined me to finish the job. They thanked me afterwards."

"Didn't you say you'd be back as soon as the party was over?"

"Yes, but the janitors have families waiting for them, too, and besides, I must do my share of manual work."

It was the only story of Ali's Sara ever checked, and it was true. The janitors told her that this had never happened before, that Ali was a kind man. It was his private way of practicing Marxism, she had thought at the time. But later she understood that this was Ali's kindness and his way of practicing justice—it was more emotional than ideological.

Once a month Ali fixed a big Sunday breakfast for acquaintances, doing his best on a limited budget. But with his uncompromising political arguments he would occasionally hurt or anger a guest he had labored to please. Once Sara intervened and patched up the damage, just as Ali was about to ask a guest to leave their apartment. It was then that Sara began to understand Ali better. Only when it came to politics did he become obnoxious and forget other people's feelings.

They walked in Riverside Park silently, until they sat on a wornout bench facing the river. Sara held Ali's hand. "I know you love your home and want to go back, but why now? If it wasn't for the immigration problem, wouldn't you stay to finish school? Are you through fighting here?"

Ali said, "I told you I'd do my best, but I felt a knife in my back pressing me to challenge the judge, and I forgot about us. Why did I blurt that out about aliens in court?" Sara shook her head. "It seems as though fighting the police, the judge, the capitalist dogs all around is coded in my genes. I can't help it," Ali said sadly. "I got mad, I threw everything into the fire. My work in school and on the job and in the student groups, and my promise to you are now turning into ashes all against my will, honestly. No matter what you think, I love you, but I can't censor myself. A part of me, the best part, would die if I stayed under the judge's gag order. But leaving you is like leaving a part of me here. I can never be really gone with you here."

Sara said, "You're not going to appeal?"

"No," Ali said. "I won't bend to the courts and I can't bend them."

"You know," she said, "there are other ways to stay and finish your studies without compromising. The Immigration Office can't touch you if you marry me. It would be a marriage of convenience. When you're ready to go home, with or without me, I won't object. Just say goodbye, and I'll say goodbye, too. Please consider it. It would work."

Ali looked into Sara's wet eyes and engraved their every detail in his memory. He said softly, "Sara, I can't put it off. And I can't marry you, even if it is as you say. I won't avoid reality, and this marriage can't be real for us now. Nothing is the same after the bust and what happened today. When Abbas was killed, I decided to devote my life to opposing injustice, but now it is more than that. All political victims around the world are my brothers."

"Is revenge so far above everything else?" Sara asked gently.

"This isn't revenge. Don't individualize it, Sara. It may sound ridiculous, but can you believe I may be guided by love? Even if my brother hadn't been murdered and I hadn't been born in Iran, I think I'd still be a revolutionary in some country, facing U.S.-supported carbon copies of the Shah. Look at Latin America; there are thousands of me there. You see, it's not just fate or circumstances, it's what is inside me that compels me to struggle against what isn't right.

"I'm glad I came to the U.S. to see and feel it at close hand. In the past couple of months you've seen the coercion, the corruption, the injustice here. It's worse in Iran, Sara. We couldn't hide from it there, like we did looking out the window in your apartment here. You aren't prepared to face what goes on there. It wouldn't be fair to you to be married to a revolutionary far away who probably would never return. I'm not even sure I am prepared to face what I must face. What can I tell you? You've heard all this before."

Sara looked at Ali sadly but admiringly as he continued, "Sure, Sara, it would be wonderful if I married you, because then I'd just have to face the most exciting woman in the world. But I can't give up or delay my goals, Sara, not for you, not for me, not for us. The revolution is the only thing in my future, the most important. I love you, Sara, but it's the revolution I'm married to. I will never marry anyone but you as long as you are free, and if I survive you can have me, as Persians say, as your life-long slave." They both smiled.

Sara's eyes glistened with tears she tried to control, to spare Ali her own fears. She said, "Why can't I go along? Teheran is full of Americans. Why can't I be of some assistance without being a hindrance? I would follow you if you want. Nothing is holding me here. Why should I think of safety first in Iran? I want to be with you or at least close to you, no matter what."

Ali seemed not to hear Sara's objections. He hoped she would understand and love him as he would depart. He felt old, older than she. He felt tired, yet he was burning inside with the desire to carry out his dreams. "I have to stop the Shah. It's an emergency. I can't be a lover, a husband or a father and still be a revolutionary. I must go now, and I must go alone. That is all."

He concluded, "I'll never forget last night beside you. I wished time would have stopped. I loved you then, just as I love you now, as I will always love you. I wish I could be with you forever. I wish Abbas hadn't been murdered. I wish there were no injustice. I wish you could come with me. My wishes have no end. It's a pity. Our wishes have no end but our possibilities are so limited."

Tears streaked Sara's saddened face. Ali saw them, but he really didn't see them. Sara felt the moisture but didn't notice her sobbing, a new feature of her life since she had met Ali, who would not bend to a storm that could break him in half. Sara looked at Ali and saw a man possessed by ideas, lost in grief over Abbas' tragedy, and enslaved by one single drive—to create a revolution. His ambition was beyond his reach, Sara thought. What happiness he could grasp he threw away. "It's no use trying to persuade him," Pirooz had told her. "Ali is a multidimensional man, but he has squeezed himself into one dimension and wants to squeeze everyone around him." Sara's tears dried in her blue eyes like a pond under a glowing sun.

Ali saw a beautiful Sara who, though conscious of the cruelty of the world around her, could not understand his commitment to end injustice. This thought solidified Ali's feelings for her into an iceberg which floated away. Why couldn't Sara accept a cause so right, so just and so obvious to him? That was why he did not notice her tears until he was in prison. The two were still worlds apart, as they had been at the beginning, but now their nerve-ends had been stitched together by the surgeon of time and love.

Sara fell silent and resigned. She had no choice. Her wishes were in conflict with Ali's goals. "How are you going home? When? Will we ever see each other again?"

Until now Ali's going home was just talk about the future, but now the future crashed into the present. With apprehension on his face, Ali said, "When, how and if we see each other again? I don't know, Sara. I only hope. Should I know all of that right now? That son of a bitch Dixon will send me a letter. Dixon's letters are a dead man's call for companionship. Sara, it torments me to think about leaving you. Your questions are snowballs shattering in my face. I curse the passing of time now. Please, let's be in the present, let's just be together."

Ali softened. "I never want to let go of you. I've never known or tasted anything so good, so reassuring. The last few months have been the best time of my life. I love you, Sara. I love your loving me, but I can't let that be a shackle for me or become a prison for you. I can't say everything you want to know now. With some space and time between us, I'll write and let you know.''

Sara said, ''This is a goodbye?''

''A goodbye for now.''

They spent the day together, holding back the abyss that threatened their love. Sara held Ali's hand and guided him through unfamiliar streets. She longed to come closer to him as the seconds drifted away, taking Ali back to Iran with them. For an instant she recognized her jealousy of the nation Ali wanted to rescue. They would take her love; they were taking him away even before he left. But not wishing to bother Ali with her thoughts, she said, ''Take me to a movie tonight. Let's go see *The Battle of Algiers.*'' It was the story of a man and his comrades valiantly opposing injustice in vain.

* * * * *

Helena organized two protest demonstrations with both Iranian and Latin American students. Sara participated and Ali showed up, but they created very little publicity. Ali's case did not become a big case but remained unknown, as Ali said, like unknown immigrant farmworkers.

The few remaining nights Sara lost herself in Ali's arms. The lovers drew ever closer to each other, became one flesh, as time waited impatiently to cut them apart.

CHAPTER 8

Lovechild

Ali dropped his briefcase at the Pan Am gate. Having already left Sara in tears and said goodbye to Pirooz, he ran back to her, leaped over a bench and hugged her madly, so hard that her bones were nearly crushed.

Tears ran down his face and onto Sara's neck. She had never seen Ali cry; he twisted like a tornado. "I must kiss you one more time," he said. Frozen in Ali's arms, Sara watched him as others watched. They kissed and slow minutes passed. The flight attendant's eyes shouted at the last passenger, What are you waiting for? Sara whispered, "Ali, please, you have to go."

Ali let go. He looked back once more from the gate and shouted, "I love you, Sara!" The cry echoed up and down the corridor. The sounds and the words echoed in Sara's mind.

Pirooz stood like a statue and watched Ali disappear. Sara walked to Pirooz' waiting arms and said, "Ali has left me in ruins."

Pirooz held her gently and whispered, "We can rebuild." They spent the rest of the day together comforting one another.

For days afterward, Pirooz put on a good face, kept busy and tried to lose himself in Helena's tender care and exciting glow. But he missed Ali and felt as homesick as when he had arrived alone in New York. "I was a fool to become so attached to a fool," he told Helena.

"Come on, Pirooz. Ali is not a fool—he knows what he wants and goes for it. You just miss him. I am sorry for you."

As though talking to himself Pirooz murmured, "A commitment to a cause should not overwhelm everything. Ali sees the world, history, life, even joy through the eyes of Marx. I wish he would open up his own eyes for once and see the political fiction for which he is rushing to put his life on the line."

Helena's accented voice, not so lovely this time, demanded, "What political fiction?"

"The fiction that an ideology, no matter how complete and good, and a new economic system brought about by revolution, can change the reality in Iran," Pirooz said gently.

"You mean Ali is wasting his life for a fantasy?" Helena asked.

"No, just for an impossible hope of curing a historical malady of a nation in one's own life time," Pirooz replied.

Helena responded, "I think he knows this too. But Ali fights for his convictions; he does not just talk about them like us."

Pirooz felt hurt and shook his head disappointedly, "I am not sure. But listen, I am also afflicted with Ali's ideopathy, only my case is not fatal, so I choose to stay with you and Capitalism. I wish I could go with Ali, and take you, my books, and all of Manhattan along. I love Manhattan like the Devil loves hell."

Helena said, "You Persians are so funny. You criticize everything in Manhattan, but yet you say you love it. I hope you don't love me the way you love Manhattan." The two lovers smiled sadly.

Pirooz soon forgot that Ali was dogmatic and a pain in the neck on occasion, remembering instead the heart-to-heart talks, the chess games, Ali's bragging after soccer games, the Persian cooking contests they staged for Sara and Helena.

Pirooz knew he was lucky to have Helena to help fill the empty spot left by Ali. Sara, on the other hand, was not so fortunate. A few days later, she stood at her window and stared into dead space. The usual lively movement outside the picture window escaped her attention. Ali was gone but she still felt his tears on her neck. The wind of her mind flipped through memorable pages of her life with Ali.

Ali had left her the legacy of his ideas, and she pondered them, even though some were unpleasant. Ali's life revolved around his convictions, but Sara could not imagine how soon they would alter her own life. In history books and in the Bible there were stories of men of flesh, bone and nerves who gave up their lives for the good of others, but Sara had found a real one in her own arms. No matter if she found his ideas disagreeable, he was sincere, and now he was gone to die for an impossible revolution.

She remembered Ali's anger. On Riverside Drive, in the Baltimore suburbs where she had grown up, or at the radio station where she worked, people shed and took on ideas as though they were clothing fashions. The worth of an idea was measured by how many votes or how much profit it could win; any other assumption was unrealistic. An idea by itself was irrelevant—it could be everything, it could be anything, it could be nothing—it was just a means. Why should anyone get stuck with an idea, or risk anything for it?

Nothing mattered; what mattered was nothing. There was no debate, only slogans, no growth of ideas, only their restatement in different words.

Scientists and artists used ideas to promote the system and their careers. Broadcasters read messages convincingly and without argument; they were human extensions of the TV tube. Whoever owned the tube owned the broadcasters, too.

Ali truly had left Sara in ruins. He had, quite simply, turned most of her beliefs upside down. Sara had been taught that society benefitted when everyone competed in self-interest. Greed for power and wealth was the nature of man, proclaimed Adam Smith, the prophet of capitalism. Sara had studied this principle for her economics test. But how could her gain reduce the losses of others? How could her happiness be segregated from the unhappiness around her? Suddenly her entire upbringing seemed a lie! Sara no longer believed her parents, the parish priest, her professors, Walter Cronkite or the President. She no longer accepted an idea without first examining it for its motivation and contrasting it with the action that resulted. For example, Lyndon Johnson claimed he was for peace (the idea), but he needed to win a war (the motivation), so he bombed Vietnamese villages (the action). A TV commercial proclaimed that the oil company which had gobbled up the coal company cared for the environment (the idea), but billions in profits were to be made (the motivation), so its strip mines scarred the landscape (the action). Too often, she found, the action just did not reflect the idea.

Before meeting Ali, Sara had had a clear image of things; they were almost more real to her than people or ideas. Cars, cosmetics, clothes, alcohol and drugs were alive; they had the power to banish fatigue, pain, ugliness, loneliness and lovelessness, to bring strength, joy, beauty, friendship and love. Conversely, people were employed or unemployed like machines of flesh, then heaped into a junkyard of the permanently obsolete. On TV, commodities were turned into people and in the real world people were turned into commodities. Workers did not recognize that the commodities they produced were themselves, and that it was their lives that capitalists peddled for profit, Ali had told her.

In particular, Sara no longer accepted the national security argument for supporting U.S. foreign policy. Ali had said, "National security for what and for whom—U.S. business abroad, or the nation?" Then Ali had answered his own question: "In any case the U.S. is really not the same country for all of its citizens; Rockefeller lives in the most affluent country of the future and the hundreds of thousands of the homeless in America live in the poorest nation of the past. The insecurity of the American workers is due to fear of joblessness and poverty and nothing more. U.S. support of dictators abroad under the banner of national security is just a ploy to keep the workers of the client states insecure. Insecurity induces worker's submission and stable profits."

Sara knew Eric would give up his life for the U.S. national security while Ali would do the same for the national sovereignty of Iran. If the national security of the U.S. were in conflict with the national sovereignty of Iran then Eric and Ali, like programmed robots, would have to fight to the end, Sara thought.

Before meeting Ali, Sara had known only that communism was evil, nothing more. But how did Sara know it was evil without knowing the history of communism? Eric was in the dark, too, Sara thought. American leaders spoke of the struggle between free enterprise and collectivism, between God and atheism, between democracy and communist dictatorship, but communists were not allowed to debate on TV, in newspapers, or in schools.

But TV had time for jingles, sports and everything else. For example, "Nowhere else in the world was so much praise heaped on a greasy hamburger, a food made of sodium chloride, calories and cholesterol," Pirooz had lectured one day. "In America, the McDonald's jingle is on everyone's mind, but the hunger of millions is not."

In the rice paddies of Vietnam, poor whites and blacks were used to kill poor yellows. The soldiers of both sides slept in the mud, fought off the bugs, lived in terror of their own lives, and waited for peace which was beyond their reach. The more Vietnamese killed, the more medals and promotions for U.S. officers. Sara knew of a few draftdodgers and deserters, but she didn't know there were hundreds of thousands, and she didn't know what they had to say. "You're misinformed or uninformed like the whole nation," Ali had explained to her gently.

Knowing now the power of ideas, Sara was left with imponderable questions: Whose ideas were the truth? Which were worth fighting for? She thought of Ali and Eric. How did opposite ideas get into their heads? How did places and times create men with such different beliefs and values? Why did every group think they were right and others were not? Why were ideas so powerful? How could they produce brutality and wars? How could the government in the U.S., or the USSR, convince its citizens to kill or be killed? Were there any absolute truths, to any ideological claims, of whatever side? What would happen if each American had the chance to know someone like Ali? They would become "contaminated" like me, Sara said to herself. They would begin to doubt what they were sure of about America. She smiled when the word "subversive" came to mind. Ali was not connected with any other state, certainly not the USSR, so who was he subversive for?

The confused days after Ali's departure added up to two weeks. Like a starved person, Sara felt a painful emptiness within. Her pangs for Ali would not let up, and talking to Pirooz did not help.

When she noticed her menstrual irregularity, she attributed it to her injured emotions, but when she saw her gynecologist he announced gravely,

"Miss Patrick, you're pregnant. You're going to be a mother," as if she had a malignancy.

Sara walked from the doctor's office in shock. She repeated, "You're going to be a mother." She banged her head getting into a taxi. The red and green traffic lights stopped her thoughts, then let them flow. Ali. Life. Abortion. Death. Sara had always wanted a child, but not like this. The contraceptive loop could fail and evidently had failed for Sara. For Sara the Professor's abstractions about businesses cutting costs at the expense of quality suddenly gained concrete meaning. It was not just unsafe cars at any speed but unsafe other things, too. Sara bit her tongue. "Now I am thinking like Ali talks." Sara turned angry, a feeling she had experienced rarely before she met Ali.

Sara, the mother-to-be, longed to rush to Ali, fly to his arms, kiss him and tell him he was a father. But Ali was visiting student leaders in Europe; his last letter gave an address in Hamburg, but even Pirooz didn't know how to reach him directly. Sara knew that Ali hadn't abandoned the child; he didn't even know about it. He left to rescue his people, his extended family. It was an emergency, a nation in chains, she repeated Ali's words to herself. Sara called silently across the Atlantic, We have a child, Ali. She rushed to her mailbox as if she could tell Ali through it that he was a father. A letter waited there for her. Her face went pale when she read it.

Sara wadded the letter in her fist. Tears ran down her face as she ran to the park, past the playground and long rows of unused benches, and finally descended under the West Side Highway to the edge of the Hudson. She ran from familiar scenes as she ran away from her past. A swath of weedy grass spread from the highway to a sculpture of huge boulders and broken concrete piled in a dike, the cavities filled with beer cans and broken bottles, all sloping to disappear into the deep riverbed. The rocks were wet or dry as the Hudson adjusted to the tidal whims of the Atlantic. Even in the daytime it was foolhardy to walk along the shore, because of rapists, muggers and bottles hurled from cars zooming by.

But here Sara sat on a huge flat rock with an unbroken view of the river. The chemical refineries in New Jersey were brushing the clouds with red, blue and yellow smoke, like children playfully daubing fingerpaints on a blank poster. The colors swirled in the air currents carrying the pollution onward. When the wind erased the painting altogether, a new blank poster appeared for the industrial children to paint again.

Sara opened the crumpled letter moist with her tears. She knew the contents by heart. She looked at Ali's final words once more, to make certain they were real and her eyes not in error. "I love you, I will always love you, Sara, but it is finished between us, it is absolutely finished."

"It is finished, it is absolutely finished," she repeated. Each word was a dagger in her heart. How could Ali write such cruel words? How could he say he loves me always and then reject me for good? She murmured to herself, "To free me, to free himself." She must let go of him, even though her nerves were pulled apart. Sara understood Ali's reasons like an amputee understands the surgeon's knife. But she had seen the Democratic convention in Chicago on TV, with thousands of peace marchers beaten by the police, so how could one single man's resolve overcome the army of the Shah? It was hopeless.

She wondered once more why Ali had thrown their happiness away. She remembered his silly Persian version of a Zorba the Greek dance, the caresses, the kisses, his eyes full of love following her in her transparent red silk negligee. A thousand reasons and resignations would not suffice. Her love would revolt against the ruling of her mind. Finally she stood up and yelled at the top of her lungs, "Ali is gone. The child is mine and mine alone!"

The idea of abortion held a tight grip on her consciousness, but she refused to yield. Abortion was made illegal by the same lawmakers who ordered napalm bombing of villages in Vietnam, Ali had told her. For Sara, abortion was a sin and a crime. The life in her womb was an idea made human. This idea created jointly by Ali and her could grow and bear fruit for generations. Why couldn't her unborn become a savior of mankind? Was Jesus legitimate?

Her time with Ali floated past her imagination as she looked at the river, which carried flotsam just as time carried her fears to somewhere unknown. A dead bass tumbled in the poisonous ripples of the surface, and Sara shivered. Wouldn't the attitudes of the populace be just as poisonous toward an illegitimate child? Would her parents accept the lovechild? A voice rose from her heart, "I love my child. I want to keep it!"

Sara thought of the child's father moving farther and farther away, perhaps toward his death. Her simple life had suddenly become the complex one of an unwed and unprotected mother. She loved her unborn; it was a part of her, a part of Ali. Abortion was out, but what of adoption? The idea grew more painful by its mere presence. Tears flowed down her cheeks as she shook her head, whispering, "Impossible, impossible."

Sara wiped her tears with the sleeve of an Indian cotton dress, a gift from Ali. I couldn't bear to live while my daughter existed only in my imagination, she thought. I couldn't bear just guessing what she looks like, if she's happy, if she learns the cello or piano or ballet. I want to watch her chase pigeons in the park with her ponytail flying behind her.

Sara's thoughts carried her to images of the future, to when her daughter was already raised by adoptive parents. What would her daughter be told when she asked about her real mommy and daddy? What would Sara's daughter say when the grandchildren asked, "Where is our grandmother?" They would never know Sara was their grandmother, and Sara would never know they were her grandchildren, even if they met.

The word "grandmother" pushed aside Sara's despair. Grandmother, indeed! Am I going out of my mind? she asked herself. How can I think of being a grandmother when I don't even know what to do with my daughter? My daughter, I say. How biased. Maybe him, a boy? My boy won't play football—soccer will do just fine. Would he be like Ali? He is Ali's son, too, but he won't be Ali. He'll live with me, she thought, he'll be an American. He'll have no quarrel with the Shah.

At that moment a decision came to her without warning. Unwavering, Sara whispered, "I will keep my child, no matter what! I want to breastfeed him, teach him to swim in the tub with tiny plastic ducks jumping around. I'll love him, play the guitar and sing for him and see him delighted, hear him laugh, watch him sleep. He won't just be in my dreams, like Ali now, but in my waking, in my arms. I need this child."

The river would keep her secret, Sara thought. She could shout her defiance here, but in truth no one must hear. The pregnancy, a secret to all, stirred an angry fire inside her veins. She must cover it up, cover her sorrow and cover her joy.

Sara wanted to confide in someone, but who? She ruled out Pirooz and her friends. She would talk to a priest, but she needed a plan, not forgiveness, she concluded.

She would not tell Ali, not yet. She would protect him. She wondered in apprehension how he would react if he discovered he had been kept in the dark. But what would he do if he was consulted? Would he abandon his revolution and run back to help her change diapers? Sara smiled at the image of Ali changing diapers. Then she remembered the week she was sick and Ali took care of her. No one, not even her mother, had been as gentle, thorough, patient and attentive as Ali. The soup he made was tasty, the Omar Khayyam he read for her exciting, the gift of a Segovia record soothing, and the roses optimistic. They were such good days of illness she had wished to stay in bed longer. He would change diapers, Sara thought as she wiped away a tear.

She squeezed the letter and her love in her fist and threw it with the strength of her anger far out to the river, to let the current carry it away. Then she grabbed a rock and hurled it. She threw another and another, watching the choppy water swallow the ripples of the splash. She threw more stones into the river, trying to raise the water to bury Ali's words, "it is absolutely finished," and to carry away her loneliness.

Finding no more stones at hand, Sara turned and fled across the six lanes of highway traffic roaring past at sixty. She crossed the park, mounted the stairs to the Drive, and found herself once again in her apartment.

She picked up her guitar and sat by the window. Her will spoke through her fingertips, and the instrument responded. No man-made tool could ever play the guitar like Sara's fingers, Pirooz had said when she played on his birthday.

She sang almost inaudibly. "Where have all the lovers gone? Where have all the daddies gone?" Exhausting the songs she knew, Sara played spontaneous chords and melodies. The new sounds invaded her thoughts, stimulating new creations. Thoughts into music, music into thoughts; the feedback grew until Sara lost herself, missing the sunset, the moonrise, the Hudson bulging with the tide and the sails rising to catch the moon.

The telephone rang. "Surprise!" Eric's voice at the other end did surprise her. Eric had been in Washington with the Agency for International Development. His calls, letters, flowers and birthday card had arrived on schedule. He had offered to help Ali with the extradition problem, but Sara had gently told him Ali wouldn't accept. Sara did not want to hurt Eric, so she had not said much about Ali. She would not hurt anyone by revealing an irrelevant truth. She felt free only with Ali and Pirooz.

She wished that Eric would fall in love with someone else. Yet he persistently called and called, reporting his successes and confessing his concern. Once he had alluded to the marriage that they had talked about before Ali's appearance. Sara always replied that she cared for him, as a friend, aware of her increasing distance from Eric and from her own past.

"I'm in New York for a few weeks. I have great news. But first let me say this and get it over with. I know you're hurt about Ali's leaving. I understand. I don't feel good about your leaving me for him, but I won't hold it against you or mention it again. Okay, Sara?"

Eric was relieved. He had practiced the words as he did his arguments for mock court. He meant what he said, but he could still never understand Sara's preferring Ali to him. Even so, Sara was under no obligation and had not said "I do." Not yet. Eric asked cautiously, "Can I take you to dinner tomorrow, Sara?"

Sara said, "Let me take a rain check."

Eric continued to talk. He announced that he had obtained a position with a prestigious consulting firm dealing with VIP's around the world. He managed to say he would be making big waves and big money. Eric rarely got excited but he did on the telephone, "Imagine, Sara—I always argued in favor of national security and now I can do something about it."

Eric was as tenacious about Sara as about his career. He wanted her for her assets: her taste, intelligence, accomplishments and attractiveness. He wanted her eyes that lured all eyes to her. She would complement him; she was lively where Eric was a bit stiff. But he also cared for Sara deeply; he loved her quiet seriousness, her wit and her grace. He wanted to share his life with her and make her happy. He could be serious about marriage now that he could provide the material comforts which he considered an important part of wedded bliss, and now that Ali was out of the picture.

Sara listened without comment. Finally Eric said, "Are you there, Sara?"

She said, "Congratulations on your new job. Yes, I'm here, but I have to get off the phone now." They said goodbye.

Two days later, Sara took her savings and left for Stony Brook to stay with her old friend Jan, who had also become pregnant out of wedlock but was now happily married to her lover. Sara needed her friend's support and the solitude of the seashore, and she could do without fingers pointing at her in a few months. She had told Eric that she needed to think things out, and her parents that she would not be home to see them as planned.

Sara had written two letters to Ali hinting of great changes in her life, but without mentioning the child. The letters were sent to the Iranian student headquarters in Hamburg, but Ali had already left the city, so he never got them and never answered.

"It is absolutely finished." She knew Ali's words were final. He had never said what he didn't mean. The Professor told Sara that if Ali said it was finished, then it was finished. Pirooz had been very understanding, but they did not talk about Ali. Pirooz knew it was too painful for her, and, not knowing she was pregnant, he thought Sara had left Riverside Drive to distance herself from places of memory. He had helped her move to Long Island and he called to ask after her from time to time.

Sara went for long walks barefoot along the beach, splashing in shallow waves as the summer grew old and the ocean got warmer.

Her doubts cleared, but her fears hung on. She had resolved unpleasant ambiguities. Now she needed all her resources. She knew the best for her was out of reach, so whatever was best for her child must be good enough for her. Sara knew she could not raise the child alone and give him all he deserved. Her father would cut off his financial support when he found out about the illegitimate child. She would have to find a job to finish school, and she might have to quit school, too. Either way, she would have little money and little time to devote to the child.

She began becoming sick in the mornings. She also became sick of the thought of the compromises she must eventually make. Her new liberating ideas had to be buried under the exigencies of her life. Necessity devoured her wishes and ideas.

The relentless Eric finally convinced Sara to have dinner with him. They had a few dinners during the next two weeks until Eric's birthday arrived just in time. He invited Sara for dinner, but this time in a most exclusive restaurant and beforehand he hinted at his trump card: "He had something important to say!" Sara suspected that more than a dinner was at stake this time, knowing Eric.

She decided to tell Eric about the child. If he wanted to marry her, he must accept the child. Eric was good, serious, decent, ambitious, kind, reliable, level headed, even tempered, and normal. He was a devout Catholic and would be a responsible father. Sara's image of Eric was the same as before she met Ali. Eric had all the qualifications; he just didn't set her on fire as Ali had.

It took more than an hour of driving before Sara and Eric found themselves in a Swiss restaurant on East 64th Street, where each waitress, dressed in a village costume, served two tables only. Eric ordered wine, all the while beaming at Sara like a young boy with a new toy. Sara felt sick inside. How would Eric react to her revelation? By contrast, Eric shone in anticipation. After a few glasses of wine, he was relaxed and confident.

"I love you, Sara, and I want you to marry me. My feelings haven't changed since last fall." He reached across the table and took Sara's hand with fingers chilled by the wineglass. He stroked her hand, hesitantly at first, then more forcefully, looking into her eyes without a word.

Sara said, "I can't answer you until I tell you something you don't know about me." Sara withdrew her hand, closed her eyes and gathered her strength. Her lips couldn't form the words. She stammered, "You're proposing to a mother."

Eric was shocked. "What do you mean?"

"I'm pregnant," Sara replied tearfully. She turned aside and patted her cheeks dry with a napkin. Relieved and strengthened by the truth, she said firmly, "I'm pregnant. I'm going to keep the child, no matter what. That's all I have to say."

Eric knew without asking who the father was. The news buried for a moment his guilt and hatred for Ali. He tried to be cool; he couldn't afford to say the wrong thing. He spoke with control. "I understand. Why don't you go to the powder room, and we'll talk about it later." Sara nodded, reached for her purse and left.

With Sara gone, Eric sighed. In his second year at law school, a case of the mumps had forced him to postpone his finals. A check-up afterwards confirmed Eric's fears: the mumps had left him sterile. Eric wanted a family, but he knew that the children could not be his own. He had considered marrying a divorcee or a widow with children, but he worried that the children might reject him.

Eric knew Sara loved children; he had seen her hug and play with friends' children in the park. Even so, he had kept his secret from Sara when he proposed to her. He realized now that his secrecy had paid off. He would welcome her back and forgive her. She carried the child that couldn't be his, yet it would be.

The problem of Ali was over. Eric's offer to help with Ali's court case had endeared him to Sara. Sara had a child, but what if it didn't look like either Sara or him? He dismissed the idea from his mind; his father had dark hair like Ali. Eric pushed himself to be positive. No one must know that the child wasn't his, not even the child. He'd have to find out from Sara if Ali knew. It was important that Ali be kept in the dark for the sake of the child, Eric reasoned, and so Ali would not have a hold over the family.

Sara returned calm and restored. She had said what she had to say to Eric, and that was that. Now it was up to him. Eric immediately took charge, lest the opportunity slip away. "Sara, everything is going to be all right. I want you, I've always wanted to marry you." Eric carefully made Sara feel at ease, until he could get the facts.

He asked her, "By the way, does the father know about the baby?" Eric refused to mention Ali's name, hoping he would fade away by becoming nameless. The name Ali must not be used in their house.

Sara sighed. "No, no one knows, and I've promised myself not to tell Ali until he's finished what he has to do."

"What's that?"

"Revolution."

Eric grinned but felt a pang inwardly. A revolutionary in Iran was as good as dead, Eric thought. The CIA was strong enough to neutralize the trouble makers operating against U.S. allies. "I think the child should never know, but I won't insist. We'll wait until the revolution," he whispered. "I think the child should be raised as if I were the father. Is that all right?"

"Yes," Sara said.

"Well then," Eric continued, "that settles it. We should get married as soon as possible."

Sara hesitated. "It's too sudden, Eric. I need more time to get used to the idea. You may want to reconsider, too."

"Do you really have to think it over?" Eric asked.

"Not thinking really," Sara said, "just waiting to see how I feel in a few days."

"All right," Eric agreed, "but time isn't going to resolve anything. You can't get to know me better and I can't get to know you better. You know I've never thought of anybody else since I met you. I hope your heart will convince your mind."

"I hope my mind will convince my heart," Sara thought to herself.

"I'll tell you soon," she replied. "The baby is growing. But what will people say about the rush?"

"We can deal with that later," Eric said. "They aren't getting married, we are."

Sara hid her emotions from Eric. She had things to do now, and she would do them without regret for what could never happen. At least she could be that strong, for the child and for Ali.

Eric talked about the consulting firm, the partners in New York and Washington and the former partners who were now in the Cabinet, ambassadors, chairmen of blue ribbon panels and university presidents. He described lucrative contracts with foreign governments, complex bargaining over American aid, working with distinguished men of wealth and power.

But Eric withheld one important fact. He had been recruited into the Central Intelligence Agency on Professor Wharton's recommendation. The Director of Central Intelligence had placed Eric in the firm, which had secret contracts to gather intelligence through its overseas offices. Eric's real job was to produce political and economic intelligence on Iran. Eric talked only of world travel and how the two of them—the three of them, he hastened to correct himself—would live like royalty abroad, with servants swarming about them. Sara listened, but did not ask a single question.

With great pleasure Eric paid the tab and left a big tip to impress Sara. After driving her back to Long Island, he stayed for coffee before returning to Manhattan. Sara was distant, but Eric was accommodating and patient. Sara wished to be left alone. She was accustomed to solitude. She had no more empty words for anyone. She endured Eric's attention politely, but finally her melancholy drove him back to New York after they agreed to meet next week.

In bed, Eric felt a hot sweat and a turmoil in his mind. How could he convince his mother to accept a quick wedding? If Sara's pregnancy showed, his inquisitive mother would notice it. Would he be able to tell her the truth, Eric worried.

Eric was a good sleeper, but that night he kept writhing like a wounded man. Brief but horrible nightmares woke him in terror. He saw his mother chasing him with a broomstick, the priest refusing to forgive him, his new CIA boss putting a numbered placard around his neck, "This man is wanted." And the next night the nightmares refused to go away. He dreamed of Ali pointing a finger at him, "You threw me to the wolves and kidnapped my unborn child." Later at the church, Eric confessed again and his sins were forgiven again. The priest told him, "It is the best for the child to be raised by a Catholic family."

Eric put on a bathrobe and sat at the desk holding his head in his hands. Nothing but an evil infatuation had gotten Sara in trouble; she was still good. On a torn envelope he scribbled, "No one is perfect, no one is perfect." He could still call it off, gently letting Sara go the way he had let others go. The thought upset him and he discarded it, but it kept sneaking into his mind. How could he let Sara, his best chance, the woman he loved, the only woman he ever loved, get away? He would never find anyone like her. Few men would not fall in love with her if they were given a chance, Eric thought. True, he was more excited about her than she was about him, but once she lived with him and experienced his goodness and commitment, all the past would be forgotten, all the future would get better, she would become used to him, attached to him, and he would make sure she stayed attached.

But will I resent the child? Eric mused. Won't he remind me of that intruder? Eric kept repeating the same questions over and over again, but there were no good answers. He scribbled, "Nothing is perfect. Everyone must make compromises."

The child will love me, he thought. To him I will be his daddy, and I will get used to him, become attached to him, and feel like the real father. Eric smiled sadly. A moment of creativity cleared the fog. Sara will grow fond of me as I will grow fond of the child. It is the best for all of us. "Sara and I will make a great team," Eric scribbled on a sheet and underlined it five times. He almost called to tell Sara that everything would be great soon, but it was four in the morning.

If only that communist hadn't ruined my relationship with Sara and I hadn't had the mumps, I could have had Sara clean. But would she have married me anyhow? Eric dismissed the painful question from his mind instantly, but jealousy of Ali, whom Sara loved, wrung his brain, tormented his soul. He rushed to the shower and turned on the cold water to rinse away the unwanted thoughts and undesirable feelings that pressed him so relentlessly that long night.

Cool and calm, Eric's opportunism finally overcame his personal and religious inhibitions and his fears of his mother. "Mother will eventually see that Sara is a great catch," he scribbled, and then went to bed and fell asleep just before sunrise.

Sara cried without anxiety, a cry of relief upon reaching a destination after being hopelessly lost. She whispered to herself, "If I won't have romance, then I will have love, the love of a child and a family."

She had started going to morning mass regularly. She found great comfort in confiding and confessing to the priest. She wanted him to advise her directly, but he never did, he only emphasized that the child must be kept and be brought up in a Catholic family. In that way, Sara understood the priest's approval of her marriage to Eric.

Sara spent the next day thinking, careful not to dwell on the impossible —life with Ali—no matter how she longed for it. Silently she cursed the deans, Dixon, the judge, everyone who had separated Ali from her. She cursed the Shah as well, who was a stronger enemy than she was a lover. When faced with hard decisions, Ali had said that it was helpful to list the most valued goals and all the possible alternatives without passion. In the face of uncertainty, the chances of success had to enter the final choice. "Finally," he said, laughing, "you'll do what you wanted to do in the first place." He added seriously, "If you don't make a decision, someone else or circumstance will."

Sara wrote down her options. More than anything else, she wanted to give birth to the child and keep him. But how could an unwed mother, a student with no income, support a child? If she worked fulltime, someone else would bring up the child; it wouldn't be her feeding, her upbringing, her loving. Then there was Eric, who seemed to have all the attributes of a good father eager to assume responsibility for her and her child. With Ali's words, "It is finished," ringing in her mind with an icy finality, what was left for her but her unborn, the most wonderful feeling? It was not logic but necessity: it was not her feelings but the welfare of the child that made her decide to marry Eric.

It was love, to preserve and protect her progeny, which evolution had stamped on her being, that guided Sara. But what of the child's choice? Could children choose their parents? Would her child choose Eric as his father? Sara had to make the decision for the unborn. It was on her shoulders, just as it was in her womb.

She was sure only that any better solution was out of her reach. Ali's words—"It is absolutely finished"—and then his absolute silence after her two letters had crushed the last of her hopes. "He hasn't answered my letters; he's irresponsible. I will always miss Ali, but the hell with him. I have a child to raise," she decided angrily.

Sara wept softly, the last tears she would shed for quite a while. She reflected that with her love gone, she could give the rest of herself to Eric. There was no point in postponing the only decision she could make. She still held ideas shared with Ali—they were no less hers and Ali's than the child inside her—but the motivation for carrying them out was missing. She emerged from her dilemma stronger, but also emptier. She would safeguard the child, who would be given the best upbringing possible.

Sara decided to marry and live with Eric, as many wives do in America, for everything but romance. Her life had suddenly turned into a typical one: a brief encounter with a dream that now had to be enough. She would abort her own life, put herself up for adoption, to prevent the same for the child. A few nights later, Sara called Eric to accept his proposal. She avoided the word "marriage" as Eric avoided the word, "Ali."

Eric efficiently assumed the burden of planning for the wedding, for dealing with everyone and everything. He would protect Sara, and he would protect the child—their child, he reminded himself. He arranged a small church ceremony, just Eric's parents and Sara's parents and brother and sister, followed by a fancy dinner out. To make everything look right, Eric organized a shower for Sara's friends in New York and a formal reception in Washington for Eric's new business associates after a honeymoon in Bermuda. Pirooz and Helena were not invited.

The night before the wedding, a stab of painful thought ran through Sara. How could I picket the immigration office on Ali's behalf and three months later marry Eric—the Establishment itself. Why should I be forced to do this? And to top it off, I can't even be frank with Eric about why I'm marrying him. In a couple of hours, Sara managed to suppress the resurgent thought before she changed her mind. She went through her wedding gracefully but joylessly, while Eric beamed in his own success and the happiness that he was marrying the only woman he ever loved.

Pirooz, hearing the news, complained to Helena, "The idea that Eric and Sara are back together is like a full blown football—I cannot swallow it. Can you imagine the sweet Sara marrying Eric before she could even make up the bed she shared with Ali? I asked Sara why. She just stared coldly past me without the bat of an eye." Pirooz then raised his voice, "Holy Statue of Liberty! Sara acted like her businessman father: blocked from the most profitable route, she quickly switched to the second best. Helena, I am telling you, Sara is back in the fold."

"Of what?"

"Imperialism."

Helena asked, "Don't you think Ali is also responsible?"

Pirooz replied, "Of course. But Sara wasn't forced to jump into the sea of reaction just to get even with Ali, or replace him, or start a family, or whatever else prompted her."

"I guess not." Helena continued, "So you and Sara are not friends anymore?"

"Not as long as I feel so disgusted with the whole affair."

Sara loved and hated Ali. Day by day, side by side, her opposing feelings quarrelled beyond her control. She slept in Eric's bed out of duty, but thought of Ali every single night for many lonely nights. She remembered Ali whistling Rachmaninoff's Second Symphony by heart, never missing a passage. Ali brought tension and color into life. He turned an ashen day into a stormy gray one or a sunny bright one.

Eric, preparing to be posted to the Middle East, was learning Arabic and Farsi. Sara studied Farsi, too, just for something more to do, and in case she should someday want to teach it to her child.

Her son was born in Washington, and only then did Sara begin to overcome the loss of Ali as she devoted herself to bringing up their son, the lovechild she named Cyrus, over Eric's objections. He insisted on the name John Patrick, but Sara argued, "The Bible calls Cyrus a good Persian king who freed the Jews and other captive people."

She finished school at night and worked as a freelance journalist. Eric became protective of the child just as the U.S. was protective of Iran. His protectiveness led to fondness, love, and possessiveness as Cyrus began to call him "Daddy."

CHAPTER 9

Iran

On the first Friday of September, 1968, a bus zigzagged, climbed and descended near the foot of Mount Ararat. Ali was soothed by that white peak, a phoenix rising high to pierce the patches of clouds that sailed the Turkish sky. Ali got off at the Iranian border a few miles from the village of Maku. He felt chilly as he breathed the fresh air that greeted him, and his heartbeat picked up. He walked across a dirt road to the checkpoint without incident. He was anxious about what awaited him in Iran.

His all-night talks with comrades in Europe had reinforced his belief that ending repression in Iran required a revolutionary party. Ali's resolve to embark on that path pushed him to write Sara the "it is finished" letter. Sara should not be kept waiting for him, fearing for his life. He missed Sara. He carried a heavy, nagging emptiness within him. He could not will it away, even as more distance fell between them. He murmured to himself, "No matter what I wrote her, it can never be finished for me." He worried about Sara and that his letter would cause her anger and suffering.

The guard checked Ali's papers, then nodded to two men standing beside a jeep with the top down. They approached Ali slowly. One was scholarly looking, of medium height and light complexion, with black-rimmed glasses, the other shorter and stocky, with a round face and brown skin, and jovial looking.

The man with glasses smiled and stretched his hand to Ali. "I am Shamil and this gentleman is Kamil. We are from the Iranian State Intelligence and Security Organization."

Ali stood still and unperturbed. He whispered, "Savak."

"Yes." Shamil's eyes focused on Ali, his hand outstretched. "Pleased to meet you, Mr. Keshavarz. We've been expecting you." Ali shook hands. How did they know my travel plans? Student Savakis, Ali concluded. Where were the handcuffs?

"Don't be alarmed, Mr. Keshavarz," said Shamil. "We have come as friends. It is not the past but the future that concerns us. We are all Iranians;

we all want the best for our country."

Just as Shamil finished, Kamil spoke softly and respectfully. "Mr. Keshavarz, you need not worry about getting to Maku village. Please accept our hospitality." He pointed to the jeep.

Ali said, "Are you arresting me?"

"By no means," Shamil said. "You shall be on the first available bus to join your family in Teheran." They helped him with his luggage, and Ali took the back seat. The encounter with Savak was a shock, but he believed the two Savakis when they reassured that he would not be arrested, not yet.

Shamil smiled. "Sorry you were left with no choice but to be our guest. There is a compensation, however. In the village down the road a humble restaurant puts the best in New York to shame."

"Have you been to America?" Ali inquired. They nodded affirmatively.

Kamil said, "There are no pinball machines, bars or television in this village, but other time-killers are available, some exotic."

Just to say something, Ali responded, "Every people have their own time- killers." Ali surprised himself by talking to the Savakis as if they were acquaintances rather than secret police. Could there be anything good about these Savakis? Were they instructed to smile at him, or were they smiling on their own? Ali fell silent and looked out the side window to watch huge oaks running by at the speed of the car.

Kamil said, "Here we are." The two agents walked beside Ali toward a mud hut in a valley walled in by unnamed mountains and unmeasured peaks.

To get his mind off Savak, Ali looked around and saw the sun on top of the farthest oak which grew out of the farthest hill. The glowing sun disk trembled in expectation of being hugged by the towering trees. Ali wondered how the acorn could hold the blueprint from which the roots, branches and leaves of an oak could spring up. Then he thought of an adventurous male pollen riding the wind for a chance meeting with an ovum in a love nest called a pistil inside a flower. Ali imagined the pollen and ovum uniting and growing to create the acorn from which the giant oaks soared to the sky and banded together into a forest to the limits of his vision. Nature must have put the blueprints in the pollen and the ovum to produce the acorn, to produce the oaks that flapped their leaves as they hugged the sun at every sunset. Why do particles band together into atoms, into molecules, into pollen and ovum, into acorns, into the oaks which catch the sun? Where and when in this process is life born? The first pollen which rode the wind and settled here must have felt lonely and insignificant, Ali thought.

He felt like that first lonely pollen fighting to survive. Could he do as well as the pollen and create a forest of men and women to bring about the revolution? Would he see the forest push the Shah aside?

Shamil interrupted Ali's thoughts. "Mr. Keshavarz, this hut has no sign, but travelers call it *Beheshte Kuchek*, 'Little Heaven.' Luckily only a few people know that the best lamb is served here."

Shamil quickened his steps to a curtained doorway. "Please enter, Mr. Keshavarz."

Ali stepped in, forgetting the Iranian custom of insisting on being the last to enter. The humble rectangular hut was made of soil carved from the hillside, the sweat of laborers and an ancient design. Silverware wrapped in napkins could not be seen on the absent tables, and there were no chairs. Instead, kilims covered the floor with tribal patterns and rich colors. The kilims covered more than a floor, they covered the colorless lives of the women and children who had woven them, Ali thought. It had become Ali's habit to think of the labor that produced what he saw. He was surprised at his own calm.

He scanned the room, like a cat in a new house. Other travelers and a few local herdsmen sat on the floor. "Little Heaven" was filled with various scents, the dominant opium smoke forcing its way through and around a curtain separating the dining room from the smoking room.

A fragile, unshaven old man, walking hesitantly, served Ali and his company kebab, cut from a leg of lamb and roasted outside in the same mountain air that the lamb had inhaled a few hours earlier. The lamb had fed on the most delicate vegetation which absorbed the rainwater, the thin mountain air and the sunlight. The lamb's flesh was not spoiled by pesticides or injections before the burning touch of the knife signaled its violent death. The lamb could have been a sacrifice for Ali's arrival, an old custom in Iran. Ali looked pensive, as he saw that the fate of the lamb and the fate of the environment under the blade of industry were similar—one meeting a sudden death and the other a slow strangulation. Ali could not help comparing life in New York and in this village. Why should a greedy generation be allowed to destroy nature for all the people to come?

Shamil offered Ali a glass filled with aragh, a Persian vodka, and Ali drank without hesitation. He took a bite of lamb. The taste brought back a delightful memory. The sweet onion on the skewer, as sweet as a Persian melon picked a bit too soon, and tomatoes, solid, fresh and flowery—how could their taste be described to someone who has never tasted them? The butter that blossomed on the piece of hard black bread exuded the fragrance of the fresh mountain herbs that fed the cow outside. Her butter was free from processing, refrigeration and transportation.

These wonderful images, tastes and scents, a flood of pleasures, overwhelmed Ali and changed his mood and thoughts which were tightly guarded by his skull and by his ideology. The scents of opium, hashish, tobacco, rosewater and freshly roasted lamb and vegetables held the Savak agents flanking the revolutionary Ali in a fleeting union of opposites, treating all to their warmth and secrets.

There were approving smiles, words of praise from the agents, laughter, questions about life in New York, as they drank and ate and inhaled the exotic air of Little Heaven. Ali was surrounded by strangers and enemies, yet he felt at home. He *was* at home, where the rhythms of the cosmos touched his perceptions as a newborn, where his memories came alive, where butter tasted the way it should, where figs hung from the tree outside, where he spoke Farsi and drank *aragh* with his enemies. The sight of agents he would have to hate, the smoke of opium he did not approve of, the smell of tobacco he always avoided, the alcohol he rarely touched, filled his lungs and nerves, conquered his mind and loosened his control. So he accepted all that he disapproved of because he was home, because all were made at home, because all were a part of him, because he was a part of them all. How could he not celebrate, not feel tolerant? He became more and more at ease, looking at Kamil and Shamil as misguided fellow countrymen. Sara left his mind for the time being.

The Savakis liked him. They thought him witty and cool, just betrayed by an alien ideology, Russian propaganda and the books of the eggheads that fill American libraries.

Ali stepped out of the hut for a few minutes in order to avoid the dirty latrine. A shepherd rested on the grass leaning against an oak, loving and playing his flute. Ali knew the music by heart. The shepherd played for himself, or whoever wanted to listen, but not for pay, not on schedule, not with printed notes, but from his heart.

A cosmic celebration awaited Ali outside; all the stars were ablaze. He fixed his gaze on the face of the sky that he had missed. He had not seen so many stars since he had left Iran. It would take eight hours or so for that magnificent night to speed over Europe and cross the Atlantic. When it reached New York City, pollution would rob the night of the stars that blinked their greetings to each other and to the minds and eyes in the universe who appreciated their fire, motion and power.

In New York, the night's beauty and innocence would be degraded, like a virgin raped. If industrial growth turned nature into poison and ugliness, then it was not progress. In the end no canaries would sing the music of evolution, no oaks would ascend to the sky to hug the sun, no eagles would descend to tear into frightened rabbits, and no man would wonder, evolve, create and love. There is no hell, but if man doesn't change his ways he will soon create one on earth, Ali thought.

The shepherd finished the song that had transfixed Ali. Ali considered running away, but where to go? He had heard that Savak first tried to get student radicals coming home not to engage in hostilities, so he felt no immediate danger. Running would only bare his intentions. He returned to Little Heaven.

Kamil and Shamil poured some fig wine, viscous, green and drugged, into their glasses, nodded to Ali and poured some for him, too. They wanted to have his confidence, to know his plans. They liked him, but they had a job to do.

Ali asked Shamil, "What is this?"

"It is an ancient recipe," Shamil replied. "It can't be described. We drink to your homecoming." The two agents took a small sip, and Ali followed with a gulp.

Step by step, through discussion of the past, through revelations of hopes for the future, their mutual understanding grew. The revolutionary and the secret police drank, ate, talked and laughed together. Ali accepted them and they accepted Ali.

Ali drank more of the wine; it tasted bittersweet. A burning wave rose swiftly to his head and warmed him from within. Relaxed in a hut which now seemed to rock gently like an ocean liner, Ali showed his well-hidden curiosity.

He asked, "Why do you have these odd names, Shamil and Kamil?"

Shamil responded, "They are not our real names. My grandfather was a refugee from the Caucasus, so I chose Shamil after the leader of Muslim mountaineers in Daghestan, who fought the Czar for twenty-five years. Kamil fought the British in Egypt. These names symbolize our untiring struggle against the materialism of the West and the atheism of the East to dominate Iran. I am sure you also put the highest value on the sovereignty of our nation. The present regime is not perfect, but under the Shah's leadership Iran will take her historic place among nations."

Ali barely heard Shamil, but the words—materialism, atheism, Shah and Iran—echoed in his head and disturbed his tranquility.

The mysterious drink had already penetrated the innermost compartments of Ali's braincells. He took another sip as his companions brought their glasses to their lips. There was no burning sensation this time, only a new wave of relief diffusing within him. Ali's eyelids felt heavy and his head fell forward.

Kamil and Shamil were smiling as they slipped away from Ali, disappearing in the smoke. The mud hut took off in his mind like a spacecraft, and he felt the queer sense of weightlessness. He reached for Shamil, but the man was already too far away for Ali's fingertips to reach. The unexpected events and the stimulating drink stirred new images of the past Ali thought he knew and old images of the future he had envisioned so often. Ali leaned on Shamil and fell into a dream.

All of a sudden Leonardo da Vinci's *Mona Lisa* flashed in his head wearing the same mysterious and unassuming smile. Lisa stepped out of the picture framework still keeping the smile. She threw her robe away and let the moonlight be her gown and signalled to Ali to join her. They danced with the music of Verdi and with the rhythm of the breeze. Exhausted, they sat on the grass beside thorny rose bushes, drank wine, ate mango and made love. The moon tickling with joy witnessed it all.

Ali asked Lisa, "Do you ever think of Leonardo da Vinci, your creator?"

"As often as you think of God."

"You wear the same smile all the time," Ali said.

"Why not? All history is the same. Greed and killing. My smile is the same even in dreams."

"In dreams?" Ali asked.

Lisa answered, "Yes, of course dreams have physics, chemistry, biology and electricity just like real things. How else can my smile happen in Leonardo's head and others' far apart in time and space?"

Then a storm blew the scene away. Ali standing on top of a hill saw people in white robes demonstrating. A huge banner reaching the sky floated above them with no one holding it. On the banner was inscribed in all languages, "We are humanity in one piece. We are humanity in many parts. Humanity above nation, nation above community, community above family, family above self."

Another banner fluttered past. On it was a picture of Jesus crucified, the bullet-riddled bodies of Che and Ruzbeh, the martyred revolutionary leader of Iran, lying side by side, Galileo behind bars in a prison uniform, and Marx with his hands tied behind his back, a huge hat on his head inscribed with all the accusations leveled against him.

Ali shouted, "There is no single Messiah or Twelfth Imam whose arrival is awaited. New prophets grow within us and among us; every era has its own prophets. Love them now, don't kill them!"

The marchers in Ali's dream were young and old, students and teachers carrying books. Workers carrying hammers and peasants with sickles hung on their backs sang folksongs. Bazaar merchants dragged their feet behind. Writers lifted a sign declaring their right to tell their stories as they pleased. Behind them mothers stood still to breastfeed infants.

Next, familiar faces appeared. Professor Pirooz carried a gigantic placard, an ant struggling to set the UN right. On it a new Ten Commandments were inscribed: "Socialism is the ideology of the twentieth century. There is no God but the human mind. The exploitation of man by man and the destruction of nature by man must end. . . ." Ali could not read the rest. His attention turned to his father carrying a flag stretched flat in a silent wind. It said simply, "God is Great."

Then Ali's sister Zaman led a mass of young women with frowns as makeup, eyes fixed and blazing with determination. They wore black fatigues, mourning women's condition. Their braids projected horizontally behind their heads, and they carried machine guns with muzzles pointing forward, parallel to the braids. They carried no flags, no words, no signs. Revolutionary songs blared from the muzzles of the guns.

He saw his brother Hussain, his mother Fatema, Sara, and hundreds of strangers in white robes holding a huge wooden coffin on the tips of their fingers with arms stretched upward. The coffin held his brother Abbas with blood pouring out of the bullet holes in his suit.

From cracks in the coffin, spheres of black smoke shot upward, piercing the clouds, turning them into black rain which fell on the white robes of the mourners, leaving parallel black stripes like prison bars.

From a distance, images and sounds, dreadful and threatening, grew and drew near. Drums of war and military marches mixed with the voices of men in the throes of violent death, springing from the crimson and grey dust.

In his dream, Ali saw Kamil turn his head and point backward, shouting, "The Shah is coming!" Ali could not tell if he and Shamil were part of the Shah's party or running away to join the people.

Now, amid a frightful duststorm, a train emerged with a piercing whistle, moving at right angles to the people's march. The Shah was at the throttle in the locomotive. He wore the blue, full-dress uniform of an Iranian admiral, with thousands of medals fixed to his chest, each a gravestone made of jewels inscribed with the name of a man he had ordered killed. Hiding under his huge coattails, U.S. technicians, CIA agents and propaganda experts stoked the boiler. Behind the Shah, in open flatcars, were his impeccably manicured generals in olive green and admirals in navy blue. On the fronts of their hats, in small letters, Ali read, "Made in U.S.A."

Police with guns strapped to their sides stood in front of a group of men in white lab coats clutching their favorite instruments of torture, including a machine for producing electric shocks and burns on human genitals. On the side of the on-off switch, Ali read, "Made in U.S.A." Executioners dressed in red, and whores of all races, naked but masked, followed. The rest of the Shah's entourage rode a flatcar whose tail end stretched back forever, to the fringes of hell. Iranian Ambassadors with heroin-filled briefcases under their arms and ministers hiding barrels of oil behind their backs preceded mullahs in long black robes, snow-white turbans and salt-and-pepper beards. They were counting their beads made from the soil around the tombs of Muslim saints. They intoned, "Pray for the Shah and praise Allah!"

But Ali saw the Ayatollahs Khomeini and Taleghani amid the people's march.

In front of Ali's eyes multitudes of human bodies with placards for heads walked alongside the flatcar. The placards were blank; the mullahs could inscribe anything they wished on them. With patched rags on their backs, carrying food for the riders on bare feet, these men were the extension of the flatcar, serving without question. The Arabic incantations on their lips were the garble of pagan worshippers of a black stone in Mecca, from a history that was dead but lived in their minds and on their tongues.

Young conscripts, with guns, bayonets and flame throwers at hand, moved behind the Shah. A squadron of vultures hovered over the locomotive. Some distance in front of the car, emanating from rotting carcasses of past massacres, a putrid odor wafted forward, a banner signifying the decomposition of the dead who had decided to think independently.

The train in Ali's mind was now alarmingly close to the march of the people, and clouds hurried to cover up the scene. The train smashed into the people, dividing the march in half, and a gigantic cross formed. Firearms unloaded to left and right, and arms of fire stretched out into the people. Instantly, thousands of springs erupted from their bodies, squirting blood like swinging sprinklers. The line of people squirmed like a single man mortally wounded. Ali saw his mother and Sara fleeing the fire, his sister fallen dead, Mona Lisa's severed head still wearing the smile. Ali could not locate his father and brother Hussain. The voices of the dying on the ground, the deadening silence of the living on the train, the dust, the falling black rain, the soaring red blood, the sight of the executioner's blade swinging, the bullets piercing hearts, flames setting faces afire, mothers' breasts cut off while in the mouths of infants, his family now lost in the crowd of tumbling dead, pounded Ali's head and he could not endure the pain. He awoke in horror to see the amiable Savak agents smiling at him.

CHAPTER 10

Zamandukht and Aram - 1968

Zamandukht had never heard such troubling words before. Her brother Ali had spoken his mind their last night together before he left for New York. His blunt challenge haunted her long after he had left.

"Your fate is to cook, clean and obey without question. You sin whenever a strand of your hair escapes the darkness of the black chador you wear. You have become a prisoner of Islam, guarding yourself. You submit to a faith that regards a man's judgement as superior to a woman's, and you accede to unequal rights because Islam proclaims that women aren't as rational as men. You veil yourself as though hiding your inferiority. You embrace a religion that tolerates even slavery and polygamy." His fist clenched, his eyes locked on Zaman's, he demanded, "How long, Zaman? How long?"

Zaman knew only that Islam was her life, breastfed and whispered to her since she was born. Zaman kept her silence before Ali, even though each word was the lash of a whip, leaving painful welts on her soul. Tears ran down her cheeks even as she felt his reassuring hands covering hers.

The next day at the airport, Ali had taken her aside and kissed her goodbye. He smiled and said, "Your name is Zamandukht. It means the daughter of time. Unlock the past that keeps you in captivity. Remember your name."

It was months before she wrote to him, promising that she would examine the articles of faith the way Persians examine their household goods before the new year, the first day of spring, sorting and cleaning or discarding.

Now almost three years later, Ali was returning home to Teheran, his studies unfinished. He had been deported by American authorities for radical activities in the United States.

It was a late summer afternoon resisting its inevitable end. To hasten

110

the passage of time in her mind, Zaman gazed from the edge of the pond at the playful interchange of the fish, some golden, others russet, ruffling the luminous surface. The fish swam through the wavering reflections of her face, her deep black eyes and soft eyelashes, her pink lips a floating rose.

As she watched patches of clouds drifting across the blue water of the pond, she reflected on her life, while the fish splashed carefree through it all. Under the lone willow surrounded by beds of roses, yellow, pink and red, Zaman wondered about herself, her place in these colors and motions. Did she know where she was heading? Should she let her nagging doubts take her where they would, or should she fight them?

She raised her eyes and saw the worn two-story structures facing one another. They reminded her of old couples who become look-alikes over the years, their small rectangular windows, like tired eyes, breaking the monotony of their rusted, well-laid bricks. With the white stucco walls to the north and south, the courtyard formed a box open to the endless sky.

Similar houses ranged on the sides of the narrow street named Vali. Tired trees and graying concrete electric poles grew out of the pavement here and there, benchmarks for children's games. Mount Damavand, a dormant volcano, wrapped in the cold of snow but boiling hot within, rose white and conic to the northeast of Teheran, witnessing the bustle of the city. The neighborhood spread behind the House of Parliament, which flanked the east side of Baharestan Square, the stage for much political violence since the constitutional revolution early in the twentieth century. The square was surrounded by shops, by sidewalks crowded with strollers, with Turkish-speaking peddlers selling oranges in winter and peaches in summer, and with beggars asking for alms. A stream of traffic encircled a park of small willows and evergreens, filling the air with poison, noise and vibration. At the center of the square a metal statue of the Shah's father, Reza Khan, stood frowning upon the House of Parliament—a symbol of the constitution.

Zaman sat staring absently at the rippling surface of the fishpond in the yard. The pensive eyes that stared back at her from the pond were her own, but also those of Ali, her brother, gone so long, so far, that Zaman thought he might not return the same as he was. She watched the wavering image of her eyes, and she knew that it would be so—he would have changed, just as she had changed. She glanced to the doorway he would soon walk through, her thoughts on the Ali who had left through that same door three years before. She had always felt close to that Ali, not at first to his radical ideas or his critical views, but to his courage. Then little by little she became closer to him in philosophy, too. Their correspondence, the books he suggested she read, and more and more her own deliberation, had put her on a rebellious path. How surprised Ali would be once he learned about all the revolutionary books she had read.

The memory of a scene long forgotten wrung her thoughts into a throbbing pain. In her mind, Zaman saw her favorite aunt slapped and kicked by her husband. "I will divorce you and take the children away," he screamed at her as she pleaded with him, "Forgive me. I will never object to your seeing that woman again." Those words would echo in Zaman's memory forever. Now, her pride had turned into a resolve to liberate women from servitude and the destitute from poverty. "Islam protects men as though they are the real victims," she mumbled to herself.

"Aunt Zaman, Aunt Zaman, it did it! The little ant did it!" Startled from her thoughts, Zaman looked across the pond to where Parvine squatted and stared intently at an ant struggling with a large piece of walnut. The little girl, daughter of Zaman's martyred brother Abbas, was clapping her hands with the excitement and joy that only her age could sustain. She applauded the ant as she ran around the pond to Zaman.

"Did you see? Did you, Aunt Zaman? The little ant took home that big piece of walnut that I left in his path. It was much bigger than the ant. He is a real champion," Parvine announced with the solemnity of discovery. "He deserves the walnut. He is going to share it with his family."

Zaman picked Parvine up and kissed the child, whispering, "I love you, Parvine, do you know that?"

"Oh, yes, Aunt Zaman, I know." Parvine giggled at her young aunt. "You tell me that every day. How can I forget?"

"Yes, and you have told me so many times that you know that I love you." Zaman's smile disappeared as she knit her brows. "Listen, Parvine, we are as strong as that little ant. We are even better: we have imagination, we have memories. The ant must accept the world as it is. We will change it to please us. We are not going to be intimidated by big tasks. The bigger the task—if it's worth it—the harder we fight."

Parvine wrinkled her nose in puzzlement. Zaman declared, "We're not going to give up, Parvine. Never." Zaman looked at Parvine and saw the reflection of her own past, reminding her of those wonderful years which had melted away. She put Parvine down gently, and the child, once free, ran around the flower garden and disappeared into the house to tell her Grandma Fatema what the little champion of an ant had done.

Zaman's memory resurrected a scene in the reception room upstairs. She was six years old, like Parvine, and it was a Friday, when she was to recite the articles for the profession of faith as a first step to becoming a Muslim before God and before witnesses.

Her father sat on a blue couch with the window behind, the mullah on his right and her greatuncle on his left, with male relatives around them. Zaman stood facing her father on the red medallion in the center of a beige carpet. Her mother, covered except for her eyes under a chador like Zaman, held her hand. The other women, also covered in printed or black chadors, conversed quietly. On the north wall a large print of His Holiness Imam Ali —the forefather of all Shiite Imams—with a lion at his feet, a sword in his lap, the Koran in his hand and a halo around his face and a colorful tapestry of Mother Mary holding Jesus in her arms on the south wall witnessed the celebration.

Zaman's father raised his hand and the room fell silent. "Dear Zaman, you may now recite the articles of faith, if you wish."

She struggled to start. At last she said in a trembling voice, "God is One; the Koran is God's inspired book; God sent the Prophets to earth; the Prophet Muhammad is the final one." Suddenly she stopped. She could not remember the rest. She could not breathe, and the whole world watched her suffocation. The sunlight set her face on fire.

The silence stretched. Finally her mother squeezed her hand and whispered, "Dear Zaman, remember: 'The Prophet Muhammad is the final one, but God favors no prophet above the other. . . .'"

Zaman raised her voice, energized by her mother's love. "Can I start over again, Father?" Her father assented by closing his eyes. "God is one; . . . The day of judgement will put good and evil in balance, and the lives of men are foreknown to God even though each is the architect of his own destiny." She finished her profession of faith in a voice filled with her heart's assent, which drew all those present into the fire of her joy and pride. She saw a single teardrop roll down her mother's face.

The profession of faith was the first of the five pillars of Islam. Zaman at six was determined to make the others the pillars of her own life: to pray three times a day, to fast in the month of Ramazan, to give alms to the poor, and to make the pilgrimage to Mecca. From that day on, the chant of the muezzin at dawn high in the minaret, sonorous and compelling, calling the faithful to prayer, was the music of heaven for her. She never ignored the call. She prayed every day, before dawn, at noon, and after the sun set, even though she could not understand the beautiful Arabic words she whispered in exact imitation of her mother.

One Friday on her way back from the mosque, she had given alms for the first time. Seeing the legless beggar forever leaning against the electric pole across from the stone lions guarding the House of Parliament, she ripped her hand from her mother's and ran to him, filling his gnarled, outstretched palm with her week's allowance. Returning quickly to her surprised mother, she said simply, "I am a Muslim; I must give alms. I shall do that from now on." Her mother's smile made her sudden resolve joyous.

Those distant events lined up like a string of rubies before her eyes. They were wonderful days filled with unqualified devotion to Islam. They were enchanting days when she chased butterflies around the flower garden and loved Gabriel, the messenger of God's truth. They were days filled with light and clarity, days when every word of the Koran held a secret treasure she was determined to discover and make the adornment of her soul. But now they were gone, all gone. Her faith in Islam had been cruelly challenged. The questions kept multiplying while convincing answers were meager raindrops in a drought.

Those days of innocence were gone when Zaman used to grasp in one small hand her mother's hand and in the other the black chador tightly under her chin, which shielded her from the eyes of strangers on her way to the shops or to the mosque. She no longer wore the chador. Zaman remembered how painful it was to accept the fact that her beloved mother would never agree with her that the chador had no dominion over faith or purity. Unable to persuade her daughter Fatema had said, "I hope your good deeds will compensate for the sin of your unveiling, Zamandukht. Meanwhile I will pray for you every night until you return to Islam's fold." So strangers saw her face, but still veiled, even to her family and friends, were her new questions and her new ideas. The days of strength and conviction supported by the five pillars of Islam had crumbled. But the memories persisted. Zaman's mind spun through time like the wind over the sea.

She remembered the proud day she had fasted for the first time. It was the first day of the ninth month of the lunar calendar, Ramazan. She had turned nine years old that day. An hour before daybreak, she felt a warm kiss on her cheek and a whisper in her ear. "Are you asleep, my love? Zaman dear, do you still want to fast?"

She raised her head from the pillow, pushed back the strands of long black hair from her eyes and nodded to her mother. She slipped out of bed, quickly washed her face and hands, and walked holding her mother's hand out to the large balcony where her family sat on the floor around a cloth covering a Kashan rug.

Zaman said good morning to her brothers, but kept her eyes on her father and sat beside him. His reassuring hand touched her hair. He said, "How are you, Zaman dear? We all trust that you will accomplish God's will. We hope that you will touch no food and no water until sunset. But if you must break your fast prematurely, don't despair. It is only your first try. Perhaps it is God's wish to test your will." He lowered his head and kissed her forehead.

Zaman had never before dined so early in the morning. All the stars of the Persian plateau looked down on Zaman, a nine-year-old girl in an irresistible rush to meet the world of adulthood and become a real Muslim. Zaman sat watching a large moth flying around the electric lamp that poured light over the cloth. Her mother served chicken and eggplant *khoresht* over rice, which she had prepared the day before, and everyone joined in eating.

Her father listened and watched attentively as Zaman ate and dreamed of the day to come, the first real test in her life. To prepare herself against hunger, Zaman continued to stuff herself at the end of the meal, with more bread, cheese, melon and grapes. She ate to the limit of her small stomach.

"Look at Zaman gorging herself," Ali had said. "During Ramazan, Mother should have no worries with Zaman's appetite."

Fatema replied, smiling, "It is not my cooking but her master plan to resist hunger."

As her mother took her hand to lead her from the balcony, Ali snatched Zaman up in his arms and kissed both cheeks. She knew then that she would not break her fast. She performed her ablutions, washing her hands, face and feet, as the Koran had prescribed more than a thousand years before. Then she said her prayer before sunrise and went back to bed, as time rushed to catch up with her journey of fasting.

She awoke late that morning to a lazy summer day, with no school, nothing to face but hunger, thirst and temptation. She came down to the yard. Younger children from the neighborhood teased her, offering fists full of sweet mulberries. The song of the vendor who carried on his head a huge barrel of ice cream with crunchy chunks of frozen cream made her mouth water. The whole world conspired to tempt her at every turn. She prayed with her mother at noon facing Mecca, and at the end of her prayer she made her first request of God, the Benevolent and Compassionate. She begged him to give her strength to overcome her thirst.

The day passed grudgingly; seconds clung to minutes and minutes to hours. The clock in the hall seemed to stand still, refusing to acknowledge the passage of time in her mind. It seemed that God held the earth in his invisible hand, slowing its rotation to test her resolve. The day was long and she was hungry. The day was hot and she was thirsty. In her discomfort she identified with the children of Imam Hussain suffering from a worse hunger and thirst in the holy day of Ashura.

On that fateful day, Yazid, the unjust Caliph, had promised His Holiness Imam Hussain, the son of Imam Ali and the grandson of the Prophet, safe conduct, treasure, and the mayoralty of Karbala if Hussain would yield to his rule. But the Imam replied that since he had conquered the fear of death, his only fear was compromising Islam and abandoning the oppressed. Instead, he urged even those not yet born to fight injustice in the city, in the caravans, in their homes and in their hearts. Stranded in the desert of Karbala, full of thorns, salt, boiling sand and evil men, the Imam's children, hungry and thirsty, did not beg their father to yield. They suffered as he prepared for martyrdom.

It was Ashura, midday, the sun's scorching rays perpendicular, when the Imam and a few faithful rode to the battlefield. The horses marched haltingly, as the sand squeaked under their hooves. Imam Hussain reined in his horse to face the men who had been paid in gold and silver to kill him. At the top of his voice he declared, "One must die somehow, but all deaths are not the same, just as all lives are not the same. Murdering me will not murder my ideas." Then the dust rose as the combatants galloped at one another.

After a fierce battle, Hussain fell, arrows penetrating his chest. The limbs of Abbas, his brother who had gone to fetch water, were cut off. Zaman cried when the mullah recounted the end of the story of Ashura. "Can you imagine it? Abbas held his sword in his teeth, fighting to the last breath."

The little girl sat in the shade of the willow tree in her first day of fasting. She would not ask for water, as the Imam's children refused to ask in Ashura. She stuck her right hand into the fishpond, closed her little fingers into a paddle and made small circles in the water, as though helping the earth to rotate so it could turn its back on the sun faster. Gradually the day, that stubborn day, did begin to fade, as if by Zaman's will. As the sun descended, its rays climbed the eastern walls, retreating into the obscurity of the infinite past. Zaman at the age of nine had conquered time, the slow pace of the summer sun, hunger and thirst. A faint yet triumphant smile spread over her face as the thunder of the Imperial cannon shook the windows, signalling the end of the fast.

Her mother's call followed instantly. "Zaman, come and break fast. We are waiting for you." She could eat and drink now, but she was no longer hungry and she felt no thirst. Zaman knew that she could go without food and water longer—perhaps forever—and she knew that she could go without many other things if she wanted to, if she had to. That she could resist temptation bestowed on her a new sense of strength. Her mind was master of her being. Zaman stood and walked toward the verandah where her family had gathered. She glanced back at the pond. Zaman had experienced the same pain the children of the Imam had suffered in the day of Ashura. She discovered that she had endured her own first Ashura.

Today, awaiting her brother's arrival, she looked at the lazy movements of the fish in the pond and wondered if she could do without that unqualified faith which had stilled her soul for such a long time, the faith that gave her strength to withstand her body's painful demands for nourishment. Could she now abandon the idea of Ashura? Could she so easily dismiss the mullah's sermons, her mother's teachings, the pillars of her faith? Could she recreate her own vision of Islam according to her own interpretations and convictions? How could Islam be so rigid that she had to be either a Muslim or an infidel?

Her will had been strengthened for years by the spirit of Ashura. Could she live without that nourishment? But Zaman had doubts. After a Friday prayer, Zaman had asked the mullah, "Why didn't Hussain's sister,

Zaynab, join her brothers on the battlefield?'' The mullah answered only, "It is God's will."

"Why is it God's will that women should not fight for justice?'' Zaman had asked. "Do not question God's judgement,'' replied the mullah.

"Why can men marry four wives?'' inquired Zaman.

"It is God's design,'' the mullah said. "Just as stallions in the wilderness have a harem of mares and offspring to protect, so men must protect their families and women must care for the young. This order of responsibility is universal."

Zaman argued, "There are too many exceptions, even in the wilderness.'' The mullah replied, "Don't worry, Zaman. In practice it is difficult to treat four wives equally, as God demands.'' Zaman insisted, "If so, then why can't women have the same rights and the same obligations?''

The mullah was shocked. "Women marrying four husbands?''

"Yes,'' said Zaman gleefully. "And be required to treat them all equally."

The mullah mumbled, "Four husbands? God punish my ears for hearing such words.'' Then he commanded, "Go and wash your mouth, Zaman. This is blasphemy."

"Why were men and women from distant lands taken as slaves?'' Zaman had asked her father. He replied, "We cannot judge the past by the standards of today.'' Then why was the code of justice so different in the Koran for men and women? Are not all people the same before God? Doubts grew to an avalanche of dreadful disbelief. Yet Zaman retained a deep faith in Imam Hussain, in Ashura, in dying to realize one's noble ideals. How could words explain Hussain's ever-shining deeds? How could deeds surpass the expectations created by his great utterances? How could anyone unite word and action better than his magnificent acceptance of death in Ashura?

The martyrdom of Imam Hussain was caused by a violent rebellion against injustice, while that of Jesus was an absolute submission to it. Zaman believed that God endorsed both alternatives of violent and nonviolent struggle to combat evil.

Zaman was torn apart as her faith in Ashura was turning into a faith in revolution. Her doubts that Islam could answer and resolve every conflict grew like a cancer of the soul.

Little by little, Zaman was being drawn to the principle of justice and freedom for all. But how could she revolt against injustice while still holding on to a veil? And how could she fight for freedom while guarding her own prison? The nation had to free itself from the Shah and the veil, from the prisons of the Shah and from the prison of its own beliefs.

Zaman's mind wandered again just as a golden fish jumped out of the water, catching a ray of sunlight before plunging back into its world. She thought for a moment: Could she return to her faith, embrace it as completely as before? Were her doubts just passing moments, like the fish leaping into the air? Then her mind swept back to the day of her first fast.

As Zaman sat to break her fast her mother had said, "Zaman, my dear daughter, your strong faith and will is a little miracle. Because of it, I feel closer to God." Ali offered her a glass of fresh grape juice and said, "My little sister Zaman is a heroine of Islam," even though his own beliefs had begun to change. Zaman saw a tear drop into the pond as she struggled with memories tirelessly drawing her back to Islam.

Those days when the formation of flying doves or the dance of falling leaves was fresh proof of God's will were gone. Her belief in Islam was in ruins. She felt that since she had questioned Islam she had to leave that peaceful and secure haven of faith.

Zaman smiled as she thought of her classmate Aram, the Armenian boy with the deep blue eyes and soft blond hair, long and loose, that he tossed back from time to time to clear his line of vision. As science students, they talked about the calculus of variations and the physics of subatomic particles as well as the closeness of Islam and Christianity. Aram had boasted that Armenia was the first nation to embrace Christianity. Zaman had teased him that Christ was not the prophet of Christians alone; he also belonged to the Muslims. The Christians wished to monopolize even the prophets!

But there was more in her heart. And then only a few days later, meeting her among the oaks under the falling leaves, he had not dropped her hands after their usual friendly handshake. He held them in his own warm hands, as they stood in the shadows of the tall trees that stood guard over the two of them. A pleasurable tremor ran through her as she felt that moment again. No one except Ali knew of her joy that was tempered by apprehension. She felt the limbs of her soul being pulled apart. Her questions about Islam fed on unceasing questions about her own desires, the meaning of her life, her growth into womanhood, and her growing love for Aram. Zaman questioned even her daydreams, which she thought of as her only possessions. She could no longer hide the terrifying gestation of her new ideas. Her doubts could no longer live inside her. They had to be expressed, they had to lead to new commitments, they were bound to be revealed to all. Who would view them with grace? Who would condemn them with disgust?

Her father's lecture came back to Zaman. "Islamic society must develop according to four guidelines: the will of God expressed in the Holy Koran; the deeds of the Prophet Muhammad recorded in history and tradition; the choice of conscience of each individual; and the collective decisions of Muslims on conflicts. By such guidelines, Islam establishes relations between man and God, man and state, man and man, and man and his own conscience. It unifies ethics and law, stability and progress. God's commands are all-encompassing.''

Zaman tried once more to convince herself of the absolute validity of Islam; she strove to cling to the past. But she was plagued by questions that defied her faith unrelentingly.

What would I do, she asked herself, if my conscious choice did not bend to the word of the Koran, to the example set by the deeds of Muhammad, to the collective decision of the religious experts as announced by the Ayatollah?

If I am not rational because of my gender, how could I, as a mother, raise men who are rational?

Why does Islam favor men in marriage and inheritance laws, and in the penal code?

Why can't I be a Muslim and not wear the chador?

Why can't I be a Muslim and not be subservient to men?

Why can't I be a Muslim and be seen with Aram?

Her questions, engraved in her mind, found no answers. She murmured to herself, ''Choice of conscience, choice of conscience. . . That is the guideline I cherish most. Weren't Imam Hussain and Christ both in the minority? Didn't they follow their conscience and rebel?''

So again and again Zaman's mind, pulled by an invisible force, would turn to her own search for truth, her own will. Whenever she let herself think her own thoughts or recognize her own desires, she found them in conflict with Islam. So Zaman turned to science and to revolutionary ideology, where men and women were equal and exploitation was the greatest evil. In the end, Zaman realized she could never live as a traditional Muslim woman like her mother. She would be faithful but appear as an unbeliever; she would not die spiritually pretending she was anybody but herself.

* * * * *

Her thoughts flew to Aram, to whom she often returned for companionship and comfort. Late in April she had gone with him to the foot of the Elburz for their first secret picnic. The mountainsides were crowded with flowers—flowers giddy and lost in a dance contest, in couples and groups, dressed in red, blue, yellow, violet, in every color but green. Water ran over the rocks, at each turn miraculously finding the shortest path downhill, rushing to the thirsty dancers.

Zaman opened her heart to Aram as they climbed the slope. She told him she could no longer hold on to the past: images of the future of her own making shattered her attachment to the past. Aram was silently attentive. At last Zaman pointed to a tree off the path. ''Aram, it looks protective, and beautiful, too. Let's stop here.''

Aram nodded in approval and broke his silence. "My sister, Anaheed, is also marching through her own painful doubts toward a rebellion that is certain to come. The other day she protested to my father repeatedly, demanding to know why she could not go out on a date without a chaperone. For her this is just a beginning."

Zaman interrupted, "Didn't your father study architecture in Paris? Isn't he broadminded?"

Aram said, "Yes, but remember, he is Iranian, too. Besides, my mother's family escaped from Turkey not just with their lives but also with their traditions."

"I see," said Zaman.

Aram continued, "Dear Zaman, the twentieth century is a time of liberation, for workers, for peasants, for women. Even subatomic particles tied in knots by the strong and weak forces are being freed by a thermonuclear blast. It is time for old walls to crumble and old locks to rust through. It is a time of liberation for everyone and everything. The world is exploding with freedom. You aren't alone."

They sat under the tamarisk tree on a yellow blanket that blended with the green of the grass. The lovers could hear a noisy brook down below, they could see the silent white mountaintop far above them that fed the brook, and in between, all around them, they could see and hear nature in full color and full concert. But they saw only each other, and heard nothing but themselves.

After the long climb, Zaman was hungry, a fact which Aram could see in her eyes. Playfully he declared to all who cared to listen, "I am a materialist. Food is matter. Without food, man would perish. Therefore, let there be a feast." He shoved his hand into the knapsack. "But behold, Zaman, this food is special. Even your mother, Lady Fatema, in spite of all her love for you, has never prepared it for you. It is not sanctioned by Islam."

Zaman was caught in the mystery. "What is it?"

His hand still lost in the knapsack, Aram grinned. "First, however, we shall have history and honor, and then calories."

Zaman, puzzled, kept her smile. Aram said, "My great-greatuncle, Malkoum Petrosian, and his brother introduced this food to the King of England, to the President of France, to the Shah of Iran, and supplied it to the Czar of Russia. They even served it to Picasso, so it is no wonder so many wonderful paintings flashed in his head."

Zaman said eagerly, "Okay, Aram, that's enough. What is it?"

"Be patient," Aram replied, continuing his speech. "I confess here at the foot of the Elburz that my honor is even greater than my uncles', for I have the good fortune of introducing this dish to you.

"Inside the dark belly of the Caspian Sea there is a fish, the sturgeon.

Inside the belly of the sturgeon are the eggs, caviar. Now this is for inside your belly," he said, pulling his hand from the knapsack and handing Zaman a piece of pita bread containing caviar and butter within.

Zaman put the sandwich down, untasted, as she put down a thousand years of tradition along with it, drawing herself closer to Aram. With a courage driven by desire, her lips met his for the first time. The two were starved for one another.

Zaman heard strange words repeated over and over as Aram kissed her. "*Jami akhtchig. Jami akhtchig.*" Finally she stopped and gently pushed Aram away from her. "What is that you're saying?"

"Just your name in Armenian: Zamandukht, Daughter of Time."

Zaman looked at the Aram she loved. "Do you think it will work?"

"What do you mean, Zaman?"

"Between us."

"Persians and Armenians have lived together for thousands of years," Aram said. "Why not us, Aram and Zamandukht?"

In a few minutes there were no more sandwiches or fruits. The taste of caviar prompted Zaman to say, "Aram, my ideas aren't sanctioned by Islam, because you are a Christian you are not sanctioned as a mate, and the caviar isn't sanctioned, yet all of you are so wonderful."

Now, later at the pond she pondered Aram's question, "Why not us, Aram and Zamandukht?" At this moment, her thoughts of the past and future intersecting in the present, she became aware of the turmoil within the house. Concerned about Parvine's absence, she called her name. Instantly she saw Parvine running toward her, smiling past her, pulling Fatema behind by the hand. Zaman turned to the bearded man who had entered their house. In a second he was clutching Parvine, Fatema and Zaman all in one bundle in his arms. Parvine was laughing, Fatema crying, and Zaman was a grain of dust in the storm of her emotions. Maryam, the old maid, and Hussain, Ali's younger brother, rushed to the scene. Maryam, who was more a member of the family than a servant, stood by as tears rolled down her face. She pushed her hand through Ali's hair from behind, the same Ali who had always insisted on more and more stories from her when he was a child.

The canaries sang of joy saved for him, the agitated fish collided, the thin, long leaves of the willow trembled in the new wind, the plump figs beneath the green boughs offered their sweetness to him. The garden rejoiced in Ali's return.

Ali held the three women for a long time. With a smile, Zaman lifted her head and looked up to her brother, as Fatema and Parvine watched. Zaman mischievously tugged Ali's beard and taunted him, "How did you grow these red, thick whiskers? Are they symbolic? Red, the color of revolution. How appropriate to my mood, to the change in our lives. I would have grown one myself if I could."

"Now you complain that you can't grow a beard, Zaman?" Fatema protested.

Zaman hugged her mother. "Why not?"

Ali and Zaman laughed. Ali then hugged Maryam and Hussain and kissed their cheeks. "Where is my father?" Ali demanded. Fatema said, "Father was praying upstairs. Let us surprise him."

"In a moment, Mother," Ali said. "We will catch up." Everyone left except for Zaman and Ali.

Ali held Zaman's hand as they stared at one another, bridging the years they had missed. Zaman said, "I am glad you have returned. When you left Iran we thought differently, but our thoughts are no longer apart. You were right—the despotic rule of the Shah over the nation and the despotic rule of men over the family must end. There is injustice in Vietnam today—the land defoliated, the people massacred. The Vietnamese have their Ashura. We need an Ashura here, too, to end injustice."

Ali spoke excitedly. "Wait, Zaman. Where is Aram?"

Zaman put her index finger to her lips. "Hush, Ali, no one knows about him yet."

Ali was taken aback. "How could you get Aram involved in your conspiracy?"

"What conspiracy?" Zaman asked.

Ali replied, "Your hiding him from the family."

"Aram did it for me!" Zaman protested. "Have you forgotten we live in Iran?" Then she added quietly, "He has asked me to marry him."

"What was your answer?"

"A big kiss and a loud 'Yes!'" Zaman blushed. "What did you expect?"

"And no one knows about all this yet?"

Zaman shook her head. "No one but you, Ali."

"Then the revolution must start at home," said Ali. Zaman stared at her hand-woven slippers. Ali broke the silence. "Aram's letters were eye-openers to me. He seems to think for himself and not accept this or that party line. Do you know what Aram said about chess and revolution, when I wrote him that I am a chess player, too? He wrote that we must approach revolution the way world champion Petrosian, Tigran the Tiger, plays chess. With every move he encircles the opponent's king a bit tighter, so imperceptibly that the opponent notices nothing until it is too late. He said we should do the same with the Shah. By the way," Ali asked, "is Aram related to Tigran Petrosian?"

"No, Ali, you should know better," Zaman said with a smile, her mood changing. "There are as many Petrosians among Armenians as there are figs on that tree."

Ali chuckled. "And I'll bet they're all just as sweet, too."

"Yes, of course," Zaman asserted, as if to defend Aram. "But he is more. He is Aram, he is fire!" She blushed again.

Ali said, "In America, no one blushes for being in love."

"I can't help it," Zaman said. "I guess my revolt is intellectual. My emotions are still backward. In any case, I am sorry that American women have forgotten how to blush."

"Listen, Zaman," said Ali, "I want to meet Aram soon, no matter how long you two play hide-and-seek with the family. He is already my comrade and my ideological brother."

Zaman pleaded, "Ali, you must help me tell Father about Aram."

Ali laughed. "You need no help. Your love for Aram is God's will, Father will say." Ali smiled. "Or else Aram could become a Muslim."

"Yes, I can just see Aram in a turban, praying in Arabic," said Zaman. "Impossible to do, impossible to believe."

Fatema's voice ran downstairs. "Ali, hurry up. Don't keep your father waiting."

Zaman took Ali's arm tightly in hers. "Let's join the others, Ali."

Ali stopped a few steps short of the top of the stairs, held Zaman tight and bent to kiss her cheeks. He pushed her face against his chest, pressing and shaking it, saying, "I love you, Zamandukht."

CHAPTER 11

Dissension in the Family

"Of course it matters. It makes a difference who is wrong and what he is wrong about," Ali exclaimed, staring at his brother Hussain. The width of a white tablecloth covered with colorful Persian dishes separated the two brothers. Dr. Keshavarz, his wife Fatema, Zaman, Maryam and Parvine listened to the siblings. The dinner that had reunited the family was over.

Hussain glared back at Ali, the thoughts in their eyes clashing like the horns of fighting bulls.

Ali's voice filled the silence, "It doesn't matter if one is wrong about whether an ant will turn left or right, but to deny evolution is to deny knowing yourself. Islam's story of creation is not so, and Islam's division of all things into good and bad leaves Muslims with little choice."

Hussain said, "Islam is the command of God. Yes, it dictates submission to God's will. It is—"

"Submission!" Ali interrupted, raising his voice. "Submission, the essence of Islam. Why submit when you can think and use science to know?"

Hussain replied, "You mean the Prophets, Muhammad, Jesus, and Moses and a billion believers are wrong?"

Ali shot back, "Yes! Remember when the whole world believed that the earth stood fixed and everything moved around it?"

Hussain shook his head. "If not God, then who made you intelligent, Ali?"

"Which god?" Ali replied. "Didn't people worship fire, idols, the Nile River, the moon, the sun with the same intensity you worship Allah? Every era creates its own God. Religion is developed by man and it prods man like an instinct, Pirooz says."

Hussain interjected, "Religion is not instinct. Come on, Ali, one must choose between good and evil every day. Islam promotes the love of God, the love of justice, stability, peace—"

124

"Yes!" Ali said. "Islam also pacifies the poor through guilt and fear. It promotes stability for the ruling classes."

Dr. Keshavarz intervened. "My sons! Don't interrupt each other. Even our best thoughts can wait their turn."

"Sorry, Father." After a pause Ali continued, "Man stands alone in this world. He must choose his goals and make the means to realize them."

"How can you be so sure?" Hussain asked.

"It makes no difference," Ali went on. "You say God created nature, our genes, heaven and hell, our destiny, and engraved all the rules of conduct in the Koran. If so, then what is left for man to discover, to do? For what choices are we responsible?

"Hussain, you're certain about everything, and I'm not. You are convinced you've found what I'm still searching for. Your life's chart hangs on the wall waiting for you to trace it, and mine is on the drawing board waiting for me to sketch it. Your God is fixed in the past, but mine is the future of man."

Hussain exploded. "You sound sure of everything. You told me life began in some soup when some organic molecules began to duplicate, and to survive they diversified into ever more complex forms. Some became plants, some fish. Then legs grew out of fins, some fish turned into mammals, and finally into man, who discovered all of these ideas you talk about. Tell me, should I believe in speculations or in God? Why do you want to convert us to Marxism, anyway, Ali?"

Ali replied, "Is everything you believe so certain?"

Hussain responded, "I breathe; this is certain. My life is inspired by Islam; this is most certain to me. I am willing to die for the cause of Islam; this is an ultimate certainty. Ali, my dear brother, I am simple, as you've said. Science is uncertainty piled on uncertainty. I wish to set my life on a more solid foundation." His face glowing with pride, Hussain took a book from his shirt pocket. It was a Koran two inches long, one inch wide, and less than an eighth of an inch thick, the printing microscopic. He kissed it and held it out, the silver cover shining in the light. "Here, Ali, this is the chart of my life."

Ali took the Koran. "How can this book hold all that can be known about the origin of life and the fate of man after death, contain a code of law for all time, and yet have enough room to specify correct genital hygiene?"

Ali's words with the Koran in his hand caused a shocked glance between Dr. Keshavarz and his wife. Dr. Keshavarz put his index finger on his lips to signal patience to Fatema.

Ali continued, "It is true that science offers only limited knowledge, but it examines itself continually. There is no uncertainty about this. Science doesn't set goals, it tells us how things are; it doesn't tell us what to do, but how to do it. Isn't it true, Hussain, that science and the concept of God and society itself are changing all the time? Remember the idol worshipers.

"Why, science seems to evoke both gratitude and terror in you, Hussain, the same range of emotions that fire kindled in primitive man. I'm not trying to insult you; please forgive the analogy. But you know, fire eventually became a friend of man. Are we going to reject science if it contradicts religious dogma?"

"Yes," Hussain replied. "Science is a great thing, but it must submit to the revealed word of God like anything else. And what about Marxism? It is no science, it's simply a doctrine with no God. Is history just a class struggle? Haven't events proven Marx's theories wrong?"

Ali nodded. "Of course. Marx was a scientist, a critic, a revolutionary. He didn't claim his work was sacred. Nothing is more un-Marxist than the fear of self-examination."

Fatema looked at her two sons and shook her head sadly. But she spoke kindly. "It seems Marx, the uninvited guest, is disrupting our supper." Maryam held Fatema's hand as Fatema struggled to regain her peaceful demeanor, which she hardly ever lost.

Dr. Keshavarz said, "Lady Fatema, let the children debate. Islam sets no boundaries on inquiry and learning, and neither should we in this household." He paused, then continued. "We can come back to this debate, but tell us now about America, Ali. How has modernization affected the spiritual life of Christians? Can we modernize without losing touch with Islam?"

Ali said, "In the U.S., millions are still hungry, homeless, and hopeless and hundreds of thousands are in jails or running away from the law. It is unbelievable that a wealthy nation with such lofty humanitarian claims can tolerate so much suffering at home and support so much brutality abroad.

"For example, look at the condition of women. In Iran women are imprisoned by tradition while in America nudity is commercialized. A large number of women are unemployed, under-employed, frustrated, used and abused against their wills in both worlds."

Zaman half stood, raising her hand as if in a classroom, not so much for permission to speak but to command attention. "Stop, Ali, let a woman speak for women."

All eyes turned to Zaman. The silence she had provoked lingered tensely. Zaman felt she had silenced herself, also for too long by keeping her new ideas hidden. Now, inspired by Ali, she was resolved to reveal herself. She glanced at Hussain, as if about to depart from him for good. "I can't accept a dogma that gives up on me at birth because I am a woman. It was men who caused Ashura and men who put Jesus on the cross. Aren't men the ones who set the living on fire in Vietnam, who waste immense resources for armaments? What kind of judgements are these, Hussain?

"What was God's purpose in giving women great abilities only to let Islam undermine them?" She raised her voice. "I'm becoming a good physicist. I am as dedicated to science, to art and to the well-being of people as any man I know. I refuse to be just an incubator, a milkmaid, and let my gender determine my life. The Shah stifles my political freedom, and Islam stifles my personal choices." She paused before she dropped the bomb.

"I am going to marry Aram, an Armenian."

Fatema reacted, "Who is he? Not even a Muslim!"

Zaman turned to her and said, "Yes, not a Muslim."

Zaman's announcement sounded like a political statement. Having unveiled her feelings and plans, Zaman fell silent, looking as peaceful as the sea after a storm.

Ali looked at his sister with the smile of a thousand approvals, with the joy of a man who, caught by aliens, finds another prisoner who speaks the same tongue. Hussain sat helpless and speechless, as if Zaman had just been buried under an avalanche. Parvine looked at her aunt in puzzlement.

Fatema repeated, "Not a Muslim!" She sat with a face of white, solid marble. Fatema was tiny and fragile. She wore no makeup. Her brown eyes were large and melancholic, her jet black hair parted in the middle and drawn back in long braids. Fatema did not know where to go, what to do, what to say, how to keep silent, how not to keep silent. Her numbness would not allow her to feel anything but numbness.

For Fatema, everything had a natural order and religious purpose. She obeyed God with ease and with joy. She had hoped Zaman would continue to follow her as she had followed her mother. Now, in front of her eyes, her daughter had discarded her faith. She had refused to become a wife and a mother to a Muslim.

How had her daughter, her Zaman, who had sucked her milk, listened to her lullaby, heard prayers whispered in her little ears, become a nonbeliever? How could Zaman challenge the revelations of Allah, the God who had bestowed on her the gifts of life, health, intelligence and beauty? Would she repent and let God's light reach her doubting soul? Would she return to the life- giving womb of Islam? Would this Christian Aram take Zaman away or would he embrace Islam? What about their children, Fatema's grandchildren? Would they be Muslims?

Then Fatema's fear of God turned to the fear of people. What would the relatives, the neighbors, and the Mullah say? How could she face them, how would she explain her daughter's going astray? She thought to herself, "I refuse to believe that Zaman spoke these words. An earthquake has struck our house and only God can repair the wreckage."

Struggling with her arthritic joints, Fatema got up from the table. Her eyes shone decisively, but the dilapidated heart of this old Muslim lady could barely carry its heavy burden. Then her familiar voice softly filled the vacuum created by Zaman's emotional explosion. "Please stay put. I will bring tea and baklava." Her family was so used to her words that they could have heard even if she had not voiced them. She disappeared into the hall.

Maryam took Parvine's hand, glanced back at Zaman to make sure she was indeed Zaman, and followed Fatema from the room.

Fatema loved to see her family together. She loved to see them debate and tease. But today was different. It had been different since Ali's arrival. He was not the same. He had grown a huge moustache. He did not talk as much. He did not tease her as he used to. He did not come around and ask for this and that, just to be spoiled at times and make her feel good. He squeezed his own orange juice, saying women should not be burdened with all the chores—those chores that she happily performed for him. Ali seemed possessed by something beyond the boundaries of Iran and Islam. He seemed possessed by the revolution, and she sensed he was in love with someone, although he never talked about it. But worse, Ali was an atheist. Her son an atheist. The idea, the words set her soul on fire.

Dr. Keshavarz looked at his Zaman, his daughter. No one expected him to say anything, and he uttered no word. He spoke only when he was sure of the substance and the effect of his words. To him even the right words and ideas at the wrong time and place were unproductive. He looked like a saint, ready to die but loving life. His remaining hair on either side was white. He wore a well-trimmed beard, gold-rimmed glasses and a gold ring. He had light skin and thick eyebrows and was medium in stature.

Dr. Keshavarz had sensed that Zaman's views were not evolving toward those of a Muslim woman, but of a modern one. He had noted small changes in her attitude, words, mannerisms and ideas which had accumulated and reached this explosive point. It was he who had given her the name Zamandukht, "daughter of time." Dr. Keshavarz already knew that his daughter, although linked by generations to the Prophet Muhammad himself, would be a woman of a new age, a woman of her time, Zamandukht. He did not expect Zaman's life's purpose to be just to serve the family and God in this world in order to attain heaven in the next. Dr. Keshavarz knew his daughter would not leave to men all the responsibilities that lay between household chores and religious commitment, as Muslim women had done before and expected to do in the future. Her utterances didn't surprise him. His silence, transparent and graceful, was neither condemnation nor approval. Zaman was beautiful, she was bright, she was in love, and she was in revolt. He loved her, he understood her, and he accepted her present state, even though it saddened him.

But all of the worrisome ideas within the house of Keshavarz penetrated Fatema's peaceful life. She rushed to her bedroom, knelt on her prayer rug of green, yellow and brown, and recited in her heart the six articles of faith as she had done before in times of distress or despair. Islam was the effervescent source of strength for her. She had no ambition but to serve and expected nothing in return. Her love for the rosebush, for the persimmon tree, for the singing canaries, for the residents of the fishpond, for the family, the neighbors and Islam was constant, unquestioning and unqualified. She nourished them with food and sympathy. Serving was not just a sacred duty, but also a desire and drive. She was possessed by love for Islam and for God's creations. She loved their old maid, Maryam, like her own sister. There was no divergence between her beliefs and her actions. She could no more compromise Islam than daffodils could hide from the spring. Islam was not second nature to her but first.

Fatema's torment of the soul dissolved in a sea of peace called "God's will." She never doubted what she believed. Her simplicity, her faith, her absolute submission to Islam gave her the strength to overcome all problems. Her keen mind could distinguish the realm of faith from the universe of reason, and any ambiguity was resolved in favor of faith.

Fatema knew something new and grave was gathering momentum in their home, but the rays of hope shone even on the stormiest days of her life. It was life-giving faith that provided security, warmth, nourishment and love.

Fatema paused for a moment, still kneeling, still feeling a prayer in her heart, the same she had recited before. "In the name of God, the Beneficent, the Merciful, praise be to God, Lord of Worlds. I ask thee for nothing. I thank thee for everything thou hast bestowed on me. If I am worthy, let thy will arise in my heart. Let thy command become my deeds. Let thy utterances adorn my tongue, and let my lips give them wing. May my family be enriched by thy presence. My Lord, I submit to the purity, peace and justice of Islam. I thank thee for the heartache that will deepen my understanding of thy wisdom. I thank thee for each breath of fresh air, for each drop of rain, for each ray of sunshine, for the gift of life and for the opportunity to serve thee. I submit myself to thy will, and I ask no more for my family but the glory of submitting to thy will." Then the old lady felt momentarily bitter. "I will welcome death as a gift if . . ." Fatema bit her tongue and as if called, she stood up in one motion and rushed to the kitchen.

Over two tablespoons of Darjeeling tea, she poured a cup and a half of hot water into a teapot and placed it on top of the samovar, which looked like a large, pregnant doll of bronze. Deep in its core, a pipe-like fixture held charcoal embers to heat the water surrounding it, and the heat from the charcoal rose to gently warm the teapot sitting on top of the samovar. In a few minutes the tea would be brewed to perfection. Fatema treated each task with the utmost care, as though it were her first or her last, but today her mind was elsewhere. She poured a little dark tea in each glass, which she set in a metal holder with a handle, and watched the tea turn golden as she added hot water in each glass to the individual's taste. Dr. Keshavarz wanted his tea light, and Zaman wanted hers strong.

She and Maryam served the tea with homemade baklava, and then

Fatema excused herself to pray some more. Let the young men and woman debate free from her presence. She went to her room again and sat with her knees folded under her. She looked peaceful. She could not look any other way. On her face there was no sign of contradiction.

Fatema's departure left the dining room in turmoil. An emotional anchor, Fatema's devotion always held the family steady. Now the gentle breeze of new ideas gathered strength, pressed against the sails and became a gale rocking and hurling the ship's passengers into each other. Family unity had disappeared.

The debate continued and the tea grew cold. Zaman declared, "If Islam demands my absolute adherence, someone had better convince me of its absolute wisdom."

Ali said, "God has shown his perfection in one way: he is the perfect hide-and-seek player. No one can find him anywhere. I want a vision. I would kiss God's footprints a thousand times." He turned to Hussain. "Show them to me."

Hussain could not believe this. "Open your eyes! Look at the bee around the rosebush; that is God's command. Look at the palm of your hand; there is God's footprint. Right there!"

"I ask for God and he points to my hand," Ali said, smiling. Dr. Keshavarz hid his smile.

Hussain said, "I beg God to forgive you, Ali."

Dr. Keshavarz held up his arm and they fell silent. "This debate is not new. Our chance of understanding God's infinite wisdom with our human reason is as limited as a doll's chance of discovering the motive of its maker. Either you have faith or you don't." He waited, then added, "I still hope Ali will tell us about America."

"I went to America to learn," Ali answered, "but I am disappointed. I certainly learned that their way does not bring out the best in man, but at times even brings out the worst."

"How is that?" Hussain interrupted.

Ali said, "Profit and self-promotion seem to be at the core of all their actions. America is a giant roaming the planet in search of loot; it is not worthy of imitation." Ali then changed his thoughts. "I don't believe that nationalism or Islam is the answer for Iran. National boundaries are scars upon the face of the earth, and religious differences are scars on humanity. Both scars are signs of old wounds; they divide us. Communism will unify mankind. I am a communist!"

The others exchanged glances. They did not know Ali had gone so far. Dr. Keshavarz kept calm. "A world without boundaries would be a wonderful place. But meanwhile what can glue together a Baluchi, a Kurd, a Turk and an Arab separated by deserts, mountains, language and culture, except Islam and Iranian nationalism?" Then he added, "Yes, you said you were a communist. Remember, the Koran commands that wealth should not be concentrated in a few hands, and that irresponsible landowners should be stripped of their property. The prophetic tradition states that fire, grass and water, the absolute necessities of desert life—as Marx would have said, the 'means of production'—must be owned collectively." The children smiled at their father's quotation.

Dr. Keshavarz spoke formally and quietly. "These prescriptions permit any degree of collectivization of property that an Islamic society finds appropriate. Marxism is just an extreme limit of a range of possibilities. Islam demands that Muslims share responsibilities, with the state as adjudicator. Duty toward God and duty toward man are inseparable, two aspects of one supreme goal, the securing of justice. Islam does not separate law and ethics as though they did not govern the same life on earth."

Ali said, "I was misunderstood. I didn't mean to belittle the importance of Islam and nationalism in Iran today, or the revolutionary role they can play, but in the very distant future we should abandon both. If each country relied on religion and nationalism, we'd never be able to unite humanity or stop war. Only socialism can provide justice and unity for all mankind."

Hussain said, "I like the idea of justice in socialism, but Islam, too, is for justice. Socialism is man-made, but Islam is God-made. That is the essential difference."

"Hussain," Zaman asked, "can you defend the necessity of all that God has made, when man is struggling to eradicate communicable diseases? On the other hand, can you dispute everything that man has made? If so, then why do you wear clothes?"

Zaman paused. "Marxism and Islam seem to conflict only because of dogmatism and lack of imagination. Islam can give moral guidance and socialism can create a rational economy, one feeding the soul, the other the body."

Dr. Keshavarz said, "Islam was revolutionary in proclaiming that land belonged to God and that its reward should go to the tiller. It was evolutionary in asking owners to free their slaves as a good deed, since instant freedom would have caused great harm to most slaves. There are only a few unchangeable principles in Islam. Since each era has its own constraints, then questions must be dealt with according to circumstances of their own period in history."

Hussain said, "We need no fusion of Islam with socialism, Father! To compromise Islam at one point is to compromise it all. A long time ago you taught me that material and spiritual lives are inseparable. So good deeds are good and bad deeds are bad whether they are illegal or unethical. It is not the Koran that must be reinterpreted but it is the individual and society who must adhere to the scriptures. There is one God, and there should be one authority for spiritual and for political affairs, until the resurrection of the Twelfth Imam." With these words, Hussain had expressed the fundamentalist view of Islam.

Zaman raised her voice, "Hussain, you're so dogmatic! You should know better. Islam deals with inheritance, marriage, the penal code, taxes, which clash with man-made institutions, laws, affairs, solutions. You can't confine the changing knowledge and the world within the fixtures of Islam. The Koran must be reinterpreted! God made man in his own image, and man creates his own destiny. If they are not perceived rigidly, socialism and Islam can merge into one." Zaman was now voicing the ideology of a forthcoming revolutionary organization, the Mujahedin Khalgh, the "People's Fighters."

Zaman continued calmly, "I disagree with Father that the main struggle of one is with himself for the purification of the soul. That is necessary, but we also need a revolution to change institutions. I also disagree with Ali, who denies the value of Islam in the life of our people." Ali smiled at his sister. "But Hussain's voice is from the past," Zaman concluded.

"For once I agree with Ali." Hussain directed his gaze at his sister and repeated his previous remark, "Don't forget, Zaman, Islam is God-made, while socialism is man-made. The two can't mix. Islam is indivisible." He knew Ali had already left the faith for good, and that his father's philosophical views were by now immutable. Only Zaman could be won back, he thought.

Ali looked at Zaman. "Islam derives energy from faith in God and miracles, socialism from faith in man and science. Islam emphasizes the primacy of the soul, socialism the primacy of labor. Islam protects private property, socialism struggles against it. How can they fuse, Zaman? It is not mental rigidity that prevents the mixture, but objective impossibility.

"And there are more problems. Our mother's Islam is absolute submission to God's will as pronounced by the mullah. Our father is a Sufi who purifies his heart in order to know the divine essence directly. Zaman wants to accept the spiritual or the better part of Islam and discard some of the traditional dogma. And you, Hussain, believe in the literal reading of the Koran and the example of the Prophet's deeds. And this diversity is only in this house. There are more sects in other countries. Which is the real Islam, Hussain?"

Ali paused for a moment, his cheeks glowing red. "Our confusion stems from trying to reconcile the conflict between science and faith, the conflict between our real physical condition and the condition of our minds. It is time to free ourselves from such shackles."

Hussain answered, "Ali, Islam is not rigid. Islamic societies in their days of glory created the most advanced science. And Muslims are now waking up again. The mullahs are rising, and Islam is becoming revolutionary, just like its beginnings. I feel it in my veins. I am a Muslim, you know."

Ali said, "I am no longer a Muslim. I want to be free! Freedom to me is the right to question anything, to abandon everything, to create, to revolt and to transcend what already exists. To create this type of freedom, communists face torture chambers and firing squads everywhere. Unlike Muslim martyrs, these communist men and women die without even the hope of heaven. They risk the dismemberment of their limbs to unite the oppressed. Don't tell me, Hussain, that they die for an unworthy cause.

"And one more thing, Hussain." Ali looked at his brother. "You talk about truth. I don't think truth can be reached, touched or held, as you do. But one can't even search for it if his freedom of inquiry is restricted. Islam doesn't permit me to question its tenets, and nationalism labels workers from other countries as aliens. So I don't recognize the boundaries of Islam or those of Iran. I have outgrown both. See? I have freed myself, and I am still alive and well." Ali finished with his fingers and eyes directing everyone to the light coming through the windows and falling onto the tablecloth with differentiated brightness.

Hussain said, "Unlimited freedom sounds good, but then this world cannot afford more than one free man. Two would clash. Come on, Ali. Life is full of limitations. How can freedom be unlimited?"

Ali replied, "In Islam people are like fish in a crystal bowl, a neat and bounded freedom. My freedom has no fixed boundaries, but it is not limitless as you poke fun at it. It is restricted only by science, by economics, and by the consciousness of the time. I respect Islam as I respect my parents. But just as we grow and must leave those who fed us, so Muslims who want to be free and use their minds must leave Islam which nourished them for so long."

Zaman interrupted, "At least we must leave that part of Islam that is confining. I agree with Father that Islam and nationalism, no matter how restrictive or contradictory, can't be ignored. But we need a class struggle, a women's struggle, a national liberation struggle all bundled in one big revolution, since a revolution that does not alter women's condition leaves the majority in bondage. Socialism treats men and women as equals, and that is a big attraction for women."

"I hear most street cleaners in Moscow are women," Hussain objected.

"So are most physicians," Ali retorted. "I won't defend socialism in the USSR, but at least acknowledge their accomplishments. Is it fair to blame the shortcomings of Islamic countries on Islam alone?"

Zaman said, "The attitude of men in the USSR has not changed yet." She continued, "I won't let the family and Islam stand in the way of my freedom. A revolution is happening in my mind, and in the minds of many Muslim women in Iran, as it happened in Europe a while back."

For a moment, Zaman felt a chill. She realized the distance that her new ideas had carried her.

Dr. Keshavarz said, "Breaking abruptly with the past is dangerous. An individual's identity is eroded in socialism by the collective abstraction and in capitalism by the commercial drive. Remember, my children, reason and science are concerned with universals, not particulars, but each man has a unique soul. Any ideology or system which ignores individuality is empty."

Ali objected. "Wasn't the individual set aside in the past in favor of religion?"

Dr. Keshavarz ignored Ali. "Science cannot and will not unite us. I won't entrust the future to the scientists, even though they have solved many problems, because they have also created bigger problems, such as the atomic bomb. Science provides means; for goals we must turn to God."

Ali objected again. "It is not science but capitalism that uses knowledge for destructive purposes."

Dr. Keshavarz continued, "I am also critical of the development of institutional Islam. I don't need a mullah to communicate with God, and God doesn't need an angel to communicate with me. We can communicate directly if God wishes. Perhaps one day we can all achieve ultimate wisdom. But, alas, God is beyond our imagination. Not one person, not the entire human race, can fully know his wisdom. No matter how far our understanding of God ascends, it will not attain to what he is but only to what is beneath him. God is the absolute, infinitely complex, infinitely simple, infinitely powerful, wise, and compassionate.

"Once more, my children, if you only pay attention to the fundamentals of Islam, you will see that it is compatible with any creative movement, be it science or socialism." Dr. Keshavarz added as an afterthought, "But I wish my new book were finished so Hussain could see the danger of unifying the political with spiritual authority."

"Father," Ali said, "Historically, faith has impeded scientific inquiry because the will of God explained everything, not science, not reason, not the search for happiness. So then in a conflict between duty and happiness, then duty, not chosen but imposed by Islam, is to be preferred. I work for revolution not out of duty but for the joy of seeing the goal, justice on earth. This happiness is my morality. It is my authority, my choice and no one else's."

Hussain concluded, "I won't be Westoxicated by the technology or ideology of the West, and I won't be Eastoxicated by Ali's Marxism and science."

Absentmindedly, Dr. Keshavarz scratched the back of his neck. "I have one more question to ask each of you, the one I have meant to ask all along. What do you think should be done in Iran?"

Ali said, "Iran is a neocolonial nation, without occupation forces but with thousands of U.S. military advisors instead. We must build a secret cadre to carry out an armed struggle while creating a party of communists from workers, peasants and progressive elements of other classes. This secret core must challenge the Shah's violence against the people with revolutionary violence, in order to galvanize our opposition. Even some capitalists in Iran who struggle against the remnants of feudalism and the competition of Western capitalists may join the struggle. We must educate and support the peasantry for collective use of the land, free of feudal obligations or the intrusion of agribusiness. We must support the workers in expropriating the means of production. We must free artists and scientists to be inspired by the masses and to help elevate their cultural standards.

"We must not become dependent on any other government or fraternal party, such as that of the USSR, as the Tudeh Party has. We must support the struggling people in the world, and our support must have no strings attached. We must learn from other communist parties and avoid their mistakes, both before and after taking power. We must lay the foundations for the socialist and democratic society. This sounds very theoretical, but there is no reason that it cannot be accomplished in Iran."

Ali had expressed the ideology of an emerging revolutionary Marxist group, the Fedayeen Khalgh, the "People's Sacrificers."

"What do you say, Hussain?" Dr. Keshavarz asked.

"I agree with Ali that the present regime must be overthrown—peacefully if possible, forcefully if necessary. American rule through the Shah is corrupt and unjust, but even if it were not, it is not legitimate. The supreme authority must lie with the Imam, like the Grand Ayatollah Khomeini. I don't believe a secret cadre of revolutionaries is the answer. We need not worry about classes, but the strength of the faith. Every good Muslim, regardless of class, should and will join the struggle. A good Muslim must not, cannot accept injustice or be its agent."

"And you, Zaman?" asked Dr. Keshavarz.

As though just awakened, Zaman said, "I have said what I wanted to say. Nationalism and Islam must be tapped. We need several revolutions wrapped up in one. For that an underground organization is necessary, as Ali says. The Shah will not go away of his own free will."

Dr. Keshavarz said, "From what I hear you have more in common than you admit. You agree that the Shah's regime must be done away with, and you agree on the supreme value of truth and justice. Let your conflicts lead to a deeper understanding of what unifies you. This family and the larger family of the Iranian people need unity to overcome the forces of evil."

They fell silent and looked fatigued, having reached a mountaintop and needing time to catch their breath.

Fatema entered the room once more to fill the unemptied glasses with more tea. It was the first time she could remember that her tea from India, brewed with such care, had been left to cool in each glass. She knew the reason.

Zaman was a revolutionary woman, a woman not of her mother's time but of her own time, her own "Zaman." Just like Zaman herself, the times were revolutionary. Ali had proclaimed himself a communist, and Hussain, the young man, was in love with and in awe of his namesake, Imam Hussain, a light and source of imitation for him, as he was for multitudes of Shiites living in Iran and elsewhere. Fatema tried to understand her children and accept the will of God.

Dr. Keshavarz, a theologian isolated from the orthodox clergy, and now from his own family, knew that even isolation would not bring him peace. His offspring would not allow that. This was a time of doubt and questioning, a time of debate and passion in the Keshavarz' family and throughout Iran, a time leading to the head-on crash of religion and ideology. It was a time of dissent, a time when the unceasing race between the necessities of life and the lure of ideas was intensified, a time when the lives of Ali, Hussain and Zaman were pulled by their new ideas, a time when the old ideas of Fatema and Keshavarz held them back, held them fast to each other and to God.

Having brought up such fiercely independent children, did Keshavarz have any choice but to accept them? The ideas of their children had to survive beyond their own lives, in the minds of others, in books and in letters. Their ideas must not die with them, but they might have to die for their ideas. The seeds of revolution had already begun to sprout in many places and lives across the nation. But unlike the Keshavarz family, few bothered with this simple question: Which revolution, by whom and for what ultimate purpose?

Months later, when all the facts of Aram's family background, his life and the length of his friendship with Zaman were known and Aram had met the family, Professor Keshavarz acceded to the marriage, provided that the children be educated in both Islam and Christianity. Fatema knew further resistance would push Zaman away for good.

Disheartened, Fatema listened to the words around her and watched her peaceful world coming to an end. She felt responsible for the fall of her children and she knew the best she had hoped for them would never come true. Months later she confided to her husband, "My elder son is an atheist and now my daughter is to marry an atheist. You know, Mehdi, I am not able to disentangle myself from the hurt that like lice has fastened its paws into my soul. I pray and pray, but the pain does not go away."

"Be patient, Fatema," Keshavarz said. "We cannot isolate our family. We must pay the price of the Nation's awakening. What is sin to you is liberation to the children. Think of them as lost lambs. God willing, they will return to the fold. You have always done your best. God knows this."

Ali and Zaman drew closer too. They knew Fatema was hurt. Ali understood his mother, worried about her and loved her more than ever even as the gulf between the son and mother grew wider and deeper. He tried not to say or do anything in her presence that would aggravate her non-healing wounds.

Through his mother, Ali had begun to comprehend the deep emotional tie between the people and their faith. No reason, no scientific evidence to the contrary could sever the tie between Islam and the faithful. How could a handful of communists bridge the wide gorge between their convictions and that of the people? How could Ali explain un-Islamic principles, goals, and means to devoted Muslims? And worse, how could he, by using words that did not mean the same thing to him and to his brother, Hussain, communicate with the masses? This realization, discomforting at first, turned to fear and then to despair. He decided to study Lenin and Mao-Tse-Tung and others on this issue and find out how they dealt with similar problems.

Ali wished he could talk to Sara. He felt a ceaseless urge to write to her, to ask for her forgiveness, to hear her voice, to touch her face. He knew he now understood his mother and Zaman better because of Sara. Zaman encouraged Ali to write to Sara, but Ali kept making excuses, "Not until these wasteful and irritating interviews with Savak are over." Students like Ali upon returning home were subjected to Savak's questionings before they were allowed to hold any jobs. Ali shuddered as he thought of his upcoming visit to Savak headquarters. How long could he sidestep hazardous Savak probing into his life and still keep his poise, he wondered.

CHAPTER 12

Tragedy With An
Easy Beginning

Ali stood at the gate of the much feared Iranian State Intelligence
Organization (Savak) headquarters. Savak, the secret police, kept an eye on
the bureaucrats, on the businessmen, on the army officers, on the police,
and on the ordinary folks. Some street cleaners, taxi drivers, hairdressers,
masseurs, workers, professors, judges, journalists, generals, diplomats, and
ministers reported to the agency. Savak rewarded the loyal with choice
government jobs and used threats and coercion to bend the will of those not
so loyal to Savak's viewpoint. Savak censored information, spread misinformation, rigged elections, silenced the outspoken, or made troublemakers
disappear. It managed political prisons and supervised torture and executions. It was widely known that American CIA experts performed a critical
role in organizing and advising Savak and training its personnel.

Outside the headquarters a large, anxious crowd milled about. Ali
asked a beggar, "What is going on?"

The beggar looked around at the crowd and said, "They hope to find
those who have disappeared."

"Family members?"

"Yes."

Pretending not to know, Ali asked, "Why here?" The beggar gave him
a long look and shook his head.

An old woman covered by a chador approached Ali from the crowd.
"Sir, will they let you in?"

Ali replied, "Yes."

"God bless you," said the woman. "Please, will you ask for my son?
Please." Ali agreed. She told him her son's name.

Ali stepped through the guarded entrance. It was his fourth interview
with Mr. Anvari, a high Savak official. For two hours of frustrating questions
and friendly persuasion from the official, Ali would spend the whole morning waiting in bleak corridors, just as he had waited at U.S. Immigration

138

and at the Legal Aid Society. The purpose here was to gather information but also to serve as a reminder, a lesson.

Savak's first step was to reduce a person's life to pieces of paper in a file. Anvari treated Ali with deference, but he wanted details, not just about the Iranian student movement in the U.S., but about Ali's private affairs which appeared to Ali of no apparent value to Savak. At first, Ali refused to cooperate, telling Anvari it was none of his business. Anvari smiled, apologized and explained that it was just routine procedure for citizens who had been abroad.

Then Ali's family began receiving anonymous telephone calls. Savakis visited his father at the university, and Zaman and Fatema noticed men following them around. This harrassment changed Ali's mind and tactics. He became a reluctant but cooperative witness, giving Anvari personal information and recounting public events, like the demonstrations in New York, but divulging only what he was sure Savak already knew. On occasion, if Ali missed something, Anvari would remind him with an all-knowing grin. Ali excused his lapses with an uneasy smile, and later with a twinkle in his eye and a shrug of his shoulders, to show that he wasn't worth close examination. "Mr. Anvari, I don't even remember what I had for breakfast," he had said the last time they met.

Ali wanted to give no useful information and to get Anvari off his back as soon as possible. Ali would occasionally alter or invent a detail to test Anvari's knowledge. Sometimes Anvari would catch him, giving Ali clues to how much Savak knew and perhaps even how they managed to know it. In this way Ali was able to learn more about Savak than Savak learned from him. Ali was learning deception, a first step in becoming a revolutionary. He could now bend a little, lie a little, smile, remain silent, laugh heartily, protest softly, whatever was necessary to get by. He withstood the pressure of Anvari's interviews, although he hated the process. In New York he had learned valuable lessons in remaining under control and he had thought them out on his return home. Ali indicated to Anvari that he had just blown off steam with his protest activities in New York. By lying, he added revolutionary discipline to his revolutionary will.

Today a servant knocked at Anvari's door and ushered Ali in. Over Anvari's shoulder hung a color photograph of the Shah with splendid medals cascading down his chest in layers of gold, enamel and jewels. His stern look focused on his officials as well as on their victims, prodding everyone to keep in line. A ceiling fan cooled His Majesty's portrait. The fan's lazy rotation seemed to slow time in the offices and halls where people waited.

Anvari stood stiffly behind his desk, thumbs under his lapels, lifting them out from his chest in imitation of a well-known posture of the Shah. The black rims of his thick glasses matched the color of his polyester suit.

Anvari preferred black even in summer, as if to mourn his lost ideals, Ali decided.

As a student in France not long ago, Anvari had admired Dr. Mossadegh and joined the dissident National Front. But as graduation approached, he began to sweat. Remaining in exile would mean a life of insecurity, while returning to Iran as a member of the Front could lead to harrassment, imprisonment and torture. Then he noticed some of his friends accepting important government posts. One, while vacationing, told Anvari that he never abandoned his ideals, but he was just working within the system to modernize Iran. The job was necessary and it paid well. So what was wrong? he asked Anvari, seeking approval.

Anvari approved. He applied for a job with the Seven Year Planning Agency, without luck. But the official there said that His Majesty would let bygones be bygones if Anvari would prove his loyalty. Insecure, homesick and alienated, Anvari dropped his conditions one by one to interviewing government officials. He finally convinced himself that neither opposition to nor cooperation with a corrupt system would change the world, and if the Shah offered security, why not for him, too?

His contact was a Savak agent in Paris, a shrewd bargainer who could estimate anyone's final price. Some students ended their opposition by bribery, some by threats, some by being ignored. Anvari was ignored, then coopted. The desperate were recruited into Savak. Anvari rationalized that in Savak he could protect dissidents who passed through his office. But he soon discovered that his own position was not safe. The insecure security officer was under the thumb of his superior, a man not to be trusted and himself under the thumbs of higher-ups, any one of whom could find Anvari's loyalty wanting. He was a man without power, pushed by superiors who were pushed by the Shah. And the Shah was insecure because he had to hide from his own people.

Savak and the bureaucracy were held together by insecurity, mutual suspicion and the rewards of corruption. Savak had its ways, and one of them was bribery. Anvari soon learned the benefits of bribery. The dream of a larger house, his wife's ceaseless demands for expensive jewelry, the charm of a new car pushed him to accept bribes, too. Another favorite Savak technique, arbitrary punishment, helped to keep victims off-balance. If possession of a forbidden book could lead to a year's hard labor, even if the law stipulated only a small fine, then one would think twice before reading the book. The trick in this scheme was that bureaucrats had to be creative and use corruption as a managerial tool. So the Shah enriched his loyal functionaries while holding them by the throat, for if caught they too could be sent to prison for corruption! When the Shah became displeased with one of his men, the unfortunate person would invariably be charged with an illegal action that most officials were engaged in routinely.

Anvari stretched out his hand when Ali walked in. Ali shook it and took the chair he was used to.

"How are you today, Mr. Keshavarz?" Anvari said.

Ali smiled. "Frankly, I'd feel better if I didn't have to come here."

"Well, national security overrides personal inconvenience," Anvari responded.

Ali softly said, "Mr. Anvari, I have to remind myself that these meetings are real and not recurring nightmares. Since you know more about my activities in the U.S. than I can remember, I don't know why we're wasting your valuable time."

The two stared at each other. Finally Anvari said, "Mr. Keshavarz, I wondered how long it would take you to reach this conclusion. The government is interested in you, that's all there is to it." He addressed Ali like a caring grandfather. "I am the first to admit that problems, errors and corruption can get in the way of His Majesty's plans for creating the 'Great Civilization.' Develop a creative tolerance toward imperfections, Mr. Keshavarz. Look at what the future holds in store for you, for us. Pull up your sleeves and join the government and reform it." Ali bristled at the words "creative tolerance."

"Your brother Abbas," Anvari said, "was a good man, but he was in too much of a hurry to change the world, so he was deceived by Russian agents. Don't make that mistake."

Anvari continued, "One last question, Mr. Keshavarz. Why did you leave Sara Patrick?"

Ali was startled at the mention of Sara's name but responded matter-of-factly, "You know about the problem with my work permit."

"Couldn't you have stayed in the U.S. if you wanted?"

"It wasn't worth it. I couldn't pay the lawyers."

"I see, but was that all?"

"Yes."

Anvari thought to himself, "We will soon know." He continued, "Now, Mr. Keshavarz, tell me about Miss Patrick."

Ali became angry but spoke softly. "Mr. Anvari, that is very personal."

Anvari answered, "In this office nothing is personal. Regulations cover everything, and I cover the regulations."

Ali replied in his mind, "Do the Shah's regulations define your sovereignty as a man?" But his voice said coolly, "I have had no communication with her since I left the United States."

Anvari insisted, "Please continue. Are you still interested in her?"

Ali answered, "No."

Anvari said, "So much the better, but you ought to know that Miss Patrick married Eric Saunders. You see, no good results from breaking the law; you stand to lose everything."

Ali was struck blind. Sara married to Eric Saunders just four months after I left her? Would she marry without telling me? How could she marry him? Have I been mistaken about her? Anvari could be teasing or testing me, trying to break my spirit, Ali concluded. Questions ran in his mind silently and quickly, then pain and anger pounded through. Why have I let my letter to Sara rot on my desk? I should have let her know I still love her. In the same moment he realized that he could not write to her now, if Savak was watching her; that would put her in possible danger.

Anvari interrupted Ali's thoughts. "You're an outstanding student from a distinguished family. Your return to the U.S. can be arranged." Anvari corrected himself, "That is, the deportation order could be rescinded. You can study for a Ph.D. with all expenses paid by the government. You could be of great help to your country, and to yourself, if you became more constructive. His Majesty needs men like you to create the 'Great Civilization.' His Majesty is forgiving, generous and progressive. We have a great leader; even U.S. Presidents seek his counsel. It is my duty to save promising young men from self-destruction. Help me to help you, Mr. Keshavarz."

Anvari paused to enjoy his eloquence. "Upon your return from the U.S. you will be welcome to join the government and to reform it. Thousands of educated men like us have done this."

Ali knew of such offers. Savak had penetrated the revolutionary opposition and tried to recruit the best. He listened patiently to the friendly persuasion. A few months ago he would have protested, but now he just said, "Thank you, but I can't hold my tongue, as you know, and I don't have your talents for becoming an agent. I won't go back to the U.S. or join the government. I've learned my lesson. All I want is a job and a family. I have no other goals."

Anvari smiled. The compliment from the serious-minded Ali made Anvari purr. Whether Ali accepted his offer or not wasn't important; it was Anvari's job to make the offer. Anvari rose as he said, "Think it over, Mr. Keshavarz." Then he changed his voice. "In any case, try to be creatively tolerant. Refrain from the troublesome thoughts, disagreeable words and wrongful deeds that caused you so much trouble in New York. Your past mistakes are forgiven. If you become interested in politics, join a legal party; otherwise, stay away from it. Our interviews are over, but my door is always open to you." Anvari added habitually, "Now, Mr. Keshavarz, can I offer you a cup of tea before you leave?"

"No, thank you, I must rush."

Anvari extended his hand. "Goodbye, Mr. Keshavarz. I hope we never meet for an interview again."

Ali thought, "And if we meet, I hope to be the interrogator." The two men fell silent and stared at each other. Ali saw Anvari as a fish caught in a jar by a playful child. The fish collided with the sides, just a leap or a child's wish away from freedom. Anvari was trapped inside the bottle of the Shah. But Ali had no sympathy for him.

Anvari saw Ali as one lost from the rest of the tribe. He hoped Ali would wise up and see that it was less painful to be separated from his ideals than from his limbs.

"By the way, a mother wants to know about her son." Ali gave Anvari the name of the son.

"I don't know him," Anvari said.

"Who does?"

"Mr. Keshavarz, if I were you I wouldn't pursue this matter any further."

Ali thought, "We'll see." He stepped into the hall, leaving the door half open. The Shah's portrait watched his departure. The three of them, Ali, Anvari and the Shah, knew that if Ali had to meet security authorities again it would be without an overhead fan, tea and sweets, or job offers; it would not be in Savak headquarters and would not end with a handshake and Ali walking out the door. Instead it would be a deadly interrogation in Evin Prison.

Anvari wished he didn't know such things. As he watched Ali disappear, silently admiring him, his thoughts turned sour. He glanced at the portrait of His Majesty, then sank into his chair and held his face in his hands. He was tired to the bone, and he could not guess the reason.

Ali walked to the stairs. His intestines contracted at the thought of Sara married to Eric. He had had to struggle not to show his emotions to Anvari. It was now very painful to think of the unmailed letter to Sara, in which he confessed his love for her. He should never have written those cruel words to Sara. He had thought it wise then to end their romance, to free himself and to free Sara. But his love had surged out of control. It could not be finished for him, and now he knew that he didn't want it finished, ever. Too late, too late. I make one mistake after another, damn it. He tripped on the last step on his way out.

At the gate the old woman stopped him. "Did you find my son?"

"I tried, honestly," Ali said, "but I couldn't get any information." The old woman's eyes grew wet as Ali's words sank in. Ali was about to go when he turned back to her. "Lady, I promise you I'll try again." Ali got her address and then fled as if Savak were in hot pursuit. He hailed a taxi, which stopped at his feet. Ali gave his address absentmindedly. He thought, I should have comforted the old lady; she could have been my mother. Then Ali plunged into his daydreams. He was glad that Savak was off his back, at least for the moment. He tried to ignore the bad news, but, unbidden, the thought of Eric and Sara together burst in his head. He remembered the night he had stepped on Sara's toes when she tried to teach him a dance, while Eric watched uneasily. Now a stitch exploded inside him.

The driver, seeing Ali come out of Savak, said, "It wasn't that bad, sir, was it?" The driver shook his head when Ali did not respond.

The taxi made its way through some of the busiest streets on the planet. Ahead Ali noticed a line of slow-moving cars, all blowing their horns at once.

"None of these screaming cars or jackhammers tearing up the asphalt or overhead wires were made in Iran. Oil was siphoned from the Iranian soil, but with equipment made in the U.S. The Shah's modernization is no different from Parvine's Lego set. All the Iranian workers do is assemble what is manufactured abroad. One little embargo and the Shah's industrial might would fall apart," Ali thought.

The taxi driver found space to rush into where Ali saw none. He lay on his horn to warn a motorcycle which turned into his path, grazed around the taxi and swerved into a side street. As he passed, the driver loudly offered his genitals to the cyclist's ancestors and progeny. The driver sped down the block, winding through roadblocks of parked cars, bicycle riders and other motorists, like a desert snake seeking life-saving shade.

Ali noted how much Teheran had changed in his absence. Food, music, air, souls, relationships, speech had all suffered from the Shah's prolonged repression and American cultural domination of Iran. There were taller buildings now, more government offices, more foreign trade representatives, more trucks, more household appliances, more televisions, radios, deodorants, cosmetics, drugs, and guns, all imported. The Shah had reduced a nation which had created great science and art in the past to a superficial imitator of the West.

The cab jerked to a halt, and Ali became aware of the driver's talking. Ali's father had urged him to refrain from political talk with taxi drivers. A good number were said to be Savak informers. Ali began instead to listen; there was no harm in that.

"Sir, I tell you, everything is becoming more difficult. Moving in this town is like carrying a headache around. There are holes in the streets just like the holes I want to put in the heads of officials. One day they dig up the telephone cable and the next day they dig up the water main. Then they put the telephone cable in place of the water pipes, and pipes in place of the cables. Then they bury them under the asphalt. To fix the error, they dig up everything again. And by this time the city has grown, so they need bigger holes to put in bigger pipes and cables. And still Teheran stretches out. I know, I carry passengers to the very ends of the city. I tell you, my father-in-law has a refrigerator now, but more food is spoiled in his house than before because there are too many power blackouts. A neighbor died on the operating table when the electricity went off last week.

"Last month I had to renew my license. I ended up bribing three officials. You can't even leave home without worrying that the police are guarding the burglar who strips your house.''

The driver talked without caring if Ali listened. ''You can't even tell a decent woman from a whore; they show their thighs as if in Miami Beach. Have you been to Miami Beach, sir? I see pictures of girls beside the palm trees, and I pray to God to send us a Castro, so I could get to the U.S. claiming to be a political refugee. It doesn't matter where I drive this metal ass. At least it would be more fun there.'' The driver glanced at Ali. Ali nodded.

''I can't understand it, Mister. Don't reporters see Teheran filled with smog and noise, beggars, secret police and foreign experts? Tell me, how is it that the more the Shah messes things up, the more praise is heaped over him? It's on the radio, in the newspapers, on the walls, all over the world. The sons of bitches. I mean the experts. The Shah can't go for a walk without foreign experts around him. They're his heart, his brain.

''The news shown on TV is phony, while real life is just baloney. I mean, look, the papers publish a government-approved schedule for orderly blackouts, but still power fails when it is not supposed to! The same is true with water rationing. The government cannot even predict its own failures right. Ha! Ha!'' the cab driver laughed at his own wit. Ali remained silent and the driver continued. ''And then the TV shows American soap operas, and, believe me, they're just shit, shit, plain shit. Even an uneducated man like me can smell shit as good as anybody. The life of these Americans has nothing to do with ours. A passenger who had been in the U.S. told me the shows don't tell much about most Americans either.''

The cabdriver turned his head, mindless of the road. ''We have plenty of shit oozing from the Shah's palace, and the palaces of his sisters and brothers and their children and their friends and the stinking foreign experts. But we have shortages all the time of onions and cabbages. You can't get cheap meat anymore, for the butchers are always out of it. Even kerosene is hard to get, and in a country sitting on oil, letting itself get screwed by whoever crosses the border. We're not allowed to complain or we get our penises electrocuted. Where did Savak get that damn idea, anyhow? No king ever electrocuted penises in Iran before. I'd rather have my eyes put out as the old kings did. A blind man can't see the ugliness.

''But we're allowed to beg, beg, beg, and we're allowed to sell our daughters. They're the only valuable possession the poor have. If the Americans say property is the foundation of the Free World, why the hell don't most of us have any of it?'' Ali became alerted. ''The foreign experts here have it all. They have the best jobs, houses with swimming pools and everything, big cars, good food, and they take our women to top it all off. The country is stripped. There's no independence, nothing to stand on, not even a good rope for a man to hang himself. There's no faith, no decency, no honor, no loyalty. There's no happiness, no security, no real greetings, no real goodbyes. There's nothing Iranian any more. Everything is imported. There's no foundation, no basis. No basis, no foundation.''

The driver slammed on his brakes hard, throwing Ali forward in the seat. Sirens wailed around the corner, and a motorcade sped through the square. In its wake a hopeless confusion of traffic suddenly unblocked poured into the square.

The driver continued. "You see that? I'll bet that was Princess Ashraf whoring around again. Because she gets a kick from diving into strange beds, she must be taken from here to there, so we get stuck with traffic jams."

Ali didn't respond. He was looking out of the window at a street peddler showing off his small, bored-looking monkey doing flips, its lips and ass tinged a light red, as though wearing the most recent and fashionable lipstick.

The driver resumed his talk. "There's no foundation, I tell you, no roots. There's no trunk, no branches, no leaves for this tree, for this nation. There is nothing. There's no place to go, no one to trust, no time to think, no privacy to touch your woman. Nothing is right, everything is wrong.

"I'm going crazy here. Tell me, sir, when the Twelfth Imam will come to right this mess. What is he waiting for? God tear my tongue out for questioning his wisdom, but where is the Twelfth Imam, the Absent Man? What is he doing now?" The driver turned his head again. "Sir, do you know who is responsible for all this? I ask you, sir."

Ali said, "Please keep your eyes on the road, or we'll be dead without finishing this conversation." He permitted himself a reassuring smile.

The driver saw the smile in the rearview mirror. He wasn't offended; he rather liked his quiet passenger. Ali added, "I don't know who's responsible. I haven't figured it out yet."

The cab veered to the curb, screeching to a stop. "Here we are, sir." Ali looked out the window at the familiar sights—the sickly but hard-dying weeping willow, the legless beggar with strong shoulders leaning against the electric pole, with one hand outstretched. Ali used to climb this pole dangerously close to the power lines, to catch bees nesting in holes near the top. His father had forbidden it, but without success. Ali paid the fare and began to walk away. He finally spoke. "This is our country. We are responsible, too." He pictured Sara smiling at this admission.

Soon he was home. The living room was filled with Keshavarzes. Parvine was making castles with some playing cards. Ali greeted the family with a big "Salaam." They were by this time used to the interviews, but they awaited an explanation from Ali.

"Well," he announced, "it's all over. They will let me alone, unless..."

Fatema anxiously asked, "Unless what, Ali?"

Dr. Keshavarz interrupted. "Lady Fatema, let's not spoil the day guessing what Savak may or may not do." Fatema agreed.

At home at last, Ali had to get things off his chest. "Every agent is a scorpion with a suit and a trace of rosewater sprinkled over him. You can tell by their grins and their poisonous politeness. They are just waiting to sting you to turn you into a scorpion."

Hussain asked, "What did Anvari say?"

"Just like Dixon in New York," Ali said. "He invited me to join in the looting or else...."

He continued angrily, "I am no one in this world. I have no treasure, no influence, no organization, no newspapers, no television or radio transmitters, no arms, no army, nothing. Yet those who have all of these try to bribe me or threaten me to change my mind."

The Keshavarzes looked at one another. Parvine stopped playing with her cards. Ali said, "Anvari seemed bothered by his own job, yet he must persuade and threaten others to join him. To live in Iran and get a share of oil revenue, the educated have to compromise, some more, some less. Anvari's case is extreme; he has joined Savak."

"I know some student leaders, even Tudeh Party members, who have done the same," Hussain interrupted.

Ali glanced at his brother and continued, "The military brass are compromisers because they have to shoot people at the Shah's wish. So are the bureaucrats who think their job hurts no one, yet they run the state machinery of the Shah. Professors and engineers are a bit more distanced from the Shah. They just don't want to be reminded how corrupt the regime is, how poor the poor are, how unjust the justice system is, much like the clergy who don't want to know how oppressed the workers and peasants really are."

Hussain frowned as Ali continued. "Then there are professionals who live abroad and keep a distance but accept lucrative contracts and enjoy all-expenses-paid conferences. Their research, financed by the Shah, ignores the mess in Iran. It is good only for their careers.

"But a few people, like Pirooz, haven't sold out. They collect petitions, write letters to newspapers, organize demonstrations at the UN. They'll do anything to overthrow the Shah, as long as it's not dangerous."

Hussain asked, "No one is good, then, Ali?"

Ali replied, "I'm just talking about the intelligentsia, those with some influence. The revolutionaries do not compromise with the regime, and if the revolutionaries succeed . . ." Ali stopped himself. For a moment no one said anything.

Dr. Keshavarz said calmly, "Dear son, look deeper into motives. Don't judge individuals by their profession only."

Fatema added, "Ali, you know how painful it is to compromise. Be compassionate to men who give up part of themselves to protect their families." Fatema was protecting her husband.

Combatively, Hussain said, "Did you tell Anvari he's a scorpion?"

Ali stared at Hussain. He felt the bitter taste of having had to lie to Anvari. He replied, "No. But you must not be honest with the dishonest Savak unless it suits a revolutionary purpose." His mind wandered. Finally he turned to Fatema and asked, "Where is Zaman?"

Fatema answered, "With Aram."

"Is he coming for supper?"

"Yes, God willing."

Fatema was more relaxed with Aram now that she knew what a good person he was, but she refused to remove her chador in his presence or shake hands. Aram understood.

What was Sara doing with Eric Saunders? The thought crashed into Ali's mind once more. If I learned about revolution at Columbia, Eric must have learned about the counterrevolution. We are exact opposites. How could Sara . . .

Interrupting his thoughts Parvine asked, "Uncle Ali, can you make a ten-story building out of these playing cards?"

"Parvine, dear," Ali said, "I'll make castles tomorrow. I'm not up to it right now." Ali excused himself.

Alone in his room, Ali picked up the unmailed letter to Sara, tore it up and threw the pieces in the wastebasket, at the same time throwing all his hopes for her away. "How can Sara marry Eric?" he repeated to himself. He felt she must have had to compromise herself. Everyone seemed resigned to compromises. But why, why don't people resist compromises? Ali remembered the Professor's words: "Everyone has principles, but unfortunately individuals, even nations, must compromise principles or disappear from the scene just like the dinosaurs who could not compromise their physiology and adapt to the environment." Ali wondered to himself, "I don't know if the society doesn't fall apart because a few individuals hold fast to their principles or because many individuals compromise them regularly." Ali felt estranged from Sara, from Hussain, from his parents, from Pirooz and from the world. He felt isolated, lonely and misunderstood. At the moment he couldn't change anything. He clung to the idea of revolution so as not to feel alone. "No one is good, then, Ali," he remembered Hussain's words. Then an unbelievable idea exhibited its hellish teeth to Ali: "Are you good to anyone? Does anyone think you are good?" Ali walked to the wall and put his face against it like he used to as a child when pouting. But now, he did it to hold a precious moment of understanding against concrete and the objective coldness of the wall.

Late that night Ali sat at his desk and filled pages of writing paper with a long-delayed letter to Professor Pirooz, who had asked Ali to write his impressions of Iran. At last the end of Ali's interviews with Anvari unblocked his mind and he began to write.

"Dear Pirooz, Forgive me for leaving your letters unanswered until now. I hope you have a bright day and are in good cheer, for those overcast days in New York were sad reminders of our uprootedness. While not yet Westernized, we have lost touch with the East. Up to now I don't feel a rightwinger or a leftwinger, but just a sidewinger. I miss the tension of New York. Teheran is more chaotic, but nothing more."

Ali wrote about the debate in the family, his interviews with Anvari. He recounted his encounter with Shamil and Kamil at the Turkish border and described his dream. He concluded, "I want to write more about my hallucination. It restructured images of the past and signalled, perhaps, the coming of future events as my wishes. I feel it is very important for me to find out how and why this dream came to rise in my head. Can ideology replace repressed experiences of the past and become the prime mover for some? Is ideology only a function of psychology, or the reverse in the case of revolutionaries? Can ideological conviction override everything else, even the instinct for self-preservation? Certainly there is no class basis for our convictions.

"The dream confused the martyrdom of Imam Hussain in Ashura with the crucifixion of Jesus and the sacrifice of the lives of today's revolutionaries. Can it be that all these sacrifices, including Galileo's scientific stand, mean the same and have common roots in my understanding? What is the difference between the communist Ruzbeh and the Muslim Imam Hussain? Both accepted the necessity of death for their ideas. We could not take justice seriously if no one were willing to die for its sake.

"I fell in love with an idea, just as I fell in love with Sara's hair, at first sight. 'Workers of the world, unite: you have nothing to lose but your chains.' What is there in those words that could turn them into a force over my life and millions of others'? Is martyrdom only suicide, or is the survival of ideas more important than the survival of the individual?

"I still have to struggle with Sara's reappearing smile in my head. The memories haunt me like an open wound refusing to heal. I feel guilty and I feel wounded. Today the Savaki told me that Sara had married Eric Saunders. I wonder if these painful words are true. You know, Pirooz, nothing could cure my agony as her touch could. Now I want to crash through the walls and throw a brick at Eric's head with enough force to carry across the Atlantic. How un-Marxist! How unhumanitarian! As she would have teased me. Sara and I parted on my insistence. How can I think myself a victim? These feelings are confusing. Isn't the revolution my passion? Do I seek it for the right reasons?

"On other battlefronts, I fear I have lost my brother Hussain to God. He is in love with Islam, and every day there is a new affirmation. I just hope his God stays on the side of the people—not the ruling class. But Zaman is open, and moving, as we say in New York, 'right on.'

"I now have a job in a bookshop. I have a lot of time to read there, for people are no longer buying books. They are all busy fighting over the little bit of oil money that trickles down to them from the top. I am on the lookout for new friends, and you can guess that they're not golf partners.

"A neighbor's son will mail this letter from Paris. I hope you are well. Extend my best to friends and especially to dear Helena. I miss a lot of things, even your 'big brothering' me!

"Wishing you the best,
"Ali."

CHAPTER 13

Silent Explosives

Professor Pirooz received Ali's letter in a few days, but not before Anvari had a chance to examine it. A neighbor had been entrusted to hand-carry it to Paris and mail it to New York, but he was a Savak watchdog. The eyes, ears and noses of Savak were attached to the walls, trees, telephone poles and people's faces. How could Ali suspect that a young man who sidestepped an ant to spare it, who smiled gently and spoke softly, was a police informer? How could he have spotted a Savaki behind his innocent face? This fellow was tightlipped and mindful of his job; his demeanor showed no signs of duplicity. Like many young men, he was a drug addict who did what was necessary to support the habit.

The letter provided Savak with the information it needed to justify its surveillance of Ali. He was a subversive now, and not just a troublemaker. Savak would keep an eye on Ali, hoping he would lead them to a revolutionary cell and organization. Ali saw men loitering outside his house, men questioning cabdrivers after he got out. But he guessed it was just a routine nuisance, like crossing the busy streets of Teheran.

He made sure, however, that no one tailed him to an apartment near the university, where he met with Aram and Hamid Ashraf, a revolutionary leader who had been underground for some time.

They discussed recruitment, publications and other underground cells that were sprouting up in Teheran. They struggled to resolve ideological and practical conflicts, and began to organize an underground party which owed nothing to any other party or country. Although no ideological line had been adopted yet, the writings of Mao Tse-tung, Che Guevara and Ruzbeh were much read and debated. They knew the theories of Marx and Lenin, and some of them were translating newer works of General Giap and Regis Debray.

Their plan was for these underground cells to carry out guerrilla actions in order to galvanize the masses. The guerrillas would counter the Shah's violence from above by violence from below and demonstrate to the people that the regime was not invincible. The slogan of the movement was "the armed struggle." But their activities were not exclusively violent. They also published forbidden leaflets, unauthorized translations of forbidden works, and an illegal newsletter and distributed them in working-class neighborhoods and at the university. Contact with the people was vital. Guerrillas could not create the revolution; they could only start the fire.

Hiking expeditions in the hills outside Teheran were helpful to keep out of Savak's sight and get to know new comrades. Gradually revolutionary tasks were assigned and the mountainsides were turned into a military training school. Friday after Friday the comrades learned to assemble, repair and use firearms. They tested and retested weapons, homemade explosives and skills; they examined ideas; and they cultivated each other's trust and friendship.

Occasionally, comrades met at the Chess Federation on Shah Reza Avenue near the Diana Theater. They bent over the boards and carried on hushed conversations, appearing to be engaged in the chess analysis going on around them. Pirooz had played many exciting games at the same tables where revolution was now discussed.

So it was that the revolution took the outward form of hiking and chess. The revolutionaries never used the telephone except for routine talk. They wrote no letters, they kept nothing in their own houses, and they hid all banned books. They disguised any evidence which Savak could see, hear, smell or touch. A mistake could be fatal to one and all.

Soon Ali was assigned to form a new cell. He would be the cell's sole contact with Hamid Ashraf, so that if Savak uncovered one link, it could not be led to others. Cell members had code names, places had code names, activities had code names. Their lives were in code, so that the inevitable Savaki who infiltrated could not go far. Each comrade was insulated from knowing those above and those below in the chain of command. All meetings were small, two to five people. They adopted successful underground techniques of the past, from the Christians under the Roman Caesar to the Tudeh Party in Iran.

The young revolutionaries made life and death decisions. But neither the complexity of the tasks, their inexperience, the need for secrecy nor the potential dangers thwarted them. Their imagination and courage made up for many deficiencies. Ali quickly learned the life of the underground.

They knew the dangers. They had heard of revolutionaries burned alive, raped by criminals, flung out of helicopters, their limbs torn on a rack, penises pierced by red-hot skewers, rectums punctured by broken bottles, chests and buttocks and breasts scarred by cigarette burns. A few surviving prisoners recounted the torture, and pictures had been published. While publicly denying its use of torture, Savak advertised it privately to induce compliance through terror, which influenced every thought, every word and every deed of the citizens.

Financing the revolutionary movement was another difficulty. They needed weapons to rob banks, and they needed the banks' money to buy weapons smuggled into the country or smuggled out of the Shah's armories. The alternative was even riskier: to go unarmed and strip the guns from police and gendarmes. Their successful activities went unreported in the controlled press, or were reported as criminal actions.

The revolutionary tasks were divided, and each cell engaged in part of an action, contributing its share to the whole. Ali was assigned to make explosives using local resources. Others used the explosives to blow up a police station or open the vault of a bank.

Ali's favorite aunt, a seventy-year-old widow, let Ali use her basement. She carried an old grudge because police had torn her chador, revealing her face to strangers, during the modernization drive by the Shah's father. When Ali asked, "Are you sure?" she replied, "What do I have to lose?" Ali trusted her to keep the secret from everyone, even her own brother, Dr. Keshavarz.

Ali converted his aunt's basement into a darkroom laboratory. But instead of pictures he developed explosives. Everything looked like a darkroom, the chemicals for explosives labeled as developers. Young revolutionaries were wishful thinkers, since if suspected, the bottles would be examined thoroughly. Nevertheless, Ali's laboratory would hide evidence from a superficial Savak inspection. Chemicals, cases of explosives, glass tubes, bottles, metal sheets, notebooks with detailed diagrams, books about explosives began to fill the basement. He smuggled his chemicals in with the groceries he purchased for his aunt once a week.

Ali began preparing a manual for making and using explosives from available materials. He asked Zaman to borrow chemistry books from the university.

Since intercepting Ali's letter, Savak had also kept an eye on Zaman and found her borrowing chemistry books without taking chemistry courses. Zaman's interest in chemistry and Ali's purchases of nitrate compounds led Savak to conclude that Ali's activity was not amateur photography.

Ali did not suspect what Savak knew, even though he noticed he was occasionally tailed. None of them yet knew the new Savak policy of taking hostages to force a revolutionary in hiding to give up—a reason many revolutionaries were forced to compromise themselves, Ali would observe painfully. The revolutionaries thought at the time that they risked only their own lives.

* * * * *

On a gloomy, overcast day Ali was surprised by Zaman barging in without a knock. She was breathless, her words coming in a rush. "Ali! We are uncovered, doomed!" Ali coolly glanced out and saw no one.

"Calm down, Zaman. What's up?"

"A short, bald man in a white silk shirt and black tie has tailed me here. He never utters a word. He's a Savaki. I saw him today in the library, but he disappeared as soon as he saw me. The librarian complained to me that he asked who was borrowing chemistry books. She said, 'It's my first day here. I'm not an informer, and I don't know who Miss Keshavarz is.'"

Ali raised his hand. "Stop Zaman. I saw him, too. He pretended to be a customer when I bought some chemicals."

Zaman rushed to say, "The chemicals, books, places, people—Savak knows it all and plays cat and mouse with us. Why?"

Ali said, "By tracing us they get to know everything we do and everyone we know. We're now Savak's unpaid informers. We must move quickly, Zaman, and inform our comrades immediately of what has happened." Ali began talking to himself. "Those bastards know now my photography is a cover and can bust us at any minute. Son of a bitch! We can't be caught redhanded. I hope they don't know that we know that they know."

"What?"

"Never mind," said Ali. "We must move before they know that we know. We have to clean up fast. I'll get a van. You and Aram come here at midnight and we'll load it up. I know what to do after that."

Zaman protested. "At midnight?"

Ali replied, "Yes. I hope Savakis sleep when they think we are asleep. Midnight is not the best time to move, but we can't be suspected of burglarizing our aunt's place."

"Okay, but you're being naive," Zaman said.

"Do you have a better plan? We have to act. Aram will stay outside, and in case of trouble he can cause a commotion to alert us. He should gargle some whiskey beforehand, so he'll stink like a drunk."

Ali and Zaman made their plans, then separated once more, a look of apprehension passing between them.

At midnight Aram stood at the head of the dead-end alley where Ali's aunt lived. The rain was about to turn to snow. Aram's flashlight signalled "all clear"—and a billion raindrops blinked with fear on their slow descent. He signalled once more, and a billion new drops twinkled. The gray and battered van started grudgingly, giving Ali an anxious moment. It was too noisy, Zaman feared. It was loaded with enough explosives to spread Ali's body over half of Teheran. A time bomb at Ali's side was set to detonate in thirty seconds when triggered. Zaman and Aram watched Ali drive off and left for Aram's father's house.

On the main avenue, Ali drove around a newly dug hole in the pavement, and heard a shout, "Halt!" Then a number of voices demanded, "Halt! Halt!" Ali's right foot crashed on the gas pedal as if fighting for its own survival. The van took off like a whipped horse. Ali narrowly missed a hole, splashing water and mud all over. He looked back and saw a car flashing its lights and blaring its siren.

Ali turned into a side street heading east and disappeared into the dark filled with raindrops. Not just his life had to be saved, but the notes, the explosives, part of the revolution.

The Savaki driver following him didn't know the neighborhood, and his rear wheel slid into the hole. There were no lights at street repair sites in Teheran; people were expected to know the ditches. Shouting obscenities, the Savakis poured out of the car and in a few minutes lifted it from the hole. Pursuit was now useless, but they had alternate plans.

Ali wiped the sweat from his face as the wipers swept aside the raindrops from the windshield. He glanced at the time bomb as he drove and then looked back and saw an empty avenue shining in the rain. He slowed down at once, fearing cruising police, unfamiliar holes and the silent explosives. He drove down Old Shemiran Avenue, turned into a side street, carefully checked the address, and turned off the motor. He scanned the area before disconnecting the time bomb. Ali's heart pounded like the pistons in the van. He changed the license plate, then put the key in the glove compartment, checked to make sure he had his notes, and walked away briskly. He was not pursued any more. A hundred yards on, he stopped and hid behind an oak tree to watch the van. He missed the explosives he had made; he was used to them. They were his.

Two men approached the van, Ali's comrades. He didn't recognize them. The darkness shielded his vision, and his ignorance guaranteed their safety. The men got in the van and sped northward. The rain had stopped, and the crystal clear air held the van as it grew smaller, becoming a dot climbing, until finally there was nothing on the road. Ali never saw the van again. His explosives were gone without an explosion, and he consoled himself by squeezing a hand grenade in his wet palm, as if to make juice.

Ali broke out in a cold sweat as he realized that now his two lives, one as a law-abiding citizen and the other as a secret revolutionary, had ended. Now Ali was forced underground; it was just hide, not hide-and-seek. His own home, the safe haven, would be a trap now. No one who sheltered him would be safe. The moon emerged from the clouds, a shy friend trying to console him. He stepped as though sidestepping a hazardous future. Sighting a cab he repeated, "Taxi, taxi" in a muted voice. The cab stopped a few feet past him. "Avenue Farhang, please," Ali said as he entered the cab.

The driver grumbled, "Agha, sir, why not ask me to take you to Port

Pahlavi? It is only a little farther." In Teheran the fare was fixed for all distances.

Ali replied firmly, "Don't worry. I'll make it worthwhile." Ali felt suddenly distanced and separated from everyone he knew. He was being driven by a worker who was not sympathetic to his cause and to comrades Ali had never met, but they would be in charge of his life. Ali felt isolated even as a worker drove him to his comrades.

The cab drove west on Shah Reza Boulevard and turned south on Pahlavi Avenue. It was almost half an hour before Ali reached his destination. He stood still as the cab vanished from sight. He walked a few blocks toward Shahpoor Avenue, then, about two in the morning, two masked strangers approached him quietly, blindfolded him, and led him to a house a few blocks away.

Inside the house they removed Ali's blindfold. A middle-aged woman in a mask greeted him, saying only, "Call me Comrade Mother." She led him to a basement room. A single bed, a desk with a lamp on it, bookshelves, a kilim on the floor, a small electric stove and large posters were all the room held. Before she left, Comrade Mother said, "Comrade, you are safe here. I'll bring writing paper. Let us know if you need anything else."

* * * * *

After losing Ali's van in the dark, the Savakis, frustrated and muddy, hurled obscenities at Ali, at his ancestors, at Chrysler which had manufactured their car, at whatever was in sight. They checked the empty laboratory and spared Ali's aunt because she was taken for a maid. They then drove to Ali's house.

An hour past midnight, a Savaki knocked on Keshavarz' door. The maid, Maryam, half asleep and complaining, walked to the door. "Who is it? Is it Agha Ali?"

The Savaki responded, "No, it's an urgent telegram."

"At this time of night, a telegram? For whom?"

"For Dr. Keshavarz. Don't delay us," the agent responded.

Maryam would not open the door. "From whom?"

Dr. Keshavarz appeared at the balcony railing. "Open the door, Lady Maryam."

Slowly, Maryam opened the door. At the sound of the unfastened latch, the agent pushed the door wide open, throwing Maryam to the floor. Four more Savakis rushed in, carrying handguns and a machine gun.

Maryam screamed in pain as the agent she had delayed drove his booted toe into her body. Parvine, awakened, ran to her grandmother, who held her tightly.

The five agents ran through the flower garden and raced up the stairs. Dr. Keshavarz left his wife and Parvine and strode to meet the agents, while tying the belt of his winter gown.

"What is the matter, gentlemen?" Dr. Keshavarz inquired politely.

The chief replied, "Where is he hiding?" He waved his gun at Keshavarz, then at Fatema and Parvine. "Where is he?"

"Who?" asked Keshavarz.

"Your son, Ali, the traitor." Another agent added, "The fairy."

Dr. Keshavarz replied, "My son is not with us tonight. We have no fugitive from the law here. Now may I ask what your business is at this hour?"

The chief, a dark man with a thin moustache and long face, his muddy shoes staining the beautiful wool and silk rug, ignored Keshavarz' question. "Are you Keshavarz?"

"Yes. Who are you?"

The agent ignored him again. "Where is he?"

Keshavarz stared at him but did not reply. He turned to his frightened wife under the chador. "Lady Fatema, take Parvine to the bedroom."

The Savaki chief raised his voice. "Shut up! You have fathered Ali Keshavarz who has betrayed God, the Shah and Iran. You have no rights. I will say who stays and who leaves."

Fatema nevertheless grasped Parvine by the arm and gently pulled her toward her bedroom. One agent with a pistol in hand blocked their path, and another snatched Parvine and threw her on the floor like a doll tossed away. Then he pushed Fatema into the bedroom and slammed the door.

Keshavarz heard his wife sobbing. He remained calm, but his voice trembled slightly with cold anger. "Why abuse a little girl and an old woman? They have betrayed no one. What is your authority?"

The canaries, protesting the intrusion, distracted the chief. Furious, he stepped to the cage, opened it, pulled out one of the canaries, and yanked its head off with a flip of his wrist. He threw the body to the floor in front of Keshavarz. "There!" he announced. "That's my authority."

The headless canary flapped up and down, smashing itself against a portrait of Keshavarz' father and spattering its blood. Parvine, horrified, sobbed. The chief marched up to Dr. Keshavarz, pushed him against the wall and pressed his gun against Keshavarz' nostril. The agent shouted, "How can you, a stupid man, be a professor? No wonder students are so rotten. No wonder they read Karl Marx and play with each other. Had you been my teacher, I would have turned out no better. This gun is my authority." He pushed the gun tighter against Keshavarz' nose. A blood vessel ruptured and spurted blood onto the Savaki's suit. "Goddamn son of a bitch has sensitive skin." He shook the pistol dripping with blood. "This gun is the warrant, the judge, the prosecutor, the law, and this gun will be your executioner if you don't shut your big mouth.''

Parvine raised her head and saw the blood covering her grandfather's face. She got up silently and kicked the chief in his shins. He pushed Parvine away. Another agent picked her up and she squirmed to free herself.

The chief let go of Keshavarz and turned to his men. "Take them to the car.'' Then turning to his men he said, ''The traitor Ali will give himself up soon; taking hostages always works.''

The agent holding Parvine set her down, telling her kindly, ''Be calm. I will help your grandfather.'' He took out his handkerchief and handed it to Keshavarz. This man, new and not yet conditioned to brutality, was a father and had a grandfather.

The man with the machine gun pushed Keshavarz downstairs. "You heard the lieutenant. Get out of the house.'' The other two Savakis smashed and turned everything upside down. One slashed the blue sofa in the guest room with a switchblade. The Savakis left the house in chaos. The lone canary mourned her dead mate while the willow, bent by the weight of the rain, silently wept. Scattered books lay on the floor. The stucco walls, pale and white, stared at each other. Maryam saw her world trampled and wondered why people inflicted more damage on people than beast did on beast.

The rain had stopped and a wisp of cloud strayed across the heavens like a lost white lamb, momentarily veiling the moon. A knot of curious neighbors stood on the street, while others peered through partly open windows and doors. Civil rights were publicized by the Shah and his media. At midnight only the walls, the canary and the moon witnessed the invasion, but they could not talk, and if they could, Savak would silence them. The neighbors kept their silence, too. The whole nation kept a sullen silence.

A Savaki sat in the police car between Parvine and Keshavarz in the back seat. In front, the chief stuck his head out the window and eyed the neighbors. "It's over. Go home, all of you." He started to say more, but the driver took off with a screech, leaving the chief to address the walls. The chief turned to the driver. "You ass-porter, didn't you see I was trying to calm the crowd?''

"Sorry," the driver replied. "I thought you were finished."

Keshavarz held the handkerchief tight over his bleeding nose as he started to cough. The chief turned on the radio to a station playing rock and roll. He had developed a taste for it while training for police work in the U.S.

Dr. Keshavarz spoke. "Let me hold my granddaughter. She's frightened.''

The chief shot back, "No! She'll survive." He turned to the new Savaki in between. "Again you've forgotten security precautions. Put his jacket over his head.''

"He has no jacket, just a robe."

"Use your brain. Cover him with your jacket."

The world of Dr. Keshavarz became pitch black and repulsive, with the odor trapped within the jacket. The bleeding stopped, but a shooting pain spread over his face.

The chief was a little Shah in his own domain, the police car considered his car, the underlings were his subjects, the suspected were his prey, and the law was his words. When Keshavarz dared to mention the law, he trespassed on the commander's territory.

In an hour Dr. Keshavarz and Parvine were put on a hard bench against a brick wall in Gezel Ghale Prison. Keshavarz sat until daybreak with an old, stinking prison blanket over his head. Parvine, her head on his lap, was fast asleep under another blanket. He was not allowed to pray that morning. He could not see the sun rise, as he did after morning prayers. The long night finally expired. Parvine awakened to the pangs of hunger and soreness, and there was nothing her grandfather could do to soothe them.

* * * * *

Zamandukht returned home before dawn and took her mother to the hospital, but Maryam refused to leave. Zaman waited for news about the family in a darkened hospital room as she gazed at her mother under sedation.

Hussain prayed before dawn and prepared to return from a religious retreat with his friends, unaware of the night's events at home.

* * * * *

Alone in his basement hideout, Ali could not sleep. Again in his mind's eye Ali repacked his laboratory, making sure that no loose ends could inform Savak. Again he replaced the explosives with photography equipment and carefully hung negatives from clothespins. He could not be sure that all was in order, but it was too late now. He would never return.

Ali stretched out on the cot and closed his eyes, pressing on his eyelids and concentrating on the blank screen of his imagination, hoping that this relaxing exercise would bring desperately needed sleep. It was not to be. On that imaginary screen passed his family, aunt and comrades, each demanding attention. He was afraid Savak might arrest Zaman and Aram, even his aunt. He had no idea of Savak's new hostage policy, but he worried about his parents' worrying about him. Ali felt more isolated yet. He felt guilty that he might have jeopardized his dear old aunt, even though he was careful to insulate her from his activities, even though she had accepted the risks. Should he worry about her? Should she be made to pay for a revolution she would not benefit from? What would Savak do to an old woman anyhow?

He sat up on the cot and turned on the bare 75-watt lightbulb. Large posters of revolutionaries covered the walls: Dr. Mossadegh, Marx, Engels, Lenin, Ruzbeh, Ahmed Ben Bella, Patrice Lumumba, Dr. Martin Luther King, Che Guevara, Castro, Ho Chi Minh, Mao Tse-tung, Rosa Luxemburg, Mahatma Gandhi. The posters showed their faces, while the bookshelf beside the desk held their ideas.

Ali looked at the somber and kind face of Ruzbeh, covered with a thick moustache, a balding forehead making him look distinguished. Ruzbeh had organized leftists in the Iranian armed forces before the 1953 coup. But even though the secret organization was uncovered later on and his life was in danger, Ruzbeh had refused all advice to leave Iran. Instead, he went underground to continue the struggle. He moved from basement to basement, one step ahead of the police. He escaped from ambushes, outfighting and outsmarting hordes of Savakis. He was a symbol of resistance, his actions celebrated by his followers. A few years after the coup, Ruzbeh was caught and put on trial, where he made a final appeal to future revolutionaries to fight for justice. He was tortured and killed. Then his body was buried in an unmarked grave. The Shah was afraid of him even in death, afraid the ideas he held could not be buried along with his body. Ruzbeh's last words were circulated despite an absolute ban.

Ali got up and walked to the poster, as if to shake hands. He said, "You're a teacher of a nation. Your murderers will discover soon you are not dead. Then you will try them. You will live longer than the Shah." Ali became aware he was talking to a poster.

Ali looked at Che, whose eyes stared back at him. Che had fought in Argentina, won a revolution in Cuba, and was killed in the Bolivian mountainsides fighting for starving peasants. Ali looked at Karl Marx, fuzzy black and white hair surrounding two piercing eyes. Marx had lived like a refugee all his life. His family also suffered; they ran before the police, were evicted from places they made home, and had to pawn their shoes to buy food. Marx, one of the most creative men, could not even buy medicine for his dying child. But he wrote books that shook the world to its roots and showed a path towards justice once and for all. Then there was Mao, friendly and cunning, who had led his comrades across the mountains and rivers of China for hundreds of days and thousands of miles. Many comrades died of cold, hunger, sickness, or from U.S. bullets supplied to Chiang Kai-shek, but the survivors marched back and hoisted the red flag atop every city, every village, and the towers of the Great Wall.

The gentle face with the thin beard was Uncle Ho's. Ho Chi Minh had washed dishes in Paris before returning home and ousting the occupation armies of the French, Japanese and Americans from his country, Vietnam.

Ali passed the two Black men, King and Lumumba, both killed because they stood for justice. Rosa Luxemburg, the only woman adorning the walls, was the champion of the German revolution of 1918 and had been murdered by a death squad, her body dumped in a Berlin canal.

Ali's eyes fell finally on a small poster of Gandhi, taped up beside Lenin's. The picture was humble, like the man himself. What about him? Ali reflected; Gandhi was no revolutionary communist. Small, too thin, sickly looking, the man carried all of India and its people on his shoulders, knowing his load was as fragile as antique china, carrying them to the summit of independence and self-respect. He commanded mountains to bend, men and women to endure abstinence, beatings and imprisonment, and he commanded the British to pack up and go home. He had no weapons and no soldiers, yet no one could resist him. How did he do it? Ali wondered. Was it possible to establish a new world without destroying the old one, as Gandhi had tried to do? Did Gandhi succeed in improving the lives of the masses? Was independence from the British enough?

What was the significance of these men and women? Ali wondered. What was so special about them? Why did they become revolutionaries? What was the source of their dedication to their ideas, their mountain-like self-confidence, their independence, their mastery over themselves and others, their love for man and for justice? How was it they were treated so brutally? What did they do? What did they say, think, feel? What did they fail to do? Why did they put social interest above private gain? Were his reasons the same as theirs?

Then Ali turned to himself. What am I doing in this basement? What will happen to my family, to comrades Savak has traced me to? Zaman, Aram? Ali needed sleep to prepare for the work and uncertainties awaiting him. But how could he sleep with so much work to be done, when time was so short, when Marx, Lenin, Che and Ruzbeh were dead, their mission not yet accomplished? They were looking to him, to Ali, to continue what they had started. Wasn't he a revolutionary, didn't he aspire to be their ideological offspring? They were the fathers of his beliefs. He needed time for self-criticism, but he was needed more to write the manual on explosives. He sat at the small desk, took his notes from his jacket, and began to write.

* * * * *

Hussain arrived home toward noon to find the door half open and the house a shambles. He went through the house quickly, looking for his father, his mother, Ali, Zaman, Parvine. All were absent. He found only Maryam, bent and sobbing quietly, in the living room. She picked up a book, took two steps, and laid it down again. She glanced at Hussain, at first fearful, then puzzled, as if he did not belong there. To the old servant life on earth was lived in the house of Keshavarz, and the other life would be lived in heaven. The order of life, the house, its furnishings, plants and the people who moved among them, had been shattered. Maryam worked to bring back order, yet she knew it would never be the same.

Maryam did not know her origin. Her face was a bit darker than the darkest face in the neighborhood, her hair curlier, her lips more pronounced, her nose flatter. But her brown eyes, benign and sad, were the same as others', and for Maryam it was the eyes that mattered. She could read people's eyes, which revealed what their tongues did not. Her eyes now showed fright and sadness. She had no home but this one, just as the fish had none but the pond. Maryam was well past seventy, of that everyone was certain, but no one knew her exact age, not even Maryam. She was not interested in the past, for the present always kept her entire attention.

Hussain saw in a glance what had happened. Chairs were thrown into the courtyard, bookshelves were overturned, book covers torn apart, his father's papers scattered around flapping in the wind like the wings of a wounded dove. Life was stripped away from Keshavarz' home. Maryam wandered with her scarf up around her face, as though searching for the dead in the wake of a cyclone.

"Lady Maryam, Khanoum Maryam," Hussain called to her. "Wake up, please, where is everyone?" Maryam tried to speak. "Please tell me, is anyone hurt?"

"No, no, no!" she said haltingly. "Agha Hussain, it was not thieves, not invaders; they were worse. Look, Agha Hussain, see for yourself." Hussain saw his grandfather's portrait on the floor, the canvas splattered with blood. Hussain heard Maryam say to him, "Why did they do that?"

He asked, "Who did it, Maryam?"

"I do not know," Maryam said. "People called them Savak. They had guns. They threw your mother to the ground, they killed—" Maryam could not continue.

Hussain paled. "Who was killed?"

"The canary. I buried him near the yellow rosebush, the one your mother loves the most. They stole your father and Parvine away. He was bleeding from his nose. Zamandukht took Lady Fatema to the hospital." Anger rose in Hussain like lava in a volcano.

Maryam raised her head. "No more questions, Agha. Ask no more. These men are cruel because they let me live and witness this. They had hearts of stone, they had minds of poison," Maryam said, repeating, "hearts of stone, minds of poison." "Now the devil has moved in, into every house, every neighborhood, into the heart of Savak."

Hussain took Maryam to her room. She sobbed loudly and pulled clumps of of thin hair from a resisting scalp. Hussain heard her chanting, "hearts of stone, minds of poison," and finally silence. He hoped she would rest now.

Instead Maryam changed the bedsheets, combed her hair and arranged her nightstand. She washed her face and hands meticulously. She put on her white cotton wedding gown, silky soft and fresh, the dress Lady Fatema, then a young woman, had sewn for her about 25 years earlier. Maryam had no children. Her husband had been killed in the Allied bombing of southern Teheran in World War II soon after their wedding. The dress still fit perfectly as she straightened her back to receive it. With the room in perfect order, she lay on the bed, her hands folded over her chest. She gazed at the black mark on the white ceiling, just as she had ever since she could remember. Maryam, the old, slow, wonderful lady, profound in her simplicity, the lady everybody loved, fell asleep. She looked like an Egyptian queen grown transparent with age, her skin soft and fragile, her face peaceful, her mouth hiding a bittersweet smile, her heart silent, her body majestic.

Hussain ran to the kitchen and gulped down a cold glass of water. At Maryam's door he called to say, "I am going to find the others. I will call soon. Please stay here and keep calm." Hussain went upstairs and called his uncle to ask him to try to get Dr. Keshavarz and Parvine released. He asked a neighbor to look after Maryam, hailed a cab to the hospital, and wondered if there were any way to help his brother Ali.

Lady Maryam no longer needed any help. Two days later her funeral was announced. Many cried for Maryam. She was the last descendant of a young slave, her grandmother, captured a hundred years before in Africa. The lineage was free at last. Maryam was dead.

CHAPTER 14

Interrogation

Morning passed as Dr. Keshavarz, still under the blanket, sat on the hard bench and waited. Sleep would not come to him, though it weighed heavily on his eyelids. Parvine slept in his lap.

At noon a Savak guard nudged him with his foot, an order to get up. Keshavarz held Parvine's hand and walked down a corridor with a Savaki as guide.

Dr. Keshavarz and Parvine were led into a room where his blindfold was removed. The daylight hurt his eyes, and he didn't know where he was. The bare room had three chairs chained to three beat-up desks under a high ceiling. On each desk sat a worn-out black telephone, like a stuffed crow.

Dr. Keshavarz looked up and saw a burly man sitting at one of the desks with his back to the window. He was short, bulging, balding, with heavy legs and heavy eyebrows over deepset eyes. The hair on his chest stuck out from his open collar. He was called "The Butcher" by his peers. "What is your name?" he said.

Exhausted, humiliated and worried about his wife and Maryam, Keshavarz remained silent. "I said, what is your name?"

Parvine responded, "My grandfather is hurt. Let us go home." Parvine paused and then, as though she had discovered something, added, "Why do you snatch people when you don't even know their name?"

"Shut up, you little rat," growled another Savaki standing beside the desk. He was tall, his eyes enlarged by thick glasses, and his head bobbed as though searching for something. He was called "The Barber."

Parvine snapped back, "I'm not a rat. Where are your manners?"

Dr. Keshavarz covered Parvine's mouth with his hand. "Hush, Parvine, keep still. This is not home." His eyes told his granddaughter, it is not safe here. He turned to the Butcher. "She is hungry and exhausted. Children don't understand the world of grownups."

The Butcher shouted, "Shut up! We're officers of the law, not your

164

students.''

Parvine replied, ''You shut up, you big monster!'' The Barber leaned across the desk and smashed his hand against her cheek. Her head snapped back, the momentum forcing her hand from Keshavarz' grip and hurling her against the cold floor. She lay dazed, a burning pain shot across her cheek, and the tissue turned color. She broke into tears. Blood oozed down her chin, mixing with tears, onto her pajamas.

Keshavarz rushed to Parvine and bent to pick her up. The Butcher came around the desk and booted him from behind like a soccer ball. The unexpected thrust hurled Keshavarz off his feet and he nearly fell on top of Parvine. He struggled to his feet and stared at the Butcher. ''She can be of no help to Savak. Send her home,'' he said firmly.

The agents exchanged glances. The Butcher said, ''That's possible, if you cooperate.''

The Butcher turned to the Barber. ''Take the child to the physician and follow procedures.'' The procedure was to report that Parvine had accidentally hurt herself. Then he whispered, ''We have no use for her. Send her home.''

The Barber picked Parvine up and left. With tearful eyes she stared back at her grandfather. The Barber stuffed her hand with a piece of chocolate and said, ''You'll be okay.''

Keshavarz managed to say, ''Goodbye Parvine. Grandma will take care of you.''

The Butcher barked, ''Sit down.'' Keshavarz limped to the chair. ''What is your name?''

''Dr. Mehdi Keshavarz.''

''No title here! I'm the Butcher, and my partner is the Barber, who pulls out body hair and even teeth.'' The Butcher grinned. ''Unlike yours, our titles mean something. Wait until your son meets the Doctor. Now, what is your name?'' the Butcher said again.

Keshavarz stiffened in his chair. ''Mehdi Keshavarz.'' He paused, then said firmly, ''I repeat, why am I arrested?''

The Butcher grabbed Keshavarz' robe, spittle forming on his lips. ''Any more backtalk and I'll break your neck.''

The Barber returned and stepped in between the two men. ''Come on, Butcher, he doesn't know any better. Don't forget, it's his son we want.'' Then the Barber whispered, ''He has a heart condition.''

The Butcher let go of Keshavarz' lapel, saying loudly, ''So what? He's a hostage. We are allowed.''

He wiped the spit with his sleeve and went back to his chair. ''Now listen, Keshavarz, you're the one that has to answer our questions, not us answering yours. Remember, criminals breed criminals, and communists breed communists. We have no respect or pity for anyone who sits in that chair. Now, where is he hiding?''

"Who?" Keshavarz asked.

The Butcher said, "You know who. Ali."

"I don't know where I am myself, let alone where Ali is."

"With this attitude you'll soon know where you are, in a grave."

Keshavarz said, "Ali lives with us, that is all I know. He doesn't report his whereabouts."

The Butcher asked, "Why does he live with you?"

"He can't afford a household, and is welcomed in mine."

"No sentiments, just give me the facts. Where is he hiding?"

"I told you I don't know." Keshavarz mumbled to himself, "But I now know where I am: the local hell."

The Butcher shouted anxiously, "Where? What did you say?"

Keshavarz calmly explained. "I'm in the local hell, where little girls and old men are beaten up without cause." Then he demanded, "Where is my granddaughter?"

The Butcher rose and a cruel smile spread across his face. "One more backtalk and I'll lose my patience."

Keshavarz said, "Don't butcher your own sisters and brothers. If my grandchild is harmed, you will meet justice in hell."

The Butcher stood over Keshavarz, covered his ears and shouted, "Stop! Stop or I'll kill you."

Keshavarz sat still, a living statue, resigned and graceful. His faith in God held the old theologian up. He wore the sad smile of a saint reflecting the tragedy of life around him. He wanted peace for all, but he found no peace in the Butcher's face.

The calm of the Sufi enraged the Butcher even more. He found Keshavarz looking into his eyes, discovering what no one must ever discover. The Butcher slapped Keshavarz, but the victim still watched him. The Butcher could not bear Keshavarz' stare, so he kept slapping him. Keshavarz' head snapped back and forth and his glasses fell to the floor. The sounds filled the room and echoed through the hall. Keshavarz sat still and defiant.

But after a couple of minutes of this, Keshavarz noticed the room dimming like a theater just before the curtain rises. Then time passed at the speed of light and two hours shrank to an instant. At the end of his journey, Keshavarz was still being slapped, only gently, and cold water dripped to his shoulders. The Barber and the Butcher were examining him anxiously. They could not permit him to die. A man in white pushed a wet cloth against his nose, filling his head with a sharp odor. His eyes opened. The faces of the Barber and the Butcher hovering over him reminded him he was still in hell.

He had seen their cruelty to a little girl, to an old woman, to holy books, to canaries, none of them a threat to anyone or anything. Keshavarz' goal was to attain peace in himself and pass it on to others, like the winter sun that slowly melts the ice. Now his peace was being tested.

Dr. Keshavarz was covered with a blanket and moved to an overcrowded, noisy corridor. He sat on the damp floor all afternoon, still not knowing the time or place. Pain raced randomly along his limbs and climbed to his head.

Dr. Mehdi Keshavarz, the old, generous man of peace and kindness, wondered when he would be kicked again as he sat under the blanket alongside others similarly covered. The blanket did not cover the sounds of terror, but it covered his shame. He was ashamed to be himself, ashamed to be a man, if man could treat his fellows this way. It was better to be a goat, a cat, a tree, a stone, a dove, a fish in the sea.

* * * * *

The Savakis would not tell him that Parvine had been taken to a neighbor's. He didn't know that she was in shock and could only repeat fragments of her ordeal. "They called him names. They kicked him. Someone call the police. Someone tell the Shah, who gave my grandfather a medal." Parvine was taken to the hospital and put in the room next to her grandmother. The hospital room darkened as Zaman drew the curtains, and Parvine at last fell asleep, her hand clutching Zaman's. The imprint of the Barber's fingers on her cheek darkened like a developing photograph of inhumanity. In her nightmares headless canaries flapped around her, looking for their own eyes, spurting blood everywhere.

Keshavarz, sitting painfully in the prison corridor, lost the notion that the state would not turn against him. But he also lost in a single night what it had taken a lifetime to put together—his family. Now Fatema and Parvine were in dark rooms, Keshavarz was under a prison blanket, Ali was hidden in a cold basement. This was the human condition, the condition of decent people in the Iran of the Shah.

Ali had criticized those who ignored injustice and made compromises. Keshavarz would never again judge his colleagues so harshly. But now, under the blanket, in darkness, Keshavarz saw his own compromised life. He had protected his family by keeping aloof from the regime. If he opposed it, he did so privately, subtly, safely. Now he saw most clearly in the darkness under the blanket what he had failed to see under the sun. His daily compromises were no guarantee of peace, or even of survival. If he risked nothing by not opposing the Shah, neither did he gain from ignoring injustice. If the innocent were made victims, then what was the purpose of remaining innocent? On the surface it was Ali who had caused this calamity, but in reality it was his own fault and the fault of the people who over the years compromised freedom for security.

Keshavarz prayed that Ali would not surrender. Ali's life was more precious than a thousand Keshavarzes, awakening too late from their sweet dreams. Keshavarz prayed that Ali would fight on, as his son Abbas had fought on. In one night, Savak had succeeded in transforming an old man of peace into one willing to sacrifice himself for freedom and justice. He might be incapable of violence himself, but Keshavarz would no longer condemn it if used in defense of freedom and justice. He now understood that nationality and religion could be used to set workers of different countries against one another, too. Ali was right. His heart welled up as he thought of his brave son.

Keshavarz surrendered the fate of his family to the will of God. They could be safe only if his friends and their friends fought injustice. He would no longer worry about himself; he should no longer worry. He was ready to die. This world was no place to live; it was more suited to his dying. He would go on a hunger strike. He would refuse food until they released him or he died.

Keshavarz smiled, a smile lost in darkness. Now he understood Abbas better, and he understood Ali's ramblings. If someone would have to risk death to end the torture of the nation's spirit and body, Keshavarz was proud that it was Ali.

Keshavarz saw Ali and himself as two parts of a single person. Keshavarz had devoted his life as a Sufi to comprehending the boundless universe within an idea, and Ali was devoting his life to transforming the world into the realization of an idea. Keshavarz sought the peace which lay beneath a tormented soul, while Ali saw the conflict beneath the apparent social order and would use it to better the world.

Keshavarz, who could convince anyone of his sincerity, could not convince the Shah's men of the truth, that he did not know where Ali was. He remained in prison. The Butcher's report claimed that Keshavarz was withholding information and should be detained not just as a hostage but as a security risk. The Butcher knew this was a lie, but no suspect was allowed to pity his tormented soul to arouse his conscience and to cause him pain. The Butcher was secure; no one could question him, he was loyal to His Majesty.

So Dr. Keshavarz' file went through channels, and Keshavarz himself was taken from Ghezel Ghaleh to Evin Prison and placed alone in a four-by-seven foot cell. The cell was damp and dead. A small tuft of weedy grass pushed through the cracks in the cement in one corner, where a single, thin beam of light penetrated from an observation hole in the wall. The grass clung tenaciously to life in that beam of light, as Keshavarz clung to a ray of hope.

Keshavarz was alone in that cell for fifteen days. He touched no food, only water, and refused to utter a single word except in prayer. He could not yield the information he did not have, as he denied the food he could have had. Except for breathing, thinking, meditating and praying, all solitary, all silent, Keshavarz might as well have been buried in a grave.

At first the hunger was painful, but in a matter of days it turned into an undemanding emptiness. He desired nothing. He accepted no favors, needed no advice, kept to himself, and withdrew from reality. He felt freer and stronger as he greeted death approaching him slowly with time. His hollowed eyes hid behind his dirty glasses, with one lens cracked, leaving him a broken vision of things lost in a fog, but yet he saw in his mind's eye what he had never seen clearly before. Through his ordeal, Dr. Keshavarz learned mankind's potential to inflict violence upon itself and also to endure it with dignity. The citizen, Keshavarz, who had refused to be corrupted or to revolt against corruption, realized that absolute innocence in all things provided no protection under the Shah. The skin of his face drew back to his bones, while his goatee grew ragged and untrimmed. After a week his legs refused his wish for light exercise as mentally he took great leaps forward in understanding the human condition in modern history and his own life.

His mind remained alert. In the deprivation of the cell his mind could focus on itself more clearly. His hunger strike would, God willing, force his release; otherwise, it would lead him to death. Either outcome was acceptable. His silence would convince his captors that he was already a dead man, that he had nothing to lose.

After two weeks, the prison officials introduced a cellmate. The middle-aged man was an agent, planted by the fearful director to encourage Keshavarz to eat to stay alive. Keshavarz listened sympathetically, but he uttered no word. He refused to share the good food the man offered him, who claimed his family had bribed the officials. Keshavarz prayed longer hours. He asked God's forgiveness for all he had done which was not his best, and for all the good he had failed to do. He asked forgiveness for not fighting more vigorously against injustice. He prayed for strength, even as his strength left him. He prayed for Ali to succeed.

Even with the intruder in his cell, his confinement remained solitary for him. It stretched long in his mind, his hopes turning into apprehension about Parvine, Fatema, Maryam, Iran. At times he secretly wished to die, to avoid being released back into humanity which had proved to be so inhumane. He did not want to know what might have happened to his family, to little Parvine, to his beloved wife, to his brave children. He silently mourned his family, realizing that, judging from the screams resounding through the prison, no barbarity was unthinkable to Savak.

His fear and his hope kept him alive and alert as they struggled throughout his being for ascendancy. His soul, the soul of Keshavarz, was the battlefield on which these armies waged their relentless war. There was no winner in their struggle, only advances and retreats. When fear advanced he wished to be kept in prison forever, to experience his own destruction. When hope ascended, he would anticipate the sweet moment of reunification with his family.

Twenty days went by at Evin. He would not eat, he would not talk, and he would not die. At length he refused to listen to the sounds of the prison, the cries of the tortured and those who survived it. He filled his ears with torn cloth. The prison physician warned him of his betrayal of his body to hunger, of his imminent death, but Keshavarz looked on as though deaf, with stuffing in his ears, a new symbol of silent defiance.

On the morning of the twenty-second day, Dr. Keshavarz lay unconscious from malnutrition and exhaustion. They had him fed intravenously.

That afternoon, two Savakis entered the cell and carried him out to a stretcher. He felt himself floating through a dimly lit corridor. As they entered the yard, the sun rays forced him to shut his eyes. He had not seen daylight for twenty-three days. He was carried through a gate. A woman who might have been Zaman—he could not make out her features—waited by a taxicab. He was helped from the stretcher and the woman helped him settle in the rear seat of the cab. A wave of energy surged through him, a delayed uplift triggered by the benefits of the surreptitious nutrient and Zaman's reassuring arms holding him. In the back seat against the other door sat Fatema, smiling through her tears and her sorrow.

With difficulty he spoke his first word in more than three weeks. "Parvine?"

"She is all right," Zaman whispered close to his ear.

"Hussain?"

Zaman nodded affirmatively. "Ali?" Zaman said nothing, trying to hide her emotions. "Maryam?" Fatema answered, "Her soul is in heaven."

Her husband was so thin and pale, unshaven and unkempt, Fatema scarcely recognized him. He fell asleep against Zaman's shoulder. The family physician was called immediately. Keshavarz was taken to his bed, where he spoke only through his eyes and his hands as he clasped his family to him.

The old man's colleagues had sought his release, quietly, without drawing attention to themselves. There was no arrest warrant, no charges, no explanations, no record, nothing. He had not been arrested officially. The Shah had approved his release when the hunger strike threatened his life. The Shah and Savak could gain nothing from his death or further confinement, and everything from a show of compassion. Dr. Keshavarz became an exhibit to the United Nations Commission on Human Rights, an example of the regime's freeing of political prisoners.

Dr. Keshavarz was given a leave of absence from the university. The dean, under pressure from the court, was insistent that he retire, and

Keshavarz acceded. He was not a criminal, but he became "lost" in the eyes of the bureaucracy; only his dossier persisted. Keshavarz withdrew from society, seeking life in prayer and in writing, reaching for a deeper understanding which was unattainable previously. No one but the closest friend read what he wrote. His work was not to be published while he was alive.

* * * * *

After his flight, Ali spent a week in the cellar hiding from Savak. He asked after his family, but his comrades didn't know yet. Knowing he could be arrested at any time, and inspired by the men whose portraits surrounded him, Ali decided to make an early start on his unfinished task. Sitting at the small desk, his notes arranged before him, he took a blank sheet of paper and wrote the title, "Explosives for Revolution."

Then the ideas for the manual that had bubbled in his head flowed easily. He wrote, "Comrades in the struggle: This manual is written for the purpose of furthering revolutionary politics only. It is to be used to disunite the enemy camp and to unite the people. Let our explosives adorn the consciousness of the people as fireworks adorn the sky."

Ali crossed off the last sentence as too romantic. He continued, "The explosives of revolutionaries must shatter the Shah's power and the fear permeating our nation. They must make people realize their own great power.

"This manual will show how to make and use several explosive devices to carry out the program of the armed struggle. Working with explosives demands that instructions be followed thoroughly and exactly. An error could be fatal. Failure to follow instructions is a waste of hard-won resources and a breach of revolutionary discipline."

Ali underlined the sentence about fatal error. He finished the manual as though spellbound, almost forty pages of detailed instructions. He checked each word, each sentence, each paragraph for precision and for simplicity, until satisfied that there could be no misinterpretation.

When he finished the final draft there was no one to shake his hand. He had sacrificed more for the project than he knew. He felt only cold and damp. The basement had a small electric stove, and Ali had two sweaters borrowed from Comrade Mother. He refused to shiver even when chilled to the bone. The cold winter of his life had arrived ahead of schedule, pushing spring, summer and autumn aside.

There was a gentle knock at the door. It was not one of the hooded comrades who came regularly with food. Ali recognized the familiar figure of Comrade Mother, even though her face was covered as always. Comrade Mother said, "Savak arrested your father and your niece a week ago as hostages to your surrender. The little girl was released with some injury, but nothing permanent. Your father remains in solitary confinement. They want you, Comrade Ali—do not mind my using your name, you are well known. If you wish to remain underground, the comrades will support you, and if you wish to surrender to save your father, we will understand that too."

Ali said, "If I may, I'd like to have my decision for you in the morning, Comrade."

"All right, Ali," said Comrade Mother. Ali then picked up his neat manuscript and handed it to her.

"Here is the manual. Please check the language and proofread it. A typographical error could be deadly. I've checked everything thoroughly already. It should do the job."

The woman took the papers and whispered, "Thank you." She opened the door leading into the sunfilled day, then turned and said, "Your efforts will spark the revolutionary movement. Your family's suffering is not in vain." The hooded woman hesitated. "Remember, Ali, whatever your decision, you have our full support."

Ali nodded his thanks with a drop of his eyelashes. The door closed, and Ali was alone once more, with only the cold light of the bulb on the wall and the pictures of revolutionary heroes staring at him. The sounds of the room were dead sounds, and the heroes were soundless. They stared at him day and night, without a moment of rest, never blinking. He missed the explosives, his manuscript; he missed writing it. He knew he now had nothing to keep him busy, to help him avoid unthinkable thoughts.

He had to wait until morning, but for whom, for what? Morning itself had become an abstraction, as there was no sunlight in the basement. His final night in the cellar passed without a benchmark, the same light bulb gazing at him continuously. The broken alarm clock, its dial forever announcing twelve o'clock, stared at him. Did it mean noon or midnight? Day never began or ended in this basement. Only night succeeded night, one after the other. The sun hid itself; there was no illumination to lighten his despair.

All that Ali had heard of Savak, the abstract, impersonal rumors, had suddenly gained dreadful immediacy, had become a personal reality. Ali berated himself for his foolishness, thinking that his family's innocence would protect them. Ali had dreaded this possibility ever since being confined in the basement, although he knew of no precedent. He had tried to ignore it, considering it unlikely, so that he could write the manual with a clear mind. Ali, the objective revolutionary Marxist, had committed the cardinal sin of wishful thinking, by underestimating the ruthlessness of the enemy.

What prey would Savak seek to devour? His family, his community, the whole nation? How could anyone think himself secure, relax, be productive, be content, with Savakis around? Ali dismissed these thoughts as useless. Still, why did the Shah understand better than the people that everyone was a potential enemy for him, that he was surrounded by a sea of enemies? Ali came to his decision. He had to give himself up to Savak to save his fragile father. His thoughts could change nothing, his wishes had no power, there would be no sympathy for his anguish and fear.

Early the next morning the sun was rising to its proper place in the sky. Ali stood in the courtyard, hugged his masked comrades, and thanked them before they blindfolded him and released him some blocks away from the house.

Ali was free and loose on Amirieh Avenue. He could not go home, he could not even sneak in over the roof. He was a marked man, a plague carrier, dangerous to anyone he touched. He went to a telephone booth to make a call.

"This is Ali Keshavarz," he said.

"Good morning, Ali," Anvari responded. "I've been expecting your call."

Ali interrupted, "My father is innocent. If you release him, I will give myself up."

"I can't promise that," Anvari said. "But give yourself up and I will do my best to see he returns home."

Ali suspected that Anvari was anxious to gain credit for the arrest. He said, "Let him go for the sake of the regime, not for me or him or humanity or God. To take an old theologian hostage is stupid. The international community will condemn this."

Anvari said, "I appreciate your calling me, but you will do better to refrain from offending government authorities." Anvari smiled. He knew how police records were falsified to cover up atrocities. The Shah's men proclaimed those who protested human rights violations in Iran were communists who invented the lie to embarrass the Shah and to advance their own evil cause.

Ali said, "I want to see my family, and I need a couple of days to myself. Can you promise that?"

Anvari replied, "I'll have to check this with my superior." After a few moments he returned to the line. The two men, then, made arrangements to work through an intermediary for Ali's surrender.

Ali visited his mother. Fatema sobbed when she learned that Ali must give himself up. She hugged him and stared into his face silently. Ali kissed her face, her hair, her hands, and asked her to forgive him for all the trouble, all the pain. She knew he could be killed before she saw him again, or she could die before he was released. Finally she spoke. "Don't let your thoughts inhibit you. Pray, Ali, and God will protect you." Ali thought,

"If God was in the protection business why was he in this predicament in the first place? Why would God not protect the people from the Shah?" It was all Fatema had to say. Fatema knew how to suffer pain in dignity. Her children had gone astray, her husband imprisoned, her world was darkening and growing ever more silent. A dove caught in the space of fighting eagles: she could only pray and she did just that.

Friends and relatives poured into the house to see Ali once more. Ali did not stay aloof that day. He was sad but warm. He shook hands and wished the best for the neighbors, as if planning a long, hazardous journey. His melancholy was apparent even though he did not express it in words. The only person he seemed to have forgotten was himself, as he kissed and hugged his family and relatives goodbye. Then Zaman and Ali exchanged news and talked about plans. Finally he asked Zaman and Hussain to take charge of the family.

Then he went to the cemetery of Behesht-e-Zahra to visit Maryam's grave. He placed a bouquet of flowers beside the modest stone as tears fell on his shoes. He remembered all the wonderful stories she had recited for the little boy Ali. Anger boiled inside him; he thought, "Poor Maryam is the first sacrifice to my revolutionary program." Ali took a piece of colored chalk and wrote on her grave, "Maryam was murdered by the Shah."

To protect his comrades, Ali informed them of all that he knew about the organization in case he revealed anything to Savak under torture.

After a routine questioning at Savak headquarters, a well-guarded van took him to Evin Prison, and Ali was in the hands of the secret police and the Shah.

CHAPTER 15

Ali In Evin

Ali was put in solitary confinement at Evin Prison in a cell adjacent to that of his father, who was growing weak on his hunger strike. Father and son worried about each other, never knowing how physically close they were.

Spiders lurked in webs in the corners. Ali watched them walk across the floor. The walls were dead, but the spiders were alive, and Ali identified with the living. Ali was left alone to think things out, to see his will eaten by fear and loneliness.

He was learning a hard lesson in compromising. Ali had given up Sara for the people, and now he had given up the people for his father. People were an abstraction; his father was real. Within this cement and steel grave that the Shah had dug for him, Ali saw that he was not a revolutionary yet. Comrade Hamid Ashraf had not surrendered when his parents had been imprisoned for two months, but Ali did not have the same option. Dr. Keshavarz' heart was weak.

These thoughts led to self-criticism and a journey into his personal life that he had abandoned to the demands of the explosives project. His father's clear, solid words came to him. "The struggle with the self is never-ending, as life's necessities constantly block the path to ideals." Ali asked himself which was more important, his family's welfare or the welfare of the nation? The anguish of choosing stayed within him for days, even though he had already made the choice at least once.

Ali had believed that by risking his own life he had put the revolution above everything. But he knew better now. He would sacrifice his own life, but not his father's. His dedication to the revolution was not absolute. A sad smile lingered on his face.

His idea of outfoxing Savak had been foolish, the twenty-one-year-old Ali concluded. He berated himself for not entering Iran clandestinely and remaining underground from the start. But his family was an important part of home; how could he return home and not see them? Wouldn't his dangerous life be a torture for them? Revolutionary romanticism had prevented him from understanding that his own life was just one element in the equation of risk and not the most important one. Ali wondered, "How could such imponderable questions be answered in practice?" So he struggled with them, he slept over them, talked to himself and the spiders about them.

The walls were indifferent and time passed indifferently. Self-criticism was necessary but not sufficient, Ali decided. He must risk action. He kept fit by exercising. At midnight, when the guards changed shifts, he secretly practiced his karate skills.

Ali began to listen to the sounds and words passing through the steel door, and began to speak to the guard who brought him food. Once, after midnight, the young conscript guard, Taghi, asked if Ali wanted water. This gesture opened them up, and they had a lot to talk about.

The next day an officer caught them talking and shouted obscenities at Taghi. Ali's comforting words later soothed Taghi, who had heard nothing but orders and insults of officers and the screams of the tortured in Evin. Taghi took a liking to Ali and said he had come close to shooting the officer who called his mother a whore.

Taghi told him the interrogation was the "period of danger" because of the torture used to extract information and a confession. The torture always stopped when the prisoner passed out, but was continued until Savak got results, or until repeated fainting caused irreparable physical damage.

Ali conceived of a plan to maintain his physical and mental integrity. His mind had to endure without permanent damage to the body, and his body had to endure without losing his mind. Ali had to control pain and not let pain control him.

To deceive the interrogator, Ali had to become a madman who held his life in low esteem. After all, what can be expected from a madman? By inviting death he could hope to avoid it, and by pretending to faint he could avoid a real fainting episode, a few of which could be catastrophic. I already consider myself a dead man, Ali thought. Savak can't kill me twice.

Ali kept reminding himself of his goals: to keep the explosives project a secret, to protect Aram, Zaman, his old aunt and other comrades, and to save himself. He assumed that his father was now safe at home. But if he talked, then he couldn't be a revolutionary, and if he resisted and experienced fainting episodes, then he would become a vegetable. He had to avoid both possibilities, by withstanding torture while his mind was alert, and then pretending to faint before pain shut off his nerves.

* * * * *

A few weeks went by. One day Ali was wondering if there was any hope. Suddenly the door clanked open. This was not a regular visit, and Ali was startled. An officer and a guard followed the sound into the cell. Ali had never seen the officer, but the guard was his new friend, Taghi, who stood stiffly with a machine gun across his chest.

The officer said, "Good morning."

Ali nodded warily.

The officer held out a pack of Camels. "Please."

Ali shook his head no. The officer lit a cigarette. "Mr. Keshavarz, we have not meant to neglect you. Important cases have been pending."

"Your job is not easy." Ali pointed to the web. "Those spiders kept me company. Now I must face humans."

"It won't be bad. You will be served tea and sweets and asked questions," the officer said, puffing on the cigarette. He handed Ali a blindfold. "Please wear it and hold onto my arm."

As though Ali's words had just sunk in, the officer said, "What about spiders?"

Ali said, "The spiders will miss me, and I will miss them. You know, you can get used to people, places, pets, even spiders."

The officer shook his head. Ali continued as he was guided blindfolded, "Why, one spider sat on my knee and stared at me. He trusts me and I trust him."

The officer thought Ali was crazy to talk to spiders, no doubt the effect of solitary confinement. "Spiders' mentality" would be a catchy phrase for his report on Ali.

The officer led Ali through the corridor, and Taghi's footsteps echoed behind. Ali heard a man bashing his head against a door; the unceasing moans of the tortured had unnerved him. He screamed, "I'm going insane. Fill my ears with lead! Beat me unconscious!" Then the man shouted, "Fuck the Shah! Fuck his sisters, his mother! Fuck Savak! Now, you bastards, come and get me. Beat me to death." Then Ali heard running steps, a clanking door, and the dull thuds of kicking. The prisoner had his wish. He was unconscious and could no longer hear the screams and moans of others. Later Taghi told Ali that the prisoner was a Turk who had shot his wife and daughter before running out of ammunition when Savak surrounded his home. He was afraid they would rape his wife to force him to spill his secrets. His Majesty had been very interested in the case, Taghi reported.

Soon Ali was guided through a door and his blindfold removed. Taghi and another conscript stood at the door and the officer left. The room looked like an empty warehouse. Ali saw two steel beds against the walls and newspapers on the floor. A large photograph of the Shah observed everything.

A Savak officer in an army uniform sat at a desk in the corner. He puffed on a cigarette, then stubbed it out in a plastic ashtray. Without looking up he said, "I am Teherani. I represent the state in matters of public security. Let me advise you, Mr. Keshavarz, that salvation in this world and the next lies in honesty. Now, will you have some tea?"

Ali shook his head. He studied Teherani, the interrogator known as The Doctor because of the surgical gown he wore while torturing.

Teherani looked up. "Your name, please?"

"You already know it," Ali said.

Teherani smiled. "Don't fight the procedures. I ask the questions and you answer them. Now, what is your name?"

Ali gave his name.

"Have you been arrested before?"

"Never," said Ali. "Just taken hostage."

"What do you mean, sir?" Teherani asked.

"No arrest warrant is issued," Ali continued. "But I am in good company with spiders, you understand."

Teherani asked, "Understand what? What spiders?"

"The spiders in my cell," Ali replied. "I am their guest."

Teherani glowered. "You may stop this silliness. Now, do you know why you are here?"

Ali said, "For my father's release. But I don't understand why he was arrested."

Teherani looked up, surprised. "You don't?" Ali shook his head.

"Well, we will help you understand."

Why was Teherani so slow in coming to the point? When would the "pleases" and "sirs" end? Ali wondered.

Teherani smiled as he rose from his seat and walked toward Ali. He talked to himself, "Guest of spiders, huh?"

Ali said, "Yes, spiders." The hanging light trembled as Teherani's footsteps echoed and the dust eddied around his feet. He stopped at arm's length in front of Ali. The two conscripts fixed their eyes on their boots, and Taghi held his breath.

Ali gazed at Teherani's face, but the inquisitor just smiled. Teherani stepped forward, raised his hand, pretending to run it through his hair, but instead he swung it at Ali's face. Ali blocked the blow with his left arm and punched Teherani in the nose with his right fist. Teherani toppled against the desk, blood gushing from his nose. Ali stood with feet apart and arms up, his eyes focused on Teherani.

Teherani wiped the blood from his face, keeping his eyes locked on Ali's. Under his breath he swore, "You'll pay for this." He went behind the desk, took his pistol from the drawer and pointed it at Ali. Without taking his eyes off Ali he barked, "Guards! Tie up this animal. If he resists, shoot him."

The conscripts were frozen. Teherani snapped at them, "Move it, you dumb bastards! Handcuff him or I'll shoot you."

The conscripts glanced at the prisoner. Ali stretched out his arms to Taghi, wrists together. They approached Ali cautiously and shackled his wrists. Ali smiled. The guards stepped back to the door, sighing with relief, their faces worried for Ali.

Teherani tossed the pistol on the desk and turned to Ali. "You whore-mother! You whore-mother! I'll teach you a lesson that even your grand-children won't forget."

He paced back and forth in front of Ali. Suddenly he swung his hand at Ali's face again. Just in time, Ali leaped away, twisted his body, and drove his right foot into Teherani's gut, hurling the Savaki backward against the desk. Ali managed to keep his balance. Teherani collapsed on the floor, dazed and shaken, his stomach aching sharply. He crawled and leaned against the desk fearful and trembling, his anger fighting to overcome the pain. The conscripts tried not to laugh.

Seeing Teherani reach for the gun, Ali hurried toward him and kicked it away. The pistol spun and came to rest against the wall. Ali stood over Teherani and commanded, "Apologize! Apologize for insulting the guards." He stepped closer, towering over Teherani.

Teherani was filled with rage. He would kill Ali now if he could, but his anger gave way to stark terror as he looked at the madman edging close. Fear forced him to say what his mind refused. "I'm sorry," he said weakly.

Ali ordered, "Tell the guards."

Alarmed that Ali's heel would crush his head, Teherani gulped out, "I'm sorry for the insults."

Ali looked straight into Teherani's eyes. "That's not enough."

Teherani raised his voice. "I eat shit for what I have done, I eat shit" —he repeated the Persian idiom for extreme penitence. "Please forgive me, Agha Keshavarz." The conscripts stood open-mouthed. Teherani, shocked and humiliated, did not command the guards. Ali could crush his head before the guards could reach him.

"Now I will interrogate you," Ali said. "Tell me the truth, or I'll kill you."

"Spare me!" Teherani pleaded.

"Has my father been released?"

"No, he is still in Evin."

"When will he be set free?"

"I don't know."

"Who knows?"

"Only His Majesty." Ali hadn't suspected that the Shah was directly involved in the details of Evin.

Teherani lay cringing and exhausted. Suddenly the door swung open. Ali stepped back to regain his balance and turned his head. Three men, clubs above their heads, burst into the room. Ali jumped, smashing his foot into the chest of the man in front, doubling him over and hurling him down to writhe moaning on the floor. At once a heavy object smashed over Ali's head, darkening his world. He felt nothing after that.

Teherani picked up the fallen man's club and smashed blows at Ali's ribs. He kicked Ali in the face, swearing obscenities. Taghi shouted, "Stop! Ali is dead. The prisoner is dead."

The news of Ali's defiance ran like a flood, filled every crevice in Evin, flowed across the yard, scaled the walls and overflowed into the roads and the city beyond. It lodged in the hearts of prisoners and guards and penetrated even the royal palace. It was believed by people who desperately wanted to believe it; it was believed by people who had every reason to deny it. His family heard it. The cowardice of Teherani evoked ridicule from subordinates who feared him, from colleagues who envied him, and from superiors who disdained him.

The news became a legend. "Ali made the savage Teherani say 'I eat shit' twenty times." "He made Teherani beg forgiveness even with Ali's hands tied behind his back." "He forced Teherani to apologize to the conscripts." "The Savakis broke every bone in Ali's body, but he would not die." "Ali has a hundred lives."

* * * * *

Ali regained consciousness the next afternoon. He opened his eyes, but he couldn't focus. His head felt heavy. He tried to move it but a shooting pain spread over his body and ruled his senses. His broken ribs commanded him to be still. Bandages over his smashed nose obstructed his view. The white walls blended into the white gowns of men with glassy eyes fixed on him. The men smiled as they vanished, as if they stood on the deck of a ship pulling away. Then his eyelids closed and darkened his sight against his will. Ali lapsed into a coma, in a life-and-death struggle. The beating had been a mistake. Ali must be kept alive at all costs to give up his secrets before he gave up his life.

The next day he opened his eyes again. He did not know where he was. He tried to smile at the nurse who held his hand. The other faces were gone. He felt thirsty and opened his mouth to ask for water. Instead of words, a spark of pain slashed across his face and raced down his neck. The broken nose, twisted thumb, cracked ribs, and external and internal bruises dictated stillness and silence with the authority of infinite pain. It was two days before he could manage to drink a little hot milk.

But slowly he gained strength as the days and weeks passed and his body mended. As spring approached, Ali was back in a damp cell, his wounds no longer life-threatening. His hands were kept tied behind him except when he urinated under the eye of a guard. The officials said he was a dangerous madman, but Ali was alive and thinking, although his plan to provoke a beating had almost cost him his life.

To survive as a revolutionary, Ali had to implement the second phase of his plan perfectly. He had to convince Teherani that he was insane. So he remained silent, or else talked to spiders, or screamed incoherently in the night, making sure someone heard him. He urinated in his pants on purpose occasionally and screamed for diapers.

Weeks passed slowly and reluctantly. Savak had banished the sun out of his life, replacing it with a bare, fifty-watt General Electric bulb. Little happened in a cell, little could happen, so his experience with men and nature was one of the past. He experienced nothing new in a silent and confined space of a cell as time passed through it indifferently.

Taghi had left a string of worry beads on Ali's food tray, whispering, "This is my only possession that may be of some use to you." Ali's thumb and forefinger touched one bead at a time, then slid it away, forever turning the beads around the white silk string. He caught a glimpse of string showing between the beads, like a beam of daylight from the peephole in the ceiling. The beads helped Ali to pass time as they helped time to pass Ali.

Taghi talked furtively to Ali despite the rules. He had to open his heart to Ali, whom he respected. Early one morning when no one was around, Taghi told about his life.

"I have four brothers and one sister," Taghi began. "My mother died when my sister was born, and my father is old. We tilled land that did not belong to us, my sister, too. Two years ago the landlord's son, the head of the gendarmerie, raped my thirteen-year-old sister. From shame she ran away to Yazd. Later we learned that she had become a prostitute."

Taghi said, "Our village is in Taft, close to Yazd. We have always been poor. Often we have gone to bed hungry and dreamt of food. I have never seen a physician. The Shah's land reform came to our village, but it passed by us as though we weren't there. We were told there were more people than there was land. It was God's will, they said, not the fault of His Majesty's government. Those who got land had twenty-five years to pay for it, and the yearly payments kept them poor, too. The land didn't help them much. We thought land reform would change something, but it didn't, not for us and not for those who got their hands soiled—yes, we call it that, soiled—for accepting the land.

"Agha Keshavarz, the conscripts know you are fighting for us, too. I will try to help you escape, even if it costs my life." Ali listened attentively.

Now the world outside Ali's cell was closed to him, life and action out of sight. Books of poetry, music, paintings, the joyful flights of sparrows, the tears of clouds, the light of the sun, the whispering of the wind, the cracking of trees, everything was shrunken, reduced to four walls. Time unmarked, space rectangular, color grey, life monotonous pressed on Ali's soul. Only his imagination was not confined. He remembered Sara, and he remembered the colorful changing paintings of nature and man outside Sara's window in New York.

One day the door opened unexpectedly and an officer and a new guard stepped in. The officer said, "Oh, can you believe it? Spring is here already. What a coincidence. Your interrogation resumes on the first day of spring, the day our ancestors have celebrated for five thousand years."

Ali turned to a web. "Spiders, do you hear? Spring is here."

The officer ignored him. "I hope it will go better this time." Ali felt a chill inside, but he betrayed no feeling.

* * * * *

The heart of Evin was a complex of five buildings connected by corridors, with an administrative section. Each building contained bare cells and larger rooms with steel cots, shackles, whips, vises adapted to hold various sensitive anatomical parts, electric shock equipment and cattle prods. U.S. companies competed to sell Iran such equipment, with the U.S. Justice Department providing technical assistance through the Law Enforcement Assistance Agency.

The interrogators called the cells "operating rooms," since the torture bed resembled an operating table. Ali stood still as two guards removed his uniform. Ali pretended that he was not there, that he was nowhere. Ali inspected the room as his wrists were strapped to the steel bed. Bloodstains on the walls had survived a cleanup, and a red spot clung to the lightbulb. He noticed a rack holding a number of whips.

Ali closed his eyes. He would close his ears, too, but he could not avoid the sound of approaching footsteps in the corridor. He began to whistle a Persian wedding tune. Two months in the hospital and broken bones had pushed Ali toward a more subtle awareness, a new self, like a silkworm emerging from its cocoon as a moth. His solitude had withered his illusions away as time peels off the seasons from the earth.

The two conscripts exchanged embarrassed glances. Men were not used to being naked in front of each other in Iran. They could not believe that Ali was whistling. They respected and even feared Ali.

From the corner of his eye, Ali saw Teherani and a physician and the two guards. The guards stepped back when Teherani approached, like nurses on the surgeon's arrival. One of them handed Teherani a white gown. Ali continued to whistle.

Teherani went to the bed and loomed over Ali. "Greetings to the wild horse. You will talk when I push you closer and closer to death. You will beg me to kill you. I will tame you so well that even old ladies could ride your back." Teherani waited. Ali continued whistling, his eyes glued to the red dot on the lightbulb.

Teherani said, "If you don't talk, you won't have air." Ali whistled, but his detachment dissolved into agitation. When Ali paid no heed, Teherani took a handkerchief from his pocket and thrust it into Ali's throat. Ali choked, writhed, kicked and jerked against the straps. His world blackened as his face turned purple. The man in the white coat stepped forward and pulled the handkerchief out.

"Stop that," Teherani shouted at the physician.

The physician said, "Follow your orders! He must stay alive to talk."

Teherani grabbed a whip of thin wires and began slashing at Ali. The physician shrank back in disgust. The whip lacerated Ali's naked chest. Another flick from Teherani across Ali's legs tore his flesh above the knee. Teherani contorted his face as if being whipped himself, shouting, "Now talk! Where did you take the chemicals? To whom?"

All of a sudden, Ali uttered a deep moan. His head fell to the right, saliva drooled from the corner of his mouth, and he fainted.

Ali's performance was perfect. The physician rushed up and ordered the guards to fetch water. He turned to Teherani and whispered, "Lieutenant, we need information, not revenge. Your first beating finished him. A pumpkin won't talk even if you chop it to pieces."

Teherani knew the physician was right, but he growled, "Shut up. I'm in charge here. If you were a good physician you wouldn't be treating suspects." To prove his point Teherani punched Ali in the stomach, then said, "Just make sure he doesn't die."

The physician ignored Teherani and threw cold water on Ali's face. The water ran over Ali's eyelids, down his cheeks, and dripped to the floor, as if Ali were crying. The physician slapped his face, and Ali opened his eyes. The whip's lashes left a burning pain across his chest and legs.

Teherani turned to the physician. "Is he ready?"

The physician said curtly, "Let him regain consciousness."

Teherani ignored the physician and questioned Ali. "Who were your accomplices?"

Ali stared at the ceiling, then looked in astonishment at Teherani. "In my aunt's place?"

Teherani hurried to say, "Yes, yes." The physician and the conscripts exchanged surprised glances. Ali was talking.

Ali said, "We played hide and seek."

Teherani shook his head. "I don't believe this."

Ali, without looking at him, said, "Ask the kids."

"Who was driving the van like a mad dog?" When Ali didn't respond, Teherani repeated himself.

Ali shouted, "I got it, I got it! A mad dog! I answered your question,

Mr. Teherani.''

The physician shook his head and whispered to Teherani, ''The man is incoherent, finished!''

Teherani gave the physician a menacing glance. Ali remained silent and looked indifferent. He was convincing. Even Teherani thought Ali was finished.

Teherani tried once more. He whispered in Ali's ear, ''I will chop you to pieces.''

Ali thought, ''You put me in solitary confinement, you break my ribs, you suffocate me, and still you can't get what you want. I am all trussed up and naked and it is you who tremble with fear.''

Teherani wanted to beat the silence out of Ali, to produce sounds, words, reactions, blood. But he was at a loss. Teherani was as the one tied to the cot, with Ali standing over him. The conflict between seeking revenge and getting information tormented him. If Teherani had kept control in the first encounter, then no one would question him even if he killed Ali. But all those ''ifs'' amounted to nothing. How could he just kill someone who could not hold his urine, who would not even know who killed him? What would his superiors think with Ali dead and his secrets unrevealed? Ali was finished, but he had robbed Teherani of his revenge, as he had robbed him of his omnipotence. Teherani had control over Ali's body, but not his mind.

Teherani betrayed no emotion. ''Well, we must test you to see how finished you are.''

Ali shuddered. He was weak, he ached and burned all over. Fear magnified his pains. For the next two days, Ali lived through torture, a descent into hell. Ali was brought to the brink of despair for his life. Electric shocks were run through his body, burning cigarettes applied to his buttocks. Ali absorbed pain, he pretended to faint, and the physician tried to revive him. The physician's contempt for Teherani had turned him into an unwitting ally of Ali. The physician hoped the interrogation would prove Teherani's mistake in destroying Ali and his information.

''Keshavarz speaks to spiders, but not to people any more. He is wild, and he doesn't care if he lives or dies,'' the physician reported to the chief of Evin. Nevertheless, Teherani knew Ali had humiliated him, had put his reputation in doubt, and for that he had to pay, to serve as an example. It didn't matter what the physician reported.

Lying naked on the steel cot, his prison pajamas in a pile at the door, Ali feared succumbing to the pain. His three months in Evin had aged him terribly, forcing the future into his life years before its natural arrival. Three hundred years seemed to have been pressed into the three months. Yet Ali had to endure still more pain. Could he remain silent? How many more days could he hold out? A cold sweat covered his body as he awaited the unexpected. Not knowing what unspeakable pain was to come was almost as unbearable as the pain itself. Now Ali had to exert himself to the limit to pretend once more that he was not there, lest he be turned into a vegetable and his masquerade become his reality. He fixed his eyes at the door and heard someone say, "The man doesn't talk or eat, and he wets himself. He's a pumpkin, he's finished. You've got him. Why don't you let him go, Teherani?"

Teherani's low voice reached Ali. "This is a lesson for all suspects. Now let's feed the pumpkin."

A tremble ran through Ali's battered mind. Could he faint yet again on cue? He shrank as he remembered the pain of the last torture. He wished to be a pumpkin and know no difference between life and death.

A guard and Teherani came in. Ali shivered. The physician was not there. Fainting might not help this time. Torture, bullets in his corpse, a coffin and a death certificate, the thought shot up and down his spine.

Teherani inspected Ali and mumbled to himself, "I'll figure out if you're a real pumpkin."

Ali trained his eyes on the ceiling, pretending he was alone. He kept reminding himself to be a pumpkin, just as Teherani said. Ali felt absolutely isolated, even more so than when he was in the dark, damp solitary confinement. Now he had to hide his painful fear or else let Teherani detect his deception. Teherani looked like the chief of an invading alien army with the mission to use men as laboratory animals. Ali wished he were dead.

Teherani ordered the guards to tie Ali up and put him in the corner of the room. Why on the ground? Ali shivered once more.

"Stand around him." The guards looked at one another, bewildered and hesitant. Teherani scowled at the nearest conscript. They obeyed. The fear of the unknown tormented Ali.

"Now water this pumpkin," Teherani continued. The guards stood still. "Move your Turkish asses," Teherani's voice boomed. They slowly opened their buttoned pants, then one by one held out their penises, glancing to the side, away from Ali, like four kings of diamonds in a deck of cards. Another bark from Teherani and they urinated on Ali.

Ali shuddered. He closed his eyes and mouth tight. Only by iron will and discipline did he remain a pumpkin. The men hurriedly finished and buttoned their pants. Teherani's laughter filled Ali's ears. "Now," he sang, "with all this water you will grow and grow and be a bigger pumpkin. Okay, gentlemen, thank you. If the pumpkin had a tongue he would also thank you. You may go now." When they were gone, Teherani pulled his pants down, planted his feet on either side of Ali and defecated on him. He said, "You need fertilizer, too, my pumpkin."

Teherani was certain now that Ali was finished; otherwise Ali would have reacted. Teherani had his revenge, even if Ali was a pumpkin. Ali was of no use to anybody any more, Teherani thought.

But Ali remained alive, and he remained a revolutionary. There were scars, some visible, some invisible, some transitory, some permanent, yet Ali's health was basically sound, his nerves steeled. Ali was more disciplined, more observant, more patient, more decisive, more wary, more dedicated to the revolution now, thanks to Evin. The cigarette burns, the marks left by the whip, the horrible memory of the last day of the period of danger remained with Ali, badges of his opposition to the Shah and of the Shah's opposition to him.

It was not the first time that the secret police had been deceived. Ali had to be absolutely truthful to the masses and absolutely deceptive to the government. The opposites of truthfulness and deception united in his life.

Just as his concern and love for his family, comrades and the people had become deeper, so had his hatred toward the Shah's regime.

Evin had also taught Ali violence. Ali, who had never struck anyone, even as a boy, would soon shoot a man in the face without a second thought.

Ali's arrest warrant was produced after months of imprisonment. In Evin, Savak routinely issued and dated the warrant after the interrogation, so a detainee could be freed without a record. And if he had succumbed to torture, he needed only a burial certificate, not a warrant. Thus the official documents covered up solitary confinement, interrogation and torture.

The detainee could withhold his signature and appeal, but he would be beaten until he signed. No one had succeeded in bringing a false document to the attention of the appeals court, which was a part of the Savak apparatus anyhow, so the Shah's regime could prove that it followed human rights accords. Only a few scarred detainees ever got away to show their wounds in exile.

The unsuccessful interrogation meant that there was no evidence against Ali, so he was charged with striking a Savak officer, Teherani, with no mention that Teherani had a gun or that Ali's hands were tied. Ali kept his silence before the military court. Every prisoner's file contained a confidential Savak report summarizing the crime. A coded letter indicated the "suggested" sentence, and the court sentence always matched the suggestion. The court sentenced Ali to four years in Evin.

Soon Ali was transferred from solitary to a group cell. To avoid prisoners who had turned informers, Ali had to keep to himself, lest Savak discover his make-believe breakdown. It troubled Ali that he could not talk to comrades, but he could not take the chance of returning to Teherani's clutches.

It was two months before Ali was allowed to see his family. He managed to convey the truth to Zaman. She told Ali that his father had been released and had been forced to retire from the university, and that Professor Pirooz had confirmed that Sara had married Eric.

Ali had plenty of time to think. The months went by slowly without events to mark their passage. The Ali who had endured torture was no longer the youthful, romantic rebel, but a steeled man who would return to the revolution when he got out of Evin, who would return to the revolution even within the walls, if it became necessary. Savak was certain that he was finished; only a vegetable could endure so much pain and humiliation. Ali had confessed to nothing, had divulged nothing. He had passed many revolutionary tests, had ascended mountains of pain, anxiety and self-criticism. He was not dead; in fact he was more alive than ever. His limbs had been treated like a side of beef in a butchery, but he was still alive, thinking, dreaming, planning, listening, risking once more.

In a few months, Ali learned much about those who shared his cell and his exercise yard. A great deal of surreptitious politics went on in Evin. The "communes" of prisoners sharing different ideologies filled the jails. There were not enough guards or torture equipment to silence the political life of the prisoners.

There were Muslim fundamentalists and mullahs in Evin who supported Ayatollah Khomeini, along with followers of Dr. Bazargan, who were good Muslims but believed in the separation of church and state. There were National Front supporters and Tudeh Party members. There were young revolutionary socialist Muslims who eventually coalesced into the Mujahedin Khalgh, the People's Warriors. They were the toughest, most disciplined group. Ali's revolutionary Marxist comrades, who eventually formed the Fedayeen Khalgh, the People's Sacrificers, were more advanced in underground and military training than the others.

There were debates, friendly exchanges, competition to win neutral prisoners over, and cooperation among the various groups against prison officials. On several occasions, hunger strikes were organized.

Many future leaders found themselves in Evin at one time or another, including Ayatollahs Khomeini and Taleghani, Dr. Bazargan, Dr. Sanjabi, Dr. Bakhtiyar, Rajavi, Ali and his senior comrades.

Gradually, Ali allowed himelf to speak to comrades. The trusted ones knew he was no vegetable, even if he spoke few words. There was a life, an understanding in his eyes, though he would not utter a single word to the Savakis.

Ali began serious discussions with Comrades Kalantary, Choopanzadeh, Sarmady and Surakey, senior comrades and communist revolutionaries of Pirooz' generation.

Ali learned a great deal from them. He promised to go to Beirut to establish working contacts between the Fedayeen and other revolutionary organizations and the helpful governments of Algeria and Libya. Ali's knowledge of English, French and some Arabic would be an asset. The Fedayeen needed finances, training, and weapons, and they planned to get them wherever they could, so long as no strings were attached.

Ali's senior comrades insisted that he remain a pumpkin, wait out his sentence and not risk escape. They had drawn blood resisting the state and were falsely accused of plotting the Shah's assassination. Some had attempted to escape, were caught, and died under torture. Their corpses were riddled with bullets and their families were notified months later of their burial.

Zaman and other members of the family visited Ali whenever possible, bringing homemade food. Zaman managed to keep Ali abreast of the activities of comrades, called "armed propaganda." He was delighted to hear that not only was his manual creating explosives, but they were being used for the objectives he had outlined.

In early 1971, several of the underground organizations, including Ali's group, united into the Fedayeen Khalgh. Soon some Fedayeen guerrillas in the mountains of Gilan captured a police outpost in the village of Siahkal. However, an expedition headed by the Shah's brother wiped out most of the guerrillas. Ali mourned his martyred comrades and saluted the beginning of the armed uprising, as did the people of Iran.

Zaman told Ali of the exploits of Aram and Hamid Ashraf. In August 1972, after the police had suppressed a strike by Teheran bus drivers, Aram, Hamid and their comrades had blown up several police stations. Two years later, they killed a factory owner who had summoned police against the striking workers which had resulted in a dozen workers' deaths. The Fedayeen announced that every brutal reaction against workers would be punished by revolutionary justice. From now on, the Shah's men were served notice that violence would meet violence.

A few months later, Taghi's enlistment was up. Ali and Taghi hugged secretly and Taghi whispered in Ali's ear, "I am a Fedayeen, too. I will join your comrades."

Ali's activities remained quiet and circumspect. But his silence did not still the hopes he had kindled in others. Ali was respected because he had belittled Teherani, the man who had belittled others.

Prisoners and conscripts alike came to trust him. Since Ali never said anything, he was safe to confide in. He discovered that he could reveal his thoughts not with words but by understanding. In this way he worked gradually to increase the political consciousness of the guards.

Once he confided in one of the guards, as he had confided to Taghi, "I have two eyes, a heart, wishes, just like you. Look at me. My skin is like yours, but now it is burned in so many places. I have brothers and sisters, and a father and mother. I have hurt no one.

"But after interrogation, I could not walk because the soles of my feet were swollen. I saw blood running from my rectum because of the wounds inside me. If I were a beast, as the officers tell you, how could I speak of my pains? Do beasts speak? And why would Savak bother to torture a beast? A dangerous beast would be killed, not imprisoned. Then why have they put you here to guard me? You guard me not because I'm a beast but because my head is full of ideas that you and I are brothers, and that you should not be a prison guard and I should not be a prisoner, that we are branches of the same tree, with one root. I am here because I don't want people to suffer. My heart is with you even if you point your gun at my heart." Ali had shed his intellectual arrogance. His prison experience had expanded his scope of understanding, patience and tolerance.

Ali did not resist dreaming of Sara, but he accepted the break with her, and would have accepted it even if she had not married. How could he expect their love to stretch across time zones, over seasons, oceans, mountains, over religions, cultures, diverging intentions, over the revolution itself, without snapping?

It had taken him over a year of struggle, but Ali had overcome his rage over her marrying Eric; so Ali no longer saw the marriage as a betrayal. There was nothing she could do that would change his love for her. Sara had stayed with him in Evin, as a lover stays at the bedside of a wounded man. Her memory stayed in his head, and the oxygen and glucose streaming through his braincells couldn't erase those everlasting impressions. His love clung to his heart, and the blood flushing by could not wash it away. He needed her memory to survive.

Several years went by. There was no conflict between the Sara who grew older and the Sara who remained in his memory, always young, always in love with him, always tossing her golden hair in the air, laughing for joy—the remembered Sara caught in the repetition of unforgettable moments. He remembered stepping all over her feet when she tried to teach him the bossa nova. She finally laughed, "You are not that smart when it comes to dancing, Ali."

He could distinguish the two Saras, the one who left him, and the one he left. The Sara he held trembling in the airport lived in Ali's head and tended the wounds of the torture. His mental Sara would never grow wrinkles on her face, would never be touched by another man. She would remain beside him, just as she was on that night in her bed when time stood still and then raced like a rabbit, the silky sheet moved up and down to the pace of her life, and her breast was illuminated by the moonlight.

Ali thought often of that perfect night, long gone. The memories of the past became the image of the future as he waited for the years of imprisonment to come to an end.

Ali was released in July, 1975, a year after his sentence had been up. He learned the reason later.

Ali the obnoxious troublemaker of the Columbia University Dean, the romantic revolutionary of Professor Pirooz, the irresponsible lover of Sara Patrick, the law-breaking foreign student of Dixon, the atheist son of

Fatema, the lost lamb of Dr. Keshavarz, the uncompromising interviewee of Anvari, the enemy of the Shah, the pumpkin of Teherani, the hero of political prisoners, and the leader of unknown revolutionaries was loose once more to shape the world according to his perception of justice and truth. The absolute isolation in solitary confinement, the extreme vulnerability on the torture cot, the pitch blackness of the coma, years of continuous discipline, and patient silence had simplified and solidified his youthful convictions. He was absolutely sure now that justice was the foremost virtue of society, as the truth was the prime virtue of a system of thought.

"A belief however popular must be rejected if it is untrue; likewise, an institution no matter how efficient and stable must be abolished if it is unjust. Truth and justice are intricately related, since knowing the causes of injustice is necessary for abolishing it, but to know the truth requires the freedom of inquiry. To overcome such imponderable obstacles to justice man must *create* revolution, because he could never *discover* it as a part of nature. We need not be overly concerned about philosophical problems of absoluteness, relativeness or even ambiguity in the concepts of justice, truth and freedom or difficulties inherent in practicing them, since they are violated so savagely and so frequently today. Thus a mere academic discourse about them at this juncture in history is superfluous. It is time for action, not debate." Ali wrote a few months later, as he pondered his experience in Evin.

The old debator, Ali, no longer debated even when contradicted. Back at home, he spoke as little as possible just as in Evin. To him, Iran, the whole country, was just a bigger prison, where one had to be on constant alert for informers. His eyes had become melancholic like his mother's and he kept his voice low like his father. He went about his secret business of revolution ever more methodically and thoroughly. He would never give himself up again, not even for his father. He would live or die with the revolution, he would be a part of it and he would lead it. The family respected and accepted the quiet change, his unspoken resolve.

He spent a month with the family, met comrades, drew plans and then left secretly for Beirut.

CHAPTER 16

One History
In Two Prisons

Early in the 1970's, Columbia University fell upon hard times and Professor Pirooz was let go. He then joined Georgetown University in Washington, where he could write letters to the *Washington Post* or appear for one-minute, "in-depth" interviews on radio or TV when a Middle East crisis developed. Pirooz had sarcastically said, "Only on U.S. commercial T.V. can one be both so brief and yet so in-depth."

Ali's imprisonment, the Shah's increased repression, the Pinochet-CIA inspired coup leading to the murder of the Socialist President, Salvador Allende in Santiago, Chile, and the continuation of the war in Vietnam by President Nixon, who had campaigned to end it, had all pushed the peaceful Pirooz into a radical political mood. So his lectures often turned into bitter denouncements of U.S. foreign policy. Once he asked, "If the U.S. is not the enemy of mankind for propping up so many violent despots, who is? And if the people in Latin America, Asia, and Africa do not topple the oppressive rulers, who will?"

His antagonistic remarks on religion, his radical lectures and his disregard for administrative tasks turned the dean at Georgetown against him. So the department chairman persuaded a few disgruntled students to write a letter and complain that the Professor digressed from the subject matter too often and was disrespectful to American leaders and institutions. Little by little Pirooz' file was filled with undesirable evidence. Nevertheless, the administration knew it would be difficult to get rid of Pirooz, because his teaching and publication records were far superior to those of many of the tenured faculty. Pirooz used to say that academic freedom is a sacred cow, revered in public but sacrificed in secret. Pirooz suspected he would be the next victim, and he was. He was denied tenure but did not fight the decision because he lacked organizational support and did not want to struggle alone on his own behalf.

He then accepted a position in a state college on the Canadian border of upstate New York. Before this job offer, Pirooz had considered driving a cab. How else could he earn a living? He didn't even know how to weave carpets, which even six-year-old girls in Iran could do. In his diary Pirooz wrote, "I chose the sadness of isolation to the anxiety of driving a taxi. I am no cab driver. I shall have to live as a gagged college professor in the heart of the snowbelt with my back against the frozen Canadian Border." To a friend he said, "I am a U.S. dissident, punished and sent to the Siberia of America." To overcome his loneliness and alienation, he turned to writing his undelivered lectures.

Helena had made a final trip to Chile to finish her research on proletarian literature. The couple planned to marry upon her return. In their last party together with friends, Pirooz had put a ring on her third finger—socialists exchange rings, too, he proclaimed. A noisy group witnessed their promises of unity forever.

But Helena disappeared in Santiago during the Pinochet coup, before Pirooz had left Washington. His dissatisfaction turned into despair.

Tears pooled in his eyes when he thought of Helena. Pirooz had gone to Chile, begged authorities, written letters, talked to Helena's friends who had not disappeared, had done everything to find her, but in vain. In a moment of madness he had stamped his foot in the office of the Santiago police chief and shouted, "You official murderer! Go on, make me disappear, too! Ship me to Helena!"

Racing his bike alone on the lonely back roads later in upper New York State, Pirooz' mind brooded over Helena and wandered over the past, as though he was watching a movie. He also raced over the mental notes for the book that evolved in his head, forever, unceasingly organizing them. One common thread stood out in all his ruminations: the effects of oppression on Ali, on Helena, on everyone he knew and cared about.

His daydreams raced free, but each one reached either a dead end or an infinite horizon. So he wrote in his head, "I want Helena back, which is impossible, and I want sanity for the world, which lies beyond my lifetime. Why must I face dead ends or never-ends? Can't I want something that is possible?"

Pirooz could never accept the facts. He heard Helena's sweet words once more, "I promise to be like your mama two hours a day to keep you happy." Pirooz remembered the day at the beach, with waves coming to their waists, when they vowed that their child would be raised as a Yankee revolutionary. Now all of this had gone up in smoke; the coup in Chile had killed his future with Helena, had killed their offspring. The image of Baback's face ripped apart like a mask haunted him again.

Now he stood by his window and gazed at the snowfall which was tapering off. The snow finally stopped, and the world was painted white, topped with crystals glittering under the sun. Pirooz jumped on an imaginary bike and raced alone to Santiago. In Santiago, where his imagination took him, it was a summer afternoon. The sun was hot and all was quiet. Pirooz imagined riding his bike from street to street, which were all alike. Everyone dozed against the walls, snoring.

"Where is Helena? Can someone tell me?" the Professor asked. He heard more snores. Then he raced to the Justice Ministry. No one was there, the offices were empty even of furniture, the fans cooled only each other. There was only a policeman, made of wax, sweating or melting, Pirooz couldn't tell which. "Where is the Minister of Justice? Where are the judges?" he inquired, pleading. "Where can one get justice in Santiago? I am starving for information, dying for one word," he insisted. The wax man, pointing forever towards a gigantic building, seemed to be saying, "There, up there, is the Hall of Justice."

In his reverie Pirooz raced there. He found thousands of men and women, high and low—janitors, secretaries, officers, judges, the Minister, General Pinochet, and his American advisors—all seated on the dais according to rank, holding their faces up and turning them from side to side. Pirooz picked up a microphone. "Do you hear me?" he shouted. They nodded their heads, Yes. "Where is Helena?" They shook their heads, No.

"Where is Helena? Where is my love? Where is justice?" he demanded, his voice filling the hall. They did not know or did not want to tell or did not care. He shouted, "It is her life, it is my love, it is your justice, you know!" The silence pained him so that he could no longer bear it. So he ran out, jumped on his bike that his mind had made, and raced alone back home.

* * * * *

Seasons ran after one another like rabbits in the meadow. Now, in mid-autumn 1975, Pirooz played the meditative tone poem of Sibelius, "En Saga," on his stereo for an entire Saturday. He looked out of the window at a hill laden with a carpet of colorful leaves on and off the trees and in midair. Each leaf was a flower, each tree a giant bouquet; they touched the sky with reds, yellows, oranges and browns on the horizon. Pirooz was overcome by the engrossing sight, and thought, "They are beautiful! They have souls. They must have names. Let's call that one the Orange Flyer. Look, Pirooz, look how it dances as it falls, how gently it lands, how softly it rolls over, how gracefully it dies. Another tint in the carpet. Listen to it Pirooz! It whispers a story without words. Learn, Pirooz, learn to land gently, to roll softly, to die gracefully. Look how the leaves join in death as if they were together alive. Look, there is no hesitation and no reservation on their part.

"What else? You can't change the world and you can't change yourself to accept the world. The world can't change you any more than it can itself. Bury your head in that pile of leaves until fall passes; bury it in snow until winter passes; bury it in rain until spring passes; bury it in heat until summer passes. Bury the hope of undone works, bury your ideas. Bury the hope for Helena. Wait until nothing is heard, nothing seen, until you fall, too." Pirooz felt that this was the autumn of his hopes; his ambiguities colorless and silent, his ambitions colorful and sacred, were both falling around him. Now they fell without Pirooz' resistance or reservation. His loneliness was his soothing friend. It helped him accept the fall—the falling without reservation.

* * * * *

Weeks later, with the chill of winter upon the land, Pirooz lectured about the old in America, those abandoned to Social Security, to an old-age home, their names turned into nine-digit numbers in a computer bank which sent them meager checks periodically, sometimes even on time. Later, at home, he thought, "Because I feel the chill of my own winter I have begun to discuss the politics of aging, of retirement, of dignity in dying."

Pirooz felt isolated and abandoned. He wrote, "I miss Ali, I miss Helena—the one buried alive, the other dead with no proper burial. I'm neither dead nor alive, not behind bars, yet not free. I wish Helena were here to drag me out of my loneliness and excite me with her own excitement. I miss her boldness and need her inspiration."

He gazed at the snow that filled the world, brilliant and melting. Pirooz raced alone, now and then, all in his mind. He raced from place to place, from person to person, from idea to idea, from Ali to Helena, from sadness to sadness, from tragedy to tragedy, all by himself. I'm going out of my mind, racing alone for so long to places which have disappeared, to people who have disappeared, to events and times which have all, all disappeared.

Pirooz went to the mailbox. A package was waiting for him at the post office. He cursed. "Maybe I should write my aunt not to send pistachios from Iran by registered mail. Maybe I should just let them rot in the post office." But his mouth began to water for the pistachios, for a taste of the past, for a remembrance of home.

He got into his Volkswagen Beetle. A few minutes later, Helena jumped into his mind, laughing and wiggling. He insisted, "Close your eyes. Let me, let me," and then he pushed a pistachio into her mouth. She showed her teeth, expecting a kiss, not a nut. She chewed it as she opened her big, big eyes and in her musical accent said, "It is so good, but don't worry, Pirooz. You're still my favorite Persian nut."

The gentle old lady at the post office smiled at Pirooz. He thought of his dead mother, who used to send him the nuts. "How are you today, Professor Pirooz?" asked the lady. He answered absentmindedly, "I like the snow on the treetops, not on the roads.'' She handed Pirooz a battered manila envelope postmarked Beirut. He recognized the neat printing as Ali's. He had not received a letter from Ali since Ali's imprisonment. He tightened his grip on the package and rushed out.

His heart beat faster; now he did not feel alone. He drove downhill furiously and almost lost control of the car. At home he locked the door, sat on his old couch and breathed deeply.

The letter was fifty pages long, together with printed material, most bearing the emblem of the Fedayeen Khalgh—a hammer and sickle crossed, the sickle forming part of the outline of a globe, and in the middle an arm holding aloft an automatic rifle.

Pirooz read about Ali's ordeal in Evin. He couldn't believe his eyes, but his ears filled with Ali's cry on the cot, the cry of a chicken, its neck torn by a hungry fox. He threw a page away in anger. On it Ali had described the pumpkin episode.

Pirooz thought, ''I must tell the world what the Free World has done to Ali,'' but his hasty resolve melted away as quickly as it had crystallized. He remembered his decision not to make waves for a while, to keep peace, to gather strength to find sympathetic faculty and students in his new university. There was more strength in numbers.

He read about Ali's connections with other revolutionaries in Evin and his eventual release. Ali wrote, ''I was held a year longer than my sentence. I wonder who caused it. I doubt it was Teherani, since from his perspective what would be the use of holding onto a rotting pumpkin for an extra year?!''

Pirooz continued to read. ''Aram and Zaman were both fired from their jobs, just after the birth of their second child. Everyone knew they were excellent science teachers. The principal looked up to the sky when they asked for an explanation. Their colleagues murmured their discontent over the firing, but they would only be risking their own jobs by protesting. Fortunately,'' Ali wrote, ''Aram's father is well-off, so the couple can manage until they find work again. Now they have become more active. They complain a little about their joblessness, pretending they are just looking for work, while they do political work. You notice, Pirooz, the more brutal the Shah, the more deceptive the revolutionaries.

''Parvine is thirteen now. She has grown so much in the few years I've been in prison. I couldn't believe my ears when I found out she's been writing slogans on the walls and distributing anti-Shah leaflets. It is a big problem to keep her out of trouble. She can't forget Savak's brutality to her and her grandparents. She cannot also forgive her father's murderers who were also responsible for her mother's subsequent suicide. My parents keep to themselves now, and you can see in their eyes that they have said farewell to the world and are just waiting for the train to pull out. They knew I couldn't stay for long. We all still grieve for Maryam. The family is not the same without her care and love. The years have not helped my mother to miss her less.

"Hussain is in Iraq, visiting his beloved leader, Ayatollah Khomeini. He was back home from the seminary in Qom for a while. He looks so different now, with beard, glasses and turban, but he has changed in other ways, too. He has read socialist literature and is now more tolerant of it. Hussain talks to the poor in the slums as easily as he talks to intellectuals at the university, to merchants in the bazaar, and to theologians in the mosques. He wins people in droves to Khomeini's side. I wish he were a communist.

"Rookney, our magnificent student leader, is now in the Shah's pocket. Ghotbzadeh is wandering from Libya to Lebanon to France. Bazargan and some National Front leaders are out of jail. I think that as Khomeini gets stronger they all, except for Rookney, will gravitate toward him.

"Now I'm in Beirut. I left Iran secretly. I'm training with revolutionaries from many lands. We discuss ideology, plans and revolutions. We disagree sometimes, often heatedly, but never in anger. Just enough to learn from each other. I am mastering the use of various weapons for the revolution, what the CIA terrorists call terrorism.

"Guess who I found in Beirut? Your old friend, Dr. Chameron. He's a tough and helpful revolutionary. Chameron and I are with different groups, but we see each other often. He teased me the other day. 'Ali, you're a carbon copy of Pirooz, except for the machine gun on your back.' Then he said, 'Tell Pirooz to come to Palestine, too, to train with us. He can learn to throw a grenade, and every grenade counts.'"

Pirooz smiled bitterly at Chameron's invitation. Chameron didn't know that Pirooz would never carry a gun and would never shoot. He looked out the window at the patches of snow which had survived the weak sun. He wished to be with the two men, rather than be alone in the midst of snow and despair. He read on.

"I feel positive about things," wrote Ali, "even though our foe has everything and we have only ideas and hopes. History in this little part of the world is not completely trapped by either the U.S. or the USSR. See! I remember your theory of 'one history in two prisons.' Well, I feel that neither the U.S. nor the USSR can keep history in a prison, no matter how great their power. There are too many cracks in the prison walls in this world. As man struggles, history will free itself.

"I have one more thing to say. You know I have never allowed sentimentalities to stop me. Sara used to call me 'Mr. Obnoxious' for that reason. But prison changes a person, so I make exceptions. I missed you in Evin, and I miss you now, Pirooz. I know your soul, and I love it even if it is so nonviolent. I'll try to keep you informed. I'll also hold you to your promise. Remember, you said that your self-assigned revolutionary task was to inform the world as best you could.

"I have many questions, Pirooz, but I will not yield to curiosity. Zaman told me about Helena, and your search in Santiago. I understand. I hope you fall in love once more. Ali."

Pirooz was left in a daze as he finished reading the letter. How could Ali bear such torture and remain so upbeat about life and the revolution which could destroy him or be years away? How could anyone in Evin miss me? I thought prisoners only missed their own limbs, their own spirits, their own manhood, their own dignity, not their own friends. He put himself in Ali's place in prison for a moment; he wanted to run away, to step out of this world which could allow such events. He knew he could not endure the hardships, sidestep the hazards, survive the dangers, stay undigested in the belly of Savak, remain sane and still have an optimistic view of man's fate. Ali was unique; he was also a survivor.

Pirooz had come to respect Ali more and more, almost revering him, even though he still didn't know him well. Perhaps no one could know Ali, Pirooz thought, not even Ali. With his simplicity and complexity, his obviousness and mysteriousness, his tenderness and crudity, his originality and orthodoxy, his impetuousness and tenacity, he was a unity of opposites, Pirooz thought.

Who was Ali? he wondered. He was the one who fell in love, then threw it to the winds to fight for a distant cause. Pirooz circled his coffee table, talking to himself.

He knows my two most urgent needs. He wishes me a new love as though certain Helena is dead and reminds me to inform the world. I try to fall in love again, but Helena is too present, too attractive, too alive, too jealous in my mind. "Keep informing the world, Pirooz." His mind heated up. He decided to deliver his lecture tomorrow on the causes of violence. Ali's letter had softened his resolve not to make waves.

*   *   *   *   *

The next day Pirooz walked decisively to the podium of the lecture hall. "Today I want to tell you that exploitation is the main cause of criminal violence at home and political violence abroad."

After a pause Pirooz continued, "Without production, society would die; so much is obvious. Using nature, labor, and capital, which is also accumulated labor, a capitalist produces commodities for sales and profit. To protect his profits he creates supportive governments, self-serving laws, regulations and ethics, and uses the mass media, schools and pulpits to distract workers' attention from the essential fact that it is their labor which makes the rich rich.

"However, all this is not sufficient to maintain the status quo. Capitalists also resort to the threat of poverty and use of force. For example, the unionization in America was a prolonged bloody affair."

A student, agitated, raised her hand. "What is the threat of poverty?"

"Poverty is a form of violence because it causes hunger pangs, homelessness, winter without heat, sickness untreated, nights without light, isolation, insecurity, indignity, hopelessness, discontent, frustration and anger. A worker, a scientist or any wage earner who opposes capitalism or, God forbid, refuses to do the boss's bidding will be fired. And if the worker refuses to learn his lesson and is fired again by another boss, then no employer will recommend him to the next. He will be in effect blacklisted and banished to the hell of poverty. He may lose his car, his home, even his family. The job insecurity and the threat of poverty hangs over the heads of all wage earners, keeping laborers in line, censoring, and controlling intellectual workers and increasing profit. No wonder widespread poverty is a permanent fixture of affluent America, despite all the wars on poverty. Note that the bosses act like gods because they demand to know the employees' past." Pointing at the students Pirooz declared, "Future wage earners of America, beware and watch your intentions! If you commit the ultimate sin of opposing capitalism you shall be condemned to the hell of poverty created by the capitalists in the land of plenty."

Pirooz took a deep breath and continued, "In general, the poor are easily kept poor. Aside from the working poor, for minorities, immigrants, single mothers, the very young or very old workers, poverty is imposed by the circumstances of their birth. These people are cast out of American affluence. Yet our leaders blame the victims of poverty for lacking initiative, skills, and moral fiber. So the poor are not only deprived, they're insulted without a chance to reply. Have you ever seen a poor person tell his story on TV? Why not? There are tens of millions of poor in America, millions hungry and homeless."

A student raised his voice. "Why don't they work like everybody else?"

Pirooz replied, "Don't forget, two and a half million fulltime workers are also under the poverty line. With their families they make ten million Americans. In addition there are millions of poor unemployed who cannot find a job or have lost hope and given up for good."

Pirooz continued, "I've shown before that social security and welfare payments do not equalize income, as it is claimed. Their main task is to prevent food riots, the same as a church soup kitchen." He raised his voice. "If poverty is violence against the poor or at least a threat, what is the reaction to it? Note that for every action there is a reaction, in physics and in society."

No one said anything. Pirooz was not relaxed or witty today.

Something was eating him, and the students sensed it. Then he answered his own question, "The reaction of some of the poor to their poverty is crime—burglary, auto theft, mugging, murder and rape."

Pirooz continued, "Strong evidence links poverty and crime in America. The logic is simple: their mediocre education and propaganda have robbed the poor of the ability to understand the root causes of their poverty. The poor do not organize to fight capitalism. Instead they strike back at society individually or in small groups with crime. Another role of the media and politicians is to divert attention by blaming the individual or drug traffic originating from abroad, not capitalism. They never explain why there is more crime relative to population in the U.S. than in Western or Eastern Europe or black Africa." Pirooz thought to himself, "What do I mean by black Africa?"

Then raising his voice once more he lectured, "Given the gradual rise in permanent unemployment and in poverty, I predict that we will soon have a million Americans in prisons and many more running away from the law. Do you think a society that imprisons so many of its citizens is unblemished?" Pirooz could not have imagined that in ten years one out of every thirty-five Americans would become a law breaker.

A student raised her hand. "White collar crime can't be due to poverty, Professor."

Pirooz said, "No, but it is due to relative poverty, the so-called 'keeping up with the Joneses.' A person making fifty thousand a year may feel deprived relative to one making a million a year, so he steals to get the same things. But he risks little, since the probability of detection, apprehension and conviction is very low for white collar crimes. And even so, the punishments are minimal. Are there any more questions?"

A student stood up. "You claim that all crimes are for money?"

"Poverty is the main factor I propose, but not the only one. There are other causes, but the violence of poverty imposed on people induces violence of the poor—crime. This is not to say there aren't other avenues of escape from poverty, or that every poor person becomes a criminal. Look, the government's own statistics show that due to poor nutrition, sanitation and housing, there is a higher mortality rate, a higher rate of sickness, mental retardation, and a higher rate of poverty and crime for children of the poor. Is the child responsible for these statistical tragedies? Remember, the child didn't make this world, the capitalists did. Did you choose your parents, your neighborhood? Let's face it, our way of life in America, in spite of the wealth and glitter, is full of poverty, crime, drug use and overcrowded prisons. Do you think Americans are genetically more inclined to crime? Of course not," Pirooz answered his own question again. "It is the social and economic condition which helps to breed crime in general. It is also the constant pressure on the young and the old to achieve, pangs of job insecurity, meaningless commercial existence, boredom, and struggle for personal identity in hopeless situations like slums that impels individuals toward drugs. But our politicians blame some unknown farmer of opium or coca overseas as the source of our drug problems. Note that job insecurity, anxiety, threat of poverty, boredom, and commercial existence are not coded in the individual's DNA but in the DNA of capitalism.''

A favorite student of Pirooz asked, "What should workers do about the chronic job insecurity, unemployment and threat of poverty?"

Pirooz answered, "They should unite in one super union and take over."

"Take over what?" a shocked student demanded.

"Take over major companies, universities, and government."

"How?" a student asked from the back row.

"It can be done democratically, peacefully and constitutionally. Remember white collar and blue collar wage earners together constitute the great majority of voters in America."

His hand trembling Pirooz, too agitated to continue, said, "The causes of violence at the international level will be discussed in the next meeting." He then uncharacteristically ignored students rushing to him and walked off.

A student ran after him, "If poverty causes crime then there must be more criminals in India."

Pirooz absentmindedly replied, "The poor are not that conscious of their poverty in India and there are fewer economic targets for the poor to attack. They also join radical political parties which do win elections. But wait for the masses in India to awaken and to rise!"

Two days later, still resolved to expose the truth, Pirooz plunged into a discussion of the causes of violence overseas, by delivering a summary of his "One History in Two Prisons" lecture.

"After World War Two, U.S. domination of the Third World replaced that of the European colonial powers, and the U.S. promptly imposed its time-tested Latin American policy of domination, rule through local dictatorships, on the Third World. For example, in 1954 the French withdrew in defeat from Indochina, and the U.S. stepped in immediately.

"Statistical evidence shows that U.S. multinational companies use the Third World as a source of cheap raw materials and labor, as markets for U.S. goods, and as a source of great profits. Imagine, the United Fruit Company pays only forty cents a day to banana pickers overseas. And since many countries are indebted to the U.S. or our banks, whenever the interest rate is raised internationally the indebted foreign governments or businesses pass the extra cost on to the local poor as higher taxes or prices. So through interest rates and inflation, capitalists can also rob the poor and do it better than burglars cracking a safe." Pirooz smiled at his comparison.

"Domestically, inflation is created to push ordinary citizens into a higher income tax bracket, except for the rich, who pay little or no taxes. Then the extra revenues are spent for weapons to enrich the owners of the U.S. arms industry, and the weapons thus manufactured are used to silence revolutionaries around the world. So our taxes are used to enrich the arms manufacturers or else to create the so-called 'stable world,' so that the U.S. multinational corporations can operate freely and exploit the poor of the Third World.

"Luxury and starvation exist side by side here and abroad. No other species allows such unequal treatment of its own members as the capitalist beast does. Now do you still wonder why there is so much political unrest in the world and why so much of our taxes must be spent to keep everyone in line?"

A student raised his hand. "Professor Pirooz, you just suggested it yourself. By the U.S. supporting local dictators or by direct intervention."

Pirooz replied, "Oh yes, but to compare the domestic and the international situations, government terror creates fear in the Third World just the same as the threat of poverty creates fear in the U.S. These fears are used by governments for political control."

A student in the front row ventured, "Aren't foreigners afraid of poverty, too?"

Pirooz said, "Poverty is so widespread in the Third World that it cannot be as much of a threat as in the U.S.; the people are used to being poor. Instead, torture and the threat of death are tools of control there. In Guatemala, Vietnam, Chile, Iran and elsewhere, the U.S. supports repressive regimes. When a revolution has won self-determination for its people, the U.S. has stepped in to crush it, to turn the people's victory into defeat.

"In summary, the U.S. is trying to keep progress and even the history of many countries in a big prison called the Free World."

Someone from the back row shouted, "What do you mean by jailing history?"

Pirooz answered, "Stopping liberation movements like that of blacks in South Africa. If you were a non-white worker there, what would you think of the U.S. government, U.S. businesses, U.S. labor unions and U.S. media who actively or passively support racist policies or ignore them, and U.S. citizens who remain indifferent, or make a profit there?"

"What about the USSR and its satellites?" a student interjected.

Pirooz responded, "I am glad you asked this question."

"I call this lecture 'History in Two Prisons' because in Eastern Block countries questioning the system or the leaders is punished severely. During the Stalin reign even artistic, literary and musical freedoms were crushed, and many political dissidents were put to death. By now freedom of expression there has improved somewhat, but not sufficiently. Soviets have a long way to go also.''

A student sounding concerned asked, "How many repressive governments does our government sponsor, anyhow?''

Pirooz cleared his throat and picked up a sheet of paper. "Many. I'll read some. Pinochet in Chile, Strossner in Paraguay, Somoza in Nicaragua, Baby Doc Duvalier in Haiti, Mobutu in Zaire, the Shah in Iran, King Faisal in Saudi Arabia, Thieu in South Vietnam, King Hassan in Morocco, Suharto in Indonesia, Chiang in Taiwan on and on and on! At this moment, as I talk to you, tens of thousands of political prisoners are kept in inhuman conditions, and thousands are being tortured. The sun never sets on territories where the U.S. is not behind some government that conducts torture.'' Pirooz was nervous. His face was red; the fingers of his right hand trembled holding the sheet.

A student said, "You mentioned that everyone is responsible—"

Pirooz interrupted, "Let me give you an example of our responsibility. U.S. workers extract minerals and transport them to factories where more workers forge them into warplanes and bombs. The process is long and complex, demanding the cooperation of workers, engineers and managers, all of them just making a living. While these millions of Americans are awake or asleep, the planes drop the bombs on Vietnam or Cambodia, killing and maiming peasants, women and children, and poisoning the country with Agent Orange. Now, do these millions of Americans think of themselves as killers? If not, who killed over a million Vietnamese? Only the government leaders and soldiers? Have you ever heard a Vietnamese hurt an American outside of their own territories? They fight us because we have trampled their home. Would we not do the same against an occupation army? Don't you see that capitalism through control of the media and schools has robbed us of our objectivity, sense of fairness and lobotomized our consciences?''

A student rose and angrily said, "You've insulted the U.S. government, business, our allies, and our way of life, and still you claim that people can't speak their minds or fight the system. How is that?''

"My comments are not insults or opinions but facts,'' Pirooz retorted. Then he paused. "I was denied tenure at another University, or simply fired. I am now an American dissident, like the Soviet dissidents you hear about all the time, except that the newspapers and TV here ignore my case.''

The class fell silent, like a calm before a storm. Anger filled some of the heads; Pirooz was popular among quite a few students. Pirooz pointed at the shocked students. "I ask each one of you to search our library, to see if you can find any error in the facts I have presented and my conclusions concerning the sources of domestic and international violence. We have violence because we have unresolved conflicts between the exploiters and the exploited and not because some individuals are inherently bad. Remember the reasons for the American revolution against the British!

"Anyhow it is most important that you be critical of your professors' work, and that includes mine. And if you agree with my conclusions, then think about why my words are so hard to digest and why I was fired for saying them."

As he walked upstairs to his office, Pirooz heard two voices from the hall. "He's the best teacher I've had." "No, he isn't. He should be fired from here, too."

Now an idea burst into Pirooz' head. "Why did I entitle this lecture 'History in Two Prisons'? Not only do the U.S. and the USSR try to hold history in their zones or prisons, but the U.S. is a rayon-walled prison itself. Mustn't I be my own censor or fear joblessness or rejection by my colleagues? Why do I have to fear? Are my ideas that dangerous? I am for food for the hungry, housing for the homeless, health care for the sick, good education for deprived inner city children. I am for full employment, for a clean environment, for peace, for consumer protection, for job security and for participatory democracy in the work place as well as in the government. I am for the media that tells the truth and lets the socialists air their views too. I am for the right of other nations to choose their own form of government without interference by the U.S.A. or USSR." Then Pirooz sighed despairingly. "If pleading for love of neighbor and justice put Christ on the cross, any other idea can put a little fellow like me out in the streets. True, I wouldn't lose my limbs or life, but if I lose my job I would lose my podium, my mortgaged house, automobile, electricity and telephone services, health, and dignity."

Pirooz grabbed a yellow pad and began to write. "Ali has freed himself, and now he is hard at work to free others, to free history. I am still struggling to free myself, to be able to express my beliefs. In the U.S. I'll never succeed in freeing myself, but if Ali succeeds, then I can go home.

"There is so much deprivation, pain, so many crushed ideas, hopes and wants in the U.S. Where are the revolutionaries? The silent majority is not silent, it's dead; only death can cast its silence for so long a time. Half of the people don't even bother to vote. Why do people permit their government to support torture and death all around the world, while they march against issues like animal cruelty? Isn't Ali as good as a dog? Why has no one marched against cruelty to Ali? Goddamn it. Damn it, I am so angry," Pirooz screamed—a primal scream. "No one knows Ali; he is only an unknown revolutionary."

The professor threw the pencil on the desk and walked away talking to himself. What was the use? he asked himself. What was he writing this for, and for whom? How could students disregard the press, the priests, the President, all respectable sources of information, and believe a foreigner, a mere professor who had difficulty pronouncing 'th'? Pirooz understood his students' confusion and anger. How could he reach any one of them, much less reach and tell the truth to millions of them? Pirooz wondered.

At home, as the sun hid behind a patch of cloud, Pirooz remembered the tension in his classroom. He fell on the couch and talked to himself, becoming more practical. "I must send a letter to Ali. He is my only link with reality, the only person I can tell without reservation what is on my mind."

The Professor began to write. "Dear Ali, I am delighted you are out of the Shah's clutches. It is sad that we must become exiles before we can write to one another. You remind me to keep my promise to 'inform the world.' And I will remind you to fight to change the world. This is division of labor! You have all the risks and I have all the indifference thrown at me.

"I long to come home, to visit the family, the men and women who have grown up only in letters and pictures, never in sound or vision or touch. It is now more than twenty years since I left. I want to debate with Hussain, play another game of chess with you, throw Zaman's boys in the air and catch them squealing with delight. I used to carry Zaman on my shoulders, you know, and tell her stories when she was little. I want to meet her husband Aram. She is a revolutionary even in her private life. Why are we deprived of the joys of being close to our families?

"My hopes of getting to Iran as long as the Shah is around were dashed when I took a ten-minute plunge into the sea of American television recently. Savak will never forgive me. Let me tell you.

"Barbara Walters interviewed the Shah and Empress Farah for an hour on television. After a protest from the Iranian Students Association, the network offered ten quick minutes for the opposition. So I was invited to be on the Today Show, a national morning broadcast, together with Dr. Fatemi. I had never met him before. He is the brother of Hussain Fatemi, Mossadegh's foreign minister who was executed by the Shah after the 1953 coup.

"I had my chance to inform the world, and I did my best. Barbara Walters tried to talk about the brain drain from Iran to America, but Fatemi and I kept to the issue of the Shah's legitimacy and the repression in Iran. I talked about the corruption of the regime, and the Shah's submission to U.S. interests. Fatemi held up a United Nations report which implicated court officials and the Shah's family in heroin smuggling. I tried to bring up U.S. complicity, but we ran out of our ten minutes. So the damage to the Shah's public relations campaign and to my hope to return home is complete.

"A few days after the TV appearance, the Immigration Office began to harrass me by delaying a routine extension of my green card. I still have to make trips to the Immigration Office. They didn't tell me what is wrong.

Now I am also waiting to hear from the IRS.

"The day after the interview, most of the faculty treated me as if I had smuggled heroin, not the Shah's sisters and associates. I received threatening calls and letters telling me to shut up or ship out. And all of this because I tried to inform the world.

"I was fired from Georgetown for promoting the poor and the Bible, among other things. One day I held a banana up and asked 'Where do you think this comes from?' When no one answered I said, 'The sweetness of this banana comes from the sweat of exploited laborers working for U.S. companies in Central America.' Then I held up a Bible and said, 'Each of us has so many books, or access to millions in the libraries, but a peasant in Latin America must save for years if he wishes to buy a Bible.' Then I said, 'It would be in the interest of U.S. companies to give away free Bibles so toilers could compare their suffering with the crucifixion of Christ and feel better.' Then I said, 'By our indifference we are conspiring in international crimes which our government supports.' Believe it or not, one day I wrote on the blackboard, 'Property is theft, profit is burglary, interest is fraud.'

"In one of my lectures I said, 'The words uttered by the administration of the school about humanity, fairness, professional ethics, academic freedom and true scholarship are not quite so. I've looked and looked, but I found none of these or God at Georgetown.' I also revealed in my last lecture that the dean had been a CIA employee, and perhaps still was. And in my last meeting with the dean I told him, 'I want to teach social science, not social science fiction.'

"I am now exiled thrice: from Teheran, from New York, and from Washington. I am not even violent! From here I can be thrown down the Niagara Falls. That will shut me up for good.

"I am so sorry for Dr. Keshavarz and Fatema, those two most innocent souls, tormented because their children dared to take human rights seriously. But don't be dismayed, Ali (Look who's talking!). I'll never advise you again to be cautious.

"You see how from paragraph to paragraph my mood changes. It's like my days, sometimes full of hope, sometimes full of dismay.

"I have a few items to report. Eric Saunders started a consulting business in the Middle East. He's the executive director, based in Teheran. Can you believe it? The two of us in exile and him living in our country. A colleague of mine told me that Professor Wharton at Columbia, with connections to the CIA, is one of the directors.

"Now guess what? I got a call from Saunders himself. It seems that he found out my days at Georgetown were numbered, so he asked me to join his firm as a senior research analyst. Now listen to this! The salary would be 'more than three times'—his words—what I was making at the university, and I'd have a generous expense account for international travel. I asked him what I'd have to do. He told me he wanted some political forecasting in the Middle East and particularly Iran, things he could sell to corporate clients who were planning substantial investments and needed to know that they would be safe from a 'crazy man like Qaddafy,' again his words, taking over. I told him, just to see what he would say, that I was persona non grata. He said I would be treated like a prince. So I conclude that he must have connections with the Shah's court, too.

"I suppose the Establishment thinks I've softened up and I'm ripe for falling into their net. But I'm not, I can't be. I'm sure Saunders' outfit is a CIA front, and the CIA would love to have me show them where the fires smoulder and what fuels them, so they can design covert operations to stop them. It's amazing how scholarly forecasting can be used for covert operations.

"Sara and her son, Cyrus, have been in Teheran since 1972. We were not in touch for a couple of years after her wedding, but later she wrote to me and we have since become friends again. Sara calls me when she visits her family in the U.S. A few weeks ago she called and said the Americans in Teheran are bores, but she loves the hospitality of her Iranian friends. She and Eric live on Fereshteh Avenue in the Mahmoodiye borough, close to the mountains. She said Cyrus, who is six now, speaks Farsi better than English. Already he knows the alphabet. His friends are Iranian kids. I asked why he has an Iranian name, and she just laughed and said that she named him after Cyrus Vance, hoping he'd become a diplomat, too. When I pressed her she said it was also an American name, but she also said the boy prefers the Iranian pronunciation to rhyme with Pirooz.

"Sara knows you were in prison, but she said that Eric had told her it was for life. I wonder how he gets the misinformation and why he passes it on to Sara. Maybe he is still insecure after all these years.

"On her last trip she told me that only Cyrus and the fact that Eric is often away on business hold the marriage together. She had never opened up to me like that before. She didn't ask about you, and I could tell she was afraid of what she might hear. She said she is sure the Americans in Iran are up to no good, saying it as if she knows something specific I don't know or that she couldn't tell me. She visited me in Washington once, and now she's invited me to visit the family in Baltimore next time she comes. I may do so. I'm curious to know about Cyrus, and I don't know why.

"Your report about Parvine disturbs me. She could get shot for distributing leaflets. We must find a way to stop her. Maybe you can send her here to school. They don't shoot at you here for leaflets, thank God.

"In case you haven't read, the U.S. press has begun to report the severe health damage of Agent Orange on U.S. soldiers, but not a word about the millions of Vietnamese on whom and whose farms the chemical was sprayed. The chemical lasts for a long time.

"My greetings to all of our comrades. Thanks for the news about Ghotbzadeh and the rest. I hear Yazdi is back in the U.S. doing pharmaceutical research. Ask Chameron, Is it God's will that we have this world and all its problems? If God consulted no one and made all decisions himself, then he is a Supreme Fascist and if he did consult, who was the advisor? Don't let Chameron get the best of you but return his needlings. Extend my best regards to him. He is like Hussain, a wonderful person. Take care of yourself. Best wishes, Pirooz."

Pirooz felt more relaxed, because Ali was safer carrying a gun and so the Shah was a bit less safe. He played the Poulenc Concerto for Two Pianos on his stereo and sat back to listen. The two pianos sounded like lovers, arguing, reconciling, dancing and making love. The ballerina he imagined gliding across the floor was Helena, covered in silver and blue, like a feather in flight. Pirooz imagined springing to his feet, taking to the air, leaving his problems on the floor, but the leap was a flop, so he left Helena alone with the earth, which proved to be a flawless partner by dint of the laws of physics. On her toes, Helena's weight was precisely balanced by the push of the floor, the molecules in contact squeezing the exact amount of counterforce with an equal force. Electricity balanced with gravity. Then her right leg moved backward to the fourth position and pushed off with one foot, her arms coming in to speed the turn; she rotated ten times before gently coming to rest. No one had ever done more than eight turns. At the end, a bouquet of roses in her arms, Helena leapt upward, hung in the air for a moment of weightlessness, and let the roses fall around her. The earth balanced her momentum and responded with a saute, altering its orbit by one trillionth of an atom's width. No one could even notice that orbital change except the Professor, who choreographed the dance in his head.

Chapter 17

Fedayeen

In June, 1963, the Shah's troops killed and injured thousands of demonstrators throughout Iran who were demanding Islamic or constitutional rule. Ali's brother, Abbas, was one of the victims.

The mullahs were protesting because the Shah's land reform policy confiscated religious property and his modernization measures shrank their political influence. In retaliation in the city of Qom, some theology students were pushed off the seminary roof or roofs of homes, in full view of their wives, children and neighbors. The message was in the blood that reddened the cobblestones: neither the people nor God could save the clergy; gravity pulled them down and the ground broke their bones just as it broke the furniture thrown after them. The regime killed men of God to show the might of the Shah.

Ayatollah Khomeini responded by starting an ideological holy war. He proclaimed that "The Shah is hand in hand with the American Satan warring with God and the Moslem nation of Iran." The Shah's rule was illegitimate on both Islamic and constitutional grounds, the Ayatollah declared. Islam had no provision for hereditary rule, and absolute monarchy had supposedly been abolished in Iran.

The Shah then broke the law and tradition by imprisoning Khomeini. When the other Grand Ayatollahs intervened, the Shah sent Ayatollah Khomeini into exile in Turkey; soon Khomeini settled in the holy city of Najaf in Iraq. The Shah decided he dared not kill Khomeini, a decision he was to regret later.

The massacre of 1963 shattered the last hope of compromise. In their minds, the people convicted the Shah of murder. Some who had earlier demanded a return to the constitution now began to demand the ouster of the Shah. Small revolutionary groups sprang up underground, merged and grew to fight fire with fire.

Once more the Shah turned to the CIA for advice to counter the "red revolution" of the communists and the "black revolution" of the mullahs, as he labeled them. So the CIA formulated the famous "White Revolution," a grandiose plan to modernize Iran and to establish democracy, but the plan lacked credibility with the people and brought neither democracy nor real progress.

Some of the ex-Tudeh party and National Front members united in a revolutionary party. In 1967, this group was nearly destroyed when a trusted comrade turned informer. The leaders, including Jazany and Sooraky, were arrested and imprisoned in Evin, where Ali met them.

Without its leaders but with courage and sacrifice, the group rebuilt itself. The survivors retreated to the mountains of Gilan Province north of Teheran. They would become the heroes of the first armed uprising against the Shah at Siahkal in February, 1971.

In 1970, two revolutionary groups merged to carry out urban and rural guerrilla warfare. After each strike against the Shah's apparatus, they distributed leaflets taking responsibility in the name of the Fedayeen Khalgh, the People's Sacrificers. This name had been born in Evin at Ali's suggestion. Savak continued to capture unknown revolutionaries and dispose of them; weren't the prisoners martyred for the people?

At first the Fedayeen numbered no more than two hundred. They studied Mao, Che Guevara, Regis Debray and their guerrilla tactics, and laid the ideological and organizational foundation for a Marxist-Leninist revolutionary party. They read Comrade Ahmadzadeh's book, *Armed Struggle: Strategy and Tactics,* which urged the revolutionaries to unite and start the armed struggle in the cities and the countryside.

The Fedayeen's initial objective was to demoralize the Shah's forces and inspire the masses through both urban and rural guerrilla war, and ultimately to spark a revolution. The prime goals of the revolution were to oust the Shah's regime, end American influence in Iran, and create a socialist republic.

There were disagreements on tactics, but the group remained united nevertheless by its goals. Initially, most radical Fedayeen advocated an immediate strike against the regime while others advised more caution and more preparation. Ali had unsuccessfully argued for patient underground work. This ideological dispute did not harm the group's unity in action, however. The "mountain guerrillas" preferred to emulate Mao and Ho Chi Minh and struggle in the countryside, with ample opportunity for attack and retreat, while the "urban guerrillas" thought the Shah's apparatus must be attacked at its head in the cities. Despite other differences, such as disagreements on the correct relationship of the party to the people, on the problem of unity with other opposition groups, on the nature of the revolution and on the resolution of ideological and practical dilemmas, a consensus emerged. The Fedayeen took sides with the workers and peasants, who had no say in the affairs of state, in their own lives, or even in the programs of other national parties.

The Fedayeen looked to Cuba for lessons, where Castro's small guerrilla band attacked an army post and then withdrew to the mountains to draw the masses like a magnet. But the Fedayeen admitted later they had misunderstood the lesson of the Cuban revolution by overestimating the importance of the armed struggle and underestimating the role of the people. They must not leave the masses behind.

Despite their socialist orientation, the Fedayeen disapproved of the increasing cooperation between the Shah and the USSR. The Fedayeen were communists, true, but they were Iranian communists. They believed the USSR and other socialist countries should help them, not the Shah.

When the Fedayeen considered penetrating Savak, they found it too risky. However, revolutionary justice caught up with Savakis who penetrated the Fedayeen; they were assassinated. In 1970 Savak caught many Fedayeen, who were tortured and killed, but the Fedayeen again rebuilt.

The organization of the Fedayeen had three layers. The outer layer of Fedayeen sympathizers recruited relatives, neighbors and fellow workers or students, quietly and slowly. Some infiltrated groups like the National Front, to influence them and to recruit members to the Fedayeen.

The second layer of the Fedayeen was a semi-secret group of individuals who were more deeply involved than the sympathizers but who led ordinary lives and were not prepared to risk everything. Some were watched by Savak because of their past political activities, so their presence in the secret core, the third layer, could jeopardize the whole organization. This second layer supported the core by fundraising, distributing leaflets, writing, obtaining supplies, and, in a crisis, hiding Fedayeen fugitives.

The central core was secret, made up of full-time revolutionaries. The core Fedayeen were organized into small teams with specific tasks. In addition to fighting teams, they had communications teams, technical teams and supply teams who were responsible for information, medical care, maintenance of houses and cars, making false documents and manufacturing explosives.

The core members were expected to be Marxist-Leninists and apply the ideology to Iranian conditions, and to master the use of firearms and the tactics of attack, retreat and counterattack, karate and mountain climbing. They studied the state apparatus to disrupt it and to assassinate officials who had committed crimes against the people. This secret core made the decisions, issued directives, delegated authority and held all power. Information necessary for their decisions moved from the outer two layers into the core. A core member could perform tasks assigned to other layers, but not the reverse. The underground core had to hold the other two layers together, as gravity holds the crust of the earth and the atmosphere.

The mountain guerrillas studied geography and the life of the peasants, recruited and mobilized the peasants, and worked to create a liberated socialist zone. The urban guerrillas surveyed banks to rob and police and military stations to bomb or to confiscate arms, published newsletters, learned from the workers and recruited them, and planned urban warfare.

Most things the Fedayeen needed, they had to steal. In the summer of 1970, Fedayeen guerrillas "expropriated" $20,000 from the national bank and later hit the Iran-English Bank in Teheran for $50,000. They also expropriated funds from the Vanak Bank, took a jewelry store in Meshhed, and stole a printing press in Isfahan.

Fedayeen also bombed government installations in retaliation for specific cases of repression.

The rough terrain and thick vegetation of the Gilan Province on the slopes of the Elburz Mountain in northern Iran was an ideal location for guerrilla war. Mirza Kuchak Khan, a revolutionary, had waged a guerrilla war against the Shah's father in the same region. The Shah could not reach the Fedayeen there, but the Fedayeen could reach the peasants and even vacationers nearby. The peasants of this province were better off than elsewhere, but land reform had left many with a twenty-five year debt, a long mortgage for short lives.

In February, 1971, Savak arrested two Fedayeen in Siahkal. The mountain guerrillas, fearing that their supply sources and plans might be revealed, attacked a gendarme outpost in Siahkal to free their comrades and capture arms and ammunition. In the battle, three gendarmes were killed and nine U.S. rifles and one machine gun were captured, but there was no sign of the captured Fedayeen.

The Shah understood that the insurrection was a challenge to his monopoly of the means of violence, so he acted with a vengeance. Soon a large military force surrounded the guerrillas. In the end the Shah boasted of victory in a display of thirty dead and thirteen captured guerrillas. The state-censored radio, television and newspapers failed to report, however, that sixty of the Shah's officers and many soldiers were killed and much equipment destroyed or lost to the guerrillas.

Relentless torture killed the captured guerrillas; the regime wanted information on the remaining rebels. General Farsio then ordered the corpses hanged. Soon the machine guns of the Fedayeen, in turn, put Farsio to death.

Such gallant battles of the outnumbered Fedayeen sparked hope in many hearts. The political significance of the Siahkal insurrection loomed as majestic as the Elburz that witnessed the heroic deeds of the Fedayeen: it was the beginning of the revolution. To crush any hopes of further insurrection, the Shah ordered the arrest of National Front and religious leaders. The Iranian Student Association was declared illegal and its members were subject to harsh punishment. As a result, the anti-Shah students abroad began to wear masks in fear of retribution against their families at home.

American TV broadcasters failed to explain why students had to wear masks while engaged in legal anti-Shah demonstrations in the U.S. The students feared the Shah anywhere in the world.

Siahkal was a costly lesson for the inexperienced Fedayeen guerrillas. They had underestimated the intensity, scope, and quickness of the Shah's reaction and had overestimated the overall loyalty of the local population. Tactically they had been slow to retreat to more protected sanctuaries.

Ali realized that Siahkal was qualitatively different from the previous rural uprisings, bank robberies and hijackings because it directly challenged the might of the Shah. And although the Siahkal defeat ruined years of planning and destroyed the mountain guerrilla movement, with it the Fedayeen conquered its fear of the Shah. Siahkal did not end the armed struggle; it cleared the way for more.

The insurrection also induced a great deal of soul-searching and debate in opposition groups. Tudeh, for example, called it suicide. Nevertheless, the Fedayeen struck back, attacking a police station in Gholak, north of Teheran, and robbing several banks; and in response to the Shah's twenty-five century celebration of monarchy, they set explosions rocking the country awake.

In June of 1973, an uprising at Evin prison ended in the torture and execution of most of the imprisoned Fedayeen leaders. The Fedayeen did not believe in the hereafter, but they did believe that the martyred could not be truly dead if their goals were being realized. Their graves were unmarked, true, but these unknown graves held men and women known for their knowledge, their courage, their honesty, their struggle for justice, their search for truth, and their vision. By murdering them, the Shah had only made them more known, more admired, more loved, more emulated, more alive. Is not the publication of their names in English the proof that the men of unmarked graves are becoming better known all the time? On the other hand, would anyone write about the courage, honesty and vision of the Shah, without pay, or without having gained from his rule, even though His Majesty lies under a great tombstone known to all? Would anyone ever admire the CIA agents or their superiors who forced this Shah upon the nation of Iran?

Ali was alive, and so were the Fedayeen, and so were hundreds of new members. The Shah could kill individuals, but not the movement. Once he was released from Evin, Ali worked on farms and helped to build houses for Palestinian refugees. Ali also contacted representatives of Libya and South Yemen, and so arms and money trickled to the Fedayeen, freeing them temporarily from the need to rob banks.

Late in November, 1975, a building in Beirut was bombed, blowing many to pieces. A few days later, a Savak agent inspected a copy of the telegram that reached Dr. Keshavarz in Teheran. A PLO commander, a lieutenant of Dr. Habash, wrote that Ali had been killed and his body, burnt beyond recognition, buried in a Druze cemetery outside Beirut.

Savak gleefully spread the word that Ali was dead, in order to deal another blow to the crippled Fedayeen. "Doctor" Teherani, vengeful that Ali had fooled him at Evin, threw a party which he called Ali's welcoming party to hell.

Dr. Keshavarz had resigned himself to a life filled with tragedies; the old man's sadness was constant and deep. Fatema was visiting her sister in the holy city of Meshhed. She prayed daily at the tomb of the eighth Imam and did not hear the news. The "wall" of prayer she had constructed around herself helped her keep her peace and sanity.

Dr. Keshavarz attended a memorial service a week later. On his way out of the mosque, a woman, her face covered in a black chador, slipped an envelope into his hand and disappeared into the crowd of mourners. Dr. Keshavarz read the letter later, smiled faintly, and then prayed for a long time. The next day he left for Meshhed to reach his wife before anyone told her of Ali's death.

Ali's handwriting said, "I am alive and unharmed, but I must remain underground. I will arrange to see you and Mother in Rayy City at the shrine of Shah Abdul-Azim. No one must know of this except Mother, Hussain and Zaman. I break our rules to see you because Savak thinks I am dead. The more you mourn my death the more secure I will feel living. I miss you. Destroy this letter as soon as you read it."

On February 11, 1976, Ali crossed the border over desolate hills into Iran. He began a new life as an underground Fedayeen in Teheran. He knew the streets and alleys of his home town, and best of all he knew the people. He adopted a new identity, and only a few comrades knew his true one.

Ali kept his promise and met his parents secretly. He met his brother and sister in a mosque later. Ali was one dead Fedayeen who could enjoy the luxuries of homemade cookies and occasional watching of Zaman's children from a distance.

The underground Fedayeen team houses were scattered in Teheran and other cities. The houses served as arsenals, as print shops, as centers to distribute leaflets, as sanctuaries and places to hold meetings, work and live without risking anyone but Fedayeen themselves.

Ali was assigned to a house in the suburb of Teheran-e-Now west of the city close to Doshan Tapeh air base. The location was unsuspected, a Fedayeen nest under the Shah's nose. Hamid Ashraf, former chief of communications and now the overall Fedayeen leader, lived there, along with the Shaygans and their two boys, Nasser, eleven, and Ajang, thirteen, and another man. Taghi, the guard who had befriended Ali at Evin, and his wife Zahra lived there, too. Ali's brother-in-law Aram, while living at home, provided logistical support to sustain the team house.

Hamid Ashraf was of medium build with light skin, his eyebrows connected across his nose. A large brown birthmark just under his eyebrow over his nose was a sign to remember. His penetrating brown eyes, sharp like an eagle's, searched and focused relentlessly. He remembered places, words, faces and ideas at a glance. He had been a leader of a mountain climbing team, had been on his school swim team, and was an outstanding engineering student before the police forced him underground.

His faith in the revolution was absolute. As a seventh grader, he had told his father, a high railroad official, "Look at the rails running south —solid and disciplined. They fear no dark tunnels or deep gorges, no snow or heatwaves. Nothing stops their twisting and turning toward the Persian Gulf. I am the steel rails, and my direction is revolution."

His father had said, "Boasting again."

Hamid replied, "No more than the rails, if they had a tongue. Watch my deeds, Father!"

Hamid was one of the most courageous and luckiest of the Fedayeen. He was marked for death by Savak early in his career. Twelve times in six years Hamid had escaped from Savak's traps, brilliantly shooting his way out, several times while hundreds caught in the crossfire witnessed a Savak defeat. There had been many violent encounters, gallant retreats and fierce counterattacks. Hamid had been wounded, but never seriously; he seemed to have more lives than a cat. His parents had been arrested and his brother harrassed, but that had not stopped Hamid.

Pirooz had known Hamid's brother Ahmad since childhood. In New York he had advised him to persuade Hamid to leave Iran, since his effectiveness was compromised by Savak's relentless pursuit. But even though the Shah treated Hamid as Public Enemy Number One and death stalked his every step, Hamid refused to leave Iran. Like Ruzbeh before him, and like Dr. Arani before Ruzbeh, the courageous martyrs, Hamid stood firm.

Ali and Hamid, the two fugitives, celebrated their meeting quietly. Hamid assured Ali he had used Ali's explosives manual to detonate many revolutionary bombs. Now all they did had to be either secret or violent. The two leaders were to plan a strategy for the use of new resources obtained from abroad.

To bring him up to date, Hamid told Ali how the Fedayeen had kept the flame going in a recent strike. The workers demanding the right to form a union and engage in collective bargaining had shut down B.F. Goodrich, the Rayy City Cement Company, and other factories, and people had brought food to the strikers. Finally police and paramilitary units had forced the workers back to their jobs by opening fire, injuring many and killing twenty strikers, including two Fedayeen. The labor movement continued to spread silently, even though the Shah's reaction to its peaceful manifestations was violent.

In retribution, the Fedayeen shot and killed the rich owner of the Cotton Print Fabric Company, Mr. Fateh, who had called in the police. This was a warning to employers that whoever harmed workers would himself be harmed and whoever killed workers would be killed. Pirooz, learning about the tragic confrontations, wrote that the reaction of the Shah was no different from that of the ruling circles in the U.S. when workers began organizing there.

Action followed the warnings. The Fedayeen blew up an employment office in Meshhed whose chief had used the police to eliminate union leaders. They also bombed the city hall in Roodsar, whose mayor exploited and terrorized the peasants.

In early March 1976, two printing presses crossed the border hillsides and arrived at a hideout south of Teheran. The next shipments brought automatic weapons, including U.S. M-16's left in South Vietnam, identical to those the Shah had bought from the United States. A few machine guns, hand grenades, ammunition, and medical supplies began to flow to the Fedayeen.

One of the presses was delivered to Aram's team house. Ali, Aram, Taghi, Hamid and the other comrades carried the crate to the basement, opened it and celebrated. Aram promised he would learn to use and maintain the machine. Hamid said, "We thank Ali, the people's ambassador, and the workers who built this machine. Now we can answer the Shah's lies with the Fedayeen's truth, and his repression with our revolution." The young men celebrated as the black machine watched them silently, waiting for work.

The next day, Comrade Mother and other leaders gathered for a meeting. More people were being recruited so military training needed to be reorganized: the program had to expand without spreading organizational secrets. Ali proposed training the first groups while wearing masks, and the trainees would in turn train their own team house members. Practice could be undertaken during mountain climbing "picnics." Ali also offered a handbook he had prepared in Beirut from his own experience and from translations. He asked Aram to read and edit it carefully before printing it on their new machine.

When he was done, Ali said, "We are going to have the know-how, the weapons, and the means to get our message across just like the Shah. But we have resources he doesn't have. We are prepared to die, we will have the people on our side, and we are armed with socialism."

Hamid smiled, "It is good that Ali has Yankee experience. From the Americans we must learn management, improve on it, and use it against them, as the Japanese do in business."

Later Ali, Hamid and Aram discussed the course of the revolution. The economic deterioration in Iran, the spread of corruption, and the discontent of thousands of mullahs and millions of citizens were beginning to undermine the Shah's grip on the state apparatus, Ali reasoned. But he also suggested that they visualize Iran without the Shah, something few had tried. The Fedayeen debated the need for and the relation between the nationalist and the socialist revolutions in Iran: the first one would free the country from U.S. imperialism, and the second would free workers and peasants from the bourgeois ruling class, the domestic exploiters. Russia and China had both established bourgeois democracy before the socialist revolution, but in Cuba national liberation and the socialist revolution had been simultaneous, excluding the bourgeoisie from power. Ali made the point that Zaman believed that a socialist revolution would not be sufficient to free women from their traditional role. There was a need for a cultural feminist revolution, too. The future of the country should the revolution succeed was far from clear.

Ali wrote, "The U.S. has learned from history. If Castro, Mao or Ho Chi Minh, who began with few men, had been wiped out early there would have been no revolutions. So the Fedayeen face a greater test to survive and win the revolution. We are marked by the U.S. whose technology, finances, and counterrevolutionary expertise will be used against us."

But there were also reasons to be hopeful. The core of the Fedayeen had grown to exceed a thousand, while the outer layers now numbered over seven thousand. Furthermore, the Fedayeen had taken over Iranian student leadership abroad and the head of the confederation was now a comrade.

But Ali knew the Fedayeen were still an elite group. The underground Fedayeen could not establish widespread contact with the people because of the need for secrecy. So in spite of great effort the Fedayeen had not yet attracted the masses, who did not comprehend socialism. Nevertheless, Ali was convinced that only the Fedayeen could secure the revolution for the people. But he saw that it was not socialism but what he called "Islamism" that was attracting the dispossessed.

In mosques and seminaries, his brother Hussain and other mullahs were organizing the masses at a furious rate. Hussain moved from house to house, from mosque to mosque, from city to city, like a bird flying from treetop to treetop, singing the words of Khomeini, the gospel of the Islamic revolution. The poor, the merchants, the teachers and students, the civil servants, the workers and the peasants all had begun to whisper the name of Ayatollah Khomeini, to talk of his views, of his eminence and to espouse his vision for Iran. But few followers bothered to ask questions about Khomeini's vision and fewer yet bothered to read his books. Ali worried about this sudden tremendous love for Khomeini and lack of knowledge of his views on government.

Zaman had joined the Mujahedin Khalgh, an Islamic socialist party. She served as a liaison between the two revolutionary groups. She did not approve of the Mujahedin's conservative view of the role of women in society, but she realized that compromises were necessary to defeat the Shah. The Mujahedin hoped that a combination of Islam and socialism would be better understood and accepted by the masses. With the blessing of Khomeini and the financial support of the bazaar merchants, the Mujahedin grew in numbers. But the marriage of socialism and Islam was not happy, and an internal struggle soon split the Mujahedin. One faction merged with the Fedayeen, and another drew closer to the mullahs.

Ali's struggle with Savak and his experience in Lebanon had changed him into a disciplined Fedayeen. To prevent repeating mistakes, he established guidelines for Fedayeen to follow. No paper, no weapon, no secret was to fall into Savak's hands. Savak was to be allowed to capture only burned-out files or blown-up team houses. Where retreat was impossible, only death would be acceptable. No Fedayeen was to be captured alive. Savak was to be allowed to torture only corpses. Even a courageous revolutionary could crack under torture, Ali knew, but the dead could reveal only silence. Never again will I allow myself to be captured alive by Savak, Ali vowed. If death is cold and dark, life in Savak's embrace is colder and darker.

Any informer or agent of the Shah who caused the death of a Fedayeen would be automatically condemned to death. Ali wanted to make sure that the rules were clear to everyone, friend and foe. No mistakes were allowed, and there was no forgiveness for a Fedayeen who jeopardized the movement. There was no life for the Fedayeen except the revolution, and no life would be spared if the revolution demanded it. Abbas Shahriani, an informer for Savak who had reached the Fedayeen leadership, was one executed under the new regulations.

As the Shah got tougher and more brutal, so did the Fedayeen. As he received shiploads of weapons and experts from the U.S., the Fedayeen received a few of their own. The odds were against them, but their hopes were solid and growing.

So in the spring of 1976, people went through the motions of celebrating the new year, March 21st. On the surface, the police state had reached the zenith of its power, bent on destroying all opposition; even the moderate National Front, with its mild demand to return to constitutional monarchy, was not safe. The Shah cracked down on the National Front, on the clergy, and on the Tudeh, Mujahedin and Fedayeen. Ali did not celebrate the new year. There was not much an underground revolutionary could do except to survive and recruit more revolutionaries.

And the Fedayeen were busy recruiting, training and also printing. Since censorship is useless unless it is absolute, the regime was threatened. The Shah could not tolerate even the miniscule Fedayeen newsprint competing with his monopoly of the media.

In a report summarizing CIA and Savak intelligence, Eric Saunders concluded that the Fedayeen were the most dangerous group to the Shah and to U.S. interests in Iran, and must be destroyed. These revolutionaries must be uncovered, and telephone bugging could accomplish this objective. Eric saw the project implemented, and his career took off when the bugging resulted in Savak's pinpointing three team houses. The Shah began to use the most sophisticated counterinsurgency methods the U.S. could offer him. Telephones were bugged and mail was opened on an ever wider scale. A census authenticated legal residence when the existence of team houses was suspected.

Thus, on May 16, 1976, several thousand army soldiers, police and Savak attacked the three suspected team houses. The Shah wanted to wipe out the Fedayeen and regain the feeling of absolute security for his men, and in the process show the citizens that revolution was useless.

Ali, Hamid, Taghi, the Shaygans and the others were finishing a breakfast of sweet tea, feta cheese, bread and fruit. Aram was to come to discuss the Fedayeen newsletter, but he was late. Zahra was visiting her mother.

The telephone rang just before eight a.m., and Ali answered. He heard Aram's accent more pronounced.

"Watch out, Ali! You're surrounded."

Ali became alert. "Talk, Aram, tell me more."

Aram said, "There are hundreds of police and soldiers surrounding you. I can't get through. They've blockaded all three roads to the house." Suddenly the phone went dead.

Ali raced back to the others. "Attention!" he shouted in a voice solid and penetrating. His face flushed. He collected his thoughts and almost whispered, "We're surrounded on three sides. We must follow the retreat procedures."

Without delay, the Fedayeen set about a well-practiced operation. Each grabbed a weapon and reached into an ammunition box for clips and into another for grenades. Hamid and Mrs. Shaygan collected the documents and one of the comrades took them to the courtyard, threw them into a metal garbage can and set them afire. Each person checked his pockets for the cyanide capsule.

Ali took charge. "Taghi, to the roof. Tell us quickly how many there are and how close." Taghi dashed off. Hamid went about the room calmly to check the weapons and offer encouragement.

Ali turned to Hamid. "I'll slow them down. You all leave."

Hamid smiled bitterly. "I haven't been killed for a long time. Leave with the Shaygans immediately. Take the roofs to where Narmak Simetri Street turns east," Hamid commanded. "Don't be shy; use your weapons. We'll join you at Comrade Mother's house."

From the roof Taghi shouted, "Grenades!" The patio filled with teargas. Everyone took cover as a fragmentation grenade exploded in the yard. The fish pool and its inhabitants splashed in a gory fountain, raining debris onto the pavement. The burning papers took flight like fiery doves, the ashes settling lazily back into the grimy water covering the yard. The comrade who had set the documents on fire fell, screaming, as he rolled over the burning papers, his eyes blinded, his left arm severed. Hamid commanded, "Now everyone to the roof. I'll take care of him."

Ali led the four Shaygans to the roof. He gave a white handkerchief to Mr. Shaygan. "Hoist it when I give the signal." No one questioned him.

Hamid rushed down and dragged his wounded comrade up the stairs. But it was no use; the Fedayeen was dead. Another grenade exploded, and Hamid dropped to the floor, glass shattering over him. Then he scrambled to the roof and shouted to Taghi, "I'll cover the east and south, you take the west."

Hamid saw Ali disappear over the roofs. "Let's follow them." As Hamid started, helmeted soldiers emerged to the north. He felt his heart pounding. Sweat and ashes dyed his face; his hair looked grey. Taghi and Hamid were surrounded on the roof.

Ali and his comrades ran over the flat, connected rooftops, slipping behind the troops just before they were cut off. Ali quietly encouraged his comrades. "Come on, Nasser. Hurry, Ajang. The police are afraid of blood."

They reached the roof whose edge fell off into the street. Ali crawled up and looked down a nine-foot drop. A police car was parked close by with a view up and down the street. An officer leaned on it holding a walkie-talkie. Ali felt for his two grenades. He took one and lobbed it at the car. The front of the car and the policeman blew up. Another policeman in the back seat, shocked and in pain, got up and sprinted away.

Ali swung over the roof and dropped nimbly to the pavement. He caught his balance, pointed the machine gun toward the fleeing man and opened fire to scare him away. Then Ali caught the children who hung on to the roof, then dropped into his arms. He shot volleys, one right and one left, as the rest of his group fell to the pavement.

Ali turned around at a sudden sound and raised his machine gun once more. Students were rushing from a school across the street. Ali's eyes searched. The children cheered, seeing that the rumors about the gallantry of Fedayeen were true.

No one paid attention to the wounded officer shuddering. The headmaster of the school, who knew Nasser and Ajang, thrust his way through the crowd, pointed to a car and shoved a key into Ali's pocket, saying "Go quickly." Ali smiled. The Fedayeen rushed to the Paykan, a stripped-down version of a Hillman car assembled in Teheran from finished parts shipped from England.

As the car sped away the riders shouted, "Long live the Iranian revolution!" to the cheers of the students, who were learning a new lesson. Their chants propelled the Fedayeen out of danger. "Allah-o Akbar! God is Great! Allah-o Akbar!"

A few minutes later a squad of soldiers reached the roof's edge. An army officer looked down and muttered, "The police are stupid cowards." The injured officer was whisked away.

At the other end of the block, a black sedan pulled up behind army vehicles, and a blond man stepped out and walked to the command post.

"Colonel, how did the operation go?" he asked in English.

"Five escaped. Some are dead, some resisting. I have twenty-two casualties so far. It is not good."

The American peered at the destruction. "Have you identified the dead?"

"No, there is resistance, Mr. Saunders."

"I see." Eric walked back to the car. "Damned incompetence," he snorted. He had been assured there was no chance of escape. He knew that Ali was still alive and had hoped that Ali would be killed this time, or put behind bars for good. Only then would he be free of the fear of Ali's claiming his child, or maybe even Sara. He remembered how Ali had spoiled his relationship with Sara. Now the Fedayeen's success and Ali's political triumph could spoil his own career. He got into the car and ordered the driver to return to his office. Eric had been informed by Israeli secret police that Ali had in truth not been among the dead revolutionaries in the Beirut explosion set by their agents.

The car with Ali behind the wheel, Shaygan beside him, and his wife and two boys huddled in the back seat emerged from the narrow street onto Damavand Avenue. Ali wanted to make sure he was not being followed.

In half an hour they had crossed Teheran and were driving north when two cars, sirens wailing, approached from the opposite lane. The first car squealed to a stop in front of Ali's car. Ali hit the brakes and stopped fifteen yards away. An officer leapt out holding a gun. "Halt!" he demanded. A bystander Savak agent in the crowd had reported the license and description of the car, and the headmaster had been arrested.

Ali whispered, "The handkerchief."

"Okay." Shaygan waved the white handkerchief, and the officer relaxed. Ali slipped out the door and dove to the pavement. His machine gun riddled the lieutenant and then the muzzle turned and blasted the police car windshield. The driver slumped over the wheel.

Ali turned to the second car across the road, aiming his weapon at it. The three officers in that car were already in flight. Ali watched them until they vanished onto the sidewalks.

Since the police knew their escape car, Ali commanded his comrades, "Into the police car!" The Fedayeen rushed across the pavement and into the empty vehicle. Ali turned on the siren and sped away.

Time flew by as Ali made his way west along Eisenhower Boulevard. After several moments, Ali spoke what they were all thinking, "I hope Hamid and Taghi made it out safely." Ajang said, "No one can capture Comrade Hamid. He kills the enemy or else he disappears into thin air." Ajang had no idea that Hamid was doing both, taking out a platoon of the Shah's agents and then disappearing into thin air.

Behind the wheel, Ali thought of Comrade Mother's house. The Kan sanctuary had a small printing press but no automatic weapons, just two grenades and a single handgun. He bitterly regretted having to lose the big printing press.

The Fedayeen headed toward Shahyad Square with its immense central tetrapylon and vast surrounding space. Suddenly Ali veered to a curb and stopped. He bought a bundle of newspapers and sped off. "We need the papers to cover our guns," Ali explained. Just before reaching the square, Ali swung left onto Firuzeh Street and pulled up behind a taxi rank. The Shaygans hid the machine gun under the papers and then filled a cab. Ali watched them disappear. Soon the Shaygans reached the house of a cousin, whose home was assigned as a sanctuary; now they were fugitives like Ali.

Ali cautiously slipped out of the police car and walked away to hail a cab.

"Kan Borough, please," Ali said, "and step on the gas. I'll compensate you." The taxi lurched northwards into Mohammed Ali Jinnah Avenue. The driver accelerated, hurling curses at other drivers and hearing curses for his recklessness. The driver apologized for his language. "Everything is getting worse and uglier: the air, the look of the moon, the other taxi drivers, the passengers, the government, and my curses. Worse and worse," he said, trailing off.

The cab passed Sassaniyan Square and turned west on Ataturk Avenue, a few miles from Kan. Soon a policeman signalled the cab to a stop. Ali reached for his revolver.

The policeman said, "This road is closed."

The driver, frustrted with closed roads, demanded, "What's going on now?"

The policeman answered, "A war! An old lady is throwing grenades, killing officers of the law. Imagine!" he snorted. "Instead of praying and raising grandchildren, she turns into a terrorist." To most Iranians, the place of a woman was home and her main task was housekeeping. For a woman (in Iranian eyes), over forty, to be a revolutionary was equivalent to the end of the world!

Ali shook his head sadly. He thought, "Their cause is hopeless, they have no ammunition."

"Do you want to walk the rest of the way?" the driver said.

Ali said, "No. Take me to Avenue Farhang."

"That's a long way."

Ali interrupted him. "I'll pay you extra. Hurry, please."

* * * * *

Hamid and Taghi tied down hundreds of men till noon, when their ammunition ran low. As the shooting subsided, the invaders burst into the yard, their bullets biting into the walls. The two Fedayeen lobbed grenades into them and lit up the battlefield; shooting drowned the screams.

Hamid stood and fired at soldiers storming across the roof. The bodies shivered in pain or terror, and moans and curses filled the space. He shouted to Taghi, "They want us alive."

Taghi tossed grenades into the clusters of Savak and police below him. He lobbed the last grenade thirty yards over a wall shielding officers. The leaderless troops then stood frozen. One remaining officer mumbled, "It is too much." Then he ordered, "Throw your grenades to the roof."

"We may hit our own men, sir."

"Throw them, I said." Grenades exploded on the roof and inside the house, reducing it to a ruin. Fragments of hot metal sliced into Hamid and Taghi, and they crumpled on the roof.

The next day, newspapers hailed the death of Hamid and manufactured stories of Hamid's sex orgies. Forged documents proved the Fedayeen were agents of Iraq. But two years later, at the dawn of the revolution, people would rename a major street in Teheran after Hamid Ashraf.

By noon after the attack, Ali was in the house on Farhang Street, where more fugitives arrived worrying about their comrades. One asked Ali, "Shall we call the other team houses, Comrade?"

Ali said "No!" Then he wondered, "How could I have missed the clicking telephone sounds?"

A comrade said, "They always make noises."

Ali was not convinced. "I should have known better. I heard them when Professor Pirooz' telephone was bugged in New York. We get wrapped up with big problems and neglect critical details. The revolution demands tighter security." Ali continued, "Telephones are not to be used. Better to be inefficient than be dead." His face was tormented. He said, "We must assess the damage, help our comrades and their families."

The discussion lasted long. A knock at the door electrified the Fedayeen for an instant. They stood alert, revolvers in hand. The comrade on watch announced, "It is Comrade Zahra."

The Fedayeen relaxed. The young woman stepped in, her eyes tearful.

Abruptly she announced, "Comrade Hamid and my husband Taghi are martyred. So are Comrade Mother and the three other comrades and the Kan house. The house in Niazi Street was attacked, too, but our comrades there aren't hurt. After a successful retreat with his family, Comrade Shaygan went to assist other comrades and was shot to death. It appears no Fedayeen documents were captured. The rumor counts more than seventy government men killed and two hundred wounded."

The Fedayeen looked to Ali as tears filled his eyes. With clenched fists he announced, "The Shah and the U.S. steal our resources, steal our freedom, force us underground, and then they kill us for being underground revolutionaries. They killed Comrade Mother, the oldest, and they killed Hamid, the bravest of us. The Shah will not have rest. The CIA who bugged the phones will be punished. The police casualties show we can punish the murderers." He paused, then his voice rose. "We'll make a thousand more grenades, a thousand more bombs. We will build again. The revolution will succeed. It must."

The face of the officer shattered by his bullets flashed in Ali's mind. Ali, the son of Dr. Keshavarz and Fatema, the most gentle souls, had murdered a man—had murdered him without a moment's hesitation. He felt as though a handkerchief was again being pushed down his throat. He hid his face in his large hands, his elbows resting on the square dining table. Comrade Zahra stood in a corner sobbing. The other comrades solemnly left the room.

Ali walked to Zahra. He held her and whispered in her ear, "Taghi saved my life twice, once in Evin and once today. He and Hamid stood and fought hundreds of enemies. They saved the Shaygan family, they saved part of the revolution." Zahra, seeing the room empty, cried louder and pressed her mouth against Ali's shoulder to mute the sound. In a few minutes Aram walked in and Zahra left the room. Aram and Ali spent the evening planning to rebuild, the losses strengthening their resolve.

Later on Ali wrote in a newsletter, "Kings and Presidents lay flowers at the mausoleum of the unknown soldiers and praise their gallantry for the sake of the nation. But in general the death of the soldier, on either side of the battlefield, is in the interest of the ruling classes and the warring rulers. Upon the revolution, people must build the tomb of the unknown revolutionary, who unlike the soldier is not drafted into service, but has offered his life voluntarily for the cause of revolution and the interest of the masses. Just as rulers praise the unknown soldier, the people must praise the unknown revolutionary."

CHAPTER 18

Time One

On the night of December 29th, 1977, Ali and Zaman exploded a bomb at the Iran-American Society building in Teheran. It saddened the brother and sister since they had once studied English there, but the Fedayeen had to protest the unholy alliance of the Shah and the U.S. during President Carter's New Year visit, and they wanted to ensure that the Western press accompanying the President took notice.

Although it was planned to avoid injuries, the bombing slightly injured three bystanders, but damage to the building was considerable. The CIA and Savak seemed not to hear or see the explosion, or understand its significance; they only investigated the case routinely. The Shah and Jimmy Carter also pretended not to notice as they drank together and praised each other for the media. Ali wrote, "Revolutionaries must use each confrontation to mobilize the masses for more confrontation. We must transform the general discontent into unity and then unity into general uprising."

On January 9th, 1978, trying to freeze the rising revolutionary fever, the Shah's police killed twenty demonstrators in Qom, and many more were injured. On the 26th, more than 300,000 demonstrated against the deaths and injuries. Grand Ayatollah Shariatmadari condemned the police violence and called for Ayatollah Khomeini's return from exile. Prime Minister Amuzegar's only response was to present a record-breaking budget increasing salaries of civil servants.

Early in February, Dr. George Habash, the Palestinian leader, sent the Fedayeen a telegram, "Long live the martyrs of Siahkal," to commemorate the seventh anniversary of the uprising. He urged Ali to work harder yet. Later in the month, the fortieth day of the Qom incident was mourned across the country; Shiite Muslims mourn the fortieth day after the death of a loved one as a remembrance. But each mourning procession became a self-perpetuating event as the regime claimed new victims from each procession. Troops fired into demonstrators in Tabriz, and in retaliation protesters set fire to banks, cinemas and hotels. More were killed and injured, and 650 were arrested. One of Ali's close comrades, who had been sent on a Fedayeen assignment to Tabriz, barely escaped serious injury. The various revolutionary groups learned to work together to pour fuel on revolutionary brushfires across the land to connect them into a gigantic blaze.

On February 27th, under the leadership of the Fedayeen, students occupied the Iranian embassy in East Berlin to protest the Tabriz massacre, and the Shah broke relations between Iran and East Germany. The revolutionary fires had now crossed boundaries. On the 28th, Amnesty International accused the Shah of human rights violations. On March 3rd, the Shah blamed Islamic Marxists for the Tabriz incident.

Revolutionaries turned March 27th, the fortieth day of mourning for the Tabriz massacre, into a day of rioting. Troops opened fire again; in Yazd more than 25 perished. On March 31st the Shah's Rastakhiz Party began a propaganda campaign denouncing the alliance of Marxists and Muslims, and on April 8th Savak death squads, calling themselves the Committee for Revenge, bombed the houses of opposition leaders Sanjabi, Bazargan, Moqaddam and others. The next day a pro-government rally in Tabriz organized by Savak announced that "People's Committees" would conduct "surveillance" on subversive elements. Ali moved from house to house, from neighborhood to neighborhood, from city to city near Teheran exhorting supporters to organize and prepare for revolution. Day by day he lost the fear of becoming uncovered, as did thousands of revolutionaries. The Shah's grip on the state had begun to loosen.

On April 16th the Shah told the *Times* of London that only ignorant people opposed him and that torture in Iran had been stopped. Two days later his death squads bombed more houses in Teheran. On the 25th, thugs paid by Savak beat up students at Teheran University for distributing leaflets. Aram escaped with a minor injury. Protests and clashes on other campuses followed. On May 9th and 10th, more rioting rocked Qom. Two theology students were killed and more injured when police attacked the houses of Grand Ayatollah Shariatmadari and other clergy.

By May 11th, the people's demands had escalated to the point that a large crowd, including Ali, Zaman and Aram, called for the Shah's abdication. The Shah reacted by promising constitutional rule. But shortly thereafter, his troops stormed the University of Teheran. The Shah soon left his uneasy city for Eastern Europe, where he would be welcomed by communist friends! It was a relief to be away from his subjects.

On June 6th the Shah dismissed General Nassiri, head of Savak since 1965, and sent him to Pakistan as ambassador. In a pamphlet, Ali concluded writing, "a soft punishment for a hardened criminal. In any case, the Shah should have sent himself to Pakistan first."

On June 17th the fortieth day of mourning for the death of the theology students in Qom passed peacefully.

On July 3rd the Shah accused his own men of corruption, hoping this act would convince people that he was personally innocent of years of looting and repression. He also announced a new "code of conduct" for the royal family. But on July 12th Ayatollah Shariatmadari nevertheless demanded free elections by June 1979, or else the nation would view the present parliament as illegal. But since the Iranian people had never respected the rubberstamp parliament anyway, the Grand Ayatollah's pronouncement was irrelevant. Shariatmadari was behind, not ahead, of the revolution.

On July 23rd and 24th, forty people were killed when police attacked the procession mourning the killing of Ayatollah Ahmad Kafi. Massacre, mourning, repression, rioting, more killing, more mourning—the cycle continued. No city, no village, no home was so secure or so remote that it could escape the bloody sequence. Finally on August fifth the Shah offered free elections and constitutional guarantees, but by this time his gestures fell on deaf ears.

On August tenth, the great cities of Isfahan and Shiraz again were scenes of turmoil and protest. Ali, barely disguised, exhorted students at Teheran University: "The victory is in sight, work together, work harder! Pressure the Shah. Don't give him a moment of rest, a second chance; he doesn't deserve it!"

On August 14th the armed forces were put on a state of alert because of the constant protests. Vengeful Savak agents soon burned 430 moviegoers alive in the Rex Theater in Abadan. The Shah blamed religious fanatics for the massacre to discredit the supporters of Khomeini. The Shah then dismissed Prime Minister Amuzegar and later Sharif-Emami, who had pledged to outlaw gambling and prostitution and return to the Muslim calendar which the Shah had abandoned. Ayatollah Khomeini from his exile denounced the new administration and called for its overthrow.

On September 4th a large demonstration in Teheran demanded the return of Ayatollah Khomeini from Paris. On September 6th the government banned demonstrations, but the people defied the ban; the power of the Shah and the people's fear of Savak were eroding day by day.

CHAPTER 19

The Safe

In the middle of August, 1978, Eric Saunders sat in the large and opulent Teheran office of the United States Ambassador, William H. Sullivan.

Eric was now a man of many boots. He needed them to climb different mountains, solve diverse problems. Eric had done well for himself. His telephone bugging operation to destroy the Fedayeen and his connections with the Imperial Court, Savak and the CIA brass had propelled his advancement to Chief of Station, the top CIA man in Iran. Eric was thirty-five years old but looked forty-five.

However, his thirst for success was not quenched. Eric wanted to remain the real power behind the throne, and if he succeeded he might one day become Director of Central Intelligence. But this revolution was clouding his dreams.

This morning, Eric was trying to get the Ambassador's support for his final blow to the opposition. He called his plan, "Operation Sweep."

Eric had interviewed former and current Iranian officials, religious and tribal leaders, intellectuals, businessmen and heroin smugglers, and concluded that nothing but Operation Sweep would work.

Eric rightfully argued that the Shah's strategy of limited violence alternating with limited concessions only fueled the revolutionary fires. Operation Sweep would knock out the opposition in one big blow, much like the CIA operation in Indonesia had done in 1965. The quick arrest of opposition leaders, a massacre of demonstrators, and a few moderates brought into the government would terrorize the people, split the opposition and isolate Khomeini, who was the most feared opposition leader.

Eric knew a big demonstration was planned for September 4th, the Fetr holiday. But Operation Sweep would have to wait for the next opportunity. There was no lack of demonstrations; indeed, they were growing bigger all the time.

No American politician would object to an actual bloodbath to stop a hypothetical one which would follow the Shah's downfall. The Shah, of course, had to be assured of continued, unqualified U.S. support, since the planned massacre would burn all bridges between him and his people. The August 13th restaurant bombing injuring a score of Americans and Iranians gave Eric the excuse to press his drastic plan more aggressively, even though it was Savak, at Eric's instigation, that had planted the bomb.

So a few days later Eric took a long time softening up Ambassador Sullivan, who listened attentively. Sullivan left his chair to pace the office and finally stood in front of Eric. "I am convinced, but you need to convince the chiefs in Washington. Why not market your plan there, Eric?" He smiled.

Eric said, "Yes, thank you for your time." He left after a firm hand-shake. Eric knew that Princess Ashraf had persuaded the Shah, and General Oveissi and others would go along with his plan. He just had to convince the CIA Director, Admiral Turner, who would then convince President Carter.

Eric's spacious office was on the second floor of the chancery building. This was the nerve center of the CIA Iran Station, restricted to personnel with access to "Special Reporting Facilities," meaning CIA agents only. No Iranians were allowed past the CIA guards, not even those on the CIA payroll. The heart of the station was the communications room, through which passed all embassy messages. Eric's cover at the embassy was Narcotics Control Officer.

Eric asked his secretary to book him on the first flight to Washington the next day before he called the office of the Minister of His Majesty's Court to arrange an audience that day with the Shah.

"Impossible today, even for you, Mr. Saunders," the Shah's minister replied with solemn finality.

Eric persisted. "Then may I talk to His Majesty on the phone for a few minutes? It's very important. His Majesty will understand."

The minister replied, "Are you in your office, Mr. Saunders?" "Yes." "Then wait for my call." "Thank you, Your Excellency."

In half an hour, Eric Saunders was on the telephone to His Majesty, the Shah. Eric promised the Shah that he could secure the approval of Admiral Turner and the President for Operation Sweep. Eric asked the Shah, if he wished, to discuss the project with the President.

The Shah did not respond directly and only said, "Mr. Saunders, we appreciate your loyalty to the throne. Princess Ashraf often compliments you to us."

Eric, understanding that the Shah had just said yes to Operation Sweep and no to a direct discussion with the President concerning the project, said, "It is my privilege, Your Majesty. Thank you." Eric heard the faint voice of the minister say, "Thank you, Your Majesty."

Then Eric sent coded cables to CIA headquarters outlining his plans and arranged a meeting with the Director in Washington. Eric did not inform Ambassador Sullivan of his conversation with the Shah. Eric, as Station Chief, was often more effective than the ambassador.

Eric reviewed his notes for the trip. He would brief the Chairman of the Senate Foreign Relations Committee and some other key Congressmen, and he would meet informally with his personal contacts—National Security Council staffers, people in the Pentagon, the Office of Management and Budget, and the State Department. He would also brief the Iranian Ambassador, Ardeshir Zahedi. And, as a contingency, he had material prepared to leak to the *New York Times* in support of his project.

CIA agents were not allowed to contact the opposition leaders, so as not to upset the Shah. The truth of the causes of the people's rebellion would contradict President Carter's praise of the Shah as a "great leader of the Free World." So the President cooperated with the Shah and kept the CIA and U.S. citizens in the dark by referring to the revolution as the Shah's "temporary difficulties." However, Eric did not want to be a scapegoat for someone else's mistakes, not even the President's in case the Shah was deposed. In particular, he had to protect himself against misleading superiors who in effect demanded to be misled. And so he had prepared an explanation for Operation Sweep, justifying the CIA actions before they even took place.

The Shah had also protected himself by planting a couple of Savaki spies in the U.S. embassy. Later it was revealed that one of them had xeroxed secret documents for the Shah. The Shah didn't trust the Americans, who he felt would support him only while he was useful to them. His safeguard was to be the richest man in history, in or out of his own country. President Carter protected himself too, by ever so slightly distancing himself from the Shah even as he continued to praise him in public.

Eric arrived home looking pensive. He had to break the news of his trip to Sara and Cyrus. It was not easy to conceal so many private and professional secrets from them. Sara had been briefed on Eric's position and ordered not to question his activities. By consent, by necessity and by deception, she was kept in the dark like the Americans back home, she quipped to a friend. But as she suspected, more and more her disapproval showed.

After dinner, Eric looked at Cyrus. For a nine-year-old boy he was bright, assertive and inquisitive. He had a tutor in French and was learning to play the guitar from Sara. He spoke Farsi without an accent and was indistinguishable from an Iranian boy. Before kissing Cyrus goodnight, Eric announced, "By the way, Cyrus, I'm going to Washington tomorrow for a few weeks. Is there anything I can get you from home?"

Cyrus looked quizzically at his father and said, "Nothing, Daddy. Besides, this is our home." Cyrus smiled and added, "I still have those silly

Oriental toys you brought me from Bangkok.''

"How about some books, then?'' Eric said as he moved to hug Cyrus.

Cyrus interrupted as he shrank from his daddy. "Do you have to go, Daddy? Mom and I are alone a lot.''

Sara interrupted. "When you grow up Dad will explain everything.''

"No,'' Cyrus demanded. "I'm grown up already.''

"What do you want to know?'' Eric demanded.

"To start with, what do you do? Where do you work?''

"I'm the chief narcotics officer at the U.S. embassy. I've told you that before.''

Cyrus asked, "Is that why you go away so often?''

"Yes,'' Eric said.

"What do you do on your trips?'' Cyrus asked.

Eric replied patiently, "I inspect places, write reports and attend meetings.''

"What's in the safe, Dad?''

"What safe?'' Eric was taken aback.

"In your study.'' Cyrus had watched Eric open and close the safe a few times, but Eric always managed to obstruct the boy's view.

"Just dull government papers.''

"Can I read them?''

Eric frowned. "No, it's against the law.''

Cyrus shook his head. "Either I'm not old enough or it's against the law.'' He hugged Eric good night and goodbye. His dad was not the same anymore, he was too busy with other things, and even at home he seemed to be somewhere else. But Cyrus still loved him. Cyrus kissed Sara and went to his room.

Sara stared at her napkin. "He's more curious than I am.''

"He's more concerned,'' Eric retorted coolly.

Sara protested. "Would it make any difference? Every question I ask bounces off regulations. I'm fed up living in a web of deceptions.'' Their eyes did not meet but their minds struggled. Sara raised her voice, not realizing that Cyrus could hear. "I'm fed up with being an accomplice to a spy in the murder of innocent people I love. I don't want to lie to my son as I did tonight. I'm not a spy and neither is he.''

Eric, tired and off guard, lost his composure and raised his voice, "You're in love with a dead man. There's no room in your heart for me.'' Then he got hold of himself. He could fight with Sara later. As though nothing had happened he said, "Sara, I'm too tired and too busy to enact an old scene. I have to pack. I'm leaving early in the morning.''

"You'll pack yourself, as usual?''

"Yes, thank you for considering it.''

"Then good night,'' said Sara.

"Take care of yourself and Cyrus," Eric said.

Sara had no more to say. Their day-to-day conflicts were all variations on a theme—the theme of fate forcing them together against their will. Sara got up and took a couple of steps before stopping and saying assertively, "We must have a serious talk when you get back."

"Okay, we will," Eric said absently, his mind already working on the details of how to persuade his superiors to approve Operation Sweep.

In a hour Eric was in bed, but he couldn't sleep. He was bothered by the light like the edge of a knife emerging from the crack of Sara's bedroom door which was not quite shut.

How long would Sara's concern for Cyrus and fear of Eric keep her with him? he wondered. Eric knew that with Sara it was finished. Their already separate lives pulled farther apart with each sunrise. Sara shunned Eric's friends and associates. She occasionally even contradicted him in public. Their conflicts could no longer be covered up, even by an undercover agent. Sara cheered for the revolution and Eric tried to crush it, both secretly. Husband and wife stood apart on many issues, yet all was kept hidden from Cyrus. Sara was a freelance writer under a pseudonym, but her pieces critical of U.S. policy went unpublished. She no longer merely wondered about but now seriously suspected Eric's influence.

Eric thought, When would the right time come to leave Sara? Money was not a problem, but he had to have custody of Cyrus. When the boy was a couple of years older, the courts would look favorably on granting Eric custody. His thoughts stopped at the word *custody*. He smiled. It would be a lesson for Sara, for not loving him, for not supporting the U.S.A. and the CIA, and for never forgetting "him," Ali.

To get his mind off his worries, Eric thought of his fifteen-year-old mistress in Bangkok, her form so delicate, her bosom conical, firm and solid, yet so soft, her skin light brown silk, her mound like a wildflower, her voice soft Oriental music, her manner so gentle, her face a Persian miniature, the best work of God. For an instant a calm and joyous feeling ran through him. He cuddled up within himself.

Eric turned over again in bed and heard Cyrus cough. He felt the joy of his son's hug once more, even though it had been hurried and reluctant, not like old times. Eric was addicted to being called Daddy. Cyrus was the only person who accepted him without qualification. But now even that was endangered. Eric was puzzled by Cyrus's change in behavior. Cyrus did not tell him to take care of himself, did not respond to his offer of souvenirs. But he suspected the cause; when would Eric be able to play with Cyrus again, to repair his recent neglect of his son?

But, damn it! he thought. Stopping the revolution, getting rid of Ali had to come first. Eric was sure that Sara was turning the child against him. Sara, his own son, the servants, the Iranian people were all bent on his destruction, it seemed.

His fears and doubts advanced menacingly toward him. He struggled, turned over, tried to shake them loose, but they clung to him like fleas under a cat's skin. His professional life, his personal life and his extra-curricular life were all approaching a crisis, a point of no return. Despite all his political power, he seemed powerless over his own life. The ladder of success was rotting away under him; things were crumbling around him, all because of Ali, because of Sara, because of the revolution. His future, the future he had meticulously worked for and eagerly anticipated, was being threatened at every turn. The revolution threatened his career, Ali threatened his possession of Cyrus, Cyrus's questioning threatened his love, and Sara threatened his home.

On occasion he thought of running from home and family, from CIA responsibilities, from secret entanglements. But he was attached to his success and to Cyrus. He needed to turn things around to save his neck and his career, even if it meant massacring the innocent in Operation Sweep. But how long could the CIA hold the Shah on his throne? And how many people would have to be killed? He had begun to lose respect for the Shah. Without his own supervision, he believed the Shah would lose the country to the communists or the religious fanatics.

Although never alone, Eric felt isolated. Nowhere did he feel at home. He would never be at home in this alien land where his wife and son had set down roots. To him it was just an assignment.

When would he have the chance to enjoy his hard-earned money, to make a bequest to the church? Eric was still religious, still attended church, still gave money for good causes. And when would he be able to build a respectable memorial for a not-so-respectable, alcoholic salesman—his father, who had put a bullet into his head rather than ask him for financial help?

Eric thought of Ali and shuddered. The man came back every time Eric thought he was rid of him, just as the revolution came back stronger every time it was repressed. Whenever a secret seemed secure, there was a revelation. Now his own son was asking about the safe. He would have to do something about the safe when he returned. How long could he keep his secrets from everybody?

His mind returned to his upcoming meeting with the Director of Central Intelligence. How best can I convince him of the Operation Sweep project? What objections could he make? What should I say, how should I say it?

Sara could not sleep, either. Everything had turned bitter between her and Eric. He avoided talking to her. He was always busy, tired, or else it was against the rules. A drunken agent at a party had shocked her with news of Eric's affair in Bangkok, but even that could not hurt her.

Sara loved Cyrus, but that was no longer reason enough to stay with Eric. This marriage had to end, it was bankrupt. But in his indirect manner, Eric had made it clear that he would never give Cyrus up if they split, and she had felt his deadly seriousness. Eric was a powerful man and he was attached to Cyrus as to nothing else. Yes, nothing else, Sara thought. Cyrus was his precious, irreplaceable property. She feared something unknown in Eric. And Cyrus was attached to his daddy. How could she separate from Eric without hurting or losing Cyrus?

She yearned to take Cyrus and run to Ali. But Eric had told her that Ali was dead. Sara had had these thoughts before, but every night she inched toward a resolution. Living with Eric was unbearable. She wrote to her mother, "I am living with an enemy, with the enemy of people I love."

Eric left early in the morning before Sara and Cyrus were up. When Cyrus didn't join her for breakfast on the verandah surrounded by geraniums, Sara called to him, "Cyrus, hurry up. You'll be late for school."

Cyrus burst out onto the verandah waving a revolver in his hand pointing it at Sara. "Look, Mom, look!"

Sara was terrified. "Put it down at once, Cyrus! It may be loaded."

Cyrus laid the gun on the table and looked somber.

Sara asked, "Where did you find it?"

Cyrus said, "In Dad's safe."

"Wasn't it locked?"

"Yes, but I watched Dad open it a couple of times. He doesn't know it, but I know how to open it, too. Do you want me to close it again?"

Sara said, "No, I just want you to have breakfast and go to school. You are forbidden to enter his study unless I tell you, okay?"

Sara took the gun to the study and put it in the safe. As she was about to close the safe she had an idea. She left it open, locked the room behind her and took the key. She came back to Cyrus. "No one must know you have opened the safe. Do you understand? Do you promise?"

"Yes," said Cyrus.

Sara said, "Your word of honor?"

"Yes."

"Why did you open it, Cyrus?" she asked.

Cyrus said, "I don't know. Dad looks upset, and he doesn't seem to care for us anymore. A couple weeks ago, I got up in the middle of the night to go to the bathroom, and Dad was walking downstairs in the hall with his hands behind his back as if they were tied up. And you two don't even sleep in the same room anymore. It used to be fun to come and wake you up in the morning when I was a kid. Remember?"

Sara shook her head. "Okay, dear, that's enough. Please finish your breakfast. We'll talk about it when you get back from school. Just as you promised to keep the safe opening a secret, I promise that I'll do everything

I can to make things right again.''

Cyrus nodded. "That's okay, Mom.''

When the chauffeur drove Cyrus to school, Sara hesitantly went up to the study. She took the pistol in her trembling hands for a moment, fearing Eric's sudden return, then put it down on the desk.

She looked into the large safe. It had several compartments. On a shelf above a file drawer Sara saw three large bags of white powder. She took a big gulp of air and stood up. She guessed what it was. Heroin. She hurried out of the room and asked the maids not to disturb her for the day. Then she rushed back and locked the door behind her.

She looked in the safe once more. She picked up a file. It contained UN reports documenting the involvement of the Shah's court in the narcotics traffic, the same reports that Pirooz had shown on Barbara Walters' *Today Show*. Sara saw Eric's handwriting in red pencil on the cover of the file. "Princess Ashraf is angry. Pirooz will pay for this.'' Sara was instantly worried about the safety of her old friend. What would Eric do to Pirooz? She forced the new worry aside and took out a leather briefcase and opened it. Her eyes grew wide in spite of herself. Bundles of hundred dollar bills filled the case, perhaps a million dollars all told. She closed it in a hurry, as if the money were contaminated. She found a passport. It had Eric's picture, but he was identified as a Professor Eric Blommestein from Belgium.

Her hands and eyes were in constant motion, searching quickly as if she had no time. There was a journal in Eric's handwriting. She skipped through it, reading names she didn't recognize and events she had never heard of. On one page Eric wrote, "Frank Norman committed suicide. The cops found him on a lonely road in a Mercedes with the parking lights on, in a puddle of blood with a new rifle in his hands. He had a Bible with the DCI's business card. What a way to go. Too bad his friends had to neutralize him.'' Sara had difficulty reading Eric's scribbling. "General Buckley in Hong Kong, had to try to keep Frank's death out of the newspapers, had to order the shredding of tons of documents, what a waste.''

Then Eric expressed his views about Frank Norman's operation and the heroin connection that had led to Frank's death. "If I had ordered my agents to hurry up and shred the stuff, if I had threatened them with sixteen years in jail and their wives shredded, and if that got into the papers, I would have killed the motherfuckers myself. All this mess just because Frank was selling phony certificates of deposit (CD's) to Americans in the Philippines and Saudi Arabia. My business will never come to that,'' Eric wrote. The words "my business"' were underlined. Sara put her hand in front of her mouth stopping herself from shouting, "What business?'' She calmed herself down and read the material fast, not knowing exactly what was being described or why. She felt queasy. How murky Eric is, she thought. All her worst suspicions were being verified. Eric was a despicable person, involved in ruining people and maybe even countries. How dangerous could he be? Sara stared at the wall for some time and tried to calm down. She looked in the safe and found a file folder with the word "Princess" on it and another file entitled "Bank." She looked at the bank file.

The bank was part of Eric's old consulting firm. Coded telexes proved that Eric retained control of the firm on behalf of the CIA. The firm had dozens of subsidiaries in places like Panama and the Cayman Islands, including an international investment bank with assets of half a billion dollars. In a directory of company officers Sara saw the names of Eric's CIA colleagues, and some acquaintances she hadn't suspected of being agents. There was a retired general who had once directed the bombing of North Vietnam, a former Senator, an officer of the Rand Corporation who Sara knew had recently retired as Eric's immediate superior at Langley, and Professor Wharton of Columbia University. One item caught her eye: an uncashed check for $20,000 from the firm to a former CIA director attached to his note on the letterhead of a big New York law firm.

The file also contained a top secret memorandum to Eric marked "Eyes Only," detailing the transfer of several million dollars from the CIA to the Committee for Revenge in Iran, and other similar groups in Thailand and South Africa, and a note showing that one of the recipients was a rightwing Cambodian guerrilla army. Sara remembered Eric's saying he felt sympathetic toward the black people of South Africa. My God! she thought bitterly, that was in the radio debate with Ali ten years ago.

On a list of the bank's clients, identified only by number but with their names inserted by Eric, Sara read the names of the Shah's close relatives, officials of the Imperial Court, top military and secret police officers, businessmen, members of parliament, and former cabinet ministers, each name followed by figures of hundreds of thousands or millions of dollars. Reading the file carefully, Sara understood its meaning. Rich Iranians were taking money out of Iran by investing it in dummy subsidiaries of Eric's firm. The dummy businesses thus appeared to lose money, but the money was actually transferred out of the country and credited to the investor. The investor drew interest on the account, and any withdrawals would appear on the books as loans.

Other material showed that the firm passed along bribes and kickbacks from U.S. corporations seeking contracts with the Iranian government. A sheaf of documents detailed payoffs to high Iranian officials, princes and princesses for arm sales. The figures were unbelievably high. There was also a partnership contract between Eric's firm and Princess Ashraf containing a long list of armaments and notes on negotiations with Rhodesia and Indonesia. One document identified Eric's firm as a partner of Prince Panya Souvannah Phouma of Laos in the "Sky of Siam" cargo airline. Sara remembered meeting a Sky of Siam pilot who boasted of his former job with

Air America, the CIA proprietary in Laos. According to these documents, Sky of Siam was flying heroin from Thailand to Iran, where it was hidden in shipping containers bound for the U.S. at a dockside welding company owned by Princess Ashraf. Accounts showed hundreds of thousands of dollars at a time paid for opium to General Kham Sa of Burma and the "Mr. Asia" syndicate of Singapore.

There were also three gold medals, together with certificates signed by the Shah, issued to Eric. There was also a CIA service medal that Sara knew nothing of.

Sara pored over the files, taking notes. She took some of the papers to Eric's small xerox machine. Time dragged on; the machine was painfully slow and made noises she had never heard before. Suddenly, Sara heard the stairs creak. Her face went pale. She jumped to the door, held the door with a trembling hand and peeked out. It was only Cyrus's cat playing on the staircase. Locking the door, she sighed and walked back to the safe and put the files, the briefcase, the pistol carefully in their place.

Buried under some files, she spotted a black diary. Her heartbeat picked up as she held it up to look inside, but a file beneath it caught her attention; scribbled on it was Ali's name. With trembling hands she took the file and opened it. She glanced at a letter turning yellow with age. Sara whispered, "My God!" and felt a knife tearing her from within. It was a copy of Eric's letter denouncing Ali to the immigration officer in New York. Eric's offers to help Ali came back to her. All pretensions, all lies, all a trap for her and for her son.

She hurriedly turned to another page, running away from the words that had forced Ali out of her life. It was a long letter to the head of Savak, dated 1974, demanding that he keep Ali in Evin Prison indefinitely due to the danger Ali posed to the American community in Teheran. Eric quoted Ali's now ten-year-old words said in anger in New York, "I am mad and I will stay mad until all the CIA agents and their bosses are buried in one big grave of history," as though Eric had had them on tape.

Sara banged her fist on the safe. Sweat gathered on her forehead as if the room were overheated. She forced herself to continue. Keep calm, finish the job, Sara, she thought. Savak's reply stated that Ali was a broken man and no threat to anybody. He would be held beyond his sentence on Eric's recommendation, but further detainment was useless and not cost effective. In the margin, Sara found a handwritten note, "He has gone to Lebanon." Another note dated February 1976 read, "He was killed in an explosion yesterday."

Sara sighed and tears pooled at the corner of her eyes. Ali was indeed dead. Eric had told her the truth. But then why hadn't he told her Ali had been released from prison and had gone to Beirut? Did the notes in Ali's file really refer to Ali? She opened Eric's diary and went to the date that Ali had supposedly been killed. At the end of the page, Eric had underscored, "Cyrus is mine now. He is a Saunders, and his childen will be Saunderses."

As she continued reading in the diary, she gasped in disbelief. Her suspicions about Eric were true, but she was discovering that they were just the tip of the iceberg. In an entry later in the spring of 1976 there was a single sentence. "Damn it, he's not dead." Sara shouted, "Who is 'he'?" Was Ali dead or alive? How foolish to have believed Eric! Sara thought. She realized that Eric had not mentioned Ali's name in ten years, just a "he" on the few occasions Ali was discussed. She felt a pain in her abdomen. Why didn't I find out for myself? Why didn't I intervene when I knew Ali was in prison? She remembered Eric's advice, "It would complicate his case. He would be worse off if Savak knew you were interested." Why did I believe Eric? He has been trying to murder the father of my son for ten years.

Sara flipped the pages mechanically wondering, "Where is Ali now? Will I ever see him again?" She found no more entries about Ali. But she did find a blue file with the title, "Operation Sweep" and the words "Top Secret" stamped in red. Inside, she read alternative plans for crushing the opposition specified by various dates. Eric had underlined September 8th.

At last she put the files back in the safe and closed it with a shudder. She took a last look around the room, grabbed her notes and copies. She locked the door behind her and ran to her bedroom, where she threw herself on the bed and cried all the tears she had held back for years.

Her pillow became damp as she lay exhausted. She had hardly slept the night before. Eric was not just a conservative, religious patriot and CIA chief, he was a dangerous criminal in white silk gloves. Did the millions stashed in Eric's secret Swiss accounts belong to the government? How much of what Eric did was authorized by the CIA? Did they instruct him to smuggle heroin for Princess Ashraf to compromise her or to finance other operations? Was Eric after Ali because it was his duty to get rid of communists wherever he found them, or was it . . .? Sara couldn't finish. He's worried about losing Cyrus. At least Eric loved one person.

Sara clung to every shred of evidence to convince herself that Eric was not as dangerous as he appeared. But her heart would not accept her rationalizations. It was a new world, a part of Eric's life she did not know, a still and silent Antarctic. Sara could not believe her eyes, could not trust her memory. She could not confide her findings to anyone without being accused of treason. Now it was as dangerous to stay with Eric as it was to leave him. Sara had to find a way to free herself from their unhappy entanglement. This new, forbidden knowledge endangered her, she knew. She was afraid, but determined to fight to survive, for herself and for Cyrus, in order to tell the world what she knew and to see Ali once more, if he was still alive. She knew the end of her marriage was near. Soon things had to be settled one way or the other.

Sara finally drifted into an exhausted sleep, to be awakened by Cyrus's gentle voice and caress. She felt Cyrus's presence as if he were just a voice. But she did not hug and kiss him today as she invariably did upon his return from school. Her mind was still with the safe.

"Mom, Mom, are you awake? Can I ask my friends over to play?"

"Yes, yes, you may," Sara said.

At the door Cyrus stopped and asked in concern, "Do you want me to close the safe now?"

"Thank you, I've already closed it, darling," Sara answered.

Later that evening, Sara stayed with Cyrus and read short stories by Saroyan, one about the little boy Aram. She had not read to him for a long time, for Cyrus read by himself both in Farsi and in English. But that night was special, a return to old times for mother and son. Cyrus understood why his mother wanted to read to him, but he kept it to himself. Later Cyrus read from Blake's "Songs of Innocence and Experience." Soon he was asleep on the couch. Sara lay beside him, holding a lock of his black hair bundled behind his head in her fingers, and fell asleep beside her beloved son, the son of her lover, Ali.

CHAPTER 20

Die Before You Die

The Keshavarz children seemed to have been shackled at birth, a challenge they had to respond to daily. A day without struggle for freedoom was a waste, just another rotation of an aging earth. But the children learned love from Fatema, and the wish to search for truth from Keshavarz. They were impelled to give the same gifts back to the nation of Iran.

In the summer heat of 1978 the revolution began to simmer. The children of Keshavarz and other revolutionaries throughout Iran were putting flesh to the bones of their ideas. Their parties swelled with recruits who sensed the Shah's end.

Ali wrote an article on the ordeal of the peasants in Iran, which Aram printed in the basement.

"The U.S. dominates our industry and now seeks new arenas for profits. With the help of the Shah, U.S. agribusiness is invading our farms. The Shah buys U.S. grain with oil revenues, then sells the grain in Iran at low prices. Farmers are unable to compete, so they go bankrupt and sell their land to agribusiness waiting in the wings. The peasants are pushed into urban slums to become cheap labor for U.S.-dominated enterprises. Their bodies and lands are put on sale by their own government. This double depletion of oil and agriculture must be halted. The Fedayeen must take advantage of this revolutionary condition."

Hussain, at the same time, gave sermons in the mosques about the deterioration of faith. "No conqueror is as dangerous or as deceptive as the Americans, who hide behind the local puppet. The invasions by the Greeks, Turks, and Mongols were physical and temporary, since beneath the institutions of conquest our spiritual life flowed unimpeded, but the U.S. invaders have come not only to loot, but to destroy our values and rob us of our faith in God and our will to resist. Look at the bribery, gambling, pornography, prostitution and heroin traffic, unprecedented in our history."

Local committees headed by mullahs multiplied across the land. They

239

were the roots of power for an Islamic Republic that mushroomed underground without much notice by the Shah.

Zaman worked with the progressive wing of the Mujahedin Khalgh. The spirituality of Islam and logic of socialism mixed in her mind; her beliefs were a bridge between Ali's and Hussain's. For Shiites, Imam Hussain's heroic stand against the usurper, Yazid, was revolutionary, but it also expressed God's will against injustice. The Shah was being compared to Yazid more and more. Zaman sought justice by resorting to socialism as a weapon.

When Mojtuba Taleghani, the son of Grand Ayatollah Taleghani, the revered spiritual leader of Teheran, declared himself a Marxist-Leninist, the father surprisingly respected his son's convictions.

The Keshavarzes were like the divided opposition, each with a different ideology, but they came together as a family and as revolutionaries. Other families were similarly divided. And so the nation, like the Keshavarzes, was becoming a politicized family.

Early in September, 1978, Ali, dressed as a laborer, got off the bus in the slums at a dusty square surrounded by jerrybuilt shops. One of the shops stood hidden behind stacks of radios, clay water jugs and cheap imported goods. A plastic billboard full of foreign brand names rose above the merchandise, and other homemade signs encircled the square.

Ali made his way through the crowded, noisy marketplace. Peddlers spread their wares out in the dust. Vendors sold Pepsi-Cola and chewing gum, and some sold secondhand goods. A youth with a filthy portable burner shouted, "Mothers, fathers, beggar children, come, a dish of rice for only eleven rials." A hunched-up old man stirred a black pot of soup made from the head, feet and tongue of a sheep. Another peddler sold glasses of tea from a samovar.

An old beggar sat at the foot of a lamppost. The man's shirt failed to cover a bloated, hairy stomach. Two girls and a boy in rags sat beside him, their eyes lifeless. A tin can of water and another with some coins sat at his side. Spittle clung to his lips as he shouted, "Pity my children for the sake of the children of Imam Hussain the Martyr."

Ali felt the misery of this poor district. Even those who were not beggars looked like beggars, and those who were not sick appeared in pain.

The slums extended south from the railway station to Rayy City. A million factory workers, day laborers and unemployed lived here in crowded shacks. Some young migrant workers lived alone and sent money back to their villages.

Ali was on his way to Daulat Abad, to the small hut of a laborer named Reza, a Fedayeen whom Ali had recruited. Reza worked in a brick factory, enduring dangerous pollution, industrial accidents and the arbitrary rules of the boss. Independent unions were illegal.

Ali entered a short alley with an open sewer down the middle and puddles of rain and waste water here and there. One-story mudbrick huts lined up as though in mourning. Some roofs had caved in in the heavy rains, and now broken walls stuck out, or flattened oildrums became new roofs. The area was called Tin City.

There was no electricity except for a few streetlamps. Ali heard a woman buying water from a tank truck tell another, "Imam Khomeini will give us a well, electricity and a new roof. He is for the dispossessed." Rats and flies infested the huts. In winter the shacks became iceboxes, and in summer the tin roofs turned into broilers. Young women, their faces wrinkled, sat in front of their shacks. The fumes and dust outside were a relief from the insects inside.

"The untreated sewage of the city comes to the surface in Tin City," Ali later wrote. "The factory owners live in the beautiful northern suburbs but let their untreated sewage empty into the poor district. Profit for the owners, and sewage for the workers; the exchange is enforced by the Shah's guns and tanks."

Ali came upon two young girls, barefoot, dirty and dressed in rags. Each held two empty tin cans, banging them together at intervals to make some music. They smiled shyly when they noticed Ali's attention.

In the summer of 1976, Ali had hidden in the slums until the foul air had aggravated his asthma. One night he couldn't breathe, so a comrade had to risk taking him for shots to Firooz Abadi Hospital, poorly equipped and staffed but serving a million. The hospital was supposed to show that the Shah cared for the poor, but it managed to cure only a few among the thousands needing help. After that, Ali returned to the team houses in the north of Teheran.

Ali did not feel very comfortable among the poor workers, he admitted in self-criticism. He knew the importance of a close relationship with the workers, but it wasn't as easy for him as it was for Hussain. For one thing, Ali had difficulty remembering names, while Hussain seemed to know everybody. Ali handled explosives, abstract ideas and agitated university students with the same deft touch that Hussain used to change diapers, console the poor and help the sick. It was Hussain, like his leader Ayatollah Khomeini, who understood the language and thoughts of the slum-dwellers. Hussain was a social worker, clergyman and revolutionary in one. He found jobs and shelter, and guided migrant workers through the ordeal of urban uprootedness. He patiently wrote letters for illiterates and served as matchmaker, an important function in a society which arranged marriages. When people asked why he wasn't married himself, he would smile and say, "I'll get married when the Shah is ousted."

Hussain carried his ideas in the traditional role of a mullah, while Ali had to struggle in the unfamiliar new role of revolutionary socialist. Hussain moved among the people like a fish through water. Even the air pollution in the slums caused him only an occasional sore throat and itching eyes. And Hussain enjoyed an important advantage over Ali: very few of the slum-dwellers would become socialist revolutionaries, but many would march voicing Khomeini's demands, and Hussain had only to ask. No wonder Khomeini has such a large following, Ali thought, with supporters like Hussain.

Now walking in the slums, Ali overheard an older boy saying to a young one, "Let's go to the railway station for some fun."

"How will we get there?"

"Hang on to a bus."

"What is there?"

"Trains, lots of noise, a man who plays a flute for a snake, a huge poster of a man smoking a big cigar. Wait until you see it all."

The poor were trapped and their children were trapped, too, until the revolution freed them. This district was like a leper colony, with destitution eating into souls as well as bodies, Ali thought with anger.

Farther on, the alley opened onto an area of abandoned brick kilns. In one deep clay pit, families had dug caves into the sides and roofed them over with tin. Women washed clothes in a foul-smelling stream nearby. Children were scavenging in a garbage dump alongside skinny dogs with open sores also searching for scraps of food. Crows flew about in search of carrion. Decay pervaded the scene. Ali grew angry every time he thought of the people suffering in these conditions while the Shah and his men lived in splendor.

Off to the side of the unpaved road, Ali saw people sitting in the dust. In the middle, a mullah led an Arabic chant. The women slapped their faces, wept and tore their clothes under their chadors. On either side of the path a piece of black cloth fluttered from a stick. It was a funeral service for a child.

Ali passed two women squatting over a portable stove outside a hut, boiling potatoes and chatting. A baby played in the dirt at their feet. A boy kept asking, "Is it done? Can I taste it?"

A skinny prostitute of about fifteen sat at the door of a brothel. Ali was reminded of the prostitutes in New York. A toddler wandered into the path, and Ali took her to her grandmother, who said, "God bless you. I hope you live to be 120 years old."

On the way to Reza's hut, Ali anticipated seeing his family once again. The young Keshavarzes had not met for several months. They planned to meet today, the day after *Aide Fetr,* the celebration of the end of a month of fasting. It was always a big risk to meet because Savak watched Hussain and had questioned him, and Zaman and Aram still lived in fear of arrest. Ali was officially dead. He hoped they would be safe meeting at Reza's slum dwelling.

The religious processions of *Aide Fetr* had turned into a great anti-Shah demonstration yesterday. Ali had stayed away to prepare the Fedayeen paper, and he was eager to hear about the march.

Ali was the first to arrive and sat alone in Reza's hut. Reza stayed outside, and his family had been sent to a neighbor's a few shacks away. The front room was ten feet square, lit by a narrow window beside the entrance, and furnished with only a simple kilim covering the dirt floor. Behind a curtain lay a cooking and storage space, with a hole in the roof to allow some light and ventilation. Ali pondered the rising influence of the mullahs. He feared they were becoming more successful than the Fedayeen at arousing the poor. The idea of the Islamic Republic disturbed him, even though it was succeeding in mobilizing the masses. The mullahs were revolutionary anti-imperialist organizers, and their activities were crucial. But he wondered how Islam's compassion could survive what he saw as the mullahs' urge for power. Ali had asked Hussain if the mullahs would tolerate progressive views, or if they would force communists underground once more and massacre them for their atheism.

Hussain had explained, "While Islam and communism are not compatible, an Islamic government will tolerate differences. A trickle of opposition will not threaten Islam, any more than a trickle of streams can stop the flow of a great river. A stream can join the river, but it cannot force the river to join it. The Islamic government will be legitimate; its power comes from God. It will not fear freedom," Hussain assured him.

But Ali was not convinced. He knew that Hussain was sincere, but intentions and policies could easily diverge. The romance of revolution no longer dominated Ali's emotions; he was more concerned with the logistics of mobilizing the people to end the Shah's brutal reign. He doubted the mullahs could hold power for long. For Ali, political power rested not on party platforms but on the relations of social classes, on economic interests expressed politically. The mullahs were just an interest group, so what class would they ultimately turn to for support? Ali wondered. He doubted they would ally themselves with the workers, but then how would they manage?

Hussain arrived in the early afternoon to find Ali lost in reflection. Hussain wore a small white turban, black-rimmed eyeglasses, a short black beard and the black mullah's robe over a white cotton shirt and black cotton trousers. Ali had grown accustomed to his brother in this outfit, but it still amused him. The brothers hugged one another wholeheartedly. "So how is my Che?" Hussain exclaimed, clasping Ali's shoulders to get a good look at him.

"And how is my Muslim revolutionary, the only one I love like my own eyes?" Ali responded. They laughed. Ali said, "I'm a little worried and a little hopeful. How are Father and Mother?"

"They are holding up," replied Hussain. "They miss you, even if they never speak of it. You know you're the undeclared favorite."

"I miss them, too," Ali said. "I'm envious that you live with them and enjoy the cookies Mother bakes."

"Here are some rice cookies, your favorites." Hussain handed Ali a package.

"And here is my gift." Ali handed Hussain a letter for his parents, written so that it could not jeopardize anyone. "How is Parvine?"

Hussain shook his head. "She is fine, but she's recklessly involved in revolution. I can advise anyone else, but not Parvine. She wanted to see you, but she had to distribute Mujahedin leaflets." Hussain asked, "How is your underground life?"

Ali said, "I suspect my secret is no longer a secret. I've always worried that the Israeli secret police would discover who was really killed in Beirut. And what the Israelis know about Iranian revolutionaries, the CIA will know, too, and then so will Savak. I must be cautious."

Hussain asked, "You think Savak knows you're alive? Do they know you're in Teheran?"

Ali nodded. "Perhaps."

"Then you really must be careful. Remember, Ali, that our mosques can hide even an elephant from the prying eyes of Savak. They are better sanctuaries than your team houses. We have people inside Savak, you know, so we know what they are doing, too."

Ali was interested. "What do you mean?"

'Well," Hussain answered, "a few Savakis have renounced their past but have kept their posts and turned into informers. Keep this to yourself, Ali."

"Of course." Ali thought, if the Fedayeen had informers, many lives could have been saved.

Hussain went on, "Some army officers and lots of conscripts are coming over to us, too. To some, Ayatollah Khomeini's commands are more persuasive than the salary increases the Shah is throwing at his security forces. Young air force cadets and technicians are also beginning to come over." Ali knew this, because the Fedayeen had also been successful with the air force cadets.

Hussain continued, "Some household servants of American personnel and Iranian government officials are reporting to us also. In some cases we have more information than the Shah. We know what he's doing but he doesn't know what we're doing."

Ali interrupted, "They don't know what they're doing themselves, either, or what they should be doing, it seems."

Hussain laughed. "We know who visits whom between Iranians and the U.S. and British embassies. We know how often the two ambassadors visit the Shah." Ali listened. "We even know about some of their conversations. We listen through keyholes and on telephone extensions and pick papers from wastepaper baskets. Anything to remove the evil from Iran. The rest is a state secret." Hussain smiled mischievously.

State! Ali thought with alarm. If the mullahs take over, they could use the same techniques to rule. He said, "You mean you won't tell me everything?"

"There's really no more to tell," admitted Hussain. "The Shah is so desperate he can't take a drink without consulting Ambassador Sullivan. The Shah grovels while he compares himself to Cyrus the Great. Ha! You were in prison when the Shah celebrated the 2500 year monarchy in history. He said, 'Sleep in peace, Cyrus the Great. We are awake to safeguard the fatherland.' He is awake all right. He keeps Sullivan awake with his late-night calls. That's why he asks King Cyrus to sleep."

"Yes," Ali added. "I'll bet they'd rather see the whole nation asleep, so they could steal about in the dark like carpet thieves."

A knock at the door interrupted them. Zaman's reassuring voice rang out. "Anyone home?"

Ali sprang up, grabbed his sister's hands and pulled her to him. Their cheeks met. Aram came in behind Zaman as Hussain stood to greet them.

Ali looked to Aram, smiled, and loosened his grip on Zaman. "Zaman, you're more beautiful and more revolutionary than ever. See what a Fedayeen husband can do for you?"

Zaman said, "More revolutionary, perhaps, but I haven't done a thing to improve my beauty. Now ask Aram what a Mujahedin wife has done for him."

Ali said, "Zaman, can't you let a remark go by?"

Zaman laughed. "Why should I?"

Ali turned to Aram. "How are my nephews?"

Aram said, "They are fine."

Reza stepped in and, seeing his guests all accounted for, announced, "Tea is ready. I'll be outside with this." He held up a whistle.

Hussain said, "Thank you, Reza. But Savak comes with an army. It will be the end."

"Not so!" Reza retorted. "We are a million! Stones will fly, guns will roar." He flushed for telling a Fedayeen secret.

Ali smiled at Reza. "Hussain can keep a secret, but be careful."

When Reza left, Hussain turned to Ali. "Are you arming the people?"

Ali said, "Yes, our promise is to arm the people, but guns here are for training. Would you arm them with prayers?" Ali asked.

Hussain said, "I hope the revolution never turns into fratricide."

Ali said, "I hope not, but the Shah's men are no one's brothers. Since they are armed, we should be, too."

Hussain said quietly, "Soldiers will soon obey God's commands, not the Shah's."

The talk turned to recent events, especially the August 20th fire at the Rex Cinema in Abadan. All of Iran was still shocked that the doors were locked from outside while hundreds burned inside.

Zaman frowned. "Can you imagine murdering all those children, lovers, laborers, people, just to blame the mullahs or teach a lesson to striking oil workers? The Shah didn't care who the dead were. He blames the rescue equipment, but the locks worked perfectly, trapping everyone. The Shah can spend billions on weapons but he can't afford a fire department. Immediately Savak finds someone to confess to the crime, then the culprit unconfesses. The regime can't even come up with consistent lies."

Hussain added, "It has been one week and still people are battling the police in Abadan. They shout at the police, 'Arsonists! Arsonists! The fires of hell are waiting for you.'"

Ali interrupted, "Tell me about yesterday."

Zaman explained, "The demonstration was magnificent! The foreign press estimated half a million participants. Before dawn I went to the Masjed-e Shah [the Mosque of the Shah], where a large crowd chanted in unison, 'God is great.' Just that. Even Aram chanted, 'God is great!' A thousand tales were hidden in those words. We celebrated our togetherness and mourned the martyrs."

Hussain followed up. "Fifty thousand marched into Ghaytariah Square and the crowd grew like a snowball. They merged with others in Jaleh Square holding the picture of a martyred boy."

Zaman continued, "People spilled out into the thoroughfare, stopping all traffic when we stopped to pray. The city became a giant house of worship. This Ramazan has transformed the religious fervor into a political resolve, converging the will of individuals into the one of the people.

"Onlookers showered us with flowers, rosewater, food, drink and pastries. And then the most amazing scene. Some marchers offered the soldiers sweets, and threw flowers and blew kisses to them. I rubbed my eyes to be sure it was true. The soldiers looked pleased. Some would have joined us if they did not fear a court-martial. Loyalty to the Shah is an addiction, but it can be broken."

Hussain looked at Ali as though his point was proven that faith, not weapons, was the crucial factor in the Iranian revolution.

Zaman went on, "Further back a portrait of Ayatollah Khomeini spoke more than a thousand slogans. There was no doubt this was a political demonstration, not just a religious procession as the Shah claims."

Ali asked, "No slogans?"

"Oh, yes," Zaman replied. "It was wonderful to say them out loud, after hearing them in whispers for so long. Let's see, we chanted, 'Our movement is inspired by Imam Hussain,' 'Free political prisoners,' and also 'Oh, army, you are one of us, don't shoot at your family.' Then we chanted, 'Khomeini, Khomeini,' louder and louder. I saw children carrying water for the marchers, as if the marchers were their children. Each person put himself at the disposal of the whole. *Aide Fetr* was more than a religious celebration, it was an ascent toward unity."

Then Zaman grew pensive. "But there were ugly scenes, too. A man chanting 'Long live the socialist movement' was beaten up by Party of God thugs. Is this sanctioned by Khomeini?" she asked Hussain.

Hussain answered, "No! But I will find out who is behind them."

"And another thing," Zaman continued, "they shouted to women, 'No more than a crack for the eyes to see.' Everyone recognizes the chador is a political symbol, but to make such a fuss about it is wrong. Then toward the end some of the same men chanted, 'One leader, Khomeini, one party, God's Party.' No one took up their chant, because no one was sure what party of God meant."

Ali said, "The Shah is trying to split the opposition, and that plays into his hand. Savak is printing leaflets with the Fedayeen emblem attacking Islam and Ayatollah Khomeini."

Aram spoke up. "Maybe a CIA trick."

Hussain added, "It could get dirtier."

"Most likely," Ali answered. "The CIA is good at it. Remember the Watergate scandal. But something new is in the air. Just look around. We could be symbols of the mixed opposition. I'm Fedayeen, Zaman is Mujahedin, Hussain is an Islamic fundamentalist, and Aram represents minorities."

Aram laughed. "I'm a communist before I'm an Armenian."

Ali agreed, "Of course, but look, we don't argue; we disagree but only gently and constructively."

Hussain interrupted, "My God! Ali, a diplomat! I must examine my ears."

Ali smiled. "Seriously, Hussain, it wasn't like this before. The Shah has united us."

Zaman said, "Such unity is good, but what about women?"

Aram nodded and added, "What about minorities?"

Ali turned to Hussain. "What do you think? Is Khomeini ready to emancipate women, treat religious minorities equally, and give home rule to ethnic nationalities?"

Hussain rolled his eyes to the ceiling before looking at Ali and Zaman in turn. "Muslim women shall not be a commodity as in the U.S. or a means of production as in the USSR. They will be dignified mothers with responsibilities not inferior to those of men. And, different nationalities and religious minorities are also citizens and have the same responsibilities and privileges as anyone else."

Aram said, "What if they are not Muslims?"

Hussain replied, "There will be special laws to protect their rights, such as those related to appropriate representation in government."

Zaman rolled her eyes to imitate Hussain. She was not convinced but she would not argue today. Aram spoke. "I wonder what will happen tomorrow? Martial law forbids demonstrations."

Hussain answered, "The religious and National Front leadership have cancelled it to prevent bloodshed, but the people have their own mind."

Ali said, "If the Shah kills more, the people become more resolute, and if he loosens his grip he also encourages the revolution. It's too late to undo what he has already done, and too late to do anything new. The monarchy is finished. What historic times! The world will watch on T.V. as we kick the last Shah out. But we must think beyond the Shah. The workers and peasants and lower civil service make up 85 percent of the people. The power must belong to them, to the people."

Hussain said with a smile, "You're still enchanted with a workers' and peasants' paradise, while the rule of Islam will achieve a peaceful society without compromising faith."

Ali grudgingly admitted that the mullahs were more successful in mobilizing the people than the Fedayeen; after all, they had had more than a thousand years' head start. And perhaps, against all odds, an Islamic Republic could deliver justice and freedom.

Aram declared, "But I'm not convinced and I'm still worried about what an Islamic state might do to religious minorities." Zaman interrupted, "Women, too." Hussain said with a smile, "We just covered this ground."

At that moment, Reza brought a tray with a yogurt and cucumber dish, hardboiled eggs, salad, feta cheese, bread and grapes. At the end of the meal, Ali said, "Remember the time we couldn't agree on anything?"

Zaman sighed. "Yes, and my love for Aram had to be underground. But, just as we are united now"—she extended her arms to include everyone—"so will be the nation."

Ali said, "But still plenty of work must be done."

Zaman turned to Hussain and asked, "What is going to happen tomorrow?"

Hussain looked skyward as if to say, I have done my work, now it is God's will. He said calmly, "We must die before we die."

Aram asked, "What does that mean?"

Hussain answered, "It is an injunction from the Holy Koran. 'To die for a cause is better than to die without a cause.'"

"A communist can accept that," Aram said as he repeated, "Die before you die."

The four got up and joined to say goodbye. Reza joined them, too.

"Die before you die" linked them more than common genes. Aram and Zaman came closer still, the five became a solid bundle of human flesh and cartilege as they hugged each other, refusing to let go of the moment. They formed one surrealistic organism, both male and female, with ten eyes, fifty fingers, one goal.

At length the real world beckoned them once more. Quickly and silently they left one at a time. After a brief word with Reza, Ali hugged him and left. Reza watched him from the doorway as the shadows swallowed Ali. Reza felt lonely and wondered, Will I ever see them again?

CHAPTER 21

Black Friday

Ali and Parvine

After dinner the family read Ali's letter. Hussain sat pensive. Dr. Keshavarz asked, "What is it, my son?"

Parvine demanded, "Yes, Uncle Hussain, what is it?"

Hussain said, "Savak may know Ali is alive. This jeopardizes all of us."

Keshavarz said quietly, "Yes, I know."

"Savak is preparing to round up thousands in one big crackdown. We don't have the list but we're sure it includes all opposition leaders. Also the Committee for Revenge, Savak's death squads, are about to increase bombings and assassinations. Father, you should go to Meshhed. Mother loves to be with her sister there and visit the Imam Reza shrine every day. Please consider it, Father."

Dr. Keshavarz reflected a moment, then said, "I have avoided confrontations all my life and compromised my soul to have peace for my family, and now you tell me to flee my home?"

"But Mother's safety is at stake, too," Hussain said.

Keshavarz said, "She can go to Meshhed alone."

"You cannot refuse safety, Father," Hussain said assertively. "Even the Prophet Muhammad took flight from Mecca to Medina for safety. From that hijra [flight] the Prophet returned in triumph."

Dr. Keshavarz looked at his son gently, understandingly, but his mind was made up. "My life has been one long hijra. Now I have returned!" He paused, then said, "Take Fatema to her sister. Remember what Ali said once, 'As long as there is injustice, every day should be an Ashura.'" Keshavarz looked into Hussain's eyes. "Allow me my Ashura. Let me die before I die."

Parvine said, "Uncle Hussain, let Grandfather stay home. Let everyone

250

do his best for the revolution."

Fatema turned her face to hide her tears and left the room.

There was a finality to Keshavarz' mental farewell; he was speaking as though taking leave of the worldly things and people one by one.

The Fetr holiday demonstration had washed away the people's fears of the Shah like a rainstorm as masses now demanded the Shah's death.

The Shah then banned demonstrations, but even the threat of machine guns and tanks could not slow down the momentum of the revolution. Ayatollah Khomeini asked people to avoid confrontation but the masses were moving ahead of the leaders. When it became known that neither fear of the Shah nor respect for Khomeini's wish could stop the planned demonstration, the leaders decided to go along. Dr. Bahoner, Dr. Moffateh and Ayatollah Ghaffari were assigned to lead it.

A network of tactical communications crisscrossed the whole of Iran; Savak could not monitor the mass of simultaneous calls announcing the time and place of assembly. The revolution commandeered the telephone system for its own use and nothing could stop it. Audio cassettes emerged as a critical revolutionary means of carrying the voice of the beloved Khomeini to the people. But even without the mass media, the masses could be mobilized instantly. For the first time in history, an underground mass media was organized so the revolution moved at nearly the speed of light.

And so on Thursday morning, September 7th, once the signal was passed, a huge crowd gathered in Gheitariyeh, a borough in the northeast section of Teheran.

One by one people filled the avenues until they were two million strong, journalists wired their astonished editors. Monday's march was being recreated on a larger scale and without a religious pretense. The slogans were fearless. "Oh shameless Shah, quit the throne" and "Death to the Shah" were prominent on banners overhead. "Freedom, independence and Islamic rule" echoed like waves across the villages, cities, mountains, deserts, to the shores of the Persian Gulf, the Caspian Sea and over the borders into the world.

The army could not remain disciplined while exposed to such slogans; the Shah knew it and the people knew it. A trickle of desertion had already begun. The impact of the movement on the armed forces was being universally understood.

On Thursday evening the Shah replaced the "government of national reconciliation" with martial law. Strikes would be considered rebellion, and public assembly was now illegal. Two persons out together were illegal; a mother and child or a married couple on the streets were subversives. The curfew allowed no one out between 9 p.m. and 5 a.m. More troops moved into streets and were put on alert. The arrest warrants piled up. The siege was an attempt to cut off the opposition's head.

Savak did indeed know that Ali was alive and a leader of the Fedayeen. When Teherani had heard this, his undying hatred like Ali's corpse arose, now that he had been fooled twice. He ached to have Ali back in his operating room.

On the same evening, Hussain rushed to Aram and Zaman's house north of Amjadiyeh Stadium and off Roosevelt Avenue. The children had been sent to stay with Aram's parents. Hussain announced, "The government has begun a major crackdown, just as we suspected. No one is safe. You should take refuge with some Armenian friends. I'm not going home tonight myself."

Zaman said, "Aram and I will see you in Jaleh Square tomorrow, won't we?"

"Yes, that is still on," said Hussain.

Aram asked, "What about Dr. Keshavarz?"

Zaman replied, "He sounds like Ali ten years ago, unbending. He believes his stand is in the ultimate interest of Islam and revolution. He knows what he wants, Hussain. Don't bother him anymore."

Aram said, "It is hard to imagine him as a revolutionary."

"What about Parvine?" Zaman asked.

"The same with her," Hussain said disappointedly. "She is headstrong like her grandfather. Everyone in the family has become stubborn."

Zaman said, "Like the nation."

"Like Ayatollah Khomeini," said Hussain.

Suddenly a shattering crash, and then the sound of footsteps rose upstairs. Aram exclaimed, "Quickly, over the roof."

A teargas bomb broke through the glass window, just missing Zaman's head; it sailed across and exploded in the far corner of the room. Aram pushed Zaman out as acrid smoke pursued them into the second story foyer. The clamor of an invasion and a command drifted up, "Catch the rats, don't kill them."

The three rubbed their eyes as they raced to the opposite end where a stairway led to the roof. Aram went first, opening the door to the flat roof. He stepped out into the open sky filled with stars. Instantly a waiting hand hurled him to the floor, and Aram looked up into the muzzle of a rifle pointblank in his face. "You are under arrest on a matter of national security."

Without delay, Zaman slammed the door shut behind him and secured the bolt. She and Hussain ran downstairs, but Savakis waited there with drawn guns. There was nothing to do but surrender.

"Handcuff them," ordered the officer. The three were led downstairs and thrown into a van which sped off into the gathering night.

At Evin the prisoners were put into a large room filled with the smells and noises of a vast crowd.

* * * * *

A state of siege ruled Teheran on Friday, September 8th. People had to abandon the streets to the armored cars. Threats, warnings and propaganda poured out of the state radio.

At first the revolutionary leaders urged people to stay home, but the people were their own leaders now. Telephones rang, the word spread, the Shah would be challenged in Jaleh Square. "No compliance!" was the slogan.

Cordons of soldiers guarded entries or stood inside the square, their gasmasks on, bayonets fixed, rifles loaded.

Demonstrators trickled from side streets. But the army stood still as though it was not there. Why no arrests? For each unarmed demonstrator there were a hundred armed men. Why were the officers letting the marchers violate martial law, passing by the cordons into the square?

An army officer explained to a French reporter that His Majesty might wish not to enforce his own law. Another instance of the Shah's saying one thing and doing another, people murmured. Still, they were puzzled by the impassive soldiers.

A rumor spread through the city like a plague, bleak and black, that three hundred Israeli counterinsurgency men had arrived to save the crown. The sun rose hurriedly over the city, over the dust and the sounds of armored vehicles, over the people to witness a great event. The square was filling up with a disciplined mass on this Friday.

Conscious of the risks but defiant, people marched past the troops. They greeted the soldiers as they had on Monday and Thursday, but the mood today was different. The people had been fortified by their suffering, their determination and their faith in Islam and revolution. They were armed with slogans, bare hands, voices now silent, prayers, solidarity, courage.

The banner at the head of the procession carried no slogans but was not blank. The bloody clothes of victims and pieces of underground papers were affixed to it, eloquently summarizing the conditions of life and freedom under the Shah. Other banners bore slogans in English, so the foreign journalists could see that the Shah was being rejected by his own people even though he was the darling of Jimmy Carter and Barbara Walters.

But nothing was the same as it had been on Thursday, especially the soldiers. Jaleh Square was surrounded by new soldiers who had been selected not to waver but to follow their orders without hesitation. Some had been flown into Teheran just yesterday. They were conscripts from the ethnic provinces, people naturally suspicious of the urban inhabitants of the capital. They spoke little Farsi, so that the crowd could not persuade them, and they had been indoctrinated that the demonstrators were traitors.

Today there would be no love between the army and people as before, no thinking for these conscripts, only obedience. The enemies of the crown must learn how weak they were and how strong the Shah was.

The soldiers looked frightened, but ready to carry out orders without hesitation. Today was to be no holiday; no saints watched over the people. As the crowd gathered, hoping to persuade the soldiers to join them, other soldiers were busy in the Beheshte Zahra cemetery, digging mass graves.

It was 8 a.m. Side streets fed people onto the median of Shah Reza Avenue which led into Jaleh Square.

A teargas grenade flew over the people and burst into smoke toward the rear of the line of march. The crowd tensed; some ran down alleys, expecting bullets next. But quickly they returned. Handkerchiefs of all colors covered faces as makeshift gasmasks. No rubbing eyes, advice moved like a wave. The marchers resumed their positions in lines, defying martial law, the army behind the laws, and the Shah.

Suddenly a loudspeaker blared, "Disperse or face the consequences." The crowd responded, "This is our city; disperse yourselves!" "The Shah is a murderer!" "We want an Islamic government."

Ali, a route marshal, directed marchers toward the center where the leaders would speak. A number of Fedayeen were among the marchers. Ali was worried because Aram had not shown up, but his duty kept him busy.

On the side of Shah Reza Avenue, in front of the police lines, a small knot of onlookers included Shamil and Kamil, the Savakis who had met Ali at the Turkish border. They were posing as journalists. The two were not in the upper echelons of Savak, yet they were free to work without much supervision and had access to certain files. They were reliable but not imaginative. They had not engaged in extortion and bribery like many of their colleagues who had salted away fortunes in foreign banks. When they heard Ali was still alive, they actually felt good.

Shamil focused his eyes thirty yards away. "Look there! Who do you see close to the electric pole beside the girl with the white scarf, eh?"

Kamil whispered in excitement, "My God! It is him, and right out in the open. If only Teherani could see this!"

Shamil interrupted. "The Israelis were right. Ali is alive." He continued to stare at Ali. "So what do we do now?" he asked.

Kamil grabbed Shamil's head and yanked his ear to his mouth and whispered, "We do nothing, understand?"

Shamil fought his way from Kamil's grip and protested. "Can't you just whisper in my ear?"

"Yes, I could," answered Kamil. "But I wanted you to see things upside down, the way they are now. No heroic actions, nothing. I don't want medals or pay raises anymore. I've heard rumors the Shah is fatally ill and that he will abdicate. I won't put my life in the hands of his son Reza, just a hotshot teenage pilot. If the Shah reaches a compromise with the opposition, who do you think they will throw to the wolves? The hated Savakis.

They have already used General Nassiri, our head, as a sacrificial lamb. The past is gone. No one will watch out for us but us."

"Yes," Shamil said. "But what if the troublemakers are subdued? The U.S. would not let the Shah fall, would it?"

Kamil shook his head. "Maybe, but the Shah is not indispensable, and if he runs, we must run before him."

"Have you lost your head?" Shamil inquired.

"Yes, I have," answered Kamil. "What do you expect? Look at Keshavarz, out in the open as if Savak were dead. No one fears us anymore. I've lost my fears, too. I'm not afraid of Anvari or the Shah. So we won't report Ali and no one will know we haven't."

Shamil added, "I kind of like the son of a bitch."

"I do too. Something about him."

Shamil interrupted Kamil. "Look at that pair."

"Who?"

"The blondes with cameras."

"Foreign correspondents."

"I thought they were banned."

"I guess we have to let that go, too."

By 8:30 a.m. fifteen thousand marchers had filled Jaleh Square. Troops circled the people.

Ali stayed at the entrance of Jaberi Street close to a protective doorway. He had spotted Parvine and had her stay near him. "I beg of you to go home now," Ali insisted.

"Why should I?" Parvine repeated.

Ali said, "Revolution is not for the very young."

"Uncle Ali," said Parvine, "it is my beliefs, not age, that matter."

"Your grandparents may need you."

"They're your parents, too."

"I'm not just your uncle but a senior comrade," Ali said assertively.

"But you are a Fedayeen, not a Mujahed." Parvine continued, "Uncle Ali, I would do anything for you but leave."

Ali sighed. "Will you stay close?"

"Yes," Parvine replied.

The chant of "Allah-o Akbar" arose. Ayatollah Nouri had arrived. He was a fragile yet courageous man, soft with words but steeled within. He stopped to assure the commander that the demonstration was peaceful. Then he walked to the center. He raised his arms and the square fell silent. "Nation of Islam, be seated." The demonstrators sat on the pavement.

But before the Ayatollah could speak, teargas grenades landed among the crowd. People ran in panic, expanding outward, protesting, coughing, tears running down faces.

The gasmasks covered the soldiers' tension as the crowd moved closer.

Newspapers were rolled up and lit as torches to lift the smoke. Helicopters flew overhead. The air sizzled in the morning sun's rays.

The chatter of a machinegun sailed overhead—warning shots. Fear and smoke mixed, and the crowd was again stilled. Jaleh Square trembled and the people trembled with it. The mass moved as though glued in one piece. Men and women vanished and emerged from the smoke, coughing.

Then the soldiers raised their guns on command, pointing them into the crowd. Ali shouted, "Flat on the ground" and dove to the hard pavement tugging Parvine along. She strained to free herself.

Dressed in black, two men and a woman defied Ali's command. They stayed up, staring into pointed guns. The men tore off their shirts, revealing bare chests. With the woman between them, hands over their heads, they moved toward the guns. The woman threw her scarf away, her long black hair hanging down, then lifting with the breeze. Defiantly the three marched forward. The crowd held its breath as the masked men poised their fingers on the triggers.

Parvine jerked herself free, stood up, threw her scarf away, and ran to the three. Ali reached for her skirt, but she was gone. She joined the woman in black. Under her breath the woman ordered Parvine, "Go back, young woman, this is not for you."

Parvine said, "No." A bitter smile covered the woman's face. Without stopping, her hand sought Parvine's. She held it tight.

Ali, crouching, moved forward, hoping to snatch Parvine away. Others rose, forming a line behind the four. Someone shouted, "Follow the courageous ones!" Ali countered, "Stay on the ground."

The four now were fifteen yards from the guns. The soldiers, like clay walls in the desert, stood rigid, dry, hot and indifferent, awaiting the order to shoot.

Silence ruled as an instinctive discipline gripped the masses. The four stopped. One of the barechested men addressed the masks holding the guns: "Here is my heart," pointing to his chest. "Shoot." His heart palpitated like a deer in a trap.

One of the French newsmen leapt to a cartop. The other was hoisted onto the shoulders of a man while steadied by others. Like the guns, cameras were also trained on the four. The sun watched, the smoke ran to the sky, eyes were wet and throats dry. Ayatollah Nouri was whisked away.

Calm and detached, the four inched forward as if their skin were bulletproof. Farther back a half circle of men followed the four. Ali, now standing, moved forward. He wondered how the same soldiers who earlier had eaten their pastries and thrown kisses back could now shoot at the heart of an unarmed man. Once more the barechested man addressed the soldiers. "Reach for Allah. Praise Khomeini, join us—join your brothers and sisters." But these new conscripts, frightened now, could not understand the Farsi words and saw only four traitors, with a huge crowd behind them, threatening them.

An officer commanded, "Now!" The soldiers pressed the triggers, the roar of gunfire echoed through the square, hearts splashed and heads shattered, intestines spilled onto the pavement. The four fell dead. Parvine's fingers trembled, as if reaching for Abbas, her father.

More volleys tore into the crowd. A hail of bullets passed over Ali's head. The Frenchman dove to the ground, his face covered by the dust and the blood. He grumbled, "I'm a fool."

The fifty seconds of firing seemed like fifty years, as many aged and died. As the living ran from death and from the dead, the troops heard a new command: "Shoot the wounded." An extended round echoed as the square fell dead.

As the people waited to see whether the shooting had ended, a soldier moved behind the line, and a single shot echoed around the world as it felled the commanding officer onto the ground like a great tree crashing down from the sky hit by lightning. The soldier shouted in Azeri, "Long live the people!" and then jammed a bayonet into his own heart.

His camera swinging, the Frenchman ran to Ali and helped to drag Parvine away. Parvine looked peaceful. Gravity could not hold her soul to the ground, as she joined her martyred father.

The newsman and Ali got out of the square into Jabari Street. The square was quiet, like a graveyard with the dead thrown up by the ground. The soldiers left the survivors alone for the moment.

His hands trembling and his eyes filled with tears, Ali laid Parvine near a curb. The Frenchman snapped shots of Ali and Parvine. His voice breaking, Ali said, "Report that the Shah shoots children. Report the officer's execution and the soldier's suicide. Report the massacre of the unarmed and innocent."

Ali then whispered, "Ashura." The journalist said in Farsi, "I know Ashura. I will report it."

Death rattled and echoed across the pavements and walls. The demonstrators set tires aflame. Columns of smoke, grey and solemn, rose around Jaleh Square. Knots of people straggled past bearing the dead and the wounded. The soldiers watched silently. The unarmed civilians would not and could not attack the soldiers, for there would be more bloodshed.

Kamil and Shamil kept their eyes on Ali, who had sidestepped the piles of broken bones and chunks of flesh. They saw Army trucks enter the scene, then soldiers loading the dead and dying into the trucks.

Someone seeing the reporter with Ali yelled, "American! An American murderer!" An old man dragging the corpse of his son stopped, took out a knife and lunged toward the reporter. Ali jumped in between and said, "He's French, a reporter." The old man fell to his knees and sobbed for his son.

Ali ordered people to clear away. Two young boys would not move. They stood by their mother, torn apart. Ali told them, "Go home, go home. We will take care of her." A woman came up to Ali. "I will take the children home," she said, pushing the boys down the road. Only then did the children begin to sob out loud.

Suddenly a motorcycle roared up toward the square. Ali signalled it to stop. "Take this reporter to safety," Ali ordered the cyclist. "Now leave, leave." The Frenchman jumped on the back seat as the cycle took off away from Jaleh Square.

Ali's eyes fell on the opposite wall. In fresh blood it read,

"Death to the Shah, Death to Carter."

Kamil and Shamil continued to watch Ali. Now they saw a jeep racing toward the square, its horn blowing, scattering people before it. The jeep ran toward Parvine's body lying on the curb. As Ali dove to push her out of the path, the jeep hit him on the side, smashing him against the wall as it fled.

Ali now lay unconscious beside the body of his niece. A deep gash on his forehead spilled blood over his face, the blood running into Parvine's blood and painting the pavement red.

"Is he dead now?" Shamil inquired of his partner.

"I don't think so. It just grazed him."

"Shouldn't we rescue him?"

"Not just yet, it is dangerous." answered Kamil. "Let's see what happens next."

A U.S. army truck marked with Imperial Army signs followed the jeep. From the tailgate, six paramilitary uniforms jumped out and divided in pairs. Like garbage collectors, each pair picked up a corpse or unconscious body and hurled it onto the truck. Parvine and Ali were thrown in. The men jumped on the truck and moved on to the next pile of corpses.

Soon the people discovered their dead were being whisked away. "Stop the thieves!" someone shouted.

Shamil asked, "What now?"

"We'll follow the truck, that's all."

Shamil held up a white handkerchief and waved it to the troops. The commander verified their Savak identity. "We need the proof of one of the dead, a refugee from the law, Colonel," said Kamil.

"You're too late." Then he whispered, "The trucks are headed for Beheshte Zahra cemetery, mass graves, you understand, no bodies, no martyrs, no funerals, no demonstrations later. You had better hurry." The colonel walked off.

Mehdi and Fatema Keshavarz

His praying over at dawn this Friday, Dr. Keshavarz watched the sun cast light on familiar surfaces. A call from Zaman's neighbor earlier had informed him of the arrests. One more dagger into his heart! He was worried, angered and saddened, but more so because he had to practice dissimulation in his own household now, keeping the secret from his wife. Bitterly he recalled the proverb, "A harmless lie is better than a trouble-ridden truth."

Professor Keshavarz had withdrawn from the world since his imprisonment and forced retirement. He spoke, ate and slept little and showed his love for Fatema and Parvine in quiet, tender ways. He rarely left the house, and he saw only close friends. He understood the past; did not await the future; and lived in the present only as an obligation to Islam, to Fatema and to Parvine. His grown-up children no longer needed him; they were themselves needed by the revolution.

Once a friend pressed him for an explanation. He said reluctantly, "I cannot stop the sins surrounding my home, filling my country. I can't remove the past and I can't move the future, so I shall live disjointed from both."

Keshavarz kept close to God and to himself, the window of his imagination a one-way mirror; no one could see him but he could see all. He read, prayed and meditated; he occasionally wrote, but not for anyone else's eyes. In the last chapters of the book he was writing, he discussed the historical conflicts of church and state in Europe and the triumph of their separation. He pondered how that experience would relate to Iran. Ayatollah Khomeini's argument that it was possible to unite spiritual and political leadership disturbed him. Zaman kept a copy of her father's manuscript in her father-in-law's house.

His gentle persuasion had failed to keep his granddaughter at home that morning. Parvine had insisted, "It is my life, I must go." But there was more than Parvine's safety at stake. The theologian's teaching of peace and Sufism had failed to persuade even his own granddaughter. Parvine was a rebel like Abbas, who had vanished except from his father's memory.

At the age of ten, Abbas had discovered the thrilling knowledge that the center of a circle was equally distanced from all points around. Abbas came to his father. "Baba," he asked breathlessly, "who invented the circle?"

"God has conceived of all things," Keshavarz said.

"Did God invent the circle for the wheel?"

"Perhaps! Man may discover and make use of God's creations."

"Why can't I discover God?" Abbas then asked.

"You will."

"When?"

"When you are ready."

"When is that, Father?"

"I do not know. Only God knows."

"How?"

"God is revealed in many ways. He is compassionate and generous, he knows your wish; do not be impatient."

Now Abbas was gone, and his brother, Ali, had vanished twice, once into prison and once underground, always running from the police, risking his life and the lives of those he visited. The father's longing to see his second son conflicted with the necessity for safety.

And now Hussain and Zaman, together with her husband, had been arrested, had perhaps disappeared forever. What could he do to help? His friends were as powerless as he.

Dr. Keshavarz loved Aram, his Armenian son-in-law. Aram was more like him than any of Keshavarz' own children: he spoke little, yet felt and understood much. Indeed, Keshavarz felt like a minority of one in his own family—in his own country.

Keshavarz' thoughts were interrupted as Fatema's voice rose up the stairs to the study. "Mehdi, it is lovely. Come out to the patio."

There was no answer. She brewed some tea, and soon her voice reached him again. "Would you like some tea and biscuits in your study?"

"Thank you, Lady Fatema, I just wish to read." Fatema understood; his will was hers.

He sat on a prayer rug, striving to make his thoughts a mirror for the Thought of God. His hands cradled the sacred book, his lips touched the old cover.

Keshavarz opened the book and read, loud enough to hear his own voice.

"In the name of God, the Compassionate, the Merciful—

" Whoever does deeds of righteousness,
  be he man or woman,
  and has faith,
  then he will enter into Heaven,
  and not the least injustice will be done to him."

Just as he finished, a blast shook the study as the front doorknob was blown away by a death squad. Keshavarz knew what to expect, for it had happened to people he knew well. He fixed his eyes and his mind on the Holy Book. He read,

" Whoever does deeds of righteousness,

be he man or woman,
and has faith,
then to a life that is good and pure
We will bestow on such a one
rewards according to the best of his actions.''

"Leave your house, old woman,'' a voice reached Keshavarz.

"This house is a gift of God in my trust for now. I should not leave it unattended,'' Fatema protested.

"Out, I said.''

Fatema responded, "Don't interrupt his praying. Shoot me if you must shoot someone.'' Fatema's protests faded away as she was carried into the street. Heavy footsteps climbed the stairs.

The door to Keshavarz' study slammed open and two men in civilian clothes rushed in. One pointed a Smith and Wesson pistol at Keshavarz, shouting, "We are the Committee for Revenge. You will be spared if you tell us where to find the traitor Ali Keshavarz.''

Keshavarz paid no attention. He knew their intentions as he knew his own. Keshavarz replied, "Ali is responsible for himself, as I am for myself. I do not know where Ali is, and if I did, I wouldn't tell.''

"Is this your final word?'' Keshavarz nodded. The man took a tin can and a clockwork device from a handbag. Keshavarz saw and understood, his eyes returning to the Koran in his lap. He read, though he knew the Koran by heart.

" God will punish the unbelievers and the hypocrites,
men and women,
and God turns in mercy to the Believers,
men and women,
for God is oft-forgiving and most merciful.''

The words from the Koran drew anger. One of the men said, "Listen, old man, you won't be able to pray if I burn you alive, will you?''

Keshavarz continued to read the Koran, the Arabic words flowing steadily from his lips with flawless diction and cadence. "It is not fitting for a Believer . . . when a matter is decided by God . . . to seek other options.'' He dismissed the men from his mind and focused all his attention on the Holy Book. He was reciting to no one but God. His words filled the room, his resolve filled his voice, but the vigilantes heard nothing but defiance.

The man with the bomb said irritably, "Let's finish this show.'' Keshavarz closed his eyes and began to recite by heart verse after verse, till the Holy Words filled his mind, blanking out the two evil men, the world, life on this earth.

He smelled the odor of gasoline and heard the liquid poured out and felt the cold wetness soaking through his gown, over his neck and down his back. He made no move; his lips whispered God's words. A match rushed against the sandpaper, and the sound of ignition surrounded his voice. The old man fell on the Holy Koran, protecting it with his chest. He died before he died, just as he had wished.

The murderers set the timebomb and fled downstairs, but they heard shouts of "Savakis! Savakis!" coming from the street. The neighbors had been alerted by Fatema's cries. The two vigilantes turned and raced up to the roof where they moved north to the adjacent roof leading into an alley, but angry neighbors waited there, too, firing bullets at the Savakis. They ran back to Keshavarz' roof to turn west. The growing crowd took up the shout, "Catch the Savakis!" The vigilante driver, seeing the two surrounded, took off in haste.

The bomb exploded, blowing the ceiling apart and tearing into the bodies of the two desperate perpetrators seeking escape. The fireball in her house burned Fatema's memory to ashes, and the explosion blew the ashes away. As she fainted, her world darkened and stayed dark. She was carried away. She wore no veil this morning. The next day in the hospital, when she regained consciousness, she had no memory—just a veil over her past life.

Neighbors formed a line to douse the fire and then tried to reach the old man as fast as they could. The fire was put out quickly, but smoke forbade entry to the study. A man said, "The bomb has shattered what was left by the fire." More and more people poured into the house trying to help, trying to understand. Someone said, "It is too late to save Keshavarz."

Smoke rose through the shattered glass, and sheets of water cascaded down the damaged walls like the tears down the neighbors' cheeks. People were shocked to see a family go up in smoke. One woman, sobbing, asked, "How many sacrifices must Keshavarz offer?" "God sends the hardest trials to the best of men, for he knows the strength of the brave," a man replied.

A bearded man emerged out of the second-floor study, his face darkened by ashes, his hair falling wetly into his eyes. He choked and rubbed the ashes from his eyes as he walked out onto the balcony. Without a word he had the attention of the people staring up at him from the ground below. The silence moved into the street, where those who could neither see nor hear became hushed, too.

The man held a book over his head, exhibiting it to those below. "A miracle, a miracle!" he exclaimed. "Muslim people of Teheran! A miracle in the house of Keshavarz! The professor is dead, God rest his soul." A murmur of sorrow spread through the throng as quick and violent as the fire which had consumed Keshavarz. "God rest his soul," they intoned solemnly.

The bearded man continued, "But the fire—" he paused for breath and cleared his throat—"the fire and the water stopped at the edge of the Holy Koran, not to harm it. Look! The book is untouched though it was attacked by fire, water, even an explosion! The elements respect the Holy Koran."

Cries—of sorrow, of wonder, of faith and of mourning—mingled together, a hundred voices hushed by the passage of God through their midst. "A miracle in the house of Keshavarz!" "The martyred Keshavarz has shown us a miracle from God!" "The elements have bowed before the Holy Koran!"

Another man emerged from the smoke-filled study of Keshavarz. He had seen the evidence himself, had witnessed the Koran taken from under the charred body of Keshavarz. In life Keshavarz had held the words of the Koran in his heart, and now in death his heart had held the book safe against the flames and water. The miracle was the faith of Keshavarz, not the book, the man thought.

The men wrapped Dr. Keshavarz' body tightly in a heavy white bed-cover and placed it in a scorched drawer from one of Keshavarz' chests, covered it with a board and secured it with a rope, a home-made coffin. Then the men carried the coffin down the stairs, people parting to make way. The coffin, held over the heads of the mourners, went out of the house into the street, into the light of morning. Women hidden in chadors stood motionless and wept as the coffin left the scene. An old lady said to her granddaughter, "See, child? He was a saint. He died for us."

The news of Keshavarz' death traveled more swiftly than did his cortege. It spread through the city and to the edge of history, a wave rolling across the sea of people in Teheran. The underground worked without rest to inform one and all of the miracle in the house of Keshavarz.

"The flames stopped at the edges of the Holy Koran!" "Water ran uphill to avoid soaking the Holy Book." "The house was completely engulfed in flames, and only the Holy Word of God survived intact." "The flames encased the Holy Book like a red giftwrap, the gift of God to the martyred Keshavarz, who so loved the Book." "It is Ashura in Teheran." "A new martyr, a new miracle for the revolution." "Allah-o Akbar. Allah-o Akbar." "Fire and water would not harm the Koran; only the Shah tries to destroy it."

Keshavarz, who detested violence, became in death a focal point of one of the bloodiest demonstrations in the history of Teheran, on a day that would go down in history as Black Friday. Keshavarz was now both a martyr and an agent of revolution. For miles and miles his body followed behind breathless tales of his martyrdom. He was borne aloft on the shoulders of students, teachers, workers, peasants, engineers, lawyers, doctors, paupers, people he had never known, young and old, to places he had never been.

An American woman hidden behind a chador, taking notes of the demonstration, asked an Iranian woman passerby, "Whose coffin is this?" "Dr. Mehdi Keshavarz is the martyr." Sara wept under the chador as she rushed home, wanting to see Ali more than ever before.

Zaman, Aram and Hussain

Aram and Hussain shared a single cell that morning, and Zaman was put in a cell in the women's wing in Evin. Each corridor contained fifteen cells with up to a hundred prisoners. There was a single filthy toilet and one sink at the end of every such radial corridor in Evin.

Hussain and Aram sat in shock, staring at the eletric bulb which stared back at them. At last Hussain broke the silence. "What are the lines on the wall, Aram?" he asked.

"Marks for time filled with dread of torture." The word "torture" gained a force of its own, each letter a thorn pricking his side. Aram shivered as he said, "I fear I may break. I know about two team houses."

Hussain answered, "Your comrades are alerted by now. But is this your only worry?" Hussain asked.

Aram said, "No! I worry about Zaman and the children who may never see us again."

"I understand," Hussain said.

Aram asked, "Have your informants told you what Savak's plans are for people like us?"

"They could kill us, like the government killed half a million in Indonesia, but that won't work in Iran. The Shah will have to murder the whole nation." Hussain thought for a moment and added, "And if we are hostages for Ali then we are in trouble."

"Then we are doomed," said Aram.

"Well, not for certain. How much do you know about Ali's activities?"

"Some. Why?"

Hussain replied, "We may be safe if all we know can't lead them to Ali."

"Perhaps, if they believe us," Aram said. Then his voice became bitter. "We don't know what to expect—this is the deadly power of torture. Ali told me Savak puts prisoners in the sun under a black blanket, without water, food or toilet use." Without allowing Hussain to respond, Aram added, "I'm surprised we are free to talk and see."

"That's because thousands are being arrested. Savak must be out of blankets," Hussain replied cynically.

"I wish the U.S. advisors would be treated for one day like the Shah treats his own nation," Aram said as his fears returned. "Are we going to disappear or have we already disappeared?''

Hussain replied, ''I will not disappear. God is with me! Khomeini and the Absent Imam are with me!''

Aram asked, ''Tell me, since I'm a communist. What makes you so sure?''

''You're also a Christian,'' Hussain scolded him. ''You are my brother, Aram.''

''I am not a Christian, but I am your brother,'' said Aram.

Hussain answered, ''You ask about Khomeini. Tell me, who is fighting against the Shah for the people? Not the Tudeh Party—it has compromised with the Shah. The USSR, by default, by trade, by constructing dams and steelworks, by promising to sell arms, is supporting the Shah. The People's Republic of China has offered the Shah its unqualified support. All their professed revolutionary zeal and socialist ideology is overcome by discounted natural gas prices. The communist powers have betrayed us, just as the profitmongers in the West have. Everybody is getting a cut except the Iranian people, who just get cut. Oh, how these exploiters wish there were no Khomeini, no people to challenge their looting.

''Admit it, Aram, the world has abandoned us. We are alone except for Khomeini. Like his martyred father, Khomeini will fight for the dispossessed. He knows our problems, our wishes and our possibilities. With him we will build our country, preserve Islam, create our own technology and determine our own future.

''Khomeini is unyielding except to God. He will save us in the here and the hereafter.'' Raising his voice, Hussain concluded, ''That, Aram, is who Khomeini is. He is helping us right now by inspiring us, giving us the strength to resist Savak. My dear Aram, if you knew Khomeini the way I do, you would also join him; your heart and mind would unite with his.''

''Yes, yes,'' Aram replied. ''I have read his work. I know his thoughts. I also wish everyone would read his books and learn about his political views before following him so feverishly. But I can never subscribe to the idea of a single man holding both a political and spiritual authority over the nation and being considered infallible. Your father is right: even God did not allow himself that privilege or else he would have sent his angels to earth on a regular basis to direct human affairs. But what's the use of discussing this now?'' he asked.

''But what else should we do?'' Hussain replied. ''We can convince no one here but each other.'' Both men smiled in resignation.

Aram said, ''Let's continue, or else worries will kill me.''

''You could pray, Aram,'' said Hussain.

''Why, to whom and how should I pray?'' Aram retorted. ''It is revolution, not prayer, that will save the people.''

Hussain smiled at his brother-in-law warmly, even if he didn't agree with him. "It is not God who is with us here but the workers and peasants whom I am fighting for." Aram raised his voice. "Our revolution follows the revolts of slaves, serfs, and workers, socialist revolutions and wars of liberation. We are not alone. We are part of a historical chain. Communists want to unite the world, something Christians and Muslims have failed to do. Anyhow, if you survive Evin, Hussain, you will get to live under the Islamic Republic you want and if you become a martyr you will go to heaven, right?"

"What is wrong with that?" asked Hussain.

"Nothing," said Aram. "But listen to my predicament. If Savak kills me, either there is hell or no afterlife for a non-believer. And if I survive Evin, most probably I will have to live under an Islamic Republic I don't like. I can't win and you can't lose, either way." Aram continued, "I usually don't talk much, but tonight is different; we may not survive Evin."

Hussain interrupted, "Then why are you here, if no matter what happens you lose?"

Aram replied, "I believe there is no world but this one, and I must fight to make it better for myself, our children and everyone else."

"I don't understand," said Hussain. "Is it your materialism or idealism which risks torture and death?"

Aram replied, "An altruistic bee defending the hive is not an idealist but a materialist sacrificing itself to defend the drones and his genetic pool that he is programmed by evolution to defend. Saints do the same by sacrificing themselves to defend man against inhumanity from other men. Even though building a big bridge may result in the deaths of workers, we still build them. I'm building a bridge to communism, just as you are trying to build one to heaven. I believe my cause is objective, while yours is not."

Hussain said, "I can't imagine a good deed not ultimately linked to God, yet you are sacrificing your life without belief in God."

"We cannot convince each other, but we can try to understand each other," Aram said. "Hussain, I don't blame God for our miseries, but I also will not give him credit for our accomplishments. God didn't bring us here and he won't get us out. I refuse to pray!"

Aram stopped. "The idea of God was drilled into me before I could think for myself, so that is why I have left my children alone. If there is a God, they will meet him someplace, sometime." Hussain listened in amazement. Aram had never been so outspoken.

"I confess to you, Hussain, I'm afraid. And when fear rushes to me, I rush for protection to a God I don't really believe exists. I'm ashamed to admit it, but it's true." Hussain nodded gravely as Aram continued, "I'm not like the great communist hero Ruzbeh and I'm not like Ali, either. I am terribly afraid of torture. I may not be strong enough to resist; I may tell everything, just to stop the pain. I just hope my information becomes useless by the time Savak extracts it from me."

"Listen, Aram," said Hussain. "You're not the only one who's afraid. I'm afraid; Ali was afraid, too. Everyone who has had to face the brutality of Savak has been afraid. The difference between the weak and the strong is not the existence of fear but how they deal with it. You know that Ali was desperately afraid for himself, for his comrades, but he didn't let fear beat him. When fear begins to affect my thought or action, I think of Ashura and Imam Hussain. Then the fear disappears. Fear cannot persist if you have faith in life after death. Faith in God is absolute, but fear of pain is only relative. The absolute conquers the relative, always."

After a while, Hussain lapsed into silence in order to pray, and Aram was left with his anxieties.

At ten p.m. a new prisoner, in rags with no shoes, with an unshaven face and unkempt hair, was pushed into the cell. In contrast to his emaciated body, though, his eyes were lively. He stared intently at his two cellmates, moving closer to squint at Hussain, as if to memorize his features.

Hussain smiled and extended his hand. "My name is Hussain Keshavarz, and this Agha is my brother-in-law, Aram Petrossian."

The man laughed, in spite of the despair of his physical condition. "And my name is Ali Akbar, but I am called, 'Akbar.' I thought I recognized you, but I couldn't be sure. My eyesight is no longer what it should be. You are the brother of Ali Keshavarz."

"How is it you know Ali? And how is it you recognize me?" asked Hussain.

Akbar replied, "I assisted that foul-mouthed bricklayer who repaired the steps in your house."

"I remember now," Hussain said. "That was almost ten years ago."

"Yes, that's it," Akbar responded. "I never forgot the first day. After work, Ali invited me to dine with the family. No employer had ever recognized me before, so I was afraid to accept. So I said that my clothes were dirty. Ali replied, 'You are the cleanest man I've ever met! You've never exploited anyone in your life.' At the time I had no idea what he meant, but I trusted him and had dinner with your family. You were there, too. I sat at an elegant dinner table and I had a good meal. I had never spoken before with such educated people, and I found you interested in my views, talking to me with respect, as if we were equals, or friends, and not just employer and worker. For the first time since I had come to Teheran I was treated like a person. The joy never left me. The night we finished the job, Ali and I went out for ice cream. We watched cars and people go by, heard horns blowing, but we talked whenever the noise faded. He told me about his trip to America.

"I told him that, if I could ever free my family from the slums, I would be happy. I expected him to say, 'It is God's will, be thankful you have a roof over your head, food, clothing and two hands to earn a living. Think of a sick beggar and don't complain.' But instead he said I was as good as anybody, that I deserve everything. He said God didn't create the slums, men did; God didn't build the Shah's palaces, men did. It isn't God's will but the capitalists' that I am poor!

"I tell you, Agha, I was so ignorant then that I had to ask him what a capitalist was. But his words stayed in my head. Your brother told me a lot of things that I had sensed, but he made them clear. He made my dreams sound possible. By believing him, I began to believe myself."

Aram and Hussain exchanged glances but let the man pour out his heart. So the prisoner continued.

"He encouraged me to learn to read and write in a night class because education is the road out of darkness and poverty and slums. He said that I should read as many good books as I could. He brought me some books even before I could read them. I saw Ali not long before he was arrested and then I lost touch with him.

"In two years I was reading the books he had given me. Every book was a new garden filled with flowers, vegetables and fruits; many of them I had never seen or tasted before. When I was out of a job I didn't stand around helplessly, I read or talked to people."

"Why were you arrested?" Aram interrupted.

"Wait, I will come to it," the man replied and continued like a recording.

"I didn't want to spend every morning standing around waiting for the work foreman to signal me over, my heart beating like crazy. I would talk to whoever would listen while we waited before dawn to see if there was work. I told my comrades that it was not the will of God that my wife should spend all day doing other people's laundry with our son strapped to her back, while we couldn't afford to buy soap for ourselves." Akbar continued, "Is there anything wrong with wanting to be something other than ignorant, hungry, cold, dirty and sick? Well, I kept talking about these things to the other laborers.

"Then one day two professors showed up in my neighborhood, one Iranian and one American, interviewing people for a book. I thought, this was my chance. I could let the world know how miserable we were, and maybe someone would care. But the questions they asked were irrelevant. They just wanted to know why we left the villages to come to the slums, that was all. I told them some workers didn't go back because they couldn't afford it, or were ashamed to admit they had been wrong to leave in the first place, or had been evicted from their huts in the village and had nowhere to go.

"Then I got mad. I asked if their study meant I was condemned to choose between starving in a village or trying to make a living in this hell.

Why didn't they ask me if I liked the slums, if I liked my job, if I was insulted by my boss, if I had enough food to feed my family? Why didn't they ask if I liked the Shah, if I approved of his government, if I hated the Americans for supporting him?

"The professors left but the next day Savak came and beat me up in front of my family. So, having become disappointed with everything, including God and his prophets, I joined the Tudeh party. They had helped me before, and they were doing a good job organizing workers in my neighborhood. I became an organizer, and, believe me, I was a good organizer. I know the life of a worker, and my tongue is his tongue. And I know what capitalism is all about from the knowledge I've gained from books and from living under the system. That's all it takes to recruit workers to the party: you have to know the workers and you have to know the bosses. It's that simple."

Hussain frowned. "How can you follow the line of the Tudeh Party? Don't you know the Russians are behind it?"

"All right, Agha Hussain, so what?" Akbar countered unexpectedly. "Don't they take care of workers in the Soviet Union? Their workers are better off than Iranian workers, certainly, better off than Mexican workers or Brazilian or Filipino. Or for that matter better off than Turkish workers in Germany or unemployed American workers or Blacks in America. And don't forget the Tudeh Party has given us great leaders such as Arani, Ruzbeh and others and has published many books and papers educating workers and peasants about their rights. Remember, no other party in Iran has done that." After a pause, Akbar continued.

"And another thing, you shouldn't call it 'Russia.' That's an insult. It's the Soviet Union, which means, 'Council of Workers.' That's what we need here, a council of workers of Iran who would work for the benefit of workers and peasants, rather than the Shah and his imperialist bosses. It's all a matter of who is in power. We, the workers who produce everything, have no power at the present."

After a long silence, Akbar spoke again; his voice had lost its energy and its anger. "What more can I tell you? I'm tired of hunger, of insults, of beatings. I will get a dignifed life or I will die fighting for it." Then he fell silent, as if a plug had been pulled and drained his head of speech.

"I understand," said Hussain. There was nothing more to be said. All they could do was wait for Savak. Aram, through great effort, kept his fears to himself. Time passed with heavy slowness and minimal conversation.

Around eleven that evening the cell door opened once more, only a crack. A small bowl filled with rice and beans was pushed in.

The food was prepared in a military kitchen outside the prison. By the time it got to the cells it was cold and dry. It arrived late or sometimes not at all. When there were mass arrests, the new prisoners got only the scraps from the guards' meals. There were no utensils, not even on special occasions when there was thin beet soup. The stale bread was thrown on the floor, where the cockroaches feasted. The prisoners knew they were treated this way to rob them of their dignity.

Aram awoke from his thoughts to say, "Guard, just a moment. Where is the toilet?"

One of the guards, laughing, said, "You've lost your turn for the night. Do it on the lap of your comrade." The door slammed shut, its metallic clank reverberating around the cell.

Hussain looked at the bowl of food. It could not be a usual portion for three, or else everyone would starve. Either they were being treated differently or the mass arrests had caused a shortage. Hussain and Aram convinced Akbar to take the bowl, since they had already eaten at home.

The three men reclined against the walls and tried to sleep. But the iron door opened again and fresh prisoners, bewildered and in nightclothes, were pushed in. The single cell was small, so they were compelled to stand up.

A deep voice commanded, "The two Russian spies, step out!"

Akbar responded loudly, "Not Russian, you Savak jackass, Soviet. Say it right."

"Shut up!" snapped the officer. "I'll teach you a lesson that your corpse will remember."

Akbar replied, "I'm not afraid of your barking."

"Quiet! Don't provoke him," Hussain whispered.

Teherani stepped into the cell. "Take that chattering lunatic to the next wing. We'll warm his feet in hot oil," he whispered to his assistant.

Hussain, rubbing his eyes, glimpsed at Teherani through his fingers. Teherani's voice boomed, "The Armenian faggot communist, step out."

Hussain said politely, "If you call people by name you'll have a better result."

Teherani turned threateningly on Hussain. "I don't need the advice of a mullah. Take him to the operating room and tie him up," he commanded the guard, pointing at Hussain. As he was pushed out, Hussain poked his head back into the cell and said to Aram, "Die before you die, brother," before he was yanked away.

Teherani then called Aram's name.

Teherani whispered to another guard, "Take this blue-eyed faggot to the cell next to the operating room." A shudder gripped Aram and his fingers trembled.

"It's after midnight, sir," the guard whispered.

"This can't wait. They have vital information." Teherani said to his lieutenant, "Tell Pahlavan and Ghazal to put the faggot's wife with him."

With a spring in his step, Teherani walked toward the operating room thinking, "I have Hussain Keshavarz. There will be no mistake this time."

Hussain, fastened to the iron bed, tried to concentrate on resisting. He knew Ali's trick could not work a second time, but Teherani had been raised in a Muslim family and he could not have shed all the fear of God in Evin, Hussain reasoned.

Sounds of struggle from next door interrupted Hussain's thoughts. "Why are you disrobing me?" Zaman's voice rose above Aram's. "Be strong, Aram, close your mind." Zaman kicked the big guard in the groin. He shouted, and she was overcome by the other guards. At last the husband and wife were subdued, their hands tied.

Ghazal said, "Guards, leave the room."

They tore Zaman's clothing and threw the husband and wife naked on the floor. The two men then removed their pants and stood over their victims half-nude.

"What do you want?" Aram demanded, the alarm in his voice overcoming the words.

"Everything," one of the men said, leering at Aram's nakedness. An evil laughter then filled the hall. It was Ghazal, a common criminal Savak used to rape political prisoners. In the next room, Hussain bit his tongue to keep from crying out, biting so hard that he drew blood.

Ghazal said, "I want him." The other protested, "I want him, too. Who cares about a violent whore?"

Zaman shouted, "We are Iranians, we are innocent! You can't degrade us, you only degrade yourselves. If you touch us, the revolution will tear you apart!" Zaman shouted desperately. She turned her head to Aram and said, "We can't defend our bodies. Blank your mind."

Hussain yelled from the adjacent room, "You are a man, you are a revolutionary. You are a martyr!"

Aram's screams shook the walls. Hussain shouted, "You godless animals!" Aram beat his head against the concrete floor. Just before he knocked himself out he screamed as an object penetrated his rectum.

Zaman lay silent and motionless on the floor. She closed her eyes. She demanded of her mind to think she was dead.

Hussain kept shouting, "Aram, you are a man, you are a father. Zaman, you are my sister, you are a mother."

But then Hussain heard no more from the next room. Finally he heard Ghazal say, "It's no fun anymore." A door opened and closed forcefully, leaving behind on the cold cement floor two naked bodies and two half-conscious minds, those of husband and wife, parents, citizens of Iran, humans, freedom fighters.

Hussain did not hear Zaman whispering to her husband, "I love you, Aram, I love you. You are my Imam, you are my light. Cry, my love. Children cry, women cry, men cry, revolutionaries cry too. Cry, my dear Aram. Cry for me, too. Cry for our country." With a final effort, Zaman rolled painfully over to Aram and put her head on his chest. Aram put his arm around her and sobbed like a child lost from its mother. Zaman felt her mind slipping from her, some merciful circuit breaker switching off her faculties to prevent an overload. Aram continued to sob, his head rising and falling, sending small waves through a pool of thickening blood from the gash on his forehead.

Hussain's pained thoughts returned to his own predicament. His hands and legs were fastened securely to the iron table. He could only with difficulty turn his head left and right. An officer and a guard appeared, and Teherani swept into the room behind them. The officer said to Teherani, "We must wait for the physician."

"We don't need him," Teherani snapped back. "Let him sleep. He was responsible for that bastard Ali Keshavarz' escape. We wouldn't have to be working tonight if the physician had done his job right. The national security is our first priority, it cannot wait. I won't harm him. Leave me. This won't take long," and he motioned for the officer and the guard to leave.

But the guard, a new conscript, was shaken to see a man of God tied to the steel bed. It was a scene he could never have imagined. At a scowl from Teherani, both men left. Teherani turned quickly to Hussain. "This is an emergency. I have little time. I'm tired and impatient, so I will skip the introductions. I know you and you know me. You tell me what I need to know and there is a chance for you. Otherwise I'll have to kill you."

Hussain replied calmly, "Kill me first, then ask your questions. You will get the same result."

Teherani ignored Hussain's challenge. He went to the door and secured the bolt. As Teherani walked back to the bed, he took from his pocket a glass phial he had secretly brought in. He held it up to Hussain's eyes, ordering, "Read the label." Hussain read, "sulfuric acid." He refused to believe it.

Through a haze of fear, Hussain tried to think. He had never heard of acid being used against political prisoners; it was too powerful. He had to appeal to Teherani's religious upbringing, and if that didn't work, he would actively resist like Imam Hussain.

Teherani mocked Hussain. "You are helpless, you and me alone, no witnesses. Now, tell me where Ali is and I'll let you live—"

Hussain interrupted defiantly. "You are blind! There is a witness." Teherani, worried, glanced around quickly. Hussain continued, "Look! God hears your every word, knows your every thought and sees your every deed. He is here in this room, no door is closed to Him, Teherani!"

Teherani hesitated. Hussain continued, "Who is on your side, Teherani? The Shah? Carter? Other Savakis? Conscripts? What will they do to protect you after the revolution and then in the day of judgement?"

Teherani ignored the talk. "Where is your brother?"

"It is Ali's good fortune that I don't know where he is," Hussain answered. "But knowing what you have done to him, and now to my brother and sister, how could you expect me to tell you where even if I knew?"

Teherani said, "If you don't tell me now, I will have your father killed."

"That won't help you either," Hussain said. "No one knows where Ali is, except Ali. Places change for him as times change for us. He doesn't know his next stop himself, until he is there."

"Shut up!" Teherani shouted, grabbing a leather whip from under the table and slashing Hussain across the chest again and again. "Now, mullah, let us see if God comes to your aid."

Hussain clenched his teeth against the pain. "If you remain the hand of evil, then even God's compassion will not reach you."

Teherani's hand squeezed tight in a fist and beat at his own thigh in frustration. Hussain's manner, his voice, his confidence were much like Ali's. Teherani saw Ali strapped to the bed instead of Hussain. This time there would be no wavering, no chance for Hussain to stop his revenge. Teherani bent over and whispered in Hussain's ear, "For a start, would you rather be deaf or blind?"

Hussain shouted, "The revolution will punish you, Teherani. Think before you do more. Think! I have never harmed you. My brother Ali did what he had to do to survive. You cannot blame him, and you cannot blame me for his acts. Think, think." Hussain repeated, "Think, Teherani!"

Teherani laughed. "Your brother made a fool out of me, ruined my reputation and my career. But as you see, I retain my powers and I am thinking!" Teherani pulled out the glass stopper. Then he cupped his hand over Hussain's right eye and brought the phial near.

Hussain twisted his head hard to the right, grabbing Teherani's little finger with his teeth and biting down with all his strength. Teherani screamed and jerked his hand away. The acid and blood poured onto the face of Hussain. He closed his eyes too late and screamed.

Teherani gripped his finger tightly in pain. "I'll show you, you dog." He wrapped a handkerchief around the finger to stanch the blood.

Hussain screamed through his pain, "Help! My eyes! God! My eyes!" The acid droplets instantly ate into his eyes, into the flesh of his cheeks, burned through his lips, the blood and tissue foaming over his face, their smell filling his nostrils. Hussain shook his head as if to shake the acid from his flesh to blow the smell of his own flesh away. But the acid had eaten into his eyes, now only a pair of sockets, sizzling and smoking.

Teherani stuck a handkerchief down Hussain's throat to stop his screams. Before he suffocated, Hussain saw an image of His Holiness, Imam

Hussain, appearing behind a wall of flame. He understood that he must walk through the fire to join his beloved Imam.

Hussain had been physically blinded as the Shah had tried to blind the people of Iran with censorship before murdering them as Teherani had just murdered Hussain. But His Majesty had failed. Hussain, dead in a Savak torture chamber, his toes still vibrating, had ensured the Shah's end. He had urged on, influenced, organized and recruited thousands of Iranian people for the crusade against the Shah's tyranny.

Teherani released the bonds and rolled the corpse onto the floor. He dragged him by the arms and propped him against the wall. Then he took out his pistol and held it to Hussain's disfigured face. Mechanically he pumped three bullets into the head of the dead mullah, the dead Keshavarz, and then ran and unlatched the door, waiting for the watch officer to respond.

Teherani shouted, "The prisoner promised he would tell me Ali's whereabouts if I untied him. I had my gun out, but he jumped me. He's worse than his brother. I had to shoot him."

His voice regained its usual calm. "Tell the guards to clean up the mess. We need the room." Then he stepped out, his face and hand bloody, bearing the wounds of Hussain, the wounds of all his victims. The guards stepped aside in horror as Teherani passed.

Aram sat isolated before the dawn of Friday. He had been brought to the operating room. Under threat of more rape, Aram broke down and released Fedayeen information. On Friday afternoon, two Fedayeen houses were invaded, but all the occupants had left. However, a Savaki told Aram that the information had led to the capture and execution of everyone in the two team houses. The lie was sharper than a switchblade. It left deep gashes in Aram's already tormented soul, his shattered spirit burning over the flame of guilt.

Several days later smuggled photographs documenting Savak torture appeared in a few foreign newspapers. Amnesty International once more accused the Shah of mass torture, mass murder and other violations of human rights. The *New York Times* carried the Amnesty International story, but President Carter and the U.S. government stood fast behind the Shah.

Operation Sweep

On Friday morning, Hussain's corpse was buried within Evin and Zaman and Aram were left alone in separate cells. At noon the funeral cortege of Dr. Mehdi Keshavarz passed through the streets of Teheran as the bodies of Parvine and the unconscious Ali rode toward unmarked graves in

Beheshte Zahra. "Black Friday" was thus born in history.

That morning, just as in Jaleh Square, unarmed people rallied in Shah Square in the southern slums. Government orders were the same everywhere: shoot to kill. The people's cry for justice was met by martial law. Again the people were given bullets for all their needs, but today people responded with their own firearms. Throughout Black Friday in parts of Teheran, the people resisted the Shah's army. The sounds of bullets formed a background for home bombings by the death squads drowning out the footsteps of fleeing demonstrators and the moans of the fallen. Eric Saunders' "Operation Sweep" was in full swing.

Eric was in close touch with the head of Savak to get the list of leaders who were arrested or "neutralized." He had to prepare a report for Washington showing that Operation Sweep was successful, that Iran could become another Indonesia. He grinned when he heard that Dr. Keshavarz' house had been blown up.

Later in the day, Fedayeen and Mujahedin protesters engaged in skirmishes with the troops. They were armed poorly, but they were armed. The battles were brief—after each ambush the guerrillas disappeared into side streets to regroup and appear elsewhere. The Army's reinforcements arrived too late to catch the urban rebels.

The Fedayeen learned about Aram's arrest within a few hours. They quickly abandoned the team houses that he knew about. The Fedayeen discussed an old plan of attacking Evin Prison, to save their comrades, but found it too costly. A Fedayeen call to Evin threatened the death penalty to personnel who tortured a Fedayeen or a political prisoner. The Fedayeen also discussed Ali's disappearance. Someone thought Ali had been loaded onto a truck, but nothing was certain. Two Fedayeen were assigned to find Ali.

Despite the Shah's jubilation over the victory in Jaleh Square, the generals found that their mighty army was unable to impose order in the cities. Although the tactical defeats depressed the generals, they in turn inspired the people who discovered that such urban guerrilla actions were effective. The survivors of Black Friday shed their last fears.

Barricades with Molotov cocktails and handguns behind them rose throughout the city. Old cars, tires, cast iron gates and sandbags were piled up to slow down the soldiers. The soldiers gradually tore down the barricades, but not without losses. The revolutionaries gained confidence with each success, as quickly as the army's morale deteriorated. Physicians drove from house to house on motorcycles, bicycles or cars, carrying their instruments as they dodged the bullets. Hospitals were watched by Savak, and wounded there could be arrested.

Teheran shook under the feet of freedom fighters, no longer just protesters. The survivors were saddened but ever more united to end the bloody regime of the Shah. The myth of his power crumbled, ironically, just as he succeeded in a mass execution of his citizens. The Shah had played his last card and could now only await the inevitable outcome. The initiative had passed to the people.

General Oveissi, martial law administrator for Black Friday, had been commandant of the Imperial Guard in 1963 during the massacre which had claimed the life of Abbas Keshavarz. In Friday evening's press conference for foreign correspondents, General Oveissi announced the casualty figures Eric and Savak had agreed upon: fifty-eight citizens killed and 205 wounded, explaining all as resulting from a riot fomented by foreign agents.

A few years later in Paris, General Oveissi's body was riddled with bullets by the children of his victims.

Based on inside sources and missing persons reports, various opposition groups estimated between three and five thousand dead. The foreign press, counting five hundred corpses in morgues, objectively reported five hundred killed and thousands injured. They had no time to search for and dig up mass graves.

The revolutionary leaders agreed that the Shah had destroyed any chance of compromise. He now would not only have to abandon power, he would have to abdicate and leave the country. Some demanded he be tried for crimes against the people.

On the following Thursday, six days after Black Friday, after hundreds of atrocities had been verified and publicized, after Eric had carried his report to Washington, after the emergency conferences in the National Security Council, after President Carter had preached peace and human justice in his Sunday church homily, the President telephoned the Shah to assure him once more of his sympathy, support and "sentiments of gratitude and personal friendship."

CHAPTER 22

Family Gathering

Shamil and Kamil arrived at Beheshte Zahra cemetery in a commandeered jeep and began to search for Ali among the dead and wounded. They saw trucks unloading the Black Friday victims into mass graves and bulldozers pushing dirt over them, but there was no sign of Ali. The two Savakis were about to give up when a new truck pulled up, the driver complaining of roadblocks. The soldiers threw nineteen bodies including Parvine's into a pit. At last they hoisted Ali, bloodied almost beyond recognition, and swung to throw him into the ditch.

Kamil raised his arm. "Stop! That is our corpse. We'll take him."

"Are you certain?" asked an officer.

"Absolutely," said Kamil.

"Bring him back here when you're done. We will be busy into the night," said the captain.

Kamil replied, "Good enough. Must we sign for it?"

"No, the Americans are interested in numbers, but I don't care. He's a bloody mess," the officer warned. "Where is your vehicle?"

Shamil pointed and the soldiers put Ali into the jeep. The Savakis thanked the captain and Kamil drove away.

Just beyond the gate, Ali moaned and passed out again. Shamil turned and felt Ali's pulse. "He's alive! Take him to the nearest hospital."

Kamil said, "The nearest is the worst. The Committee for Revenge will finish him off."

"Then how about Shemiran?"

"Now you're talking," said Kamil as he pushed the accelerator, whipping the jeep northward to distant Shemiran at the foot of the Elburz. "Ali was in an accident. That is all we say. Remember, Shamil."

The next day, on the morning of September 9th, Ali awoke thinking he was back in Evin's hospital, even though Shamil and Kamil had told him of his narrow escape from death. The tortures in Evin, locked in his mind,

277

would torment him as long as he lived.

Ali's head was covered by a bandage, his ribs were bruised, and his left leg, bound in a cast, felt like someone else's. He had a fractured femur.

He thought of Parvine, and her hair streaked with blood. Her white scarf a red flag flapping at her side aroused anger in Ali. What had become of Aram and Zaman, of his family, of his comrades?

As his pain diminished, his agitation grew. He had to hide, to survive for his family and the revolution. He felt exposed and helpless despite the assumed name Kamil and Shamil had given him. The hospital was unsafe, and he knew Kamil and Shamil's loyalty was thin.

But at the moment, they were all he had. Ali waited impatiently for the two Savakis. Every minute counted. But where was he to hide? The crackdown made the team houses risky, and he would burden his comrades. He would not be able to move quickly during the six weeks he would have to wait until his cast was removed.

The images of Teherani and the bust at Columbia and the anxious faces of Pirooz and Sara in the New York hospital passed through his mind. Pirooz had written that Sara was living in Teheran and that she had asked about him. But Ali could not risk revealing he was alive. Could Sara help him now? Ali shrugged off the idea, but it forced its way back. It was impossible; Sara was married to Eric Saunders, CIA. But what choices did he have? Eric was an enemy, but perhaps Sara could find a way. It wouldn't hurt to ask; it was worse not to. He lifted the receiver beside the bed and dialed a memorized telephone number.

"Hello, Saunders' residence." Her magic voice rang in his life once more. "Saunders' residence," Sara repeated. Ali felt fire run inside him.

"Hello, Sara, this is Ali."

"Ali who?" Sara asked.

"Ali Keshavarz, Sara."

Sara declared icily, "Mr. Keshavarz is dead. I have no time for this."

Ali interrupted. "Wait! Sara, I always saved the biggest cherries for you."

"My God, Ali! It is you." Ali heard the telephone fall and hit the tile floor. Sara returned to the line. "You're alive."

"Yes, but I need help to stay alive."

"What can I do, Ali?" Sara asked.

"I am hurt. I'm in a hospital now, but the secret police will find me here soon. I have nowhere to go."

Ten years coalesced into ten seconds. Sara was eager to nurse Ali just as she had after his release from the hospital in New York. "Yes, of course, you can stay with us. Where are you? Shall I come to get you?"

Ali did not answer. "What about Eric?"

Sara said, "He's in Washington for a few weeks."

"What about friends? Servants?" Ali asked.

Sara said, "All the servants are for Khomeini. Ali, you'll be safe here. They'll care for you like the pupil of their eye." The Persian idiom reassured Ali. "We can hide you in their quarters, away from visitors and Cyrus's friends."

For a moment, Ali was puzzled. "Who is Cyrus?"

"Our son—I mean, my son." Sara's heart almost burst through her chest, but she recovered quickly. "Now, where is the hospital? I'll come to get you."

"No, don't. Savak is too close. This phone call is dangerous and I must finish quickly. Is it all right if I get there in half an hour?"

"Yes, Ali."

"Then goodbye."

"Goodbye." Sara hung up with one question that had to wait: "Why, Ali? Why didn't you call all this time?"

Ali heard footsteps approaching his room. He feared Teherani behind the door, felt the handkerchief pushed down his throat and gasped for air. The door opened, and Shamil and Kamil rushed in, their usual smiles gone. Kamil hurried to say, "You can't stay here. Savak agents are invading this hospital, too. The wounded are being dragged out, and physicians who resist are being arrested or beaten up."

"Yes, you must get away quickly," Shamil agreed.

"I know."

"Where will you go?" asked Kamil.

"That is my secret," Ali said tersely. "All I ask is that you get me a taxi."

Kamil frowned. "Are you sure you can manage?"

"Yes," Ali answered. "But tell me, have you found out anything about my family?"

Shamil hung his head and Kamil looked away and said, "Our condolences. Your father was killed on Friday and your mother is recovering from the shock. Your brother, sister and her husband were arrested, but we have not located them yet."

Ali saw his father praying, just like the portrait of Imam Ali in their guest room. He saw the sword of an unbeliever strike the Imam from behind. Kamil finally penetrated his daze. "Ali, are you all right?"

Ali whispered, "Yes. Can you help Zaman, Hussain and Aram?"

Kamil said, "We will do our best, Ali. But first let's get you to safety."

Ali commanded, "Then call a taxi."

Shamil left the room. Ali got Kamil's telephone number and asked him to collect his medicine. Shamil returned to say, "I have a taxi."

Ali ordered, "Give me the crutches." The two Savakis obeyed the revolutionary without hesitation. With Kamil's help, Ali lifted himself onto the crutches and took his first awkward steps. Shamil held the door and the three men left the room.

A nurse blocked their path. "This patient is not released," she scolded. "We have orders."

Kamil thrust his Savak identity card in the nurse's face, and she jumped back as if she had seen a cobra. "Now please move away," he ordered.

They helped Ali into the back seat of the taxi. When the engine roared, Ali said, "Hold on," and called to Kamil and Shamil at the curb. "Thank you. You've saved my life."

Shamil asked, "Will we see you again?"

"Maybe," said Ali. "I have your number. Listen, help the revolution or get out of the country. Khoda Hafez. Goodbye."

As the cab pulled away, Kamil and Shamil said together, "Khoda Hafez."

The driver said, "Where to, Agha?"

"Fereshteh Street. Near the Hilton." The car drove south along oak-lined Pahlavi Avenue, away from the snowcapped mountains. It was a beautiful September day.

The driver began to talk. "I hope your injury is not serious. I've had more wounded than healthy passengers since yesterday. The whole nation is wounded."

Ali hid his face in his hands, tears flowing under their own power. He imagined Parvine calling to him, "Cry for me, Uncle Ali, but fight to the end," his father counselling patience, his mother praying, Maryam watering the flowers, Hamid Ashraf saying, "You go, get away. I have not died for a long time," Zaman, Aram and Hussain, wherever they were. Ali thought of their fate. What an insane world! He had just lost his family, and in a few minutes he would see the woman he had dreamed about all these years. He was saddest at the time he thought he would be the happiest.

The taxi driver interrupted Ali's thoughts. "Agha, here we are." He helped Ali onto the sidewalk. When Ali paid, the driver said, "Thank you. May God heal you."

A large iron gate creaked open. A man came to help Ali inside and across the yard. A woman stepped from behind a huge oak. "Hello, Ali."

With difficulty, Ali faced Sara's voice, the same voice which had strengthened him in the darkest hours of Evin. But now he heard the voice with his ears, not just with his mind. "Hello, Sara."

Sara reached out a hand, and he felt it quiver and let it drop. He would not hug her in front of the servant.

Sara spoke hesitantly. "It is good to see you, Ali."

"You, too, Sara," Ali said. They smiled guardedly.

Sara said, "Please help the gentleman to the guest room,

Mohammed."

"Yes, Sara Khanoum," the man responded.

Ali started. "You speak Farsi."

Sara said, "Cyrus speaks it without an accent. I'll have to tell him about you. Nothing can happen around here without his knowledge."

Ali said, "Are you sure that it is safe?"

"Absolutely," Sara answered without looking into Ali's eyes. "He can keep a secret. He's as revolutionary as his Iranian friends."

They went into the guest room, where Mohammed helped Ali into a round couch which imitated the curvature of the window behind it. The red velvet upholstery of the couch and chairs captured and reflected the light streaking through a sheer white curtain. An etagere against the wall held a collection of porcelain dolls Eric had brought back from his numerous trips.

Sara said, "Thank you, Mohammed." When Mohammed had left, Sara stared at Ali for the first time. Ali appeared older, more solid; his eyes looked not like an eagle's, but like those of a hunted deer. He looked like a father, a teacher, and not the college student that Sara remembered. The warm sunlight engulfed them both and fell on a light blue Kashan rug with a bouquet of roses woven in the center. Sara had lived long without the love of a man. She was starved for a gentle glance, a trusting touch. She sat at Ali's feet, took his slender hands in hers and shook them. "Ali, are you all right? Stop looking at the dolls. Look at me." She talked as if to fill the room with words, to push Eric's lies out of her life.

Ali felt secure in Sara's soft, comforting grasp, yet he had to struggle to speak. "My father was murdered, my niece executed, my brothers and sister have disappeared, and a grave has almost devoured me. Forgive me, Sara, for being cold for not recognizing my dream has come true. I have so much on my mind." Ali then drew Sara close and embraced her whole-heartedly, as much in pain as in joy. Sara sighed and then she trembled in his arms. Ali felt it and let her free. He then asked, "Tell me what has happened to you. Let me just listen."

Sara said, "What can I tell you? Eric told me you were dead, but my love for you never died. I understand why you couldn't tell me you were alive, knowing my husband is a CIA agent. Just as you are in trouble, so am I, Ali. Cyrus is my whole life. I am his mother, and also his friend, his sister, his political ally, but he is my umbilical cord to life. I am married to a man I do not love. That is no secret. He loves his career more than anything else. I don't sleep with him, and I don't sleep with the CIA."

Sara clasped Ali's hands. "Your fingertips touch mine. I feel I am an extension of you, Ali. I wish I could take your hand and Cyrus's and run away. I want freedom and I want love. I have missed you."

Sara kissed his palms again and again. She buried her face in his hands and sobbed. Her blue eyes full of tears, her heart palpitating, Sara lifted her head and looked into Ali's eyes.

"But how can I burden you with my tedious days, so numerous I cannot tell them apart? It is you that must talk, Ali. Your family is mankind; your food, work and dream is the revolution. You haven't lost your goal, for it draws closer every day. I have come to love Iranians and I admire their struggle, just as I loved you and your struggle."

Ali whispered, "You make me feel I still have a family, Sara."

Sara fell silent. She sat with her back against Ali's leg and her head bent over her drawn-up knees; the wave of golden hair glittered in the sun playing hide and seek with the Persian clouds. The dreams, the new hopes and fears, the sun streaming through the window held the two of them.

The sadness in Sara's voice had pushed aside Ali's own grief and fears for a moment, and he felt loving and protective. His fingertips reached for her hair, that golden hair, but withdrew after a touch. He still loved her. Ali's two Saras—one a memory, one married to his enemy—merged into the same woman. Whose tears, whose lips touched him now? Whose golden strands spread all around him?

Ali choked back a sob as he held in his anger, his pain, his grief and his purpose. It would have been safer to endanger his body elsewhere than to torment his soul here. He should not love this woman who cried silently, watering the love roots that he thought had dried up.

"Sara, I have committed two crimes: I have loved you and I have loved the dispossessed. I am in love with a woman in a trap. I am also trapped: I am wounded and I am a communist taking refuge in the home of a CIA agent," Ali said. "I am in my own country, but I'm also in enemy territory."

Ali said gently, "Khanoum Sara, *gerye kon, gerye kon, baraye hameyeh ma*. Lady Sara, cry, cry for all of us."

Sara turned to put her tear-streaked face on Ali's knee, holding his ankle tightly. She said, *"Man ham yek zendani hastam.* I am a prisoner, too."

At length, Ali smiled and said, "This doesn't look like a prison. What prevents you from running away?"

Sara answered, "Eric has threatened to take Cyrus if we separate. He is the CIA station chief—he's a powerful man with powerful friends."

Sara got up and dried her eyes, then pulled up a chair and looked straight into Ali's eyes. "What do you know about Eric's activities, Ali?"

Ali replied, "Only that Professor Pirooz wrote me that Eric was probably with the CIA."

Sara answered, "It's worse than that. I will reveal a secret to you that I cannot tell anyone else. A few weeks ago I was able to look into his safe which he always keeps locked. He's not just the CIA chief in Iran, he's involved in heroin traffic in partnership with Princess Ashraf." Sara then gave

Ali the details.

Sara said, "Remember Pirooz' party when I tried to teach you to dance? Well, I read in Eric's diary that he was very jealous over that. He sensed my interest in you before I knew it myself. He is good at sniffing things out." Sara smiled. "You told me then when you danced with me you forgot everything else. I thought you said that to all the women that night."

Ali smiled teasingly. "I did just that."

Sara smiled, too, as a stubborn teardrop rolled over her face. "You remember that, after what you've been through?"

"I remember everything about you."

Sara finished telling Ali Eric's secrets. "There, now I'm guilty of treason."

Ali reassured her. "Don't worry about treason, worry about Eric. This isn't just CIA stuff, it's Mafia crime. The son of a bitch!" he exclaimed. "He's been out to get me from the start. His ideology, profession, family relationships all match." Ali concluded, "Then fear holds you together."

Sara replied, "I married a lawyer, not a mobster and spy." Sara looked into Ali's eyes. "We are friends, yes?"

"Yes, at least friends." Ali smiled.

A man's words rang into the room. "Lady Sara, the room is ready."

"You need to eat and rest, Ali," Sara said.

She helped Ali to his room. A small desk against the wall stood beside a bookcase with a radio on the shelf. A blue blanket over a white sheet mimicked the colors of sky and clouds. The pillowcase was covered with delicate needlepoint roses curling across it. Sara observed Ali admiring it. "It is my needlework," she said. "They are the red roses of Iran."

Ali lay on the bed, exhausted from his injuries and exertion. Sara said, "Should I call a doctor?"

"Thank you, but I have medicine." Ali smiled. "There is no cure for a dead man."

Sara smiled back and said, "How about some pastry and capuccino?"

Ali said, "Yes, I'd like that. I've missed the taste."

Sara ordered the maid to bring a tray.

"Capuccino here?" Ali inquired.

"It just takes a small machine."

"You don't miss anything, Sara."

"But I feel as if I miss everything."

Sara could not wait to tell Ali about Cyrus. Feeling guilty for keeping the secret so long, she forgot that Ali needed rest. She had thought Ali dead, never knowing he had a son, and Cyrus never meeting his real father. Sara trusted Ali; she would not keep secrets from him. He had been resurrected to her, and she felt a stirring in her heart for him. He had always been truthful to her, and she was going to be truthful to him—always.

"I have a secret. God has saved you to hear it."

Ali said, "God?"

Sara waved her hand. "When I see a miracle, I can only think of God. I love you, I love Cyrus, and I love God. Will you accept the facts?"

"Yes."

Sara took a deep breath. "Cyrus is our son."

Ali said, "Yes, I know that."

"No, you don't know!" Sara exclaimed. "He's your son, not Eric's."

"Mine?" Ali tried to stand, but a shooting pain crippled his effort and compelled stillness.

Sara said quietly, "Yes, yours. He looks just like you. He speaks Farsi like his classmates. Wait, Ali, wait and see." Sara sighed. "At last I am free of this burden."

Ali, dazed by her revelation, stared at Sara and whispered, "Cyrus, my son." Sara allowed him a moment to adjust to the shock of his new fatherhood. "Tonight I will prepare him and tomorrow you try to tell him who you are, if it is all right with you," she suggested.

Ali said, "How?"

Sara said, "Simple. Tell him you are his Baba. Tell him you love him." Trembling, Sara stood and sought Ali's shoulders. "Tell him he is your *pessar,* your son."

A knock on the door pushed Sara away from Ali. A maid entered carrying a tray with two demitasses, a dish of pastry and a big bowl of apples, pears, grapes, cucumbers and apricots. Sara took the tray and placed it close to Ali. With a cup and a cookie she sat on the edge of the chair.

Ali asked bitterly, "Does everyone know this except me and Cyrus?"

"Just me, Eric and God," Sara replied. "I kept Cyrus a secret because you wanted to work for the revolution. I tried to free you for revolution and tried to do my best for Cyrus. Cyrus is everything to me, and he has also been your living memory.

"I married Eric to give Cyrus the financial support and protection of a father. Eric was happy since he couldn't have children of his own. I found this out, of course, later. Anyhow, Eric made me promise him at first not to tell you or Cyrus."

"Forever?"

"Eric wanted that, but I didn't promise it."

"So he stole my son just as he is trying to steal my country," Ali said. Sara said, "At the time, I thought—"

"Mohammed, where is Mom?" A boy's voice rang out from downstairs in Farsi.

"Upstairs, not in the main building," the gardener replied.

Ali waited anxiously. Sara sat frozen.

Cyrus asked, "Why is she there?"

"She has a guest," replied Mohammed.

Footsteps rushed upstairs. There was a knock, a shout, "Mom!" and the door flew open.

Sara struggled to compose herself. "You must knock, Cyrus."

"I did knock," Cyrus protested.

Ali concentrated on the child in the doorway. Cyrus looked like a photograph of himself at ten.

Cyrus looked at Ali. "Mom, who is he? Does he speak English?"

Sara stammered, "Yes. His name is Ali. You may call him Uncle Ali." Cyrus stepped toward Ali and asked, "How do you do?"

Ali replied, "I am fine, how are you?"

"I am all right." The two weighed each other momentarily; then Cyrus abruptly turned to his mother. "Guess what I did today."

"What?" asked Sara.

Cyrus fumbled in his pocket and held up a piece of red chalk. "I wrote, '*Marg bar shah*. Death to the Shah' on the school wall." Ali smiled in disbelief.

"You were forbidden," Sara said firmly.

"Don't worry, Mom. The kids hid me. No one could see."

"Still, it is wrong."

"All the kids do it," Cyrus replied.

Sara embraced Cyrus. With resignation and a trace of impatience she said, "We'll discuss it later."

Cyrus said, "Okay, but that won't change anything."

Sara said, "I don't want to change your opinion, Cyrus. It's your actions that frighten me."

Cyrus said, "Mom, do you remember Agha Djafar, Mr. Jackson's gardener, who brought us white mulberries?"

"Yes."

"A helicopter shot him yesterday." Cyrus shook his head sadly. "It is so unfair."

Then the words tumbled out in a rush as he glanced at Ali. "Agha Djafar made us hold a big sheet under a mulberry tree. He would climb the tree and shout, 'shaking time.' Then he would shake the tree filling the sheet with mulberries. Once, when a big one wouldn't fall, Djafar shouted, 'I'll get you, you sucker.'

"He was so funny. Once he pretended to be a scorpion, singing, dancing and climbing a wall. He made you feel he was a scorpion."

Cyrus looked at the floor. "He is dead. His kids have no baba now. People are calling it Black Friday."

Sara said, "What is that?"

"Yesterday was Black Friday, because of all the people killed. Now you know why I wrote on the wall. If the Shah is dead, he cannot kill anymore people.''

Cyrus turned to Ali. ''Does your leg hurt?''

''A little.''

''How about your head?''

''It is getting better. What about you, Cyrus?''

Cyrus said, ''I'm fine, except for the killings.''

Ali smiled at Cyrus, ''I agree. But good things are happening, too. The people are rising up.'' He wanted to grab Cyrus, hug him tight and say he loved him. Cyrus talked as though he knew the Shah had murdered his grandfather, uncle and cousin. ''If the Shah is dead he cannot kill people,'' Ali repeated in his mind. Cyrus was like a wonderful dream after the nightmare of Black Friday.

Cyrus asked, ''How did you break your leg?''

''I was hit by a jeep.''

''Did they shoot at you?''

''Yes. But listen, Cyrus. You must not talk about me to anyone, not even to your friends.''

''All right.'' Then he asked, ''Do you know my dad? He's in Washington now.''

''Yes, I know him.''

Cyrus felt comfortable with this man who had fought the Shah. ''Uncle Ali, when you are well will you play catch with me?''

''We won't have to wait for that. Do you play chess?''

''A little. My friend Manoucher—he lives next door—taught me. I like chess, because you don't have to be lucky to win.'' Cyrus added with a twinkle in his eye, ''Besides, I like to attack the king.'' He thought, then added, ''You know, calling you Uncle Ali sounds funny.''

''Cyrus,'' Ali said, ''I agree. It's too sudden, and I'm not your uncle, anyway.''

''Then what should I call you?'' Cyrus asked.

''Are you ready to hear the biggest surprise of your life?''

''Yes, yes.'' Cyrus turned to his mother, who nodded her approval.

Ali said, ''Okay, Cyrus. Hand me that mirror.'' Cyrus brought the mirror and sat next to him on the bed. Ali drew Cyrus close and held the mirror out so that both faces were reflected side by side. Cyrus threw Sara a puzzled glance, but she just smiled.

''Look at your eyebrows,'' Ali said.

''They connect like yours,'' said Cyrus.

''And the cheeks?''

Cyrus responded, ''Mom, look! He has a dimple like mine.''

''Yes, Cyrus, I know,'' Sara said.

Ali slid his shirt off his right shoulder to reveal a birthmark. A similar mark showed from under Cyrus's shirt. Cyrus nearly upset Ali's balance, shouting, "The same color. The same place. Impossible." He turned to Ali like a prosecutor. "Who are you, then?" He did not wait for an answer. "You slouch your shoulders. I do it, too, even when Daddy reminds me to stand straight."

Ali put the mirror down. "Do you want to know everything?"

Cyrus said, "Yes, I do."

Ali held Cyrus by the shoulders. "Will you believe me?"

"Yes, I promise."

"Your daddy, Eric, is your stepfather. I am your real father, your baba!"

Cyrus raised his voice. "My baba?"

"Yes, yes, your baba." Ali pulled Cyrus close and kissed him, repeating, "Yes, I'm your father."

Cyrus squirmed to check with his mother. Sara nodded her confirmation as tears streaked her face. She had dreamed of this scene so often and for so long. Cyrus sat down beside Ali and held his hands firmly, staring at his new father. The appearance of a new father was like fireworks for him, unbelievable to a person who had not seen it before, yet it was so colorful, so noisy, and so real. There was something special about the bearded man. Cyrus was convinced.

Sara said, "It's true, dear. He is your baba, your real father. Your daddy took care of you as if you were his own son."

Cyrus asked Ali, "Why did you leave us?"

Ali said, "I was ordered to leave America before you were born. I didn't know I had a son."

Cyrus glanced at his mother, and Sara wiped her tears and whispered, "Everything your baba says is true."

Cyrus asked, "Why didn't you come to us in Teheran?"

"The Shah put me in prison, so your mother thought I was dead."

Cyrus turned to his mother. "Mom, now I will write 'Death to the Shah' on every wall." He looked back to Ali. "How did you get out of jail, then?"

"I served my sentence, and then I went into hiding."

Questions crowded the child's head, demanding attention all at once. Before he could ask any more, Ali said, "Cyrus, you trust me, just as I trust you to keep my visit a secret, yes?"

"Yes," replied Cyrus.

Ali said, "Then I'll tell you everything soon. We have a lot to learn about each other. If I had known you were my son, I would have come to you sooner. We cannot change the past, but we can change the future."

Sara sat on the bed and held hands with father and son. Their fingers intertwined, reaching for the unity which they had never had. Sara had never felt happier; she wanted the moment to last, wanted to put their hands on her heart to feel the new beat of life.

Cyrus insisted, "Will you play catch with me?"

Ali said, "As soon as I can." He pulled Cyrus to him. Cyrus did not resist. He wanted to be hugged by his baba. Ali said, "We will play whatever we wish. Also, you will tell me your stories, like the one about Agha Djafar, and I will do the same. Okay, Cyrus?"

"Okay." Then, hesitantly, Cyrus repeated, "Okay, Baba."

A maid knocked and stepped in. "Agha Cyrus, your friends are downstairs."

Cyrus looked at Sara and Ali, one at a time, deciding whom to ask. "Should I go?"

Sara said, "If you want to."

Cyrus said, "I promised to play, but if I had known my baba—"

Ali interrupted. "Keep your promise, Cyrus." Sara nodded.

Cyrus hugged his baba and heard Ali whisper, "I love you, Cyrus, more than anything else."

Cyrus ran to the door, then turned back to look at Ali. "See you, Baba." Cyrus's disappearance was as sudden as his arrival.

Sara sought Ali's hand once more. Above the sounds of the children drifting up to them, Sara said, "Remember, Ali, you need rest."

Ali, exhausted, agreed. "Sara, my comrades will be looking for me. Please call this number from an outside telephone and say, 'Ali is alive but recovering from a wound.'"

Sara smiled. "Yes, sir."

"Now I need a glass of water."

Sara brought it and helped Ali take his pills. He lay down and she covered him with a sheet and adjusted the pillows. Ali felt secure with Sara at his side.

She said, "I will call an Iranian doctor to see you this evening. Don't worry, he's a close friend. There will be no visitors, and I'll make sure you're not disturbed. We'll have supper with Cyrus later. Call me if you need anything."

"I haven't felt at home for such a long time, but I do now. Thank you, Sara." Then Ali's thoughts pushed through his words. "Is it true, Sara? Is that bright ball of fire my son?"

"You know it's true." She kissed his forehead. "Now rest, Ali." Ali fell into a deep sleep.

Sara went out, leaving her heart in the small servant's room, taking with her a crisscrossing of emotions—love, fear and a desire to be free. She left to make the call for Ali.

Cyrus ran to play football, running away from unbelievable to familiar scenes. But he couldn't keep his mind on the ball or on anything but unsettling questions. He tried to concentrate, as Eric had coached him, but today he dropped passes.

Baba was a welcome word, a secret desire of Cyrus's. All his friends had babas. Cyrus had learned that more children in the world call their father baba than any other word, but Eric demanded to be called Daddy. Cyrus loved Eric, but no man had ever hugged him like his baba Ali, no one had whispered in his ear, "I love you more than anything else." He ran to his mother's room when the game ended. He had many questions and he asked them all.

At dinner that evening, father and son talked of the past and the future. Ali told about mountain climbing as a boy, when he and his friends had discovered huge steel pipes being installed to bring water to the Niavaran Palace. They pushed a pipe down a slope, creating havoc. The headmaster at Alborz High School had to intervene to keep the police away. Cyrus admired his baba's bravery. His eyes were fixed on Ali as though trying to make up for the lost time.

Quickly days ran after one another like sparrows in flight. Ali became a fixture in Sara's and Cyrus's life as father and son spent much time together. Ali's role as a father grew on him, and he grew in Cyrus's mind as a baba. The truth of their relationship had leaked out to son and father despite Savak and the CIA. Every day brought nourishment to attachments starved for moments that ought to have happened already. Father and son were twin stars attracted by the gravity of love. It was hard for Ali to keep up with Cyrus, but it was harder to say no. Cyrus treasured the time his baba had stored up for him. But Cyrus also had begun to worry about his father leaving them after his wounds healed. The boy knew his father could not stay there permanently.

But father and son were prisoners walled in by bricks and by the fear of Savak and a certain CIA agent. But there were no limits to the terrain they could explore about each other. They were free to play, to talk, to agree or disagree, to laugh, to sit together in contented silence, to dream.

So they played lots of chess, and Ali balanced himself on his crutches against the wall and caught tennis balls from Cyrus, or stood in front of a table with the carpet rolled up and played goalkeeper, while Cyrus kicked a tennis ball through his legs, cast and crutches.

Sara watched the joy fill the house and garden, as father and son's laughter ran over the flowers and filled her heart. She had waited many years to hear that laughter.

The house was built on two acres. The main yard at the south held a fishpool at the center, with a fig tree, two persimmons and a cluster of oak trees rooted several feet from the white stucco walls of the house. The family quarters spread north of a patio. A large, square hall at the center connected to the family room, guest room, dining room and kitchen and held an open staircase twisting to a second-floor balcony with bedrooms and Eric's study around it. To the north, a small yard separated the main building from the plain brick servants' quarters, where two maids, a cook, a chauffeur and Mohammed the gardener lived.

From an outside balcony, the garden looked like a huge flowerpot, the colors and scents competing for the attention of men and honeybees. Mohammed worked from dawn to dusk to please these seasonal guests with different names—rose, begonia, carnation, tulip, chrysanthemum, aster, marigold.

This setting to Ali was a Garden of Eden. Despite the nagging feeling that he should be fighting alongside his comrades, he had not been this content in years. He informed his close comrades of his whereabouts, and they ordered him to stay put until his leg healed and the search for him cooled off.

As Sara had predicted, her servants took great pride in aiding the fugitive revolutionary. At Ali's request, Mohammed regularly phoned Kamil, and through him Ali learned of Hussain's death and Zaman and Aram's imprisonment. Kamil promised to try to include Zaman and Aram in the list of prisoners the Shah planned to pardon for publicity. Ali discussed politics with the servants and they drew close to him.

Ali wondered, "How long can I fight back? When will it be my turn to join the dead?" Images of his brothers, father, Parvine and Hamid Ashraf appeared and disappeared in his mind. But the great emptiness left by the death or disappearance of his family and comrades was filled by Cyrus, who proved the best medicine for him. Ali's head healed and his leg grew stronger.

Whenever he was not with Cyrus and Sara, Ali thought, read and wrote about the tasks ahead. Sara delivered to a comrade a short article of Ali's which was published in a clandestine Fedayeen newsletter. It was an invitation to oil workers to stop production for export, to limit production only to domestic civilian needs.

At dinner Ali laughed at the irony that the CIA was sheltering him and helping him stop the flow of oil to U.S. military bases around the world.

One evening as Ali lay on the bed, Cyrus sat on his chest, put his thumbs under Ali's armpits and threatened to tickle him unless Ali raised his hands in surrender.

"Resign, Big Baba," Cyrus demanded again and again.

"Yes, yes, Cyrus, I resign." When Ali raised his hands Cyrus tickled him a little.

"Please, don't tickle me any more. I can't breathe with you on my chest." Ali laughed and squirmed, half from the tickling and half from joy.

Cyrus said, "Okay, but promise you won't tickle me if I let go."

Ali said, "If you free me I'll tell you a Persian story."

"It better be good." Cyrus sat with ears open in anticipation.

"This is a story from the *Shahname,* the Book of Kings, by Ferdowsi, a famous poet. It took him thirty-seven years to compose the history of Iran in one long poem. He starts with the adventures of legendary heroes and finishes with real men, events, wars, victories and defeats. The *Shahname* preserved tales which might otherwise have been lost in time."

Cyrus asked impatiently, "Are you going to tell me all of it?"

Ali said, "No, just one tale. It's about Rustam, the most powerful man who ever lived, and his son, Sohrab, whom he had never seen." Ali explained the tragedy of Rustam, who killed his son in battle, thinking he was the enemy general. Cyrus said, "We are luckier. We found each other and no one is hurt."

Afterwards, sitting at the edge of the fishpool and playing with the water, Cyrus looked at Ali and said, "Baba, I have to tell you something. Do you promise not to tell anybody?"

Ali said, "I promise."

Cyrus said, "My daddy isn't a lawyer—he's a spy. My mother called him that one time when they thought I was asleep."

Ali replied, "I know, Cyrus. But remember, your daddy has cared for you. He may be my enemy, but he is not your enemy."

Cyrus said, "I know. I just wish he weren't a spy, and you two could be friends."

Ali said, "I wish so, too. Maybe your daddy will change so we could all be friends."

On Friday, October 28th, the doctor removed Ali's cast and a cane replaced the crutches. Ali was strong enough to walk into the dangerous world once more.

Eric was due back on Monday. The weeks had gone quickly but had allowed father and son to travel a great distance together. Ali dreaded leaving, and so did Sara and Cyrus, but there was no choice.

On Saturday the servants went to march in a demonstration. Although the servants visited their families regularly, rarely did they all leave on the same day. Cyrus reluctantly went to play chess with his friend Manoucher, leaving Sara and Ali alone in the house for the first time since Ali's arrival. Ali's rekindled love for Sara was stronger than ever, making their solitude on this day especially painful for Ali. A brief affair with a revolutionary woman had ended conveniently when he had left Beirut. Since he had arrived at Sara's, Ali's strong will had had to struggle with the impulses of his heart and body prodding him to go to Sara in her nakedness, to squeeze her loveliness in his arms, to brush her silky whiteness with his burning fingers leaving invisible words of love on her skin. Only with constant effort had Ali kept his distance from Sara since the sudden embrace on the day of his arrival. It mattered not that Sara did not love her husband or that she loved Ali, or that Eric had stolen Sara, his son and country from him. And it did not matter that the marriage itself was no more than paled words on a dried-up, wrinkled legal document. What stopped Ali was that Sara was someone else's wife in the eyes of his new friends, the household servants, and—most importantly in the eyes of his own son and himself. Ali felt the trappings of Fatema's upbringing and heard in his mind the alarm bells ringing. Ali kept reminding himself that Sara was taboo as he tossed and turned in his small bed night after night.

It was Ali's honor that forbade it. If the people learned all about his life, he wanted to be able to acknowledge every bit of it without reservation. Making love to Sara, another man's wife, at this time would not be something he could admit to. Sara understood Ali's principles, inflexibility, and capacity to absorb pain or to inflict pain on others, to demonstrate by example the life of a revolutionary. Sara accepted Ali's will, her own will, and made it easier by distancing herself from him. She acted as though she had also been nursed by Fatema. So the two lovers stayed at arm's length, and planned how to deal with Eric. Ali and Eric had to agree to share Cyrus; there was no other way.

Ali would surprise Eric upon his arrival, before he could order Ali's arrest. Sara knew that Eric was always unarmed, and Ali would cut the telephone lines. Sara would arrange for a Fedayeen to wait outside the house in a car, in case Sara could not take Ali away herself. They could give Eric no opportunity to trick them. Ali had Cyrus and Sara on his side, but Eric had the armies of the Shah on his. Sara assured Ali that Eric would keep quiet because he could not afford the scandal of a fugitive revolutionary in his house, and because she would threaten him with the heroin connection if he didn't cooperate.

Finally at 10 a.m. on Monday, October 31st, Eric arrived home. Ali hid in his room; Cyrus was in school. In the guest room Sara announced, "Eric, we need to talk. Something has come up that can't wait."

"Very well," Eric said reluctantly; he was tired from the long flight. "What is it, Sara?"

"Ali is alive!" Sara stared accusingly into Eric's eyes and continued, "And you know it."

Eric was taken aback at Sara's knowledge. He controlled his voice despite his anxiety. "Where is he?"

Sara said, "Here."

"In Teheran?"

Sara said, "No, here in this house. The father and son have been together and love each other."

Eric exploded, "What father? What son? Cyrus is mine!"

"We've covered things up for too long." Sara became softer. "You will always be Cyrus's daddy, but Ali is his real father, and you are the step-father."

"He's my stepson, is that it?"

"Yes, what else?" Sara answered.

"Where is Ali?"

"He'll be here shortly."

"A terrorist in my home!"

Sara responded angrily, "Stop it! Who is the terrorist? I know your Operation Sweep wiped out Ali's family. Ali thinks you are stealing his country as you stole his son."

Eric turned pale. "What Operation Sweep?"

Sara replied, "Stop the pretension. I know everything."

"The U.S. will consider it treason," Eric whispered.

"What if the Agency finds out about the heroin dealing?" Sara retorted.

Eric's ears turned red. "How did she know?" he wondered painfully.

Sara said, "Let's not fight, Eric. You and Ali must decide what is best for Cyrus. Cyrus loves you. But think. If you destroy his father, you will destroy his love for you, too."

Only an icestorm could cool Eric's initial anger, which now was turning into fear. His world was indeed coming apart. He couldn't be secure in Washington or Teheran. Even his mistress had acted strangely the last time he was in Bangkok. "Okay, Sara, let's get it over with."

When Sara left to get Ali, Eric went to the telephone, but it was dead. He fought to remain calm. Ali could not take Cyrus; he was a fugitive. Eric decided to be agreeable, get the facts, and plan his action later, the instinct of a trained CIA agent. At worst, he could whisk Cyrus away to America, where in time he would forget Ali.

Besides, Eric might be able to pry political and private information from Ali. Eric had been told in Washington, quite bluntly, that his head would roll if the Shah went down. The CIA brass was under fire from politicians and the media that it had underestimated the power of the revolution.

Eric's thoughts were broken as Ali followed Sara into the room. He was ten years older, a bit heavier, with a mustache, but Eric recognized him instantly and tensed. The presence of Ali in his own house made Eric painfully aware that even his own small personal goal in Operation Sweep—to rid himself once and for all of his rival—had failed. The two men stared, weighing each other, both having mastered secret lives. Eric stretched his hand to Ali with a smile like his father's greeting a customer. "How are you, Ali?"

Ali waved him away angrily. "I have no time for pretensions. You know the facts; now Cyrus and I know them, too."

"Well, then?" Eric asked.

Ali took a breath. "Cyrus and I must spend time together, and he should eventually choose his home."

Eric said tersely, "That sounds okay. What else?"

Ali glanced at Sara. "Cyrus stays in Teheran until the custody settlement."

Eric taunted Ali. "What custody? You're a fugitive."

"Don't worry about that. Soon, when the people seize power you will be the fugitive."

Eric ignored Ali's insinuation. "What do you propose then?" Ali and Sara exchanged glances.

"Cyrus will be safer with an Iranian family. He is no longer safe in the house of a secret agent. I will find a secure place for him and Sara."

Anger raised Eric's voice. "That's impossible. No communist will take my family away from me."

"My politics is my business." Ali waited a moment, then became conciliatory. "You do not deny that Cyrus and I have rights?"

Eric took a deep breath, regretting the argument. "No, I can't deny that, can I? But I've been a good father to Cyrus, and a friend to you."

"A friend to me!? A good father to Cyrus!? You've had a hand in murdering his grandfather and banishing his real father to Savak."

Eric glanced at Sara, but she looked away. Sara must have told Ali everything. How did she know? Ali's voice brought him back. "You have worked to destroy everything that is good in this country."

"I serve America and freedom, Mr. Keshavarz. But do you think subversion and terrorism serve Iran?"

Ali said, "Ha! Remember Operation Sweep! The CIA's maiming of people goes beyond the many bodies and souls of the victims, it bleeds the roots of humanity." Each of Ali's words was a stroke of a handsaw on Eric's spine. He went pale and numb. So Ali knew about Operation Sweep too, Eric thought. But no one else knew the safe's combination, no one. How could he know? Someone in the embassy? Eric's mind wandered frantically from place to place, from person to person to pinpoint the culprit.

Ali cursed Eric in his mind, "You son of a bitch, you motherfucking butcher!" but he only said, "No amount of money can make a man accept the sacrifices I have had to make. But you are a bloody mercenary! What is your price for murder, Mr. Saunders?"

"You'll never stop lecturing, Mr. Keshavarz."

"You'll never learn. The CIA never learns," Ali shot back.

Eric said, "You're a Soviet agent. I don't have to listen to you!"

"When will you give up using that stupid myth to rationalize foreign revolutions and U.S. setbacks, Collector of Intelligence? Listen, no matter where in the world I would fight for freedom I would find the guns of the local CIA henchmen in my face. This is true terrorism, Mr. Saunders! But your game is up in Iran."

Eric retorted, "These riots will not succeed."

Sara interrupted, "Gentlemen, talk about Cyrus."

Ali replied, "The nation's fate and Cyrus's are related, for both are hostages of the CIA. Listen, Eric, Cyrus knows everything. If you take him away, Cyrus and I will never stop searching for each other."

Eric felt cold, as if Ali were reading his thoughts. He mumbled, "There is little trust between us."

Ali said, "No trust on my side. Can't you be on the level for once, for Cyrus's sake?"

"What else do you want?" Eric responded.

"Cyrus stays in Teheran."

"Okay," Eric said to get Ali off.

Concerned, Sara said, "Ali, we must go. We will work out the details later." She turned to Eric. "Don't do anything foolish." She and Ali left the room quietly.

The sound of the car driving off filled Eric's ears as hatred for Ali burned within him. Everything was falling apart. He began to pace up and down, talking to himself.

"I'm betrayed and isolated. My work, my family, my secrets and my future are turning against me. Sara has abandoned me. My child, the only person who loves me, is about to be snatched away by a man I hate. Cyrus is the only good thing I have, the only thing I don't have to cover up. I feel as possessive of Cyrus as the CIA does of Iran." The word "stepfather" entered his head. "Stepfather." It had a pricking ring to it; Eric was used to others thinking he was the real father.

"Failures are mounting on failures. Iranians haven't bent to the Agency's schemes. Nothing is the way it is supposed to be. On the TV it didn't even look like Carter believed his own words calling the Shah 'a great leader of the Free World.' Only the Swiss bank accounts have stayed put. But worst of all, Operation Sweep backfired. It seems to have linked these Iranian people together in a steel chain.

"I'm no criminal, I'm no murderer, I'm no spy," Eric thought resolutely. "I will put my money to good use, and I'll leave it to Cyrus."

He ran down the hall and stood before the mirror. He was getting bald, his stomach bulging like his father's—too many fancy dishes and too little tennis.

His eyes peered deep into their reflections. It had been a long time since he had been able to look anybody in the eye, he thought. Not Sara's eyes, with the cheating and the lies; not Cyrus's eyes, for he had thrown Ali to the wolves; not his subordinates' eyes who didn't know their work was a CIA cover; not the eyes of the Ambassador and the Director, for he dreaded that they would get wind of his heroin connections and his unauthorized reports to Princess Ashraf and the Shah.

"I'm a secret millionaire and station chief. I'm a narcotics officer, but I smuggle heroin. I'm a U.S. official, but I must deceive the IRS. I've covered up everything, even my despair and confusion. I'm not on the level with anyone. The son of a bitch Ali has a point."

He had to cover up everything now, including his own glances in the mirror. He looked away out of habit as his own eyes stared at him accusingly. He forced himself to look again. Then he opened his mouth wide, as if for a dentist, hoping to see what was inside, his inner self. He saw his teeth, stained brown from cigarettes. The bloody face of his father emerged from his mouth. At the end his alcoholic father who could not sell cars had shot a bullet in his own head rather than hear another "No" from another customer and be ashamed by his own son, Eric.

Eric's eyes clamped shut as he struggled to erase the painful visions. All the ugly secrets were bubbling to the surface, with the stench of a leaking sewer. Hideous revelations bulged from the mirror, reflections in a concave mirror, he told himself. But his tongue stuck out on its own accord and growled, "Reflections of your life, Eric!"

"What is your price for murder?" Ali's words were branded on his brain like the scar tissue on prisoners burned with sulfuric acid. What must the communists pay a man to stand in front of a tank? Who is Ali subverting for? Why? How can he suffer through torture and injury with no financial reward, no medals—nothing.

Eric was not the only one with thwarted ambitions and split vision. Thousands of U.S. agents were propping up the Shah with nothing but wishful thinking. They thought the revolution was a whirlwind, destructive but temporary. But with enough revolutionaries like Ali, the Shah is doomed, and my career is doomed, Eric thought. The CIA, the President and the Shah have underestimated the power of the people. I will resign from the Agency before the Shah is overthrown. I have money and I can make more money as a legal and financial advisor to the Shah's men in the U.S.

All of a sudden, Eric felt absolutely alone. He murmured, "All is lost, but I'm not going to lose Cyrus. I know what to do with Ali." He looked away from his disturbing reflection in the mirror.

* * * * *

As she drove the car away from her home, Sara broke the silence. "It is too late to convert Eric, don't you think?"

"I was foolish, I admit, but how can I keep cool with that murderer?" Ali responded. Suddenly the pain of leaving Cyrus struck him. Ali wanted to live for Cyrus, for Sara, and for the revolution. Cyrus loomed as tall as the revolution, and Ali smiled at the thought. The hardened revolutionary had turned into a soft father, the discipline of years disappearing in a few weeks.

Sara asked, "Did you write the letter to Cyrus?"

"Yes. Here it is," he said, handing her a bundle of folded sheets from his jacket pocket.

"May I read it?"

"Yes. Please type it for him, but give him the original, too."

"Okay." Sara smiled at him. "Nothing has changed. You're still a political man before anything else."

Ali said, "Sort of, Sara. Although I think of you and Cyrus no less than the revolution." He felt relaxed, even though in danger. He always relaxed when Sara's eyes, mouth and cheeks beamed reassuringly at him.

Sara asked softly, "Do you think Eric will live up to his word?"

Ali said, "No, but he may surprise us. We mustn't rely on his good faith, though. We must plan. He may try to get Cyrus out of the country."

Sara said, "But I could win custody in the U.S."

"It would take time. And Eric could take Cyrus and disappear with him. Just don't leave Cyrus alone with Eric. Remind Cyrus what to do in case Eric tries something. Try to reassure Eric we want the best for Cyrus, not revenge," Ali demanded.

"I'll do my best." She pulled to the curb behind a taxi which would take Ali back to the revolution.

"Stay in touch and remain alert," Ali said.

"Yes, of course. Don't worry about us, Ali." A tear formed in the corner of her eye. Ali got out cautiously. With the cane he looked like an old man who had refused to age.

Before Sara could say goodbye, Ali leaned inside the car and drew her close to him, letting his lips reach and hold hers. The two lovers stayed together for a long moment. Then, before Sara could move, Ali was out of the car and gone.

Her last impression was the sound of the taxi taking off. Sara was left still shuddering from their last moment together. And Ali, in the back of the cab, shuddered too.

CHAPTER 23

Time Two

Operation Sweep proved to be a big blow to the monarchy, but not to the revolution. It was, in fact, the spark that ignited the largest fire of the revolution. The Iranian jurists' organization immediately denounced the massacre of Black Friday, the human rights violations and the Shah's imposition of martial law. But on September 12th Savak arrested more opposition leaders. Then the Shah reacted to the conditions he had helped to create by ordering Savak to arrest some of his own men for corruption. His majesty's gesture was no answer to history or to his own deeds; it fooled no one.

On the 14th, in the face of mounting civilian casualties, Ayatollahs Khomeini and Shariatmadari urged nonviolent resistance.

By September 17th parliament had approved the Shah's demand for martial law and a week later 10,000 oil workers went on a strike which spread to the factories. To prove his commitment to reform, the Shah banned the royal family's profiting from government contracts. But the Shah's admissions of past wrongdoings were "too obvious, too comical, too irrelevant, too desperate, too little, too late," Ali declared in a demonstration in southern Teheran.

On October 1st, a one-day nationwide strike in support of Khomeini showed the world that the people were after the Shah's crown, not just surface reforms. From the 3rd to the 8th, more strikes frayed the Shah's nerves. Public workers joined and shut down post offices, public transport, schools and government offices. Only the armed forces appeared loyal to him.

The Shah reacted in desperation. Again well behind time, he granted amnesty to dissidents living abroad, including Ayatollah Khomeini, and more political prisoners were released.

On October 6th Khomeini left Iraq to go to France. The conditions were not ripe yet for his return home. He knew he could be assassinated at the Shah's order.

On October 10th President Carter repeated his strong support for the Shah. In a leaflet, the Fedayeen accused President Carter and the Shah of being co-conspirators against the will of the people.

On October 11th the government censor shut down the conservative newspapers *Kayhan* and *Ettela'at*, and in retaliation printers struck *Rastakhiz,* the government paper. While no legal newspaper could publish as usual, the illegal ones flourished. On the 13th, censorship was lifted on the condition that the press not criticize the Shah or the army. The Fedayeen quickly denounced this exemption of the Shah and army. Ali wrote, "The Shah is Enemy Number One of the people, and the army is his instrument of murder; neither can be exempt from criticism, from responsibility and punishment."

On October 16th a one-day general strike protested the massacre of Black Friday. To stop the crippling strikes, the Shah increased the salaries of civil servants by $100 a month. But on October 22nd police fired into the crowd in the city of Hamadan; killing many people. The protests continued. As the Shah strived to demonstrate his power and his compassion the monarchy went one step forward and two steps backward.

The Shah dismissed many senior officials of Savak, and, ignoring the fact that he had recently announced that there were no political prisoners left in Iran, he released 1451 prisoners, including Aram and Zaman. There had been no formal charge against them. A few days later 37,000 oil workers went on strike again. Without large daily oil revenues the Shah couldn't pay the army or buy arms from the U.S., his twin sources of support. The noose began to tighten. On November 1st, the Shah released Grand Ayatollah Taleghani from prison, and the people celebrated his freedom. On the 4th troops fired on students who tried to topple a statue of the Shah in Teheran. On November 5th more rioting rocked the country. Prime Minister Sharif-Emami resigned and the Shah replaced him with General Azhari, the chief of staff who was the darling of the U.S. National Defense Council. On the 6th the Shah went on TV, admitting mistakes and asking forgiveness. The world outside Iran also began to learn that the Shah was desperate.

From France Ayatollah Khomeini and Dr. Sanjabi, a National Front leader, in a joint statement ruled out any possibility of compromise with the Shah. Even Sanjabi, a moderate, demanded the Shah's abdication. On November 30th, the Shah approved another pay increase for all 700,000 civil servants. But two days later demonstrators marched in Teheran and other cities in defiance of martial law and the curfew.

The revolutionary leaders began a new attack on the Shah's ultimate support, the armed forces. Ayatollah Khomeini, in Paris, called on soldiers to desert if ordered to fire on the people. When the oil workers acceded to the Ayatollah's demand to remain on strike oil production fell by almost half. Revolutionaries began to intimidate the security men, and threatening words appeared on the front door of homes of generals, police officials and Savak chiefs. They were told to abandon the Shah or else.

In the U.S. former Undersecretary of State, George Ball, led a task force to investigate the causes of the Iranian crisis. On December 5th Prime Minister Azhari, not daring to accuse the Muslim leaders, blamed foreign-controlled saboteurs for the national discontent. Far away Professor Pirooz commented, "The only foreign saboteurs are thousands of Americans propping up the Shah, unless they no longer consider themselves foreigners. In that case, they are just local saboteurs of the people's struggle for freedom."

CHAPTER 24

Ashura

Ayatollah Khomeini chose December 11, 1978, for an unprecedented demonstration. He commanded a peaceful march whose only theme was to be unity against tyranny. From Paris his words reached everywhere and everyone. The people were now easily mobilized; their commitment to revolution appeared absolute. The massacre of Black Friday had sharpened the people's resolve, with not one in a thousand willing to compromise. The whole country, from small villages to large cities, had risen up to march against the Shah, to demand their rights and an end to his repression.

December 11th was an appropriate day because it was Ashura, the holy day commemorating the martyrdom of Imam Hussain. The mutilated body of the martyr lay buried beneath the windblown sands, but his ideas lived to nourish the souls of the faithful. In remembrance of Hussain's wounds, some devout men slashed their foreheads with knives and whipped their shoulders with chains until blood soaked their white robes. Onlookers wept to remember both Hussain's tragedy and that of their relatives and comrades who had recently fallen on Black Friday.

Fearing damnation on that first Ashura, the usurper Yazid had given orders not to kill Imam Hussain, but to no avail. And in 1978, fearing damnation, the Shah, whom the people now called Yazid, ordered his troops not to kill demonstrators on Ashura. But this Ashura in Teheran was different: the minority seeking justice had become the great majority.

The Shah faced a dilemma, for banning religious processions on Ashura would threaten his legitimacy as a Muslim leader. So he lifted martial law for one day. He had by this time made new promises of reform, lifted the censorship, freed hundreds of prisoners, exiled his brothers and sisters, and jailed his officials, even his favorites, Hoveyda and Nassiri. "No king has done all of this," he said to Queen Farah.

"I've even asked my people for forgiveness."

But the people were not forgiving. Before dawn on Ashura, they came from all directions to gather at the mosques to pray, regroup, plan and coordinate their march toward Shahyad Square.

Assigned to the Hilton area, Shamil and Kamil watched from the lobby both the procession forming and the bystanders. An American arms salesman cursed at being turned back at the airport. He complained, "Goddamn it! We used to run this country."

The U.S. Embassy advised Americans to stay off the streets. Eric and Cyrus stayed home. But ignoring both the Embassy's and Eric's admonishments, Sara left under a chador to report the demonstration. Sara was sure Eric couldn't take Cyrus away that day because the airport was closed. Eric forbade the servants to join the demonstration, but they disobeyed. They risked their jobs, but no king or CIA agent could stop them. No one could resist the urging of conscience and the command of Ayatollah Khomeini on Ashura.

The servants, in fact, had no love for the master of the house. With his unexplained disappearances, his secret telephone calls, his suspicions of them, and his treatment of Sara and Cyrus, he was up to no good, they figured. But they loved Lady Sara, and especially Cyrus, who treated them as family. His smile, the large black eyes, the eyebrows growing right across the bridge of the nose, the mischievous intelligence flooding from every glance could win any heart. Cyrus protested when Eric treated the servants harshly. The gardener once asked Sara whether Americans in general were more like her and Cyrus or like Eric. When Sara answered that she didn't know, he said, "If all Americans were like you, we could love all two hundred million of them."

On the same day, despite the Shah's edict, troops opened fire on marchers who had caught a death squad arsonist in Isfahan. The once peaceful marchers then broke into two banks and set fire to theaters showing pornographic American movies and the four-story building of the Grummann Aircraft Corporation, which trained the Shah's F-14 pilots. No Americans were hurt, but many demonstrators were killed and injured. After the Isfahan killings, Persian hospitality to Americans could no longer be assumed.

From the Teheran mosques, millions of the faithful poured into the streets. The leaders marched in front—National Front, Fedayeen, Mujahedin, Tudeh Party, followers of Ayatollah Khomeini—forty abreast, their arms linked like the civil rights marchers in the U.S. in the 1960's.

Behind them the line of protesters came into full view of the world —the longest and largest political demonstration in the history of mankind, three to four million in Teheran alone. Never on so vast a scale had there been such a showing of unity of political and religious commitment, such physical and spiritual oneness, harmony, and compactness.

Ali wore the white armband of a marshal and directed Fedayeen and sympathizers. Aram was among them. But the rape in Evin had changed him. Some days he was energetic, while other days he was depressed or even delirious. Zaman and other women Mujahedin marched under black chadors.

The people swept forward like a river, carrying Ali, Zaman and Aram —and the Shah—into the sea of history, where each person would arrive at his own specific destination. Soldiers stood motionless like trees along its banks.

The orderliness of the march was a triumph of planning and hard work carried out despite the months of martial law. Marshals and mullahs directed traffic, led the chanting and intervened at the first sign of disorder. People moved or stopped, sat on the pavement or stood up, on signal. Some dispensed food and water, and first-aid stations treated the old and children for exhaustion.

The rhythm and power of voices and footsteps shook the walls, the soldiers and the Shah reaching Mount Damavand. Gigantic banners filled the streets from curb to curb, their messages repeating the chants.

"Martyrs are the heart of history."

"Workers, peasants, students, clergy: Long live the unity of the people."

"American mercenaries must be expelled from our land."

"Death to the Shah! Death to the murderer!"

"The struggle will not end until the birth of the Islamic Republic."

"God is great, God is great."

The immense line moved toward Shahyad Square in northwest Teheran. The procession continued to fill the vast square until it overflowed with a million marchers. Hundreds of thousands had to stop on the boulevards leading to it.

The demonstration proved that ideas could overcome matter, that the struggle for justice could overcome the Shah's weapons and men. His arsenal lay unused, as Teheran and other large cities were taken over on this holy day by the marshals of the people, by the leaders of the people, by the people's physicians and nurses and by the people's unity. The people of Teheran unanimously approved a resolution at Shahyad Square, on December 11th, 1978, summarizing their demands: the Shah's abdication, the return of Khomeini, political freedom and economic justice for all.

Khomeini called the march a referendum, indicating that the people had indeed caused the abdication of the Shah. And he warned that when the people seized power, no international contract with the Shah's regime would be automatically honored, since the Shah represented no interest other than his own and those of the Americans.

For His Majesty Mohammed Reza Pahlavi, this day of Ashura seemed interminable, stretching painfully forever. He watched the demonstation from a United Technologies' "Huey" helicopter whose whirling blades kept him aloft while distorting and drowning out the chants below. But he could feel the pulse of the masses, could see that the revolution had its own soul, its own body, its own force and motion, its own mission. He realized that no one, nothing, could challenge its momentum, while at the same time no one could know its final destination.

From the north, the helicopter approached a gigantic Square, which the Shah had constructed and named "Shahyad" meaning the "remembrance of kings." At its center stood the modernistic arch, a tribute to Cyrus the Great, to Darius, and to the Shah himself. The structure rose high into the future, as the Shah had envisioned. But to his people it symbolized a hated past to be rejected. Shahyad, the memorial to the Shah, would be renamed the Plaza of Liberty after the revolution. Today masses converged on the square just to curse him, just to wish him death. The crowds did indeed remember the Shah, but as a thief and a murderer.

The banners were so enormous, the Shah imagined he could stick his hand out the window and touch them. "The regime has answered our cries to Allah with bullets," he read. From the helicopter, Shah Reza Boulevard appeared to slide in slow motion. The Shah was awestruck that the millions below him were so different from his census statistics. He mumbled, "I didn't know I had so many subjects. Why have they turned against me? Didn't they read in the textbooks that I am the nation's father? How dare they rise against their father?"

As he flew over streets clogged with demonstrators, the Shah felt estranged from his people and from his land. He didn't realize that if that American-made helicopter blade had stopped for a second and forced him down among his own subjects, they would have hung him from the nearest tree.

He commanded his pilot, "Fly closer."

"Your Majesty, it is dangerous."

"Fly closer!" the Shah barked.

Now the Shah could make out the huge portraits of Ayatollah Khomeini, his former prisoner, punctuating the movement of the people. The Shah then saw a picture of Dr. Shariati, the Muslim scholar he had ordered poisoned for denying the Shah's legitimacy to rule. Shariati was one of the modern architects of Islamic ideology, in which Islam and socialism were merged together, faith and science met peacefully, and ethics, law, and politics intermingled harmoniously to create a utopia of Islamic justice, peace, and prosperity. To Shariati, Islamic revolution embodied the revitalization and modernization of Islam. His ideas were of course too radical for the Shah, but not sufficiently fundamentalist for Khomeini.

Shariati's work was being translated into many languages as he was being buried.

The Shah also remembered Ruzbeh, who before his execution demanded that the Shah stand trial, not him. He remembered Takhti, the famous world champion wrestler, whom the Shah had ordered killed by injecting air bubbles into his veins. He remembered Dr. Hussain Fatemi, Mossadegh's Foreign Minister, tortured and then sent before a firing squad. They all had one thing in common: they had questioned the legitimacy of his rule. But now the people were honoring his vanquished adversaries by calling them martyrs.

He wondered, "Why did I order that journalist set on fire in jail? I can't even remember his name. I have killed many whose names I don't remember, but the nation is still alive and even stronger and now wishes my death."

The Shah saw a coffin being carried on the shoulders of demonstrators in what looked like a funeral procession. He wondered who lay inside. He did not know the coffin was empty, that it was meant to be his and that of the monarchy. Unbidden, the faces of all those killed by his father or himself through the years came to mind while he gazed at the coffin.

He remembered the Rex Theater in Abadan, the people recently locked inside by Savak and set ablaze, turning hundreds of workers and family members into charcoal. His sister Ashraf, high on heroin at a party, had said, "The Rex fire is a fitting memorial to the twenty-fifth anniversary of the 1953 coup. Let the oil workers know who is the boss. Let them know what could happen after another strike."

The Shah asked the pilot, "Why is that big group wearing white robes?"

"In case they are martyred, Your Majesty."

"But they know I've ordered no violence today."

"Your Majesty, they are prepared just in case."

"You mean they don't trust my word?"

The pilot kept silent. The Shah continued, "Why is that group toward the east dressed in black?"

"Your Majesty, it is Ashura, and they are mourning the death of Imam Hussain and the recent martyrs."

The Shah shot back angrily, "I didn't ask your opinion." The pilot bit his tongue.

Then the Shah's mind took him to the past, a defense to lower the pain of the present. "So what if the demonstrators don't want me? They are not the people who matter. The Chinese, the French, the Japanese, the British, the Americans, the Russians, Kings, Queens and Prime Ministers all praise me and boast of my friendship. No other leader has the trust of the Americans, the Russians and the Chinese, all at the same time. Who else enjoys the support of both the Israelis and the Saudis, as I do? I've befriended every important person in the world, and every government is on my side, even the goddamn communists. Who made Iran the 'Island of Stability' Carter brags about? I sell gas to the Russians and the Americans applaud me. I help wipe out Marxist guerrillas in Oman and the Russians toast my health. I sell oil to Israel and the Iraqis sign a peace treaty with me. I am the greatest diplomat in the world. Everyone is my friend.

"Yes, I'm the richest man on earth, too. The computer printout of my investments abroad is a thick book. I can't even remember them all. That's all right. I'm a king, not a businessman. My money has bought powerful men and beautiful women." He smiled painfully. "I can buy everyone else but I can't buy even one smile from my own subjects. I'm an anticommunist, I am just, I'm a modernizing leader," the Shah said to himself. He thought of all he had done to calm the people, to get things back to normal. But no one believed him anymore or appreciated his great deeds. "Why can't my subjects see what the whole world sees in me?" he asked as he looked up at the spinning helicopter blades.

"What more can these people demand?" he wondered. "The generals get all the arms they want, the security forces and bureaucrats get money and privileges, the intellectuals are wallowing in research funds, the businessmen have prospered for many years until the last couple of years, a lot of the peasants now have land, the clergy—except for Khomeini's followers—have been taken care of, the skilled workers live like princes. People now have cars, televisions, refrigerators, vacations—everyone can become rich, like in the U.S., thanks to me. Everyone," the Shah repeated to himself "—yet nothing works. I gave each Savak agent a bonus of ten million riyals, $150,000, to buy a new house, yet some are still wavering." The Shah would have been shocked to know that Shamil and Kamil had befriended and helped Ali Keshavarz, who had not given them a penny. It was all too baffling.

The Shah sighed. "Peasants driven into bankruptcy and off the land by the White Revolution during the last ten years are now emerging from the slums to demonstrate against me. I've been generous to all who supported me, although it is true that I have had to silence those who have not. It seems I can't satisfy anyone here. Even top bureaucrats are calling me corrupt now. Merchants call me unfair for favoring foreign capital; students and teachers accuse me of brainwashing the nation. The workers accuse me of exploitation, the peasants call me a loan shark. The clergy call me an unbeliever. Citizens call me a traitor, an agent of U.S. Imperialism. I'm tired of being called names.

"I still wield great power. I could still order the troops to shoot, to clear the people from Shahyad Square and force them to flee for their lives. But I cannot make them admire me, respect me, forgive me." The Shah exclaimed, "Nothing works! Threats, torture, bullets, fire, apology, bribing, nothing works."

"Pardon me, Your Majesty?" the pilot asked.

"Keep quiet." A moment later his thoughts again emerged from his lips to murmur their protest. "I've tried everything, and nothing works. Nothing has worked, nothing will work. Damn it!"

The pilot said, "Your Majesty?"

"Nothing. Carry on."

"The prisoners I released are probably now demonstrating against me," he guessed bitterly. The Shah was right. Aram and Zaman, who had just been freed, were in the crowd along with hundreds of others.

The Shah should have known from the beginning, but did not know that "uneasy lies the head that wears the crown." His own propaganda and the praises of his men had convinced him of his greatness and invincibility. As God had praised Himself in the Koran, so the Shah praised himself in his book on the White Revolution. He could no longer distinguish the truth from his own lies. The American press and President saw his programs of cosmetic modernization as progress, but not his own subjects, and now only he, himself, was still fooled. When his policies had failed to reform society, he had ordered his statisticians to re-form the data. "But all governments manipulated statistics," the Shah reasoned to himself. "Even in the U.S., the true unemployment rate was much much higher than the official one. Is there one ruler that does not—that does not have to lie," the Shah admitted to himself gingerly!

Still the Shah's mind wandered. How is it that American television can convince the people, and my television can't? The people have become deaf to their government. If only they listened to me instead of to the mullahs.

The Shah watched the procession flow below him. Though he was hovering over the people, he felt they were marching over his body, over him, over the monarchy. "It doesn't really matter anymore, anyway. They don't need to wish my death," he thought ironically. "The cancer will do it for them. Pincer movements of pain from within and without signal my approaching doom. The surgeons can't cut out the rebellious cells threatening my life, and I can't cut out the revolutionaries threatening my crown. There is no cure for either malignancy. My kingdom is in ruins, and my life is coming to an end."

The Shah looked down at the throng of people. "They deserve a worse punishment than just imprisonment and torture," he decided. "I will deprive them of my leadership!" The Shah was right again. Many people who had risen against him regretted it later. At last the Shah entertained the idea of abdicating. "But how would foreign leaders, even my own family, treat an ex- Shah?" His Majesty worried.

He noted with satisfaction the lines of soldiers with fixed bayonets and officers with holstered pistols shielding his palaces and those of his family and his Court. They also shielded the road to Karaj, with its factories and offices of American corporations idled by workers who had joined this march. The Shah looked westward to Mehrabad Airport, which seemed to wait for his final departure from Iran. Could the soldiers save his crown? Khomeini had proclaimed that God's commands overruled those of the Shah, that the troops' loyalty oath to the Shah, who was corruption on earth, was contrary to Islam. "I should have had Khomeimi executed instead of merely exiled," the Shah thought regretfully. "How long will the men I have generously taken care of hold fast to me? Khomeini has forced me to compete with God for the loyalty of my army. So far the soldiers confronting unarmed people have held fast, but once the people arm themselves, all might be lost."

The Shah thought of his greyhounds, to whom His Majesty fed steaks flown from Europe. "They are faithful beings I can rely on," he thought. "But no one is forever loyal; even my greyhounds would tear me to pieces if I stopped feeding them."

His wandering mind focused on immediate problems. The Shah thought wearily, "I can't trust anyone. My supporters are fleeing with their money. They're not short of excuses. Sabeti, my new Savaki chief, has just disappeared to Israel or the U.S. The army is wavering, my police and secret police are wavering, my crown is wavering, my life is wavering. Back in 1953 the generals came to me as their savior, their symbol of legitimacy. Once I was everyone's hero, and now what am I? What could have happened to all that might and glory? It's not my fault," he thought, his teeth clenching. "I did my best. I am still the Shadow of God, still 'Aryamehr,' the Love of the Aryans. Are these marchers Aryans or Arabs?" The Shah stopped wondering for a moment, then continued.

"The trouble is that too few of my men shared my vision. My family, my prime ministers, my generals, my old Savak chief, Nassiri, are the ones who brought about my ruin. I should have stopped the heroin smuggling after the UN report. I should have kicked Eric Saunders out. The mullahs blame me for all that pork eating, dog loving, hotpants, gambling, drinking, prostitution and corruption under my rule." The Shah's downhill slide was ripping away the mask of self-confidence he had worn since the coup of 1953. As though he had already abdicated he asked himself, "Can I save the throne for Prince Reza? Can the people forget the past, forgive me and look to the future?"

The Shah was weary. His burdens were becoming too great. He shouted over the roar of the helicopter, "Back to Niavaran."

The pilot answered respectfully, "Yes, Your Majesty, we are almost there."

The Shah needed to hear praise. Like a battery worn down, he needed recharging. He wanted a taste of those glorious days when he celebrated the

2500 years of Iranian monarchy, with the world still in his hands, applauding him.

As the Shah walked briskly across the palace lawn, he acknowledged the salutes of the generals, security officers, court functionaries, even his old friend Fardoos, as he swept by. He marched past the situation room, where his top men were assessing the progress of the demonstration, to his office, followed by his private secretary. He demanded that calls be placed immediately to the British Ambassador, Sir Anthony Parsons, and the American Ambassador Sullivan.

Ambassador Sullivan got on the telephone. He was tired of the Shah's endless complaints, doubts, fears, despair. His Majesty sometimes called in the middle of the night, when he had conceived of a new idea while suffering insomnia. What could he do for the old boy now? Sullivan asked himself. His instructions were clear: no wavering from official policy. Sullivan was to assure the Shah that the U.S. government was behind him, that they expected him to carry on. The Shah was not to learn that the Embassy was in touch with the moderate opposition leaders and was planning to support a government without the Shah.

At their last meeting, the Shah had detected impatience in Sullivan's eyes, and in Sir Anthony's face, in their superficial sounding words, even in Sullivan's assurance that, "The United States always honors its obligations." But "what were 'the U.S. obligations' to me?" the Shah began to wonder.

Today, while listening to Sullivan's empty promise on the phone, the Shah thought of Eric Saunders. "I shouldn't have listened to that American jackass," he decided bitterly. "His Operation Sweep, Black Friday, was a disaster." The Shah became angry, bitter, revengeful, and said to Sullivan, "Operation Sweep was a stupid mistake, I see it now."

Ambassador Sullivan replied, "It wasn't my idea, Your Majesty."

"It was that SOB's, Eric Saunders!" the Shah shouted. "Send him away. I don't want him in Iran!" The Shah spoke as if he were commanding his own ambassador. Sullivan thought to himself, "The poor Shah is out of his mind. He's forgotten who is the boss."

The Shah hung up thinking angrily, "The Americans are responsible for this mess. I've always consulted them, I've taken advice from Ambassador Helms, from Sullivan, from their Presidents, from the MIT SOB's. They can't abandon me; I've made sure I'm their only friend here. Their interests and mine are identical. We must pump out the oil and keep Russia out of the Gulf.

"I wish I could stay home after a failure like Nixon and Johnson did. Carter, the son of a bitch, is probably conspiring against me right now, plotting with my generals or National Front leaders or Khomeini's lieutenants behind my back." He remembered clearly Jimmy's dodging a question at a recent press conference. Asked if the Shah could survive, Carter said, "I don't know. I hope so, but the United States will not get involved in the internal affairs of Iran or any other country. We personally prefer that the Shah retain a major role in the government, but that is a decision for the Iranian people to make."

"What does he want me to do?" the Shah thought bitterly. "Didn't I implement Operation Sweep?" He murmured to himself, "They've written my obituary, and I'm not even dead yet. The Chinese communists are more loyal to me than the American capitalists.

"Did I ever shortchange Carter?" he asked to himself. "I always put U.S. interests above all others. I supported them in the 1973 Arab oil embargo. I sold oil to Israel and South Africa, risking my subjects' alienation. I followed their advice in OPEC, all against the advice of my friends and my experts. I could have defied them at any time since 1953. I could have allied myself with the Arabs against Israel. I supported their war in Vietnam. I even sent my best F-5 pilots to Saigon. I patrolled the Straits of Hormuz, to secure a safe journey for American oil tankers, with my planes and ships. I bought billions of dollars of their armaments in cash, keeping their plants and workers employed at full capacity. I even built barracks and prisons instead of hospitals and schools to show my resolve against communist aggression. I always paid American technicians—just high school graduates—higher salaries than my own U.S.-educated Persian PhD's, the MIT SOB's. I instructed my UN ambassador always to vote with the U.S. I let the Americans use my embassies to gather intelligence in communist capitals. I let them install listening posts on my Russian border. I did everything they wanted me to do."

The Shah shouted, "What else could I have done for those ungrateful Americans?" A Persian expression he never used came to him: "Americans are blind cats. No matter how many favors you do for them, the next time they look at you they remember nothing. Carter is just a blind cat. I shouldn't have listened to the Americans so much. What do they know about Iran, anyway?"

An aide opened the door in alarm, but the Shah angrily waved him away. "I paid attention to the needs of everybody in the world except to those of my own subjects," the Shah concluded painfully.

Now an image related to a formal reception some years ago popped into the Shah's head. The American ambassador, Richard Helms, was beside him in the receiving line. The guests moved past them, bowing low, eagerly awaiting a confidential word from their Shah. Teherani, the Savaki, kissed his hand as the Ambassador looked on, smiling. The Shah remembered something strange—Helms was wearing a turban. "Was it a sign: could the Americans be behind all of this mullah business?" the Shah wondered.

The Shah stalked back and forth over the rich carpets. "If it weren't for

Khomeini and Marx I would have no problems." Now his home was a fortress surrounded by an untold number of enemies, his own subjects. He was a prisoner within his own walls. Like the prisoners he still held in Evin, he was now being tortured daily, by cancer and by his conscience.

The Shah's mind shifted to women. He had had hundreds of them —Persian and foreign women, peasants and aristocrats, young and innocent or older and worldly, black and white, yellow and brown. "The cancer and the mullahs have sapped my energy, have made me forget the pleasures of my office," he thought with regret.

"I wish I could be a virgin again," he thought. "I wish I could start over as Shah. I would have done things differently. I wouldn't have let the slums grow so large, I wouldn't have jailed Mossadegh, or left Hoveyda in power for so long, or executed Dr. Hussain Fatemi or Ruzbeh, or created the martyrs who haunt me now. What did all the killing accomplish? I should have consulted Khomeini, from time to time, to keep him happy. I shouldn't have confiscated religious land. I should have befriended the clergy, like the kings in the past. The clergy may be stupid, but I was stupid to forget I can't bomb their mosques, because they can talk to the people without my censor. Now every mosque is a military base against me. I wish I could burn every mosque in the country, I wish I could order my artillery to bombard them and reduce them to rubble. But I can't, and I wouldn't even if I could. I have Khomeini on my back as it is; I can't have God on my back, too."

Recently, the Shah had no appetite and could not sleep. All he could do was to show his loyalists that he was still strong, even when he wasn't. He had to keep up the appearances, or else all was lost.

"I should have killed Khomeini when he was in my power in prison. Now he has more power than I do, and the love and admiration I should have. He has all that power," the Shah marvelled, "without an Army or Navy or Air Force, or even foreign allies. He commands my subjects, tells me what to do and what not to do, and I can't stop him."

"Damn it, damn it," the Shah shouted. He threw a book at the window, shattering it to pieces, just as he had shattered so many lives. The broken glass fell to the floor and refracted the sunlight into a rainbow. "So many colors in the light of the sun," the Shah thought. He had never seen them before. He went and stared at the fragments. He wished to be hypnotized by them, to escape the pain of his thoughts. The glass fragments were broken, but they shone brilliantly, like the martyrs' memories. But he could no more concentrate on the dancing light than he could keep his thoughts on his victims, or even on one track.

The Shah hated his victims, the dead Mossadegh, Fatemi, Ruzbeh, the still living Khomeini, Bazargan, Sanjabi, the countless prisoners, the children going hungry while his dogs ate steak. He hated the leaders because the people loved them, and he hated the whole nation that followed them. He wanted that love for himself, the submission and the loyalty. But whatever he did to get it, it eluded him. "Why are all those men rising against me? Why do my own people want to kill me? Why are the Fedayeen and Mujahedin and Islamic groups against me? Why are the lice-ridden mullahs spreading lies against me? Why do they rouse my subjects against me? Why are they victimizing me? I wish I could take out their tongues and eyes, a fit punishment, as the great Nadir Shah would have done, and make heaps of eyes and tongues for all to see I am the Shah."

The Shah had not been a very good Muslim ruler; he had not performed the religious offices that the people expected of a Shah, and he had done plenty that he should not have done. He admitted he was not religious. He knew the power man could have, since he had had it. He had not needed God when his power was absolute. There just wasn't room for God in his life, unless he was sick or in trouble. God didn't help him with his thoughts now; God had no answers for him! No one had answers for him!

The Shah took a fistful of tranquillizers and went straight to bed. But even the pills would not stop the thoughts and memories from tormenting him. He couldn't sleep, even though the greatest and most magnificent demonstration in all of history was by this time over.

*　*　*　*　*

As dusk fell on Teheran, the marchers hurried home to beat the curfew, but they also hurried to plot against the Shah. They went to the roofs and chanted in unison. As the street noises died away, as the bazaars and cafes fell still, millions of people stood under the stars and chanted their wish for his death. The chant always began and ended with the same words, "God is great, God is great." The whole city chanted, carrying its message to the Shah and around the world.

Inside his palace, the sleepless Shah heard a hum somewhere inside his skull. The hum came from everywhere at once, like the sound of a swarm of locusts. Suddenly he realized it wasn't in his head, it was the sound of chanting blurring over the great distance into a hum. Even in his fortified palace, with his tanks at every streetcorner, the protesters got through his defenses. He got up and turned on the stereo full volume, but could not shut out the incessant hum.

How many more nights would the Shah hear this curse in his bedroom? How many times could he hear it without going insane? Now he was hearing it in the daytime, just as in his nightmares. He would get up in the middle of the night, unable to sleep, and immediately he would hear, "God is great, God is great. Death to the Shah."

Shattering sounds of gunfire roused up the tired Shah. He immediately telephoned Savak headquarters. Was there a prison breakout or an army mutiny? Not believing Savak assurances, he called Sullivan. Was there a coup? Should he leave Iran? Sullivan was as confused as the Shah. The Shah was frightened by gunfire that he had not ordered but that seemed so near. Savak finally found out what was happening: people had perched loudspeakers on window ledges throughout the city, the volume turned to maximum, and played tapes of machine gun fire. It was done to destroy the Shah's nerves and strike fear in the hearts of the Shah's soldiers. The people of Iran, without the slightest chance of overcoming the Shah's military might, Savak and American counterrevolutionary tactics, had brought new instruments and methods onto the battlefield. Psychological and ideological war, religious holy war, all at high pitch, all at once, were thrown at the Shah. His weapons could not answer them or destroy them.

The Shah lay on his back, listening to the distant hum of chanting. He trembled as the hum carried through the freezing air. He found himself out of bed and alone, alone with a billion cancerous cells, alone on top of an angry volcano about to erupt. He would kiss Khomeini's foot if the Ayatollah would allow it—if that would save his crown. He would give a billion dollars to the religious foundations, if they would only accept.

The Shah went to his study. A huge oil painting of his father looked down sternly from the mantle. Reza Shah, the founder of the dynasty, was an overbearing man, with penetrating eyes beneath thick eyebrows. The Shah felt ashamed in his presence. His father would never have considered kissing the feet of an Ayatollah, even to keep his crown. He would not vacillate, he would do what he had to do, even if it meant killing them all.

But now there were too many Ayatollahs, too many mullahs, too many followers ready to defend them. Even the fierce Reza Shah could not scare these foes, could not beat them into silence, could not kill them all. These men did not fear death; they welcomed it as blessed martyrdom. Maybe the Shah should just take his money and family and run away. Maybe he should follow the whispered advice of some of his supporters, which none would dare suggest to him directly. Maybe he should take a "vacation," go into a temporary exile. He would not live long in any event. And when he died, his son could triumphantly return to take his place on the throne.

The Shah slumped on the couch and finally drifted into fitful sleep, snoring beneath his father's gaze. On this Ashura the ideas of Imam Hussain had triumphed peacefully over the swords of Yazid of the time.

CHAPTER 25

Time Three

On December 13th pro-Shah gangs attacked motorists in Isfahan who did not display the Shah's portrait on their windshields. The ensuing riots killed over fifty people. Ayatollah Khomeini then threatened to cut off oil to foreign leaders who continued to support the Shah. Step by step the internal and external roots of the Shah's power were being damaged beyond repair. The Shah, in defense, took a step backward by offering to meet with some opposition leaders, including Sanjabi and Bazargan, but they responded by asking for his abdication. All attempts at compromise failed.

On December 18th, in response to a request from Khomeini, oil and industrial workers went on a one-day strike. An army unit was sent back to its barracks when some of its soldiers joined the demonstrators. Ali wrote in the Fedayeen newsletter, "The Shah will not be safe now even among his own men."

On December 24th, in the first demonstration outside the U.S. Embassy, Marines shot tear gas, launching an international dialogue. On December 26th, after oil workers had taken control of refineries, oil exports were halted and domestic consumption was rationed. The sources of the Shah's power and the critical one, the oil revenues, were drying up. December 28th saw more clashes and more killings in Teheran and Ahvaz and elsewhere.

On December 29th a sick and listless Shah replaced the prime minister, General Azhari, with his former prisoner, Dr. Shahpur Bakhtiyar. Bakhtiyar accepted the office subject to the conditions of dissolving Savak, prosecuting corrupt former officials, compensating political prisoners, increasing the government role for religious leaders, gradually abolishing martial law, and halting oil exports to Israel and South Africa. But by this time the Shah's family had taken out their huge assets, the culprits were disappearing, and Savakis were running away. Dead prisoners, moreover, could not appreciate compensation. Oil production was no longer under the Shah's control.

Martial law was disobeyed anyway. Bakhtiyar had thought these concessions would buy him the time he needed to negotiate with Ayatollah Khomeini and Dr. Bazargan, but alas, no concessions short of transfer of power were sufficient. Khomeini demanded all power for the Islamic ruler.

In accepting this position, Bakhtiyar abandoned his friends and ignored the command of Ayatollah Khomeini to decline the Shah's offer, for the brilliance of power and a burning desire to do good blinded Bakhtiyar to reality and made him try the impossible. The new prime minister, a brave son of the Bakhtiyar tribe and a National Front leader who had fought against fascism in the Spanish Civil War and with the French Resistance, and who had fought against the Shah in Iran, now had the choice of causing more death and destruction or running away from his deal with the Shah.

Bakhtiyar had difficulty forming a cabinet. He named cabinet ministers no one knew much about, including, inadvertently, a former Savak agent. He even approached Rookney, the former President of the Iranian Student Association, but Professor Pirooz urged Rookney not to accept for his own security, and so Rookney reluctantly refused a post. Soon the way was paved for the Shah's departure by the formation of a nine-man regency council. Now Bakhtiyar had the approval of a rubber stamp parliament, but not of the masses.

On January 4, 1979, the National Front condemned Bakhtiyar for betraying the revolution, while the U.S. announced it would cooperate fully with Bakhtiyar. On January 5th, with the approval of revolutionary leaders, workers in Abadan agreed to produce only enough oil to satisfy domestic needs until the Shah abdicated.

CHAPTER 26

Death In Teheran

The U.S. embassy advised U.S. citizens to stay indoors and prepare to evacuate Iran in a hurry. Sara requested to be put on the list of essential personnel exempted from the evacuation order and demanded that Eric support her application. She was a reporter, after all, she argued. Eric agreed to but asked her to stay with him until the political crisis was over. Sara declined. "Not one more day, if I can help it," she told him coolly.

Despite being faced with the loss of Cyrus, Eric secretly used his influence to deny Sara's application to stay. Suspecting this, Ali had planned for Sara and Cyrus to take refuge with Aram's father in an emergency.

Ali was worried about Sara and Cyrus, so he decided to act at once. He could not let the CIA agent steal his son again. At 9 a.m. on January 7th, 1979, a day full of small demonstrations, Ali phoned Eric to demand that Eric stop impeding Sara's efforts to stay. Then he fired his heavy mortar. "And if you try to kidnap Cyrus, I'll expose your illegal activities, Station Chief!"

Eric knew Ali was deadly serious. He searched for a move to parry Ali's threat, and came quickly to a decision. He chose his words carefully. "Very well, I'll get permission for Sara to stay, but I'll need your cooperation and Sara's. Can you come here this morning, so the three of us can get started? I want Cyrus present when we discuss his future."

Ali was alert to danger. "Let me speak to Sara."

Eric said, "Okay, but you'll have to hold the line. She's in the shower."

Ali considered the dangers of a secret meeting with Eric, but his paternal instincts overpowered his caution. "I'll come, but if you doublecross me, you'll ruin yourself, too." Eric couldn't pull any tricks in the presence of Sara and Cyrus, he figured. And Ali no longer feared Savak—they were on the run. Even so, Ali hid a small gun under his coat before he left.

After Eric hung up he formulated his plan. This was the perfect opportunity for him. Sara had taken Cyrus to the airport to see a friend of his leave for the U.S. The servants had been dismissed in anticipation of dissolving the household. Eric was alone. The failure of Operation Sweep, the Shah's wrath and the imminent danger of losing Cyrus had damaged his self-assuredness and better judgement. Eric pressed his tired mind. He felt Sara and Ali knew about more than his CIA job, but how much? Did Ali have evidence of the heroin smuggling, of the unresolved murder, of the Swiss bank accounts? Could Ali ruin him?

"Damn it," Eric said to himself. "I even offered a Savak agent a hundred thousand dollars to get rid of Ali, but the bastard answered he wouldn't kill for any price anymore." But if Ali had damaging evidence he must be neutralized. "Containment!" Eric thought. U.S. presidents used the word to justify their worldwide counterrevolution; it could certainly be used to justify his.

Eric's indoctrination ran deep, to the marrow in his bones. At home, in school, on TV, in the newspapers, in spy movies, from presidents and professors, he had learned that communism was evil. Communists had to be searched out and destroyed, as in Vietnam, or ridiculed and blacklisted at home, put under inquisition for un-American activities or harrassed by the FBI, the IRS and the Immigration Service. Eric thought, the ends can be the means and the means become the ends; who is to say which comes first and matters most? By killing Ali, Eric would be doing what the U.S. did all over the world. The image of the greatest recent CIA success formed in Eric's head and reassured him—half a million dead communists floating on Indonesian rivers. What was the difference in how Ali was disposed of—by the Shah's firing squads or by Eric's gunshots?

He pictured himself committing murder. He realized the irony of his situation: he had once been a good Catholic opposed to abortion, and now he was contemplating murder. But Ali stood between Eric and his dreams, between him and Cyrus, who called him "Daddy." Ali and his fellow communists had ruined Eric's career and conspired to enslave the free world. This man had to be disposed of; this communist, Eric corrected himself.

Eric took his pistol from the safe, snapped in a clip, checked that a bullet was seated, and attached a silencer. He brought it to the front gate and hid it in a large tub under some bushes beginning to show the effects of a harsh winter. In the mountain gorges, just a short drive over nearly deserted roads, Eric could dispose of the body. The police were too busy to investigate another corpse. No one could suspect him if Ali were to disappear, just one among thousands during these chaotic times.

Within half an hour the doorbell rang. Eric felt his hands tremble and tried to steady himself. He quickened his steps and swung the gate open. As Eric smiled thinly, Ali noticed his agitation. Of course Eric would be nervous; he had lost.

"Where is Sara?" Ali asked immediately.

"She's waiting inside. Come in, please."

Ali stepped into the yard, his senses quickening. It was second nature to a revolutionary to live always alert to danger. He looked around and observed everything. As no one else was in sight, Ali concentrated on Eric. One move from him and Ali would draw his gun.

Eric proceeded with his plan. He stopped at the tub and muttered, loud enough for Ali to hear, "That damn gardener should have taken this plant inside. I told him it can't survive the cold."

Two steps away, Ali turned around quickly. Eric said casually, "Look, what can you blackmail me with, anyway? I've got nothing to worry about."

"Yes, you have! You're a heroin smuggler. I have proof."

The second Ali saw Eric withdraw his hand from the bush holding a gun, he fell to the ground and rolled, looking for cover, trying to get his gun out. Three bullets ricocheted off the pavement close to his ear. A burning sensation passed through his right arm and shoulder and down his side, and he felt the sudden stickiness of his own blood. Reaching the house, Ali tried the door, but it was locked. Eric approached calmly, the gun in his outstretched arms pointing at Ali.

Ali shouted, "Sara!"

"Sara is gone. The door is locked. Everything is locked for you except hell. You should have been dead long ago."

Ali crouched helpless, his back to the door. His right arm was numb; he could not take his gun out. "Don't kill me! All I want is a share of my son and freedom for my people."

Eric savored the moment, enjoying Ali's hopelessness. He didn't respond, but took one more step forward.

Suddenly the gate swung open behind Eric and a voice shattered his world: "Don't do it, Daddy! Don't kill my baba!"

Ali collapsed in a pool of blood. Eric turned around to see his son framed in the gateway, with Sara behind him, both of them frozen. They had returned from the airport early because the flight had been cancelled. Eric forgot everything, as the pistol lowered his arm by its weight. His mouth agape, his eyes wide, his heart pounding furiously, he wished to disappear. The shame of a lifetime drowned him. Cyrus ran to the bleeding Ali, shouting at Eric, "You've killed my baba!" Sara's glance at Eric radiated accusation and hatred as she rushed past him toward Ali. "My God, my love."

Eric turned and slowly walked away with his eyes fixed on the ground. He went through the house and straight up to his study. Flames of fear and shame raging in him, he stood at the window and watched Sara and Cyrus on either side of Ali, helping him across the yard and into the car. A line of red splotches marked their path. He heard the car pull away in a hurry. He looked through the gate to the street, now deserted and silent. Defeated, frightened, guilty and alone, Eric had no one to turn to. No one needed or wanted him anymore, not even Cyrus. Everything was destroyed. He remembered the gun in his hand. He raised it, stared at it absently and pressed the trigger. There was no shot—the bullet stuck. He threw the gun away.

Eric knew he was a murderer at last. Ali could never survive three bullets. Eric couldn't think any longer. Horrid images rushed into his head, inflicting a sharp pain. A prosecutor, all in black, pointed his finger and said, "Murder in cold blood. Murderer of a father in front of his son." He saw Sara and Cyrus in the courtroom nodding their agreement. Suddenly Eric's father stood there beside his mother's weeping face, pointing at Eric and shouting, "This is not his first murder." Eric strained to hear, but the words were lost in the confusion. Instead he heard Sullivan say, "The Shah is mad at you, Eric. Keep away from him." He imagined Professor Wharton walking away. He heard them say, "A big failure."

Fear and shame tormented Eric. He took the heroin, the money, the bank accounts and the diary from the safe and set them ablaze in the fireplace. He had never been so fearful. His secrets would be out; MP's would be at the door to arrest him, or else the CIA would neutralize him.

He shouted, "Damn the CIA! Damn the CIA! I just cheated a little in tennis, and now I am a murderer. My son saw me murder his father. Damn the CIA, damn the CIA." He ran downstairs, found some rope and went to the hall. He stood on a chair and tied one end of the rope to a chain suspended from the ceiling, the other end around his neck. Then Eric kicked the chair from under him. The impersonal rope tightened its grip around his neck, pressing hard against his throat, blocking the flow of air to Eric's demanding lungs. Before the world blackened, Eric envisioned for a moment a poster which had hung on Professor Pirooz' front door in Manhattan. It was a fierce-looking Uncle Sam, pointing his finger at him: "I want you."

CHAPTER 27

Time Four

The next day, January 8th, the State Department announced that General Huyser, Deputy Chief of Staff of U.S. Forces-Atlantic, was in Iran, officially to bolster the support of the Iranian armed forces for the Bakhtiyar government. Actually he had been in Iran for some time and his mission was to protect U.S. interests. In particular, he had to get rid of the Shah, who had become a liability, and make sure that if Bakhtiyar also fell the military could maintain discipline, be prepared to intervene, and remain loyal to the U.S. He also wanted to make sure the leftists were destroyed.

Huyser secretly discussed the Shah's impending fate with the Iranian military brass, with the CIA, and with Ambassador Sullivan.

But Huyser had orders. So on January 8th he and Sullivan met the Shah in his study in the Niavaran Palace. Also present were General Rabbi, the Air Force Commander; General Badri, the Commander of the Army; and General Garabaghi, the Chief of Staff.

After some small talk, the Shah forced himself to say, "Please accept my condolences for the tragic death of Mr. Eric Saunders. I wanted to personally express my deep sorrow to the highest official of the U.S. government. Mr. Saunders was not just a freedom fighter of outstanding courage but a friend of our Court. He was deeply disappointed, I know, when Operation Sweep failed in its objective. He could not accept even one failure." He looked at his generals and added, "I wish my officials would learn from him."

Huyser interrupted. Sullivan had warned him about the Shah's rambling. "If Your Majesty please, when the fate of a great nation is at stake, we must accept sacrifices. The U.S. appreciates Your Majesty's sympathy, but we must look to the future. The main concern of my government is the welfare of Your Majesty and the welfare of the nation."

The Shah mumbled, "Thank you."

In two hours the plans, already drawn up by the CIA, modified by the Shah's staff and reviewed by Huyser, were finalized. Although the Shah wished to save the monarchy with or without himself, Huyser's objective was to preserve U.S. influence in Iran, and the Shah had no role in his scheme. If the Shah did what he was told, he would not meet the fate of President Diem of South Vietnam; so the Shah consented.

They agreed that the royal family must surrender their holdings in Iran to the Pahlavi Foundation. The Shah was to leave Iran as soon as possible for an "extended vacation." Huyser went along with the charade to get the Shah out of the way.

The generals present remained attentive and accepted His Majesty's decision. Still, in the palace halls after the meeting, Garabaghi said to his fellow generals, "Huyser grabbed the Shah by the tail and threw him out like a dead mouse." It was rumored in very high places that Garabaghi, to save his own skin, had already established contact with Ayatollah Khomeini.

Soon after, violent demonstrations and arson spread across the country. Ali, Zaman, and Aram worked openly and intensely, night and day for the revolution. Supporters of Khomeini began to assert themselves among opposition groups as well as in the government apparatus.

On January 16th, the coffin of the monarchy was carried into history. At a hurriedly arranged press conference the Shah announced that he would take an extended vacation. With tears in his eyes, a bag of Iranian soil under his arm, a conscript kissing his boots and a jet roaring overhead, the Shah left Iran. In his class the next day, Professor Pirooz shook his head and laughed at American press coverage. "The U.S. press reports the Shah's press conference instead of the events that led to it. An extended vacation, indeed, tears, a bag of dirt and all; what a farewell show! What is needed is a court of law to try the U.S. and Iranian officials who assisted the Shah in his crimes against humanity."

The Shah in exile was an embarrassment to his former friends. He moved from Egypt to Morocco to Panama to New York and back to Egypt. As he journeyed hither and thither, the cancer journeyed through his body. The Shah waited in faraway places for news of a miracle, a coup at home. But 1979 was not 1953. No matter where he stayed he felt like a prisoner in Evin, surrounded by guards who spoke no Farsi. He was tortured by guilt and cancer. The surgeons in Egypt butchered him as he had butchered his nation. Soon he was dead, buried near King Farouk in Egypt. But no great pyramid of stone marked the resting place of the last Shah of Iran—only a pyramid of condemnations.

The Shah and the U.S. never admitted defeat. Shahpur Bakhtiyar took power in the name of the Regency Council—a monarchy without a Shah —and pledged a new constitution, hoping the solutions of the 1907 Constitutional Revolution would work in 1979. But Bakhtiyar ruled in name only, some of his men going over silently to the opposition or melting away into exile.

The U.S., which had supported the Shah up to the last minute, now latched onto Bakhtiyar. President Carter declared the new regime the legal government of Iran and reaffirmed U.S. support. In gratitude Bakhtiyar pledged to maintain all military, political and economic ties with the U.S. Professor Pirooz commented that "A peanut farmer President has become an instant Iranian constitutional expert."

Ayatollah Khomeini repeated his intention to form a provisional government and a national assembly to draft a new constitution, and President Carter responded by reaffirming his support for Bakhtiyar. Now that no intermediaries were left, the intentions of President Carter and those of Ayatollah Khomeini clashed openly in public. On January 17th in Paris Khomeini ordered general civil disobedience and strikes and appealed once again to the armed forces to join the people. In response, ministers and members of parliament resigned, more soldiers deserted—and more demonstrations rocked the Iranian soil. Pirooz, hurrying to pack to leave for Iran, said to a friend helping him, "The people have decided not to sleep, not to stop moving until final victory."

The Iranian left fell into a tragic strategic error "almost unconsciously," as Ali had warned. The leftist groups only echoed Khomeini's anti-imperialist rhetoric, but did not propose a program of their own for democracy and women's liberation, after the Shah, to distinguish themselves from Khomeini's crowd. So the masses, finding no difference between the leftists and the fundamentalists, gravitated even more toward Khomeini, a great and familiar face, and a spiritual and incorruptible leader.

On January 20th Khomeini announced in Paris that he would return home in six days. This was the critical threat to the Regency Council, for if the Grand Ayatollah could command so powerfully from a distance, what might he do at home among his people? Bakhtiyar ordered the airports closed, and over fifty thousand people demonstrated in Bakhtiyar's support.

On January 27th Bakhtiyar offered to go to Paris to discuss with Khomeini the "future of the nation," but Khomeini would grant an audience only if Bakhtiyar resigned first! Three days later Bakhtiyar ordered the airports reopened. The U.S. government ordered the "temporary evacuation" of all American dependents and nonessential personnel. Sara had no intention of following the embassy's order. Revolution leaped forward, carrying its own creators like a storm billowing the leaves.

CHAPTER 28

Khomeini
Comes Home

On the evening of January 31st, darkness covered Paris but not the excitement of those waiting at the airport to witness the Imam's departure for home. Supporters of Khomeini called him Imam, the spiritual leader descended from the Prophet Muhammad, a term of highest respect. The Twelfth Imam had disappeared a long time ago and the faithful awaited his resurrection.

The tanks of a jumbo jet were filled to capacity. If necessary, the plane could make a round trip. Mehrabad airport in Teheran was open again, but a military coup could force a change in the flight plan.

About 10 p.m., a whisper ran through the corridors of the Paris airport. Khomeini is here! The crowd pressed forward, and some lifted a large picture of the Imam which carried the words of a French reporter, "The Man Who Rocks the West." They waved Iranian flags, red, green and white but without the symbolic lion, sun and crown. As the Imam came into view the roar of applause drowned out all other airport noises. "Praise be to you, Khomeini," and "God is great," they shouted.

His family and close associates accompanied him, including Abul Hassan Banisadr, Sadegh Ghotbzadeh and Dr. Ibrahim Yazdi. With a serene face and penetrating eyes under thick eyebrows, the Imam walked slowly. He appeared to be in meditation while absolutely alert. At the gate, the Imam turned and waved to supporters and journalists, and spoke into the microphones. "I thank the people of France for their hospitality," he said before boarding the plane.

The eighty-year old Khomeini inspected the cabin, leaned toward Ghotbzadeh, and whispered, "Only male flight attendants, no wine or liquor, and the faithful must pray in flight." After takeoff the Imam prayed in the first class lounge, journeyed into his memories, and then fell asleep.

His father, a judicial scholar and farmer, had been assassinated on order of the Shah of the past dynasty when Khomeini was one year old. The father, like the son, had denied the legitimacy of a king in an Islamic country. His mother had died when Khomeini was fifteen. From Khomein, the village of his birth, he went to study with the respected cleric Haeri at Qom. Soon he rose to the rank of *mojtahed* in Islamic law and philosophy.

For forty years Khomeini led the quiet life of a scholar and teacher. He kept his belief that monarchy was illegitimate hidden within school and home. Even so, the Shah shut down his school and forbade him to teach, but Khomeini continued secretly and trained hundreds of future leaders not only in theology but also in his vision of Islamic government.

Khomeini supported Mossadegh and denounced the 1953 coup. He became Ayatollah in 1960, and three years later, when he was acclaimed *Marja Taghleed,* Source of Imitation, he publicly denounced the monarchy as illegitimate. The Shah imprisoned Khomeini but could not bend him, and, not daring to kill a holy man, finally set him free. But following the uprisings of June 1963, Savak destroyed Khomeini's house, set his manuscripts on fire, and imprisoned him once again. He again did not yield, was released, and denounced the judicial immunity of U.S. advisors, Iran's borrowing money to buy U.S. arms, the big landlords, the White Revolution, and the Shah's regime itself.

This time, he was sent into sixteen years of exile and wandering: first to Bursa, Turkey, then the holy city of Najef in Iraq, and then a short stay in a humble house in Neuphle-le-Chateau, a suburb of Paris. His wife, son, son-in-law, three daughters, grandchildren and great-grandchildren all endured the difficult times with him.

He wrote a total of forty books and collections of lectures. But in Iran anyone found with his books faced a ten-year sentence. The Shah circulated copies of the banished books altered with forgeries to discredit Khomeini. The *New York Times* denounced Khomeini's anti-Semitism using the altered quotations from his book, *Islamic Government,* and refused to retract the denunciation after they were proved false. Khomeini was anti-Zionist but not anti-Semitic, for that would violate the Koran, which declares Jews people of the holy Torah.

Savak's murder of Khomeini's son, Mustafa, sparked the January 1978 uprising in Qom which spread across Iran and didn't end until the Shah's fall. Khomeini reacted impassively to his son's death. "There is no difference between my son and other martyrs," he said.

Khomeini's residence in the Paris suburb, his headquarters in a bungalow close by, the aides, petitioners, visiting politicians and journalists evolved into an Islamic Republic in exile. His influence was great, even in exile. A single telephone linked the bungalow to Iran, where tape recorders and a tape duplicating machine permitted recordings of Khomeini's messages to be played in 80,000 mosques, in the bazaars and in homes.

Khomeini ate yogurt and rice regularly, took short walks for exercise and napped in the afternoon. He kept his voice low, uttered only simple words and kept a humble appearance. He worked hard and long and never missed a prayer or a fast. He was messianic, his life austere. His aides and students imitated the practices of "Agha," as he was called lovingly.

Now in the plane, Khomeini awoke, prayed and granted reporters an interview. His aides sat behind him, silent when he was silent and attentive when he spoke. They carried out his commands without question, without exception. His eyes carried messages of finality, minimizing the need for words. It was very difficult to look into his eyes even briefly.

Khomeini looked out of the airplane window, studying the clouds below as if to check that Iran was still there, that it had not changed beyond all recognition in the sixteen years of his absence. He was flying over Iran, over deserts and mountains, farms and villages. He held this nation like water in the palm of his hand, could move it from side to side, change its shape or pour some out.

The reporters waited politely, but the Imam gazed out of the window and ignored them. No one, not his closest supporters, none of the hundred and fifty reporters flying with him, were allowed to know his thoughts about the birth of a new Iran. Only the most perceptive could sense or guess the life of the new state still only an idea in the Imam's head.

The Imam thought as he raced far above the clouds, "This land is a part of Dar-ul-Islam, the House of Muslims. I will protect it. I will spread God's word over Dar-ul-Islam. I will impose His will across it. I will do no less than those whose rightful successor I am—Muhammad and his heirs, Abu Bakr, Umar, Uthman, Imam Ali and his descendants to the Twelfth Imam. I will announce that all Muslims, both Shi'ite and Sunni, are brothers and sisters. All Muslims must unite to stamp out corruption on earth and the influence of the Satans of the West and East. My mission will not remain undone; no one can stop me. No pain, no sacrifice is too great in waging my holy war against unbelievers. First persuasion and then force will spearhead the Islamic Revolution. Didn't Islam explode over the world in the same manner long ago? Didn't the Prophet Muhammad, all praise be unto him, invite people to submit to God's will and then use his sword to enforce submission on anyone who would not accept the message of God? So let those who stand against Islam and my will be banished."

The reporters respected the Imam's silence. A brief moment of impatience passed the Imam's mind as he reflected on the inferior position of Muslims in world affairs. The emotion uncovered a fire of righteous anger in the Grand Ayatollah. I must change this world; I must make sure Muslims are worthy of Islam! Just then a reporter broke the silence to ask, "What are your feelings, now that you are so close to home? What exactly are your thoughts, Imam, as you gaze at your homeland after so long a separation?"

Khomeini looked up, his face unmoved. He hesitated as if he had just awakened. In a soft, barely perceptible voice, the Imam replied, "Nothing."

At last the plane landed, rolling on as if to escape the military vehicles along the runway. But it did stop, surrounded by uniforms and equipment. The impatience of the whole nation engulfed the plane, its engines still humming. Airport workers moved the stairs to the plane, and Ayatollah Taleghani mounted them to greet Khomeini on behalf of the nation. After a long wait, Khomeini stepped out and the two Ayatollahs embraced. Despite press censorship, word of the arrival flew across Teheran, across the country, like a flash of lightning. "The Imam has arrived." "God is great." A roar of cheers, praise and prayer filled the Iranian landscape. The celebration moved on the lips and in the minds of the faithful. People embraced, kissed and cried for joy.

Khomeini stepped down to the earth of Iran, and Banisadr, Bazargan, Ghotbzadeh, Yazdi and other aides followed him. Khomeini knew that no leader commanded the loyalty of a nation as absolutely as he did. He was not a head of state nor a war hero returning home; he had an ordinary passport and wore sandals. Still, a presidential escort had taken him to the Paris airport hours ago, and now he saw a mass of people waving welcome, all ready to obey him, to give their lives on his whispered command. He felt the joy in everyone's soul, he saw the light in their eyes and heard the words of praise in their voices. He responded with assurance, waving his right hand over his head, the fingers wide open. He sensed eyes moving, and minds and bodies, in harmony with the movement of his own fingertips.

A primordial sea greeted him. It boiled here and there, certainly, but it was warm and it was full of new life. The life was not that of a simple cell but that of a whole nation. The Imam thought, "I shall turn their faith into an irresistible force to establish Islam as a living reality: martyrdom as the essence of life. God's wisdom transcends all things. We owe our very existence to him. I shall demand absolute obedience to God, and total surrender to his laws, to his will. I shall carry the true message of Islam to the world, believers and unbelievers alike."

Public concerns interrupted the Imam's private thoughts. As a microphone was presented to him, the chanting ceased and people awaited his benediction. His simple, muted words took flight, were amplified, and echoed around the world.

"In the name of God, the All-merciful, the Compassionate....I praise and thank the dispossessed of Iran, the workers and peasants, merchants, civil servants and students, all who have fought bravely for their country and for Islam. The Shah is gone, but his ouster is just the first battle of our struggle. The dynasty has ruined Iran and we must reconstruct it. I command you to safeguard our precious unity, which is the secret weapon for the battles awaiting us. Final success will come when all foreigners are ousted.''

The Imam finished and then moved quickly into a waiting blue Chevrolet Blazer to set out twenty miles across Teheran to visit Beheshte Zahra cemetery, which was now called the Martyrs' Cemetery.

The tears of his followers on his route could fill a river bed. Some journalists estimated that the crowds who stood for hours to catch a glimpse of him were three million, others, closer to five million. "His welcome is a miracle," one wired. "Never have so many welcomed an old man with such passion."

More than forty thousand Islamic marshals, who had directed the march of Ashura, kept the throng in check, but their thin lines were broken often when exuberant onlookers pushed close to the Imam's vehicle.

Close to Pahlavi Square, a few miles from the airport, Ali and his Fedayeen comrades carried red flags emblazoned with hammer and sickle and watched the motorcade. Ali had emerged from underground and no longer needed to pretend to be dead. His gunshot wounds, more superficial than Eric had realized, had just about healed, leaving more scars on his body. Sara and Cyrus were safe with Aram's father, and Ali saw them frequently. He smiled as he thought of the night before, when Sara had held him tight and kissed him gently until he fell asleep.

Ali saw the throng so full of joy, wanting to pay their respects, to touch Khomeini's gown, to express love and admiration without fear.

There, there was Khomeini, the exalted leader, waving his hand. The Imam's words no longer flew from cassettes; now it was his own lips that gave them wing. His face was no longer just pigments printed on posters, it was made of flesh. The once absent Imam had reappeared, descending from the clouds.

In a moment the motorcade flew past. People shouted, "God is great, God is great," the chant reaching the heavens. They roared, "Imam, Welcome," "Yankee go home," "Now that you are with us, Khomeini, establish the Islamic Republic," "Islamic Republic, yes, monarchy, no."

Khomeini seemed to frown at Ali and the Fedayeen. Ali waved his flag but remained silent. He remembered the U.S. flag draped over Eric's coffin as it had boarded a plane for home. U.S. imperialism was gasping its last through the lungs of Prime Minister Bakhtiyar. A few mistrustful glances of Islamic marshals fell on the Fedayeen and their communist flags, but the joy of the Imam's reappearance swept suspicions aside.

The dreams of Ali's life were threatened by the chants of the masses. He had fought the U.S. and the Shah, but the adversary seemed to be transforming itself. What if these masses, now shouting, waving, crying, praying, enchanted with the Imam, were not ready for a workers' state which would end exploitation? What if the revolution split apart, one faction devouring the other? Could he and the Fedayeen tell the people that it is not the will of God, as declared by the Imam, but their own will that must shape their lives? How could a few thousand Fedayeen be a match for the millions that the Imam commanded?

More than a thousand years ago, the followers of Imam Hussain were outnumbered on the field of Karbala, but now they were great in numbers and about to grasp state power. But today, the Fedayeen, in contrast, were but a handful. They seemed on the periphery of today's joyous demonstration. Would the revolution for which they had worked so hard be stolen? Ali wondered. He thought of Lenin, whose small party triumphed; of Mao, who retreated ever deeper into the mountains only to return in victory, of Castro, always a short step away from a firing squad, before marching into Havana at the head of the people. But Ali thought also of the many unknown revolutionaries who had died in failure, and they filled all of history.

What if the cherished dreams of the people occurring now in their awakening were a deeper dream, a nightmare? What if the Imam's idea of democracy was not what many expected it to be? What if the Imam does not approve of the Fedayeen and turns the people against them? Unsettling questions swirled in Ali's mind like a storm trapped in a canyon.

Like Khomeini, Pirooz had also returned home, one of the thousands of exiles pouring back to Iran. His hair was graying and receding, his face sadder than when he had left. Now he stood beside Aram and watched the motorcade. They didn't exchange many words; they just shook their heads. They shared a bittersweet feeling: the Shah was out, but who was in? Pirooz whispered to Aram, "God save the country from the mullahs."

Aram whispered back, "God save the minorities from the mullahs."

Zaman whispering said, "God save the women from the mullahs."

A bystander, overhearing their whispering, added, "God save the Muslims from the mullahs."

Pirooz added, "And God save the communists from the mullahs!"

Aram said, "Amen!"

Midway through his journey, the Imam was taken to a waiting helicopter to complete the trip to the martyrs' graves. At two in the afternoon, the Imam stepped from the helicopter and went to sit on a platform, while around him a crowd of political and religious leaders knelt in anticipation. The voices of two children chanted the words of the Koran. Finally all fell silent as the Imam spoke.

"Martyrs are the heart of history. I feel very sad. Those who have given so much to Islam shall be rewarded by God. The nation rejects the Shah and Bakhtiyar, who has neither supporters nor legitimacy. I invite the military to join the people. I shall send the guilty to the courts of justice. Let everyone know that we are not against progress, only its abuse. We are not against the freedom of women, only prostitution. We are not against foreigners, only imperialism. We demand to be masters of our own house. Guard the revolution!'' The Imam took a breath and lowered his voice. "I shall appoint an interim government to set the law in motion.''

After he had returned to his home in Qom, he made clear his position: "We shall uproot the Western influences that have ruined us. We shall establish the Nation of Islam.''

It was now only a matter of days before U.S. influence in Iran was to be buried in history. The Imam had the people, and the people had the Imam. After Khomeini whizzed by, Ali left to spend time with Cyrus and Sara, but his tasks remained unfinished. Ahead of him lay the struggle against Bakhtiyar's wavering authority and against the remnants of the Shah's military machine, especially the hated Immortal Guards, who were well indoctrinated, well paid, well dressed, well disciplined, much feared within the military and absolutely loyal to His Majesty. Ali believed that the Shah's Immortals could be eventually subdued, though he would not know at what human cost.

Nevertheless, looking beyond the Shah's collapsing apparatus, Ali saw dark clouds, furious and angry, gathering momentum and roaming toward the Fedayeen and the multitude of wishful thinkers who today cheered the Imam's magnificent arrival. Ali thought of the arrival as a wedding party of the Imam and the people that was catered by God's angels. The Imam vowed to be faithful to the dispossessed and to the diverse groups who had supported him; and he perhaps meant it. But there were too many brides, so to speak. Not even the Imam could keep them all happy! So some of the marriages would end in divorce, some in violent separation, some even in homicide! Ali hurried his steps home as he tried to repress his gloom and fear of the future by the thought of spending time with Cyrus and Sara.

CHAPTER 29

Revolutionary Tactics

On February 2, 1979, Bakhtiyar offered to form a "government of national unity" to include supporters of Imam Khomeini, but the Imam refused and asked all officials to resign.

On February 5th, in the auditorium of Alavi High School in Teheran, four hundred Iranian and foreign reporters waited, microphones and camera eyes open, senses and pencils sharpened, to witness a surreal political occurrence, to record history in its most colorful nakedness. They were now waiting for an event to unfold which would have appeared impossible only a year earlier.

On that day Imam Khomeini—a small man with piercing eyes, a very old man but a relentless fighter, a spiritual leader but a savvy politician, a former prisoner and exile, a man without an army, navy, or air force, without a political party or parliament, a man who had condemned all superpowers and neighboring states—was to name Dr. Mehdi Bazargan Prime Minister of Iran. He would tell President Carter that Bakhtiyar was no Prime Minister, and that, if Bakhtiyar did not resign, Imam Khomeini would order his arrest by the nation of Iran. Ghotbzadeh, Imam Khomeini's "other son," beamed. Dr. Yazdi wearing a thick beard stood by; Banisadr, who would become the first President, looked into the future. Other Ayatollahs and mullahs crowded around Imam Khomeini, who was lost among them, yet no one failed to feel his presence. Imam Khomeini was a lone star fixed on the face of the sky; the others were satellites spinning around him. The Imam's messianic charisma held each follower in a specific orbit. He could pull them closer or push them farther away with ease.

Imam Khomeini stepped before the microphones and announced to the world, "These are not ordinary times. Our country has been robbed, wounded and pillaged. I am appointing not an ordinary government. Dr. Bazargan's authority is sanctified by Islam, and his commands are God's will. Whoever disobeys Bazargan disobeys Almighty God, and I shall punish

330

him until he repents and regains wisdom, or else I shall send him to hell."

Dr. Mehdi Bazargan, head of the National Liberation Movement, former Dean of Engineering at Teheran University, former director of the National Iranian Oil Company, and former prisoner of the Shah, humbly accepted the honor. "I beg the nation for patience, cooperation and calm in these days of turmoil. I demand Dr. Shahpur Bakhtiyar's resignation to prevent further bloodshed."

On the same day, Bakhtiyar reiterated in Parliament his refusal to step down, while fifty-seven parliamentary representatives obeyed Khomeini's command and resigned. Now Iran had two prime ministers—one appointed by the Shah and the other by the Imam.

Bakhtiyar appealed to the dead constitution and threatened the revolutionaries with a firing squad. His threats persisted as his limited power withered away. He promised to yield power constitutionally, but he could not give away what he really did not have. Bakhtiyar could not understand that he needed the people; but the people no longer needed him or any of the other Shah's leftovers.

When Bakhtiyar commanded the air force to bomb Khomeini's residence, the air force commander warned him that pilots might "accidentally" drop the bombs on his office instead. The message sank deep. Even though U.S. instructors had taught Iranian pilots to fly and to bomb, they had failed to indoctrinate them to commit murder for Bakhtiyar who, in the eyes of the people, stood for U.S. interests. One airman made a huge placard which read, "Give me fuel and I will fly my bombs right to the White House!" Knowing how the media in the U.S. would twist such boastings to sound like a real threat, Ali asked the Fedayeen for more realism and restraint in their pronouncements.

Revolutionary rumblings arose among officers who watched conscripts disappear, and air force cadets and technicians, called airmen, were close to open rebellion because they had been treated poorly and underpaid.

The first actual rebellion in the armed forces had occurred earlier at Boushehr Airbase, from which the Shah's planes patrolled the Persian Gulf. A few months ago when a general had struck an airman for opening his collar in the summer heat, the airmen went on strike and refused to service or repair the planes. The tension mounted until a hunger strike ensued. The Shah, frightened that the rebellion would spread, ordered the incident censored and the work schedule falsified to hide the hunger strike from the public, but word spread nevertheless. In the fall of 1978 as the Shah was losing control, airmen in Teheran became mutinous. Just before the Shah's departure hundreds of airmen were arrested and 157 executed; it was the revenge of a desperate, sick man.

As Bakhtiyar now issued executive orders that fell on deaf ears, State Department spokesman, Hodding Carter, reaffirmed the constitutionality of Bakhtiyar's rule and asked Iranians to rally around Bakhtiyar.

"Somebody must be eating donkey brains for breakfast," Pirooz said to himself. "Give me Gordon Liddy before Hodding Carter. Poor Bakhtiyar is now supported by Hodding Carter who has no power and knows nothing about Iran."

* * * * *

Against this background of revolt and desperation, Fedayeen leaders gathered in Reza's team house in northwest Teheran to await Ali. Zaman turned to Aram and remarked, "Ali is late."

"Traffic is slow. He has to visit many groups," Aram replied.

"Still, I'm worried."

"I understand. Be patient, Zaman."

Reza, whose house in the slums had earlier served for secret meetings of Ali's family, looked at his watch. He had fewer wrinkles on his face now than he had had in the slums, as though growing younger from three years of better food. "Hush!" Reza said when he heard a motorcycle coming to a halt.

In a minute Ali stepped into the room and went to the head of the table, while his comrade stood still at the door. "Thank you for waiting. Greetings to all of you! You've heard that Bakhtiyar won't resign. Bazargan has announced another march, but marches will not overthrow the government. Comrades, we, the Fedayeen, must seize the opportunity and strike the first blow to overthrow Bakhtiyar."

A man leaning on a rifle said, "Comrade Ali, tell us what the Fedayeen must do."

"I have a plan, but we must discuss it patiently and decide collectively. We are putting not just our lives on the line but the nation's.

"There are many things to be done. Radio and television workers are ready to join the struggle if we disperse the troops guarding the studios. Police desertion is high, so we can probably take over some police stations. We must also liberate the prisons. Dr. Chameron is planning to seize the House of Parliament. And we must capture the U.S. Embassy, not to harm Americans but to prevent espionage and counterrevolution. We must not forget what happened in 1953."

A comrade said, "An excellent idea. A hundred men can quickly overcome a few Marines who have forgotten how to shoot, and maybe even capture the one who raped our sister."

Ali retorted, "Comrade! We do not seek revenge."

Aram said, "We must also capture CIA documents."

A man with a gun added, "We must put Sullivan on trial." Another man continued, "If convicted, Sullivan must face a firing squad."

"We must take the initiative!" said Aram.

Ali said, "All these suggestions sound appropriate and just. But the Fedayeen have more important tasks than trying individual culprits. At first, we must resolve the question, 'Who rules Iran?' We must win a decisive battle against the military. The followers of Imam Khomeini will join, but the Fedayeen must strike the first blow. Army morale and discipline are weak, there are many desertions, and even the generals are not united because they differ in their private interests, their loyalty to the monarchy and their aversion to personal and political risks. Still, there is danger. The army is well armed while the people are mostly unarmed, the generals are still able to control mutinies, and the units in Teheran may be reinforced from outside. The U.S. may intervene as well; they have already sent General Huyser. We must by all means prevent a coup attempt by the Americans, but also we must make sure not to harm U.S. citizens in the process unless we are forced to."

"What do you propose?" They all waited expectantly.

"I believe the Immortal Guards of the Shah stand between the nation and liberty. So first we must crush the Immortals." Ali heard a gasp. "The Immortal Guards number eight thousand. As you know, their loyalty to the Shah is unwavering. They march around the Niavaran Palace shouting *Javid Shah! Javid Shah!* The Shah Forever! everyday! The Immortals are told that the Shah will soon return and that their sacred duty is to stop any mutiny in the armed forces. They are disciplined and will enforce discipline. Fear of these vicious Immortals is all that holds the army together, and the army is all that holds the facade of the government together.

"Comrades," Ali raised his voice. "The Immortals are our last obstacle. If we can defeat them, the revolution will march by itself. But it will be too costly to attack the Immortals at their base, at their point of strength."

Zaman asked, "How do we draw the bastards out?" The Fedayeen looked surprised at Zaman's profanity.

Ali continued, "On a signal from the Fedayeen, our comrades in Doshan Tapeh Airbase will provoke the Immortals into coming out. The airmen have planned a sneaky demonstration against the Shah on Thursday."

A comrade repeated, "Sneaky?"

"Yes, they will take over the base and the armory." Ali continued, "And if the Immortals come out, we will attack them from all sides."

"Great," another comrade responded.

Zaman then asked, "But what if the Immortals stay put?"

Ali answered, "Then we will clean out the armory and arm civilians. The longer the Immortals wait, the stronger the people will become."

Reza asked, "Have they any weaknesses?"

Ali replied, "The Americans have recently further trained them for riot control, but not for urban warfare."

"How will we coordinate everything?"

Ali said, "We will use the demonstration at Teheran University on the anniversary of Siahkal as our focal point. We have invited Bazargan to speak there."

Zaman concluded, "If we defeat the Immortals we will have defeated twenty-five hundred years of monarchy."

"Yes," Ali responded. "But Islamic marshalls outnumber us one-thousand to one. So the collapse of the regime will not automatically lead to a workers' state. I hope that after the monarchy the Fedayeen will have a breather of freedom to educate the people."

Reza added, "God willing."

Ali resumed, "We must prepare a detailed economic and political strategy and be prepared to present it to the masses as convincingly and effectively as possible. We must emphasize that we are not just another anti-imperialist group, but that we are for a worker and peasant state, for the liberation of women, for minority rights, for economic justice, for peace and progress, and for democratic rule in Iran." Ali glanced at Zaman and continued, "Fedayeen must also get ready for all of the unexpected eventualities. I remind you comrades—the future will not be any easier or simpler than the past!"

All approved Ali's proposals enthusiastically and worked on special plans and contingencies. If the battle at Doshan Tapeh succeeded, different groups knew which police station or army base to attack next, and some would train people to use the captured arms. Zaman took notes to take to the Mujahedin.

On February 6th the "non-interfering" U.S. government reiterated its support for Bakhtiyar. But General Huyser left the country as the decline of the Shah's regime became inevitable. On February 7th revolutionary forces took control of local governments in Shiraz, Isfahan and Qom and began to do the same in other cities.

On the morning of February 8th, more than a thousand airmen hid their uniforms in paper bags and went to Imam Khomeini's headquarters, where they changed into their uniforms and joined a million demonstrators in support of Bazargan. Then they changed back into civilian clothes and returned to the base. Supporters of Imam Khomeini and the Fedayeen were ready to defend the airmen if the military brass retaliated.

Bakhtiyar, who had all his life struggled for national sovereignty and democracy, was now blamed by the common people for compromising both goals for personal power and glory. His illustrious past was ruined by his ambition. Whatever he thought, said and did was too late, too ineffective.

"Bakhtiyar had come to go and he had to go," Ali remarked to his comrades.

On February 8th, as Bakhtiyar's world fell apart before his own eyes, he made a prophetic prediction, calling the forthcoming Islamic Republic "archaic and medieval."

CHAPTER 30

Day Of Revolution

It is now Friday, February 9th, the day of revolution. Two prime ministers, old friends and former prison mates, are contesting for power. Neither actually has it, and neither will ever have it, except for appearances.

Bazargan appeals to the will of the people and the will of God, Bakhtiyar to the armed forces and the constitution. They negotiate secretly but publicly flex their muscles and exhort their supporters.

A question explodes in the sky like fireworks: Who rules Iran? Teheran trembles. Muted answers arise from government offices, from the Niavaran Palace barracks where the Immortal Guards are stationed, from mosques, and from the barrels of guns and the rumbling of tanks. There is no clear answer; power is in flux. The monarchy is old and dying, but the republic is yet unborn; the angel of death is a midwife.

The battle of wills and words escalates. Khomeini threatens holy war, as Bakhtiyar proclaims he will tolerate peaceful dissent but will crush revolt. Few listen to Bakhtiyar; he might as well be talking to himself. Bakhtiyar does not realize that legitimacy and the constitution and other legal subtleties have lost all credibility with the oppressed people. The Shah has made it so. How can the new order be established without first disorder? How can the republic be born without pain?

Rumors spread that the Shah is plotting a comeback. Faked cassettes command the army to rise up and to support the Shah. General Rabii, the Air Force Commander, grumbles to himself, "Impossible! The Shah's spring is broken beyond repair."

Ambassador Sullivan fears that top secret U.S. weapons sold to the Shah, especially the F-14 Tomcat and its radar system, might fall into the hands of communists.

On all sides people wait expectantly; the revolution is reaching its zenith. Demonstrations are no longer enough; the people must seize power. But how? At what place? The Fedayeen are ready with a plan.

February 9th dawns in tension. The airmen at Doshan Tapeh Airbase are tense, for they could be the turning point of the revolution, the eye of history. Watching a tape of Khomeini's return on TV, the airmen applaud and chant, "Allah-o Akbar." A squad of Immortals on the base rushes to disperse the demonstration; they break bones with rifle butts and push a couple outside and shoot them on the spot. More airmen gather and shout, "Death to Bakhtiyar. The Immortals are U.S. dogs!" Outnumbered, the Immortals are forced to withdraw.

When Bakhtiyar hears of this alarming rebellion, his face turns pale. He consults his generals. "The army is turning on itself," Bakhtiyar announces. "The Immortals are our last hope." Discipline elsewhere in the armed forces crumbles, but the Immortals hold fast. The Immortals must crush any mutiny immediately. Poorly trained airmen and a few ragtag civilians are no match for the mighty Immortals, Bakhtiyar reasons. The Immortals will execute a few airmen and then all will be quiet. They are not called Immortals for nothing! General Khosrowdad, Special Forces Commander, will put a helicopter squadron in the air to spray death on whoever resists the Immortals. He has more helicopters than all the U.S. generals put together.

In tanks and jeeps, the Immortals leave the Niavaran barracks for the Doshan Tapeh base to put down the rebellion. One column proceeds on Arjan Avenue through Mobarakabad.

The news of their march travels faster than the Immortals themselves, alerting people along the way. An AK-47 gun hidden under his gown, a mullah shadows the feared guards. Molotov cocktails, stolen Iranian army G-3 rifles, brand new Kalashnikovs, and Star .45-caliber pistols from Spain appear as if from nowhere; they have come from the PLO, from Libya, who knows? even from the Soviet Union. Men and women, young and old, kneel at windows, climb trees, lie on roofs, huddle behind electric poles, waiting for the Immortals.

The Immortals parade as proudly today as on the Shah's birthday, but today revolutionaries, hostile and quiet, follow them. Each person is but a grain of sand, but together they are a quicksand of Immortality. The Immortals don't notice and don't care. They are impervious; they have the most advanced weapons, even flamethrowers. They are the Immortals, just as the Shah had repeated that the monarchy was immortal.

What is it that impels individual civilians to face the tanks, machine guns, armed helicopters, the fearless posture, expressionless faces hidden under masks, tight organization, and the impeccable discipline of the Immortals? Is it hatred of the Shah or desire for freedom or both?

While the Immortals march through the morning, armed civilians seize control of air bases, military outposts, police stations, government buildings, and highway intersections in Teheran and all over the country. In many cases the troops welcome the revolutionaries, or offer only lukewarm resistance. With the fall of each bastion the people capture new arms, arm new men, spawn new hopes and welcome new audacities. Revolution grows by leaps and bounds; it devours whoever is in its path.

The sky blackening, the Immortals move southward on Majidieh Avenue to the gates of Doshan Tapeh. The airmen there have killed a few officers and captured some weapons, but the armory is still guarded, and the revolutionaries need the weapons inside.

Three Fedayeen airmen ducking behind walls approach the armory, where a captain stands guard next to a machine gun. A Fedayeen jumps in front of the captain, waves a pistol and shouts, "Freeze!" The captain dives for the machine gun, but a bullet splashes his face. The Fedayeen pour into the armory and distribute weapons to all the airmen.

The Immortals arrive, using a tank to push through the south gate of Doshan Tapeh, and begin machine gunning indiscriminately. But the airmen are ready.

Fire meets fire. The airmen train their weapons on the Immortals from barracks windows, from behind trees and walls, from roofs, from anywhere they can hide. One airman lobs a grenade under an advancing tank, blowing off its treads and stopping its death march.

The Immortals are suddenly shocked—they are pinned down. The mutiny was supposed to evaporate at the sight of the Immortals! One arm of the military is trying to destroy the other. The airmen keep the Immortals at bay, but there is little hope they can hold out for long without reinforcements.

But Ali and the Fedayeen are prepared. Thousands have gathered at Teheran University on this February 9th to celebrate the anniversary of the Siahkal uprising. They march to Ferdowsi Square, closer to the Doshan Tapeh base. Zaman and the Mujahedin join them. The Fedayeen and Mujahedin lead armed civilians to the airbase to attack the Immortals from the rear.

But an even greater number of Khomeini followers move their demonstration west toward Shahyad Square, away from Doshan Tapeh. The mullahs order Muslims not to mix with the leftists, fearing that the Fedayeen will contaminate the masses and Islam will be tainted by communism. Thus even before the monarchy collapses, revolutionary unity begins to fray.

At the base the airmen are now surrounded, but suddenly armed revolutionaries sprout like weeds to encircle the attacking Immortals. Government helicopter gunships hovering overhead meet a heavy sniper fire and decide to flee, leaving the Immortals unprotected.

The fighting between military and civilians is fierce and costly. A fragmentation grenade blows up near Zaman as she fights alongside the

Mujahedin. Aram leaves quickly to take his unconscious and blood-soaked wife to a hospital south of Doshan Tapeh.

The Hilton and other nearby hotels are soon turned into makeshift hospitals that look like chaotic slaughterhouses. Casualties pile up on the floors. The nurses and physicians called out of retirement struggle to the point of exhaustion, but many injured die waiting for treatment while the dead wait patiently for graves. On this day of revolution thousands are killed across the country, with tens of thousands injured.

As the night drags on, the Immortals become hungry, fatigued, hopeless, mutilated, mortal, as bullets fly at them from all directions, even from the cracks in walls. Those who do not fall are pushed back block by block, back into history. An officer who orders his men to stand and fight is shot in the back.

* * * * *

Generals Badri, Garabaghi and Rabii meet in Bakhtiyar's gloomy office late Saturday evening, February tenth. They hear the sounds of revolution—voices, bullets, tanks rumbling in the background—and see smoke rising, as they feel time is running out.

Bakhtiyar looks pale and tired. Negotiations with Bazargan have failed. Bazargan has advised Bakhtiyar, his old friend, to resign and save his life. In silence the four men drink water and smoke cigarettes with bitter faces and bitter feelings.

Air Force Commander Rabii breaks the silence. "The Immortals won't survive the battle. They're dropping faster than ripe tomatoes in the heat of summer." He shakes his head. "Khomeini and Bazargan and the fools around them are blind! Can't they see that if they destroy the army they're sitting ducks for the communists? The mullahs can't shoot straight or do anything but pray and incite riots. Damn it, how can you tell these fools they need the armed forces in order to rule?"

Bakhtiyar muses, "If only we could bomb the lot of them."

Rabii replies, "Mr. Prime Minister, I resent that. My commands cannot override those of God, who appears to speak only to the Imam! Damn His Majesty's politicians who dragged us into this mess."

Bakhtiyar waves his hand. "Gentlemen, regrets are useless. I will ask each of you a question and I want a candid answer. General Rabii, what are you going to do?"

Rabii answers, "It is too late to fight, so I'm ready to put myself under Khomeini's command, in order to save what's left of the Air Force."

General of the Army Badri, a staunch supporter of the Shah, smashes his glass against the wall and draws his pistol. "No you won't, you mother-fucker!" He points the gun at Rabii and shouts, "Traitor! Make one move and I'll blast your head off!"

Rabii and Bakhtiyar stand frozen. It is Garabaghi who raises his arms and steps between his colleagues. "Stop it, General Badri. Killing the general will not save the country."

With visible tension, Bakhtiyar says, "I beg of you, General Badri, let's keep our heads."

Garabaghi declares, "As Chief of Staff I order you to put your gun away." Badri quietly lowers the gun and Rabii sighs in relief.

Bakhtiyar looks at Badri. "What do you think we should do, General?"

Badri, his face red hot and tense, retorts, "What do I think?"

Bakhtiyar insists, "Yes, you, General."

"I still think we should bomb the hell out of Khomeini's headquarters."

Garabaghi argues, "But that's impossible, General."

"Then I will do it myself," Badri replies.

Rabii protests, "You'll have to shoot your way to the plane, load it yourself and fly it unassisted."

Garabaghi breaks in, "Gentlemen. Fighting Khomeini will only split the demoralized armed forces and push the nation into a prolonged and bloody civil war." He pauses to let his words sink in. "It will also strengthen the leftists. Remember, Khomeini will need us to curb the communists."

Bakhtiyar asks, "So, what do you propose, General Garabaghi?"

"The armed forces must declare their neutrality, withdraw to the barracks, and accept whatever government emerges from the fighting," Garabaghi replies.

In disbelief Bakhtiyar asks, "Neutrality?"

"Yes, Mr. Prime Minister." Garabaghi breathes deeply. He has conveyed Huyser's recommendation. And thus does Huyser's plan become part of the history of Iran. While President Carter continues to declare his support for Bakhtiyar, Huyser, his own agent, has deserted Bakhtiyar in order to preserve the armed forces intact as the instrument of counterrevolution, as in Chile.

Bakhtiyar becomes as pale as a sheet. "You mean . . . ?"

"Exactly," Garabaghi concludes.

Bazargan's advice flashes through Bakhtiar's mind: "Resign. Save your honor and your life."

Garabaghi adds, "A helicopter will be at your disposal, Mr. Prime Minister."

Dazed and hopeless, Bakhtiyar mumbles, "Thank you."

Earlier that day, Bakhtiyar had pledged in a national broadcast that the fighting would not deter him and had reassured the nation of the stability of his administration. But now, Bakhtiyar, his cabinet and the Regency Council have little choice but to resign and go into hiding. Friends of the Shah and the U.S., too, go underground for safety while revolutionaries finally emerge from hiding. Thus the illegal becomes legal, the lawful unlawful.

Rumors spread through the city that Bakhtiyar has committed suicide, or has been pardoned by Bazargan, or has been captured. Newspapers, moreover, print only those rumors favored by their owners, so confusion reigns throughout the country.

The Fedayeen and other revolutionaries fight the stalwart Immortals throughout the night. The casualties are high. At dawn on Sunday, February 11th, a bullet kills Comrade Reza fighting beside Ali.

The Immortals retreat from the air base under a rain of sniper fire, leaving behind forty dead and a hundred injured. As the last tank turns to flee, Ali jumps on it and commands, "Surrender or I'll blow up the turret!" "We give up, brother," a meek voice replies, and the soldiers give up their pistols. Revolutionaries swarm over the machine, forgetting the dead for a moment as they celebrate the first captured tank in Teheran.

Ali replaces the military radio operator with one of his own fighters and then motions for quiet. "We have won this battle. Now we have a tank to liberate the radio station." People roar their approval, "To the radio station!" Ali shouts into the tank, "To the radio station." The commander, happy that he will be allowed to live, replies, "Yes, sir." The tank roars off toward the city on Ali's mission.

All over Teheran, people capture or destroy more tanks and armored cars, liberate more armories and police stations, and confiscate more weapons. Thousands of police and Savak agents flee or are captured, and a few especially hated ones are torn apart or set on fire in the streets.

The Muslim revolutionary, Dr. Chameron, a former student of Bazargan, leads Khomeini's supporters in liberating the House of Parliament. He disperses the troops defending the building, but the deputies have all resigned or run away already. Professor Pirooz stands beside Chameron. A gun has been put in his hand, but he looks like a deaf person watching a symphony orchestra in full swing.

The whole city is now in revolutionary hands. The underground revolutionaries called terrorists by some of the leaders of the Western world overnight turn into the most dedicated advocates of a new law and order because their leaders demand it. The collapse of the monarchy has energized the revolution, which now moves with its own momentum ahead of individuals.

* * * * *

In the early afternoon on Sunday, Ali and the tank join the revolutionaries encircling the radio and television studios on Jame Jam Avenue. The staff have been out on strike for days, and soldiers are in the building and at the door, nervously eyeing the tank drawn up in the middle of the square. News of the Immortals' defeat has already reached them. Ali takes a bullhorn and shouts from the tank, "Military brothers and comrades! Spare your lives and ours. The country needs us. The Shah is gone and Bakhtiyar has fled. Join us in victory!"

Ali's words linger in the air a tense moment, then white handkerchiefs float like doves from the windows. The soldiers walk out and join the crowd in chanting, "Praise be to the Imam."

Ali and the broadcast workers pour into the building. In half an hour silent radios come to life in the crowded studio. Ali sits in front of a microphone to read an announcement. The clock shows 1:45 p.m., February 11, 1979. Ali's voice, first trembling, then firm, flies across Iran and utters the words he has dreamed of all his life.

"This is the voice of revolution, the free, the true voice of the people." Then he reads a stilted but momentous bulletin. "At 10:20 a.m., in consideration of the circumstances, the Army Supreme Council ordered troops back to their garrisons." Ali adds, "The people are victorious! We must guard the revolution!"

*　*　*　*　*

As Ali finishes the words of victory, in a hospital a few miles away Zamandukht's injured left leg is amputated above the knee while Aram tries to shut out the screams.

*　*　*　*　*

In the radio studio, a Mujahedin now takes the microphone. "The Mujahedin have taken over the security of the city of Teheran." But he does not know that Islamic marshals are already gently pushing Mujahedin and Fedayeen away from key positions in the name of unity and the authority of Imam Khomeini. A Khomeini aide pushes everyone aside at the microphone and reads the Imam's words.

"In the name of God, now that victory is ours, people must refrain from destroying government offices and equipment or damaging embassies or harming foreigners. If soldiers join us, we should welcome them."

Next, Ali broadcasts a Fedayeen announcement. "Fedayeen and supporters! Until the complete defeat of the enemy, no one must disarm. Organize and lead defense committees of ten to fifteen to maintain order and security. Communicate with the leadership. Instruct the masses in the use of firearms and warn them against recklessness. Instruct citizens to serve the revolution with cool heads. Be alert for enemies; arrest them but don't harm them. No one will escape revolutionary justice." Then leaving a comrade to read further Fedayeen messages, Ali hurries off to find Zaman. Learning that her leg has been amputated, Ali feels a searing anger—like a handkerchief pushed down his throat. A part of Zaman is buried while the rest of her is still alive.

Pirooz had sat at Zaman's bedside all night, a night full of ricochets, darkness and the sobbing of a half-conscious woman missing her leg. He remembered Zaman as a little girl throwing herself into his outstretched arms which lifted her to his shoulders. He heard her joyful squeals as he trotted around the fishpool, while Fatema, busy watering the rose bushes, said, "Zaman, dear, don't tire Uncle Pirooz." Now he sees Zaman trembling. "Is the revolution worth it?" he wonders. Then Pirooz reminds himself, "I must visit Lady Fatema even though she won't recognize me." He smiles a bitter smile. Just a few days ago Zaman's little boy, Arash, had ridden on his shoulder as Cyrus pulled his hand alongside the big oaks. "Uncle Pirooz, I wish I wasn't too big to ride your shoulders." How special that boy is, the best of Sara and Ali, the best of two cultures meshed in one soul. Pirooz feels tears fall onto his knees. "Who are we? Damn it, why so much inhumanity? Why must it take inhumanity to overthrow inhumanity?" A few weeks later Pirooz would beg Zaman to let him bring her to the U.S. to get the best prosthesis that technology could offer, but she would reply, "I will make do with local resources like a thousand others."

Ali and Pirooz stay at the hospital while Aram steps into streets that are now becoming deserted and silent. Marks of destruction abound, and nothing is intact. Tired of fighting, tanks and armored cars lie still and silent. Smouldering tires melt and shed black tears as the smoke rises toward the clouds. The soot of war covers the bark of trees, while leaves tremble in fear of more fighting. Shattered windows let winter winds slash inside. Slogans written in charcoal, in chalk and in blood on walls, on the ground and on lampposts still make their silent demands. Statues of the Shah and his father, Reza, pulled to the ground by thick ropes around their necks, lie headless all over town. Not many people are about now. A few celebrate, a few mourn, a few laugh, a few cry, but most have simply gone home. No one is left to shoot and no one to kill. The day of revolution darkens as the combat slows to a halt.

The stars shine around Aram, who has become delirious. He feels he is way up in the sky and talks to himself. "I must slow my descent or else burn up in the atmosphere. I want to go to the merry-go-round where my mother used to take me, to run around, to be a boy, to be free.

"The earth is a merry-go-round as it whirls around the sun. Look! The trees, animals, man, even the Elburz, all are on the wild ride around the sun! Everything tumbles drunk around the sun, in the midst of laughter and tears, births and deaths, the ups and downs of nations. This crazy merry-go-round will not halt for a wedding or a dying, for peace or war, or to salute the stars or the great woman Zaman.

"Look at the merry-go-round, the steer munching grass, the fish chewing the fish, the beast eating the beast and look at the man devouring all. Look at man, the cannibal, the slaveowner, the landlord, the capitalist, the commissar, all over the lot all over time. They are white and they are black, they are yellow and they are green! Green!" Aram wonders.

Aram finds himself on the deserted merry-go-round in Pahlavi Square. It looks eerily out of place in the midst of so much suffering and destruction. But the ponies, the camels and the lion and all the other animals are there. He pushes the switch and jumps on the giraffe he always liked. But he is alone: his mother is dead, his wife is dying, his children are left with the maid his father has hired.

The animals come alive, begin to run, begin to dance at constant tempo. Aram speaks. "Is anyone here? Who is in charge of this merry-go-round? Who is in charge of this planet?"

But the ride lacks the joy of yesteryear, when he was a boy, when no one was dead, when the giraffe he rode was new and young, when he didn't know he was a minority, an Armenian. He fears that soon even Zaman will be treated like a member of a minority, under the rule of the mullahs! A full citizen in name alone.

Then the loneliness of being alive, the pain of his losses, the galloping of the giraffe with its ups and downs at constant tempo make him dizzy, and he begins to cry. The revolution is in danger, Aram realizes in his delirium. The dead are dead, limbs are gone, lies and truth are left unsorted, so much fire is still ablaze, so much print is in the gutters, questions are on every mind, the bullets and the grenades fly, and still the evil men of the CIA hang around. And Aram cannot forget that some prisoners still incarcerated could hear the sounds of the revolt, but could not see that all had changed.

Pirooz finally finds Aram on the merry-go-round, vomiting all over the giraffe.

* * * * *

On Monday, February 12th, Islamic marshals attack the 30,000 Imperial Guards at Lavizan base in northeastern Teheran. They kill officers and a few troops before the rest surrender. Later that day, the last dying hope of the Shah in exile, his prize Immortals, the elite part of the Imperial Guard, vanish without much resistance; they suddenly turn into frightened mortals. When the commander, General Biglari, is found shot to death at his home, it is rumored that his aide turned on him. Once the Lavizan base falls the Niavaran Palace itself lies undefended, and Islamic marshals under the direction of mullahs take it over. The Shah's former prisoners and the poor he despised so much occupy the magnificent palace, but there is no looting, even though the Shah and his officials had looted the country to build it.

When the followers of Khomeini threaten to storm the huge Qasr prison, the prison guards abandon their posts. The prisoners pour out like water from a broken dam. The next day, Ali and his comrades burn their way through the hated locked gates of Evin, now called the prison for innocents, with acetylene torches. The prisoners walk out as heroes, including Ali Akbar, the cellmate of Aram and Hussain, who has survived having his feet dipped in boiling oil, although he will never walk again without pain. Pirooz had organized ambulances and a few doctors to take the prisoners who need treatment to hospitals.

The revolutionaries angrily set on fire the torture equipment until Ali stops it. Instead, despite his repugnant memories of Evin treatment, he convinces them that the instruments should be put in a museum commemorating a place American presidents had called a part of the "Free World."

The Butcher and the Barber, the two vicious interrogators of Ali's father, are arrested and confess to countless atrocities. Before his execution, the Butcher admits he brought hell to others and deserves to go to hell himself. Teherani admits his guilt on TV and urges the revolutionary court to execute him. "I deserve the worst punishment, just as I gave the worst, surpassing the cruelty of Genghiz Khan. Shooting me is a favor," Teherani declares at his trial, "for I cannot face another human being, except for those who will execute me." The revolution succeeds in eliminating Teherani, but cannot cure Ali's recurring nightmares, since by this time he has also learned the horrifying details of the killing of his brother Hussain.

* * * * *

Bakhtiyar disappears before surfacing in Paris sometime later. General Garabaghi also vanishes. General Badri is found in his office closet, shot by his own officers. General Rabii surrenders, to be executed a few days later. The American-trained generals and police officers, many of them highly valued "CIA assets," are arrested or give themselves up. The poor devils think they are safer in the hands of revolutionary courts than among their own men, but they are wrong! Within a few days the U.S. hitmen in Iran are themselves hit. Death opens its vengeful mouth wide and black and swallows them. When people demand to see the bodies, a few are displayed from the roof of Khomeini's headquarters just east of Jaleh Square—Savak Chief Nassiri, Teheran Martial Law Governor Rahimi, General Naji the Governor of Isfahan, and Special Forces Commander Khosrowdad, pierced by bullets and soaked in a mixture of their blood. Some bodies are so full of bullets that when lifted for burial they fall apart like wet cardboard.

General Oveissi, who had commanded the massacre in 1963 in Teheran which brought death to Abbas, Ali's older brother, manages to flee, but is assassinated alongside his own brother two years later in Paris. Time and space prove no protection for the guilty.

On Monday, February 12th, Imam Khomeini asks the people to surrender their weapons to Islamic guards and not to associate with nonbelievers. To him the Fedayeen are the principal nonbelievers, and the Mujahedin are heretics. Power must be absolute, or else it is not power to Khomeini.

But when the head of an orphanage in southern Teheran demands that the children follow the Imam's instructions, a boy counters, "No mullah is going to take my gun. We have suffered too much to disarm."

When a mullah tries to disarm a young man in Shahyad Plaza, which is now called Freedom Square, the man of God is shot down in cold blood like a deer on the steppes. The revolution helps some shed inhibitions, for now.

Multitudes of adults, teenagers, even children are now armed with knives, rifles, handguns and machine guns, politics and demands. Quite a few are killed by accident as they fumble with clips and bolts.

Fearing the new regime, nonbelievers defy the Imam and do not disarm. Instead they organize classes and teach courses in weaponry. Captured army trucks filled with weapons go careening from armories to Teheran University and elsewhere. Ali urges the Fedayeen to keep their arms, to hide or bury them if necessary, and to arm and train as many workers and students as possible.

The magnificent brotherly love of the revolution thus ceases to be magnificent or brotherly. In its place a power struggle threatens to turn the revolution into civil war. Which class now rules Iran? Conflicting interests surface, united groups disunite. Ugly chaos looms at every corner. The Shah is gone, the Immortals are defeated, the generals are arrested and shot. But without a common enemy there is not enough hatred to glue the contending victorious factions together.

On Tuesday February 13th, the new prime minister, Bazargan, puts a mixture of oldtime National Front leaders, technocrats and close Khomeini aides together in a cabinet. The former student leaders in America now become leaders of Iran. Dr. Yazdi becomes Deputy Prime Minister for Revolutionary Affairs. Ghotbzadeh becomes head of television and radio (the Shah's famous phrase "my people" slipping from his lips on radio), his long-held wish to be seen and heard by all people at last fulfilled. The meditative Dr. Chameron will soon become the head of the new secret police.

On the same day the Fedayeen present a list of demands to the Bazargan administration which includes equal rights for men and women, the nationalization of all industry and commerce, the expulsion of foreign military advisors, the dissolution of the secret police, and freedom of the press and assembly. The Fedayeen also exhort workers to form councils and run the factories themselves, and demand for soldiers the right to elect their own officers. But Khomeini and his followers are tightening their grip on national life and the demands are all rejected.

Pirooz, acting as a liaison, meets with Chameron and Yazdi and several other revolutionary leaders. He begs his old friends to persuade Khomeini and Bazargan to include Fedayeen and Mujahedin in some reasonable manner in the government, in a gesture of conciliation. Pirooz believes that the demands of the Mujahedin and Fedayeen, with some moderation, would not contradict the principles of the Islamic Republic as they are understood at the moment. And he also believes that the resourceful Fedayeen and Mujahedin could be as useful in the reconstruction of the country as they were in defeating the monarchy. Yazdi and Chameron both promise the Professor to relate his suggestions to Imam Khomeini.

Although Ali has been too busy to see Cyrus and Sara during this historic week, he is not worried, for they are safe with Aram's father at the foot of the mountains. There Sara takes care of Zaman when she is brought home to recuperate. Zaman tells Sara that, just as her leg was buried, so was a part of the Iranian nation, the martyrs. Sara in turn confides to Zaman the details of Operation Sweep. Cyrus and Zaman's two boys become friends, and Cyrus loves living with his Iranian cousins. He has accepted Eric's death, realizing that Eric made a big mistake by trying to kill his baba. Pirooz spends his time with Sara and Cyrus, attempting to make up for Ali's absences doing revolutionary work. Cyrus has grown fond of Uncle Pirooz, and Sara and Pirooz have drawn close as friends.

Early in the morning on February 14th, Ali leads one hundred Fedayeen in attacking the U.S. Embassy. The purpose is to prevent CIA interference in the revolution and to demonstrate that all revolutionary groups must remain united against U.S. imperialism.

From nearby roofs and side streets a barrage of automatic weapons fire rudely awakens the embassy staff. After leaving many scars on Iran, today the embassy receives its own scars. The nineteen American Marines, clad in flak jackets, are ordered to use only tear gas in return.

Two Marines are hurt, windows are shattered, and Ambassador Sullivan is shaken. Two Iranian employees are killed, and the Fedayeen announce that they were Savakis taking refuge in the Embassy. The Embassy does not respond to this charge.

After two hours, Fedayeen attackers blast through the Embassy gates and burst into the compound, while others scale the walls. Ali races to Sullivan's office and finds the ambassador on the telephone making a last second plea to Bazargan's lieutenants for help. Colonel Holland, the military attache, stands by. Sullivan's face is unwrinkled and his hair is white, the same color as his shirt, and he has on a deep blue tie and a light blue suit as though dressed for a reception. He looks cool and composed. Ali, in contrast dark and fully bearded, points his machine gun defiantly at the two men.

"Mr. Sullivan, you are under arrest! Order your men to cease fire."

Sullivan replies, "There is no need for gunplay here. Colonel Holland and I are unarmed and I have already instructed the Marines to shoot only to protect themselves. Otherwise they are to surrender."

Meanwhile about twenty Americans who fall hostage are frisked and paraded around the compound. Ali has forbidden brutality, but discipline cannot be absolute: a couple of Marines are kicked when they resist the order to move. The Fedayeen feel the whole nation has been kicked around for too long by the same Americans.

About eighty staffers, many of them CIA agents, flee to the east wing, the site of Eric's old office. In the communications room, they begin to shred secret papers, hastily destroying everything in sight, as though the day of judgement were upon them. They throw whole bags of documents into the incinerator. A communications specialist who looks like a robot out of control wields a huge sledgehammer to pulverize every machine in sight —electronic gear, a coding machine, even typewriters.

Finally the Fedayeen reach the room, too late to capture sensitive documents. "Everyone get down," a Fedayeen commands. The Americans dive to the floor. A man with a camera is visibly shaken. "Who are you?" the Fedayeen asks.

"I'm with the *Los Angeles Times.*"

"Then why are you with these spies?"

The correspondent goes pale; his job is a CIA cover. He struggles to say, "I don't know."

The Fedayeen smiles, pointing his gun at the man. "If I ever catch you spying I will shoot you on the spot! Do you believe in Mission Impossible, where the CIA men are always the good guys and the communists forever the bad guys?"

"No, sir, no, sir, I don't," the correspondent says trembling.

The Fedayeen laugh and some of the men on the floor begin to relax. It is comical, unbelievable, that a few Fedayeen can scare to death and then tease a group of CIA agents.

Ali and his comrades put Sullivan on trial as a co-conspirator with the Shah accused of crimes against the people of Iran. Sullivan remains silent and composed, even though he knows he could be executed. After all, he is not just an ambassador but a master spy in the eyes of Iranians and partially responsible for Black Friday. He is surprised that the Fedayeen know so much about Operation Sweep. Inwardly Sullivan curses the Iranian generals for squealing, never suspecting that Eric was the unwitting leak. Sullivan categorically denies all the charges, just as General Nassiri denied his role in Savak.

Ali hears all of Sullivan's denials but believes none. He tells the U.S. ambassador to deliver a message to President Carter. The ambassador agrees and Ali dictates, "Mr. Carter, if you or your predecessors were tried in Iran, the jury of millions, nearly the whole nation, would condemn you to death for crimes against the Iranian people. This is a warning—you may not be safe at home if you continue similar policies around the world."

Twelve long, tense hours go by at the Embassy. Suddenly there is shooting again. Everyone in the yard runs for cover, ducking into drainage ditches, behind trees, under cars. But the shooting is a false alarm, all sound in the air. Islamic marshals have arrived to rescue the Americans. A bullhorn declares, "Heed Imam Khomeini's command! For the sake of the country and international law release the prisoners and leave the embassy compound immediately."

The Fedayeen oblige; Ali and his comrades leave quietly and quickly. He throws a dirty look at Sullivan and Sullivan whispers back, "You will pay for this."

Sullivan never reports his mock trial, the questions, answers, evidence and his conviction for crimes against the people of Iran. The American press forgets to report what he did for twelve hours—certainly he did not play cards with the Fedayeen.

An hour after the Fedayeen leave, Deputy Prime Minister Yazdi, with a greyish beard, a white turban, and a mullah's black gown, steps out of a Mercedes to survey the damage to the Embassy. Yazdi, the cancer scientist, has now become metamorphosed into a complete mullah. Everyone has now begun to grow a beard, to wear the traditional gown and turban, to play with beads and to pretend to be pious. It is good business: it is safe and it pays in many ways. For example, more and more people wear clerical outfits because it is a major step toward becoming a member of the new ruling group. Yazdi reports to the Imam that it will be difficult to govern with Fedayeen and Mujahedin on the loose: it will be difficult to keep the workers, peasants and students where they belong. After all, Yazdi's title is Deputy Prime Minister for Revolutionary Affairs. But it is now the counter-revolution that is becoming his affair. However, poor Yazdi will soon become a victim of his own making.

Aram's family leave for safety to Europe, and Ali and Pirooz join the others to live in their beautiful mansion. Zaman never complains about her leg, and on occasion she even becomes cheerful. Her quiet forbearance strengthens the others. Aram begins to feel more at ease. Cyrus, Arash and Baback play hide-and-seek in the beautiful gardens, enjoying an unexpected vacation from school. Sara keeps busy writing about the U.S. dominance of Iran and the legitimacy of Iranian complaints.

Two weeks after the capture of the U.S. Embassy, the new family is relaxing after supper when Cyrus sits on Ali's lap and speaks loudly. "Baba, listen. I have something important to say."

Everyone becomes attentive. "What is it?" Ali asks.

"Remember, you told me you'd do anything for me?"

"Yes, anything possible and good, Cyrus."

"Then marry Mom! It is possible and good."

Sara asks, "What is this, Cyrus?"

"Let him speak, Sara," Ali interjects. "But ask Mom first."

"She will do it, I know it."

"Stop it, Cyrus," Sara protests. Zaman, Pirooz and Aram grin from ear to ear.

"Then when?" Cyrus demands, holding his father's hand.

"Soon."

"No, now, tomorrow."

"Why now?" Ali asks his son.

"Because that is my wish and you said you'd do anything for me."

Everyone laughs out loud. Ali is cornered. "Well, Cyrus, I will do it, but not just for you, for me, too."

Sara laughs and cries and hugs Cyrus and Ali in one bundle. They are married at home by a magistrate a week later.

CHAPTER 31

Counterrevolution

The Shah was gone. His generals were captured, his Immortals were defeated, his Savakis were killed or in hiding, and his prisoners were freed. The people's revolution had triumphed, but the masses were not ready for it or united. The Fedayeen and Mujahedin wanted to push the revolution to a socialist conclusion, but the clergy wanted to control it, subdue it, arrest it, and, if necessary, kill it in its infancy, and they could do it, for they had the masses in their hands.

The U.S. quickly recognized the Bazargan government, because President Carter thought it could handle the communists. Ambassador Sullivan was stripped of his power.

On February 23rd, Ali led more than 70,000 demonstrators to demand the inclusion of the Fedayeen and other leftist groups in the new government. Even though the Fedayeen had grown to number about 20,000 members with many more sympathizers, they were ignored by Khomeini who commanded millions of followers.

On February 24th, the new government dissolved Savak and created Savama in its place. Savama organized local watchdog committees everywhere, and all ardent followers of the Imam turned informers. Everyone watched everyone else. Dr. Chameron, a good Muslim and brave revolutionary, headed Savama. He did not approve of its secret police tactics or its excesses, he confided to Pirooz, but Savama would guard the revolution as the Imam had advised.

The Shah had taken billions of dollars out of the country, but the revolution could recover none of it. On March 5th the Swiss courts rejected a government request to freeze the Shah's assets. Later, U.S. banks announced neutrality and kept the Shah's assets in their vaults.

On March 7th Imam Khomeini announced that female workers must dress according to religious standards. Gradually those standards tightened as new messages reached Teheran from heaven, until all women were shoved back under a chador, the sad, ugly scarf. The government then repealed the equal rights law for women. Women demonstrated but in vain, for nothing could change God's command. Day by day, Iran was taken century by century back in time, to the early days of Islam. The difference was that in 1979 the Islamic Republic possessed modern means of communication, modern secret police and modern means of coercion.

Supporters of Imam Khomeini formed revolutionary committees and began making life and death decisions on the local level without consultation with the Bazargan government.

The Islamic marshals were officially turned into Revolutionary Guards. They were to keep everyone in line, not just politically but in every way. Food, entertainment, news, sex, books and words had to be approved, sometimes by a young guard carrying a big gun. The guards could stop anyone in the street, could enter any home at any time and ask any questions they wished. The only requirement to be a guard was to be an unquestioning follower of the Imam. Thousands of Revolutionary Guards were ready and anxious to carry out the mullahs' commands.

A national referendum sanctioned by Imam Khomeini in March gave only two choices to the nation: the Islamic Republic or the deposed monarchy. Grand Ayatollah Shariatmadari protested that the referendum gave, in effect, no option but the Islamic Republic. With this criticism, he set himself on a downhill slide to condemnation and house arrest. (Later on the ruling mullahs would argue that Shariatmadari ought to be stripped of his title and privileges of Ayatollah—an unprecedented event.) The Mujahedin and Fedayeen, having demanded a democratic republic, also denounced the restricted referendum. But the referendum was overwhelmingly approved and Iran became an Islamic Republic on April 1st of 1979.

The day after the referendum—a day of mourning for the death of freedom, Pirooz called it—he took Zaman to be fitted for an artificial leg. As he helped her into the car in front of the clinic, the sound of the word "Stop!" slashed his ears. A young Islamic guard stood before them. "What is your name?"

"Freydoon Pirooz."

"And the woman?"

"She's Zaman Petrossian."

"Ah, an Armenian last name," the guard said triumphantly. "What are you doing together?"

"We've come from the clinic," Pirooz said gently.

"What is this? You have no right—" Zaman interjected.

"Yes, I do! I ask any question that serves Islam!" His bayonet glittered in the sun.

Pirooz explained, "Guard, she is my first cousin and needs help."

The guard said, "Don't you know it is forbidden to touch any woman except your wife, sister or mother?"

Zaman grew angry. "I have no time for this. My children are expecting me."

The guard ignored her. "You are under arrest," he snapped at Pirooz.

Pirooz tried to be conciliatory. "Listen, we are related and —"

"Where is her husband?" the guard interrupted.

"He is very sick."

"That makes no difference."

"Under arrest on what charge?" Zaman inquired.

"Corruption on earth." The guard repeated the now-famous phrase of the Imam, a phrase that had become a license to imprison or even execute innocent citizens.

Pirooz and Zaman were brought to a local revolutionary court and put in separate men's and women's holding rooms. By the end of the day Zaman lost her composure and loudly complained to the other detainees, "By pointing an accusing finger at you, the guards and the mullahs can do whatever they please." She raised her voice. "I didn't lose my leg to replace the Shah's thugs with another bunch."

As she finished the last word an undercover policewoman slapped her in the face. Blood ran down the corner of Zaman's mouth. As other detainees quickly stepped between them, the woman warned, "Don't you ever insult the Islamic Republic again!"

Dr. Chameron intervened on behalf of Zaman and Pirooz and got them released later that evening. Back at Petrossian's, the family sat around the table and worried out loud—where was the freedom for which they had fought so long? Aram said, "It's getting worse. Just last week in Kerman, the guards burst into a house and found an unmarried couple. They flogged the man in the city square until his skin tore off, and the next day they bundled the woman up in a sheet and stoned her until she was chunks of flesh and broken bones."

Zaman said, "Our Friday mullah, who once told me a man was like a stallion and his wives like mares and ordered me to wash my mouth when I objected, is now the magistrate of one of the revolutionary courts. Now he orders firing squads, not just mouthwash. I hate to admit it; monarchy was an affliction but this theocracy is a calamity. Under the mullah's rule it is a sin to be crippled, a sin to love, a sin to laugh, a sin to think, a sin to read unsanctioned books or hear unsanctioned music; it is a sin to be happy. Father was absolutely right—religion and politics don't mix."

Terrifying nightmares interrupted Pirooz' sleep that night. At last he got out of bed and stepped onto the verandah to think. He heard muffled sobbing and saw Zaman's crutches in the moonlight. When she saw Pirooz, Zaman tried to stop, but she sobbed harder when she felt his hand on her shoulder.

Pirooz sat beside her and whispered, "What's the matter? Is it what happened today?''

"Yes, but I also miss my leg."

"I understand. But you have never talked about it."

"I cry alone at night. I don't want to upset Aram or the children. Please don't tell the others, Pirooz."

"Okay, I won't." Pirooz paused, then added, "And I won't tell you not to cry. Ignorance and brutality rule our country now. I feel like crying myself."

Zaman replied, "All my life I have fought for women's liberation, and now I am beaten up by a woman bent on remaining unliberated. I am glad I do not have a daughter." The two cousins stared sadly at each other as the moon hid behind a cloud. Pirooz took Zaman's hand and a teardrop on her face splashed on his wrist. She whispered, "The loss of the revolution is worse than the loss of my leg."

Pirooz said, "Take your family and come with me to America. At least you wouldn't get arrested for walking with me." The two exchanged bitter smiles.

Zaman replied sadly, "No, Pirooz, we belong here. We have fought too long to run away now."

Two weeks later, Ali took Sara, Cyrus and Pirooz to the airport to leave for the U.S. At the gate, Ali hugged Pirooz and whispered in his ear, "Look after Sara and Cyrus for me." It was with the greatest pain that Ali said farewell to Sara and Cyrus, but he couldn't risk having his family harmed. It was now more dangerous than ever for Americans in Iran. Ali and Sara hoped that their marriage could help Ali to get a U.S. visa; as Sara's husband, Ali would probably be allowed back in the country by U.S. Immigration. Ali watched the plane take off, with Cyrus between Sara and Pirooz, holding their hands and sobbing to leave his baba behind. They were among many Americans and Iranians fleeing the country. Pirooz had never developed a taste for the monarchy, and now he had no taste for the Islamic Republic either. Pirooz preferred to live in America and at least inform the people, rather than be subjected to the repressive regime of the Islamic Republic, lose his hard-earned freedom and quite possibly lose his life.

The words exchanged between Sara and Cyrus before the plane's arrival in New York stayed with Pirooz. Protesting his father's remaining behind, Cyrus told Sara, "Baba does not care for us."

Sara had replied, "That is not true, dear! He loves us, but he cares more for the people than you, me, and himself put together."

"But why?" Cyrus inquired.

"I am not sure—saints are like that."

Ali strove to create a front between the Fedayeen and other progressive groups. But some of his comrades broke away to join the Tudeh Party, which had become busy teaching the mullahs the skills of running a revolutionary government. Some of the Fedayeen agreed with the optimistic leaders of the Tudeh Party that the mullahs were anti-imperialist and perhaps socialism could be achieved under the Islamic Republic, or if necessary, by another revolution from within. But when the Tudeh Party leaders faced the firing squad a few years later, they regretted having supported the Islamic Republic.

Tension grew daily between supporters of Imam Khomeini who had fought for the man and the Fedayeen who had fought for workers' rule and Mujahedin who had fought for Islam and democratic socialism. The political underground became crowded once again, for whoever disagreed with the regime was considered an outlaw.

The revolutionary guards, meanwhile, needed some justification to institutionalize the repression. So the mullahs created an incident, blamed the Fedayeen and other leftists and used it to crush dissent, no matter where, why, how or by whom. They would punish dissent in proportion to its severity, but those who resisted the Islamic counterrevolution would have to be put to sleep like horses with broken legs, even if the guards had to break the protesters' limbs first.

The incident was simple enough. When the landlords of Ghonbade Kavoos, an area in the north, fled, the local Turkman peasants took over the land. When the mullahs attempted to reclaim it, they met stiff resistance. This provided the excuse for the revolutionary guards to intervene, which resulted in many deaths and the defeat of the peasants. The incident was used as a propaganda ploy and was blamed on individuals and groups who had severed their ties with Islam, namely, Fedayeen, Mujahedin and the impoverished Turkmans, who were ironically stricter Muslims than the Imam himself.

Then the whole country was cleaned up to prevent further incidents. Progress in human rights only weakened Islamic control, so labor councils not under the mullahs' control were smashed, peasants remained landless as though no revolution had taken place, intellectuals had to be silenced, artists had to produce only Islamic art, ethnic minorities had to forget local autonomy or die, and Christians and Jews, who had once found Iran to be one of the most unbiased societies, had to conform and perform according to new prescriptions. Gradually, the minorities were coerced into using Farsi in their religious schools and accepting a mullah as overseer.

Thus the Islamic Republic in practice was not much different from the Pahlavi regime, except that women were put back under the chador and that the repression was now in the name of Allah rather than the Shah. Private industry to a large extent remained private, land reform was ignored, and universities remained closed, while censorship, indoctrination, torture and executions returned. Imam Khomeini's Islamic Republican Party took the place of the Shah's Rastakhiz Party, and all other parties were banned. The

Reflection of God, the Ayatollah, replaced the Shadow of God, the Shah. But throughout the establishment of his harsh rule, the Imam maintained his pure and austere life. He appeared simple, straightforward, good and all-knowing to the common man, but complex, shrewd, a brilliant politician and a demagogue to the sophisticated. He could be everything to everybody, but he was never anything but Imam Khomeini. He took a long nap every afternoon, just as he had on the day of revolution. He had more power over his subjects than any other leader, yet he kept his voice so low it could hardly be heard. The great majority waited impatiently for his wise words, waited to carry out his commands, yet he held no office. No part of society, not villagers, slumdwellers, workers, merchants or bureaucrats, not even the armed forces, were immune to his messianic power. In only ten days after his triumphant return from exile, he had destroyed the 2500-year-old monarchy.

Even though Imam Khomeini possessed the trust of the masses, he missed the opportunity to unite the nation under his protective gown. It was more important to him to have all the power than all the people on his side. So instead of getting people to comply voluntarily with his wishes, he now had Revolutionary Guards coerce them.

Iran remained a country of one-man rule; the bloody revolution had just changed the ruler. All numbers were compressed into one: there was one God, one leader, one political party, one interpretation of the Koran, and one political program, and that was called the Imam's line. Imam Khomeini reacted to dissent by unleashing his whip. The earth had to be cleaned of all corruption. Dissent was considered a type of corruption to be punished accordingly. He urged Muslims to wage holy war against those whose paths diverged from Islam, the Islam of the Imam's interpretation.

So, after the Shah's supporters got what they deserved, the Mujahedin and Fedayeen were the next targets, branded as heretics, or corruption on earth, or agents of the U.S. or the USSR or Israel or a combination, or just dangerously misguided. (Later, during the war with Iraq, the Islamic Republic purchased weapons from Israel through intermediaries, forgetting that the PLO had taken over the Israeli embassy in Teheran in the glorious days of revolution.) The appetite for power of Imam Khomeini's supporters grew with each successful extinction of another political group. The long-awaited revolution had brought not freedom, but a counterrevolution.

Separatist movements began to cause more bloodshed. Kurds, Arabs, Turks, Baluchis and others asked for cultural autonomy and home rule, but they were crushed.

On May 13th, Ayatollah Khalkhali, the chief judge of the Islamic Revolutionary courts, issued death sentences in absentia for the Shah, his family and former officials now living abroad. That same week the U.S. Senate adopted a resolution condemning summary executions in Iran without due process of law. It was a good gesture, Pirooz commented, but the Senators' words lacked credibility because they were selective. Had they taken a 25-year nap when the CIA and the Shah ruled Iran equally brutally? On May 15th journalists at the daily newspaper *Kayhan* protested after a number of Khomeini supporters blocked the entrance to prevent its publication. Consequently, May 15th is remembered as the day when the Islamic Republic put its bloody hand around the neck of the press and began squeezing it. Censorship cast its shadow over the nation like an eclipse that would not move. On May 19th more than 100,000 people demonstrated, protesting censorship and the closing of the paper *Ayandegan.* In response presses were smashed and reporters beaten up. All of this was done without Bazargan's assent.

So again Iran had two governments, the official one under Prime Minister Bazargan, which tried to keep the bureaucracy functioning, and the Supreme Revolutionary Committee and its auxiliaries, which held the power of a government. The committee ordered executions and controlled censorship, the courts, and whatever else the mullahs wished to take up in the name of the Imam, Islam and God!

Bazargan, complaining that Iran now had a hundred chiefs, could not stop the erosion of the imaginary power of his government. With the Revolutionary Guards tormenting his dreams, Bazargan, the old liberal, called himself a "weak donkey" and repeatedly tried to resign in protest. But Imam Khomeini honored the Prime Minister by praying behind him at a Friday service, and Bazargan could not refuse to continue to serve. Having fought injustice all his life, as Prime Minister Bazargan was now powerless to stop it. Finally, when he dared to criticize the revolutionary committees, he was replaced as Prime Minister. Still allowed to serve in parliament, he continued to speak out and was harrassed and insulted by the mullahs. Finally, out of office and disgraced, Bazargan finished writing Revolution in Two Movements, an account of his disillusionment with both the Shah and the Islamic Republic. In it he told of the Savak chief's visiting his prison cell to apologize for the Shah and promise reform, but Bazargan at that time would not compromise. However, Bazargan's patience with the Islamic Republic indicated his increased capacity to compromise. But Bazargan's tolerance for repression under his name was limited nevertheless, and finally he could not continue.

Deputy Prime Minister Yazdi, not being counterrevolutionary enough, was disgraced and purged like Bazargan. Foreign Minister Sanjabi resigned and went into exile. His successor, Ghotbzadeh, after enjoying many days on American TV, eventually faced the firing squad. He was too ambitious to suit the Imam. His final request was for his execution to be televised, but all he got was a Camel cigarette.

The Islamic Republic also smothered the tradition of debate among the clergy and did not allow individual interpretations of doctrine. The fanatical supporters of Imam Khomeini began to devour the moderate clergy who believed mullahs should not rule the country. Two sons and a daughter-in-law of Grand Ayatollah Taleghani, the spiritual leader of Teheran, were arrested, as a hint to Taleghani to follow the Imam's line or retire. Taleghani went into hiding to protest the repression, retired from politics and soon died. Ayatollah Khiabani of Khuzistan threatened to go into exile unless the arbitrary rules of the revolutionary committees ceased.

Dr. Chameron resigned from Savama to lead volunteer irregulars in the war against Iraq—a death wish, perhaps, Pirooz commented. Chameron was killed at the front, but it was rumored that the leaders of the Islamic Republic plotted his death. He was becoming a national hero, but instead he became a martyr, as did thousands more.

The new parliament looked like a theology school and dogma became the law of the land. Religion was no longer a private matter, one's relationship to God, but rather one's relationship to the mullahs and the state.

Ali, representing the Fedayeen, in one last conciliatory gesture wrote a long letter to Imam Khomeini. In it he said, "The people of Iran and the Fedayeen have offered innumerable martyrs for the revolution. Freedom has been more precious than life for many, but now freedom itself is tormented in every corner of the country. People have been accused of not being Muslims. For this reason the Revolutionary Guards have trampled households, piled up books and set them afire, disrupted peaceful assemblies of teachers and students and beaten up the participants. They have attacked with sticks and knives those attempting to organize workers' councils, and have torn apart legal leaflets and thrown them into the sewers. The guards have dared to call men or women tortured by the Shah's regime traitors. Religious and cultural freedoms, ethnic autonomy, even those rights existing in the dark days of monarchy are being violated.

"The Fedayeen, in defense of the rights of workers and peasants, in cooperation with all real friends of the nation, freedom fighters and intellectuals, condemn the guards' oppression, whether planned or spontaneous."

After reading Ali's letter, Imam Khomeini whispered to an aide, "This Ali Keshavarz is not following the path of Islam." The mullah knew what to do then.

They did not have to listen to Ali and the Fedayeen, did not have to listen to the Mujahedin, did not have to listen to Bazargan or Sanjabi, did not have to listen to Grand Ayatollah Shariatmadari, did not have to listen to people who moaned, who groaned, who screamed and who mourned; and they did not. The mullah prepared a final assault on dissent—any dissent.

Meanwhile, helplessly observing the tragic events around him, Ali was approaching a turning point, crossing boundaries of new and disturbing understandings. He had serious doubts about his usefulness in Iran anymore and had realized that he could not live away from Sara and Cyrus any longer. Ali finally reached his decision painfully but positively, and explained it in a letter to Sara.

Dearest Sara,

I hope this letter will find you and Cyrus in good health and in the best of spirits.

I will soon cross the Turkish border, once again illegally, but this time travelling toward you. Day by day, I push aside heavy minutes as though they were dense jungle vegetation separating us. I cannot believe how my love for you has gathered such an uncontrollable, unreasonable thrust and become so fiercely independent of my will.

I dream of a new start, a little nest with you and Cyrus, a life without fear, without violence. I vow to you to retire from soldiering in the revolution because I can no longer commit violence or accept the risk of becoming a victim of it. This aversion toward violence is forcing my previous ideas into submission! I must admit that all the violence I have had to commit—and all that has been committed against me—has accomplished nothing, for the citizens of Iran are worse off than they were before. At least then a revolution could be pulled off but now there is no chance. I realize that a person can be revolutionary in an infinite number of ways, only one of which is armed struggle. I will leave the armed struggle to the young Fedayeen who must now wait for and create the next historical opportunity, since this one is lost.

My father's book is set to be printed underground. This last project of mine in Iran is a tribute to his martydom, a living gravestone for his undying soul. My father's prophecy has come true! His profound wisdom and powerful reason proving that theocracy is unworkable and detrimental to the nation will soon become accessible to people. But once the book is out Savama, the progeny of Savak, will embark on a big head hunt like sharks sniffing and swarming toward spilled blood. That is why I must leave Iran in a hurry.

The Islamic Republic is a tragedy, a dark heavy fog of lies and half truths oozing out of the State Control Media engulfing ordinary folks, blurring their vision to the widespread coercion and murder perpetrated in the name of God.

Unfortunately some of my optimistic or opportunistic comrades have joined the Tudeh party and together with them are busy propping up this dictatorship of the mullah. They claim that since the regime is anti-imperialist, it deserves their support. But the regime is also anti-science, anti-art, anti-freedom, anti-truth, anti-justice, anti-Islam, anti-women, anti-worker, anti-farmer, anti-love, and anti-life! I think the leftists are digging their own collective grave—deep, wide, dark, and expectant—with their own hands. I am afraid a collective self-delusion is arresting the better judgement, even consciousness, of some very intelligent comrades. They perceive Islamic fascism, this monstrous reality, as a nightmare that will pass, but the mullahs consider it a dream coming true that will last forever. So the ruling Mullah is now swallowing power like a drunk gulping down wine.

In your last letter, you wrote that all my principles can do for me in Iran now is to get me killed. Now I must admit that you are right—you realized that before I was able to. Armed struggle is futile for the time being, so the left must look for other forms of revolutionary action. It is time for thinking, reassessing and planning, not shouting or shooting. I can't defeat the counterrevolution and I don't want to be cut to pieces in Evin Prison like beef in a Chicago slaughterhouse.

It is very hard for me to explain this decision on paper. You know how impossible it is for me to open up and reveal my thoughts and feelings even to you. The secret life of a revolutionary has not helped me to overcome this undesired trait—it has, in fact, intensified it.

But I, the "straight arrow" as you once called me, am bending here and there. I want to tell you of my strange thoughts and emotions which have been growing on me for some time and I dare not disclose them even to my comrades. The thoughts are not original but are meaningful to me.

It has surprised me that the annihilation of my enemies the Shah, Eric, and Teherani did not bring me joy at the end but sorrow. For years my life was linked to theirs and so I am what I am partly because of struggling against them. They were a part of humanity, a part of me too, although as cancerous limbs they had to be severed and buried. So their death is a part of my dying, as their lives were a part of my living. Because of this I wish not to repeat the past and continue as a social surgeon and fight the mullahs and their followers. If you are not shocked, I have more to confess.

I do not resent or fear the emergence of new doubts anymore; I don't push them aside—in fact I have welcomed them. They make all the pains surrounding me understandable, so I savor the presence of doubts and press them into my memory lest I forget a single one. I think of my new doubts as colorful wild flowers of a most wonderful spring; I want to establish a dialogue with them, learn about them, discover where they come from and where they intend to take me. I cherish them, respect them, love them.

So my life shall become meaningful, once again, with you and Cyrus on my side and new frontiers to march forward to. I feel as if I am about to be reborn.

I want to talk, to write, to work and play in peace and to be free from fear. I can no longer live under such stressful conditions with no hope of success and apart from you and Cyrus. I long to express my love to you, Cyrus, and to the Professor in a thousand different ways I have been dreaming about. I wish to feed the ducks during a lazy summer afternoon in Central Park. I would fly to you this minute, Sara, if I could, but I must secretly ride a humble and slow bus in a couple of weeks.

My dearest Sara, my dearest wife and my only love, I once left you for the revolution but now I will leave the revolution for you.

> With the kisses that only you know,
> I love you, Ali.

The Professor told Sara back in America, "What the CIA and Operation Sweep could not do to leftists in Iran the Islamic Republic is doing and doing it more brutally."

* * * * *

At the bus depot on the day of Ali's departure, Ali, Zaman and Aram were arrested, and in June 1981, Ali found himself back in Evin Prison. Evin looked the same as it had under the Shah, but it was not quite the same. In place of Savak officers there were mullahs, in place of a military court there was a revolutionary court, in place of conscripts there were Revolutionary Guards, and in place of tortures there were executions.

Ali's crime this time was trying to publish his father's manuscript underground, a treasonous work, as Ali knew, because the book was an open rebuttal to Imam Khomeini's argument for the oneness of spiritual and political leadership. Dr. Keshavarz had asked, How could a spiritual leader be punished for his inevitable political misjudgements and administrative errors? Dr. Keshavarz' conclusion was that in the best interests of the individual and society, of Iran and Islam, and of the here and hereafter, the spiritual leader ought not to become the political one.

But now no one dared to contradict the Imam's line, not even the dead. When the guards learned of Ali's project, they invaded Petrossian's house but found no weapons, only Dr. Keshavarz' book galleys which were sufficient to put Ali, Zaman and Aram in Evin as heretics, enemies of the Islamic Republic and possibly foreign agents, their past revolutionary valor notwithstanding.

But Ali had an additional strike against him: he had married the widow of a CIA agent. The revolutionary court knew that Sara had helped the Fedayeen and thus the revolution, but this support did not matter. The courts of the Islamic Republic needed little or no evidence, or if necessary they did not hesitate to create evidence. On certain days a hundred men and women had been executed, the Islamic Republic informed the world proudly.

Ayatollah Khalkhali was the chief justice of the revolutionary courts. His round, chubby face was covered with a short, grey beard, and his short, round body with a grey and black gown. Small, deep-set eyes were hidden behind round glasses. Every morning Khalkhali rode a white horse in the prison yard. It was reported to be the Shah's ceremonial mount.

When Ali made his second and final appearance in Khalkhali's court, he was formally charged with printing an unsanctioned book, denying Islam, and being a foreign agent. Ali grimaced as he found himself in the same room where he had first confronted Teherani and been beaten nearly to death twelve years ago. The same bare bulb dangled from the ceiling, the same black telephone sat on the desk, the same cement floor was bare and cold.

"Mr. Keshavarz," Khalkhali declared as he stroked his short beard, "The Islamic court will give you one last chance to repent or state your final defense, the time not to exceed five minutes."

After his first appearance before the court, Ali had been given a grace period to repent and inform on his comrades. He knew the proceedings were merely to meet the requirement of Islamic law of a trial before execution. Ali had heard the firing squads. The only sounds were reluctant steps to the walls, final slogans shouted by revolutionaries and a burst of gunfire. He knew there was no chance for a revolutionary to leave Evin alive, even if he cooperated. Guards stood by with loaded guns; firing squads were busy shooting scores of Fedayeen and Mujahedin every day. The mullahs fretted that the heretical views of these young men and women would contaminate the whole nation.

The U.S. press for the most part ignored the slaughter or treated it indifferently, hiding the news in the back pages; President Reagan, who agonized publicly over the discomfort of dissidents in Eastern Europe, did not seem to object to the daily massacre in Iran—even after 12,000 names and particulars of victims were published later on. Instead the President and his friends tried to make friends with Khomeini and his friends—exchanging the Bible, cake and God knows what.

In the torture chamber courtroom, Ali, knowing for certain he was doomed, replied with authority, "Revolution has bestowed upon me the freedom to print the book of a martyr and scholar for the enlightenment of the freedom-loving people of Iran. I don't regret my action," he added defiantly. "Mr. Khalkhali, I am your prisoner but it is you who should be on trial!" Ali repeated what Ruzbeh had said in his own defense in the previous regime, that the Shah should stand trial, not him. And by calling Khalkhali "mister" instead of "Ayatollah," Ali had belittled him. Ali continued, "Five minutes is obviously insufficient to review years of my revolutionary struggle and to prove that murdering me and my comrades is only aiding world imperialism. Mr. Khalkhali, you fear the guards may refuse to execute me if they hear my defense, to know the substance of my father's book and to learn the truth. The elimination of us is a tragedy, since our creativity, skills, work, and commitment could be employed to build the nation. All we have demanded from the regime is to let us express our ideas freely. And if the Islamic Republic has more convincing ideas, let the people judge."

Ali paused for a moment. Staring at the guards and raising his voice he declared, "Mr. Khalkhali, you claim that you have God on your side, that you have the Imam on your side, that you have parliament, the revolutionary courts, revolutionary guards, army, navy, and air force on your side, that you have radio, T.V., newspapers, schools and mosques under your supervision. Then why do you fear publication of one single book, the words of a good Muslim? You have everything on your side, and we have little besides our ideas and this book. Are not truth and justice virtues in Islam?" Suddenly, realizing the absurdity of trying to reason with Khalkhali, Ali lowered his voice and mumbled to himself, "I could have spoken to aliens in a galaxy far away with a better result." Then he addressed Khalkhali again, "I know you have orders to silence us just as Savak had orders to silence my comrades and my father. History will condemn the Islamic Republic for crimes against the people of Iran."

Khalkhali retorted, "Do not waste the precious time granted to you with such nonsense. Repent, nonbeliever, before death! In His infinite wisdom and compassion God may forgive you."

Ali replied, "The only nonsense I see is the revolutionary Islamic court, which is neither revolutionary nor Islamic. Mr. Khalkhali, no God would approve of this mockery of justice."

Khalkhali turned red in the face, but the redness was covered by his beard. "I will have you gagged before I read your sentence."

Ali answered angrily, "I have been gagged by Savak right in this room. I am not afraid. Mr. Khalkhali, we both know I am not a foreign agent, but who are you? Whose interest do you serve by killing revolutionaries and setting my father's manuscript on fire? His book is the culmination of the scholarly work of a true Muslim. The Shah set his body on fire and you set his ideas on fire. Let me tell you who the real Muslims are." Ali continued, "My martyred brother, an ardent supporter of Khomeini, was a true Muslim, Ayatollah Taleghani was a true Muslim, my mother is a true Muslim. They were truthful and compassionate. I accuse you Mr. Khalkhali of corruption and murder on earth!" Ali looked straight into Khalkhali's eyes and then gazed at the guards. Ali spoke as though he were in charge. "Tell me, whose agent are you?"

Khalkhali, glancing at the puzzled guards, answered proudly, "I need not tell you, but I am God's agent."

"No, the devil's!" Ali now spoke like the young Ali of yesteryear, defiant and angry.

Khalkhali ignored Ali's last comment and asked calmly, "Do you believe in Islam?"

Ali answered, "I respect and love true Muslims, but if I say I believe in Islam I will be denying my intellect and my best judgement."

Khalkhali shouted, "You are out of your mind. This court has had enough. You shall die a sinner; without repentance hell is your hereafter."

"It is justice which is out of order in your court and your regime of terror," Ali answered.

"Guards!" Khalkhali shouted. "Take this imbecile away. Then put him away before sunrise!"

Ali said calmly, "They cannot take me far. I will not be dead for long and you will not be alive for long. I will come back."

Khalkhali, thinking that Ali was threatening him, commanded, "Stop, guards! What is on your mind, condemned man?"

"Did you know, Mr. Khalkhali, that the more communists you kill the faster communism spreads?"

Khalkhali did not want to waver in front of the guards. "Communists will not multiply under the Islamic Republic. I will make sure of that. Next prisoner!" he commanded.

As Aram was brought in, he exchanged glances with Ali in what both realized was goodbye. Khalkhali looked Aram up and down as though inspecting a head of cattle. "Prisoner Petrossian, will you repent and tell us who the other Fedayeen are, the traitors?" When Aram did not answer, Khalkhali said impatiently, "What is your final defense?"

"None."

"Why?"

"Because this is an Islamic death camp, not a court of justice."

"A nonbeliever refuses the Islamic court?"

Aram shouted, "Wrong! I am a believer. I believe in socialism, which will clean up the earth of your likes. I will not honor you with a defense but I have a final comment about your regime. I used to think that the imaginary God and the real prophets were just historical curiosities of little political consequence, but I was wrong—dead wrong! The religious symbols are now used by the Islamic Republic to manipulate the masses to act against their own ultimate interest. So Islam is now more of a chain tying the citizen to the state than a spiritual link between man and God. Judging by its beginning, the Islamic society you want to create is out of step with and contrary to the scientific and spiritual progress of mankind so far and is proving to be unworkable, cruel and frankly a comical tragedy." Aram continued not like a person on trial for his life, "It appears as though the Islamic Republic is trying to put wings on a camel for space flight." The guards smiled at Aram's analogy. Aram continued, "Mr. Khalkhali, inform the Imam that Islam will not fly in the twentieth century no matter what kind of wings you put on it or what prayer you say after it. The Holy Koran, the examples left by the prophets and the Islamic tradition are not only insufficient to guide a modern society, but they are as witnessed today detrimental to it. It is unfortunate that this nation must offer so many sacrifices just to learn this simple truth: that even winged camels cannot fly." Aram, raising his voice and pointing at Khalkhali, declared, "Mark my words, executioner! Either the Islamic Republic will modernize and become humane or the people will force it to, or overthrow it."

Khalkhali screamed, "Take him away, and put him away before sunrise."

A gun butt pushed Aram, but he turned to Khalkhali as he left. "The monarchy raped me and the Islamic Republic shoots me. You are no different."

"Next, next!" Khalkhali shouted. Zaman was brought in. Khalkhali asked, "What happened to your leg?"

"It is buried. A punishment for helping evil to power," Zaman replied.

Khalkhali said, "Speak your mind, woman. Are you still an atheistic communist, or do you repent?"

Zaman shouted, "I'm pregnant and a mother of two. That's what I really am."

An aide whispered to the surprised Khalkhali, "There can be no temporary marriage after her husband's execution." The court forced temporary marriages of condemned women to guards so that the guards could rape them without sin before executing them.

Khalkhali protested, "But the guards will get restless. There must be an incentive for the young men to shoot traitors."

The aide replied, "Yes, Your Excellency, but the nurse has confirmed that this woman is five months . . ."

"All right. I understand." Khalkhali turned to Zaman. "Islamic justice gives you a last chance to repent and give us the names of the other traitors."

Zaman stared at him accusingly. "You are the traitor," she shouted back. "Put yourself in front of the firing squad."

Khalkhali answered, "You can save your unborn child and yourself if you cooperate."

But Zaman replied, "Your guards are raping teenage girls. It's a sin to waste virgins, isn't it? Now the Islamic Republic is about to execute a five-month-old fetus, a traitor, too, I understand," Zaman said mockingly. "Evil has won its rebellion against God in Iran. You are children of evil ruling my country. I would rather see my unborn die with me than live under the darkness of the Islamic Republic."

Khalkhali became furious. He could tolerate women talking back even less than men. He had been told these three revolutionaries would not repent, so he had rushed their trials. "Take her away and put her away before sunrise.''

The aide whispered, ''Your Excellency, she is . . .''

Khalkhali snapped, ''This is God's command. She does not repent.''

''But, she is foolhardy. We are not . . .''

''That is enough, mullah!'' Khalkhali exclaimed.

The guards looked at one another and escorted Zaman out gently as Khalkhali blared out, ''Next!''

The three revolutionaries had been forced to watch the executions of some of their comrades before appearing before Khalkhali, a common practice to break revolutionaries and coerce them into becoming informers. The condemned were allowed to write letters which were sent out only after inspection, a last hope for Khalkhali to gain information from the prisoners. Zaman, Aram and Ali were not allowed to see each other one last time unless they repented and informed.

The next day before sunrise, after the guards and Khalkhali had said their prayers, the three were blindfolded, taken out and put against the wall. The three heard the sound of bullets blasting their eardrums but they felt nothing, no pain, no absolute darkness. It was a make-believe shooting to terrify them and make them repent. Even the Shah's regime had not played games with the lives of its victims as the Islamic Republic did. Zaman's tears wetted the blindfold.

During three horrible and uncertain nights terminated by fake executions in the mornings, Ali kept busy remembering his time spent with Sara and Cyrus as a family, despairing that now he would never see them again. Aram fell into delirium again, regained consciousness and then fell into a depth of depression that the repeated threat of death can induce. Zaman took care of her children in her mind, prepared food for them, washed them, put them to bed, read them stories the revolution had not given her time to read to them. She repeated these thoughts over and over as she waited for death night after night. The three wanted to be shot, wanted to get it over with.

The next night, a young man was thrown into Ali's cell at midnight. Ali, leaning against the wall, heard him sobbing. He reached out and touched the youth's shoulder, but had nothing to tell him. ''What can one doomed man do for another one,'' Ali thought to himself.

''I don't want to die, I don't want to die.''

Ali heard the young man who seemed to talk to indifferent walls, to uncaring guards, and to the world beyond. Ali replied softly, ''Comrade, I don't want to die either.''

The young man looked up, their eyes meeting for the first time. ''You are Ali Keshavarz.''

''Yes.''

''Are you not afraid?''

"Just a little."

"Why?"

"I am so used to the idea of death that even if I am afraid, I don't feel it anymore. Also I have lived almost through my own death so I am almost free of the fear of death, but to conquer the fear completely one must experience death itself." Ali ignored the puzzled look of the boy and continued, "So, while to live and learn is natural, to have to die and learn is just tragic." Ali then added an afterthought, "But one can imagine dying while still living to dispel some of the fear."

"How, how?" the boy asked anxiously.

"Simple. Imagine a blindfold over your eyes dimming the light for you like in a theater before the curtain rises. Then hear a drumming, like bullet shots and feel an instant of heartburn before falling asleep forever." Ali added calmly, "I am sure you have experienced every stage of this process I just described to you. This is how we will be killed."

The boy ignored Ali's analogy and said, "But you want to live, don't you?"

"Oh yes, forever," Ali smiled bitterly.

The young man smiled too, his eyes begging for support. "You have escaped death many times?"

"Yes, I have been lucky, I have run away from death a few times."

"Why not this time? Cannot we do something before sunrise?"

"It is next to impossible. I have tried to find a soft soul among the guards, but it is futile. The guards are the Ayatollah's robots and follow his commands as though they were God's commands."

"What do you mean?"

"I mean you and I cannot reverse God's command."

"So there is no hope?" the boy asked dejectedly.

"Hope is never zero."

"What can we do then?"

"Wait, observe, think, and be ready to use every opportunity," Ali said calmly.

"We can't try to break away."

"Show me how and we will try it," Ali said sincerely. The boy's head drooped down as Ali continued, "But remember, begging the unjust ruler strengthens him as truth strengthens the searcher for knowledge." Ali then moved closer to the condemned and whispered into his ear, "You have defied the Ayatollah! Remain brave, true to yourself. Die before you die!"

As Ali repeated the Koranic injunction without batting an eye, the boy reached out and held Ali's hand, his head still down crying softly, "But I was going to be married this fall. I am a good Muslim—I haven't kissed a woman in my life, and I have dreamed so much about my wedding night." He began to cry out loud, "It is not right to shoot a man for scribbling a slogan on the wall of his own house."

Ali, trying to engage the boy, asked, "What did you write?"

"Nothing. Just. . . "

"Just what?"

"I wrote, 'Thieves of Qom, give us back our revolution.'"

Ali said to himself, "They swallowed the revolution like a boa would swallow a newborn lamb." Then Ali addressed the boy gently, "Don't be ashamed. It is all right to cry for your revolution." The youth began to sob, his body shaking. Ali held him in his arms until he gradually calmed down and fell asleep. Ali thought the young man was even more unknown than an unknown revolutionary like himself. Ali laid him gently against the wall. He thought for a long time, and a tear rolled down his cheek. He then wrote his first and last poem naming it, "Cry For My Revolution, Iran." He could not sleep that night; he wanted to live his final hours in his full awakening.

Ali remembered the words of Ambassador Sullivan: "You will pay for this." He remembered the night Cyrus asked him to marry Sara. He remembered his bullets splashing the face of the police officer during the chase and he remembered Teherani's handkerchief pushed down his throat. He thought of these most memorable moments as he walked to face the firing squad each morning, reflecting bitterly on the irony of his surviving many years of struggle against the Shah and Savak, only to die ignominiously at the hands of supposedly holy men. Was it worth it?

The fake executions took place on one more morning. But on the fourth day, bullets finally pierced the hearts of Ali, Zaman and Aram, tearing their beautiful faces and dreams to pieces. They were buried in a large, unmarked grave.

Ali had kept his word to Sara that he would marry her only after the revolution. He had kept his promise to Cyrus, by marrying Mommy, as Cyrus had wished. He had fulfilled his prophecy to the Professor that some individuals have to die or else humanity would go astray. And Ali kept his resolve to the end as he shouted in front of the Islamic Republic firing squad, "Death to Imperialism! Long live the creators of civilization—the laborers, peasants and intellectual workers of the world." And then just before the bullets silenced him he shouted, "I will come back, Iran!" He died before he died, as had his father, sister and brothers.

Zaman shouted, "Long live women's struggle for freedom and justice!" and Aram whispered to himself, "Long live the struggle for community of man!"

The names of the three victims were published in the government approved newspaper. A week later the Professor wept reading Ali's last letter. The bullets tore apart not just Ali's body but the soul of the revolution, he thought. For the time being the dreams of the nation are buried with Ali, Zaman and Aram in an unmarked common grave. Soon wild tulips with green leaves would turn the topsoil white, green and red, as on the flag of Iran. It was as though they represented Ali's prophecy—the words of an unknown revolutionary, "I will come back, Iran."

* * * * *

Some years later Imam Rouhollah Khomeini, the spiritual and political leader of both the revolution and the counterrevolution, lay in his bed and concluded that he had had enough. He had just about cleaned Iran of all corruption on earth. There was no longer any dissent, let alone disobedience; no one was left to deserve the firing squad. He thought of history, the history he had created. He thought of his ardent supporters.

Sanjabi had gone into exile, Bazargan and Yazdi were disgraced; the first president, Banisadr, had had to flee the country—too bad he got away before being flogged! Many revolutionary leaders were disgraced or had fled the country in fear of their lives, thousands were self-exiled, and several Grand Ayatollahs were under house arrest. Imam Khomeini thought of Ghotbzadeh, whom he had called his "other son," now dead and buried. He became alarmed that he might in a fit of anger order his own son killed, as the Khalif Omar had once done. The Imam remembered his close associates who had been blown up by the bombs of the Mujahedin at Islamic Republican Party headquarters. The last Keshavarzes, Ali and Zaman, had been eliminated. The Imam wondered at the fate of the Keshavarz family, wiped out half by the Shah and half by the Islamic Republic. The manuscript of Professor Keshavarz, had, of course, been put to the torch.

He thought about his own book, *A Clarification of Questions,* in which he had tried to guide Muslims to absolute purity by answering some 3,000 questions on prayer, fasting, diet, hygiene, marriage, divorce, birth and death and burial, even taxation, trade and government. The purpose was to offer the rules of Islamic living, but not the reasons behind them. His only regret was that the printers had used the same cover as on the Grand Ayatollah Borujerdi's book, God bless his soul.

He had answered Question 2,854 that profit on a loan is forbidden, unless it is to a non-Muslim, according to Question 2,080. He answered Question 2,824 that the hands of foreigners who rule Muslims must be cut off. He murmured, "The infidel communists also say it somehow, but I was the one who *did* it."

He smiled in satisfaction at how thoroughly he had explained which deed is pure and which is not. The prayer of a menstruating woman, for example, is void because menstrual blood is impure. The Imam thought for a moment, "Too bad menstruation itself exists. I will never know all of God's wisdom." Khomeini was convinced that the code of purity he had expounded ruled his own thoughts, words and deeds. That is why corruption on earth had to be rooted out under his rule. But what was the difference between his code of purity and Zoroaster's "Good thoughts, good words, good deeds"? The difference, Khomeini thought, was between "pure" and "good." He should have clarified this question, too.

But on this day the Imam doubted himself for the first time. "Yes, I preached hatred, but I also showed the way to heaven. I may have put too much emphasis on purity—even though purity is the supreme value. So many men have been treated harshly because I considered them infidels or apostates.

"I still believe Sadam Hussain of Iraq was an infidel, but why did I have to continue waging a war and sacrifice a million—give or take a hundred thousand—dead and injured trying to oust him? God, was this bloody struggle with Sadam my duty? I admit to you the war was a tragic blunder repeated day after day, minute after minute, death after death! So many dead, so much destruction! I punished my own people for Sadam's adventurism! God Almighty, God erase my painful memories of the losses and forgive me!"

Khomeini now admonished himself, "Why didn't I terminate the war in one year, in two years, in five years, or even in seven years? But how could I—peace without victory would have been an admission of lethal blundering, of continuing the war even after the national boundaries had been secured. God, was the uprooting of Sadam Hussain worth even the life of one good Muslim? I am ashamed to admit I don't even care now what happened to him! I should have preached and practiced more peace and compassion than war and hatred . . ."

Khomeini's reflections were stilled for a moment, then resumed, "If I am an Imam, and the infallible Muslim leader I claim to be, then how could I have committed such grave errors of judgement, and worse yet, how could I acknowledge them to my disciples and adherents? Would not that admission make me look wrong and Dr. Keshavarz right in the eyes of the faithful —and in your eyes, God Almighty? Would not that destroy my inspired theory of government, unifying politics and religion, law and ethics, church and state, leader and God—you and me, and subordinating science to faith, and to you, the Creator of all things perceived by man? God Almighty, God rescue me from my dilemmas, from the torments of my soul! I beg of you."

The infinite patience, tenacity, savvy, courage and charisma of the Imam which had been assiduously cultivated to oust the Shah and to turn the nation into a cloister overcrowded with tyrant mullahs hovering over toiling, insecure, bored, wounded and dying citizens had borne fruit. The Imam ruled over great suffering without challenge. But, the curses of the hungry, of the homeless, of the sick, of the lame, of the tortured and of the orphans and widows growing day by day surrounded the Imam and gnawed at his flesh, bones and senses. The nation's constant sobbing and twisting in mortal agony, and the buzzing of his own useless sectaries were fatiguing the Imam to death. The Imam covered his big ears like the Shah had done; he closed his ascetic eyes and pulled his gown over his head, but the relentless cursing of the multitude broke through like a sonic boom.

The Imam even lashed out at the critics of the Islamic Republic in his own Islamic party and his own House of Representatives, but it did not work. At the end the Imam was drained and exhausted of questions, of answers, of clarifications, of purifications, of arguments, of politics, of praises, of curses, of blunders, of laws, and of wars. The infinite weariness of a whole life of struggle engulfed him and sucked his heart's core of all hopes. Khomeini finally admitted the inadmissible, "I wanted to win the love and mind of all the faithful forever, like His Holiness Imam Ali, I wanted to conquer the territories of the infidels for Islam like the respected and feared Khalif Omar, and I wanted to unite the Shiites and Sunnis into one big Muslim family, and I wanted to show the absolute goodness of the rule of Islam, but I have only achieved the opposite of my goals. I hope God and history will judge me by my intentions and not by my accomplishments, and I hope my loyal disciples will finish what I have begun."

The Imam, having already written and sealed his will, prayed to the Almighty that he was ready to receive the angel of death. God obliged and Khalkhali appeared at the door with beard, glasses and black wings on his back saying, "Salam Agha."

Khomeini was shocked. "You, Khalkhali, the angel of death!"

"Yes, Agha. God's will."

"You, you," Khomeini repeated.

"Yes, yes, Imam. You know I must not waver, your Holiness. You have come to go like everyone else! No exception for an Imam, not even for you!" So Khomeini, a great conqueror without arms, the magnificent leader of the revolution and the unmerciful leader of the counterrevolution, passed away. Allah-o Akbar, Allah-o Akbar.

Many Muslims around the world mourned. Veiled women screamed, slapped their faces, pulled their hair and tore their dresses. But at the same time a great many people breathed a sigh of relief. The passing away of the Imam shook the Islamic Republic to its roots. Iran would not be the same, and the world would not be the same without Imam Khomeini.

*　*　*　*　*

Finishing an address to a gathering of Iranians in New York, Pirooz remarked, "The Imam is dead, God Bless him for dying! The nation may now have peace!

"Remember years ago, lifting a woeful gloom, the Imam's homecoming infused a fire of ecstasy into the nation, lulling the perception, the imagination, and better judgement of the populace. In an exhilarating dizziness people believed the Imam's announcement, 'I will soon go to Qom and begin a life of piety.' Instead, soon afterwards, seemingly comical proclamations and regulations about dressing, eating, speaking, playing, working, and everything else followed causing ridicule and laughter in some quarters. But the Imam was serious and before the people could snap out of their joyful stupor and guard the revolution, his commands gripped the nation tightly with censorship, repression, executions and war.

"The Imam, also a brilliant actor, took the center stage to turn rapture to love, love to laughter, laughter to tears, tears to tragedy, tragedy to catastrophe. Now we have seen it all, the unsuspecting audience becoming the victims in a brutal play of history.

"Iranian exiles who had lost everything at home had to lose more abroad. They were ashamed, even fearful to admit to their nationality in most countries of refuge. The Imam had stripped them of their pride by giving Iran the stigma of lawlessness and violence.

"Meanwhile, the nation was used like a herd as though there existed no connection, no emotion, and no remembrance between the dead and the living and between the living and the unborn. Every young man falling on the battlefield signaled the death of some unborn. The school children were indoctrinated: 'You are a Muslim nation—not a nation of Iran. Your history started in Mecca around a black stone.' So to rule, the Islamic Republic tore the past, the present and the future apart, dismembering the nation physically, biologically, culturally and historically.

"On the New Year's Day, every year, the Imam promised again and again that he would win the war with Iraq in the coming year, but he only conquered more territory in heaven for the new martyrs. The Imam continued to praise the dead who were his fallen ambitions, his mistakes. So each new casualty appeared like an old mistake repeated once again! Publicly the Imam condemned the U.S. satan, but privately he begged them for military spare parts. He finally struck a deal with President Reagan releasing a few hostages held in Lebanon. The first flesh-for-weapons trade between the Islamic Republic and the United States. As a consequence, little trust survived—if the Imam's word was not reliable, whose was? In truth, this great Savior whom the people believed, loved and followed has been dead for some time. Now his body too, has finally died. But I fear the Islamic Republic will continue to cover up its incompetence and corruption by deception and terror. It is now up to the people to send the Islamic Republic after its exalted creator." Pirooz heard people clapping in sadness.

CHAPTER 32

The End

In the end, the world of the Professor was full of endings. Pirooz stood at his office window and looked out on a large parking lot with pine trees on three sides. Having just finished a lecture on the nature and extent of poverty in the United States, he was agitated.

"How many times can I repeat it? The hungry are not here to learn about the cause of hunger, and the well-fed students don't care. My God, how selfish economic man is."

He stared at Ali's final letter. He had already read the execution report in the newspaper. "I must call Sara, but what if she doesn't know he is dead? God damn it! I don't have the heart to tell her."

Pirooz then picked up the receiver, and the electrons he set in motion rushed in an instant to Sara's office on the *Guardian* in New York.

He recognized Sara's voice. "Hello, Sara."

"Hello, Professor."

"How are you?"

"Okay."

"And Cyrus?"

"Cyrus Keshavarz is just fine."

"I—I wanted to know if ..."

"Yes. They killed Ali, a candle light unconquered by vast darkness. What times! A saint is killed again."

The Professor agreed, "Yes, he was a light, a real saint, like Imam Ali his namesake! But, let's not forget the others—Zaman and Aram and thousands more."

Sara hurried to reply, "Sure. And I meant to ask about Arash and Baback, their children."

"They are safe and sound in Switzerland with Aram's father. I plan to visit them as soon as I can." Then he rushed to add, "Does Cyrus know about his father?"

"Yes, Cyrus has read his father's letter. Ali wrote that the best time of his life was getting to know Cyrus, even though at the time Ali had a broken leg and a broken heart. He loved Cyrus."

Pirooz explained, "I know. Ali wrote to me that he had to wage a battle every single night to convince himself anew that he should stay in Iran one more day and not pack and run to you and Cyrus. It is tragic that just as he tried to leave the country he was cut down."

Suddenly all words dried up in the throats of Pirooz and Sara, as though the telephone had fallen dead. Finally the trembling voice of Sara changed the subject. "Pirooz, when are you coming to visit us?"

Pirooz felt she was fighting tears. He replied immediately, "How about this weekend? Is it okay with you?"

"Yes, please come."

Pirooz said, "Cyrus might need my reassurance."

Sara added, "I need it, too."

Pirooz went on, hesitantly, "I really don't know what to say, not on the phone, anyhow."

"I agree," Sara said. "But I do have something to ask you."

"What?"

"About your promise to Ali."

"Promise?"

"To inform the world."

"Yes, of course."

"Are you planning on writing a book about the revolution?"

"Yes, and I have all the material I need." Then the Professor added, "I have decided to write a novel because it would give me greater freedom than the usual social science stuff."

Sara said enthusiastically, "Great idea! A novel is just the right form, but write a few pages before you come. That would be a good start, a good gift for all of us. With school closed next week you may want to stay longer than the weekend. I'll put a desk in the third bedroom. I'll let you have all my own notes and will do all the editing and typing throughout the novel for you."

The Professor said, "That is fine." Then he added, "It is nice to get an assignment from a former student. In any case, I'll let you know about my flight."

Sara said, "See you in a couple of days, Pirooz. Goodbye."

"Goodbye." Pirooz hung up and sighed. He had not known how to comfort Sara but all had gone well. She sounded strong and resolute.

He picked up Ali's letter and read the poem once more, the first and last one Ali ever wrote. The censors had not bothered to translate the letter written in English. Such letters were usually mailed without delay, a courtesy to the dead. Pirooz began to mumble to himself. "Sure, I will write the book, but for whom?'' The Professor felt injustice squeezing his throat and tears gathered in his eyes as he thought of Ali's poem, not really a poem, but a means to endure the nights while the Islamic Republic was toying with his life.

Cry for my revolution, Iran
   Cry for my life, caught in prison or the underground
   Cry for my love, brief then, only a dream
Spring is waiting on the wings of the Caspian Sea

Cry for my revolution, Iran
   Cry for my father, set on fire
   Cry for my brother blinded alive
   Cry for my sister raped in the halls
   Cry for my mother who lost her mind
   Cry for my son kidnapped by the CIA
   Cry for the fetus that was shot
   Cry for Hamid, for Aram, for Taghi, for Reza and for Maryam
   Cry for my friends and their friends fallen dead
   Cry for Iran trampled by Islamic hordes
Spring is coming north of the Elburz peaks

Cry for my revolution
   Still smouldering under my ashes
   Cry for the last hugs I never got from my son
   Cry for Sara, for the living
   Cry for Islam, fallen astray a thousand ways
Spring is here, water the fields and wait for me
   I will come back, Iran; I promise
I will be present—present for the revolution to come.

The Professor stepped to the window, wiped a tear with his sleeve, and tried to swallow his anger. Outside the window the sun sizzled and beat on the roofs of the cars in the parking lot. A heat mirage hovered over the asphalt, blurring everything along with his fears and setting inanimate objects in motion.

Still not quite sure about the nature of the book he knew he must write, Pirooz began imagining things. He saw Hussain, Dr. Keshavarz and Fatema sitting on the roof of a black car. Hussain's ears and eyes were heavily bandaged, for he was blind and deaf; his head rested on Fatema's lap as she prayed, her hands outstretched.

Fatema said, "God forgive the murderers," and Keshavarz responded, "In the day of judgement God will balance good against evil. It is all there in the Koran.''

Atop the white car next to them, Pirooz saw Maryam, the black maid of Keshavarz' household, in her silk wedding dress, the hem floating around her in the breeze. She pointed a finger at Pirooz and scolded, "Tell the world that Christians and Muslims snatched my ancestors and sold them like cattle. Tell the world that Savak agents kicked me in the chest."

Pirooz saw little Parvine screaming and fighting headless canaries which swirled around her head. She was on top of a blue Volkswagen Beetle which trembled violently. Helena rushed to help Parvine and tried to scare away the birds. Helena turned to Pirooz imploring, "Listen to Sara. Tell the world how my father disappeared in Argentina, how I disappeared fighting oppression in Chile, just when I was dreaming of becoming your wife."

The Professor then saw Hamid, Taghi, Zaman, Aram, Ali, and a grown-up Parvine in overalls on a red pickup truck. Barrels of guns pointed at them from all sides, but they appeared unruffled. Parvine said, "Tell the world I was shot by an American gun in the hands of U.S.-trained murderers." Zaman and Aram nodded. Ali said, "Tell the world about all the U.S. crimes in Iran." He raised his hand and announced, "One more thing, Professor. You've been right all along. The overthrow of a regime is just the first step. Even if the leftists had taken over, we could also have become corrupted by power. It is sad to learn only when you are dead that revolution is complex and has many phases, and can go wrong at any phase. The revolution must first happen in the souls and minds of the multitudes or else it can go astray."

The Professor blinked, then he saw Grand Ayatollahs Taleghani and Shariatmadari, Prime Minister Bazargan, Deputy Prime Minister Yazdi, Foreign Minister Ghotbzadeh, Dr. Chameron, President Banisadr and Dr. Sanjabi like football players in a huddle. All the Imam's men raised their heads, shook them and said in unison, "This Islamic Republic is not what we fought for. Professor Pirooz, history must record our objections." Bazargan added, "I dare not say what this regime is, but with God's help it may become an Islamic Republic!" Then Aram shouted at Bazargan, "The hell with it, even if it is a true Islamic Republic! Who gives a damn about religious hocus pocus in the twentieth century? It can't work."

Suddenly, out of thin air Bakhtiyar stepped forward and pointing to Aram announced, "This young man is correct, Mr. ex-President Banisadr, and Mr. ex-Prime Minister Bazargan. Remember, I warned all of you and the nation right from the start that the Islamic Republic is 'archaic and medieval.' Unfortunately, you were all so bewitched by the Ayatollah that even God's messenger could not have changed your mind!"

"But what about your accepting the Shah's offer of Premiership?" Bazargan replied.

Bakhtiyar retorted, "The Shah was finished anyway, history had passed him by. It really didn't matter who appointed me Premier!" Baktiyar paused and then admitted, "Had I been wise and rejected the Shah's offer I would have been standing on a higher moral and political plateau today. I would have been absolutely blameless and absolutely correct." Then Bakhtiyar murmured to himself loud enough for Pirooz to hear, "My God, I nearly lost my life on that foolish deal."

At that moment another group marched with determined faces up to Pirooz' second-floor window, floating in the air. A bearded man put his face up to the glass, filling the whole window. It was Karl Marx, who said solemnly, "If you do not disclose the facts about society and raise the consciousness of the populace to change society, you are no intellectual and you have failed history, man, science—socialism, truth and justice!"

The Professor rubbed his eyes. But there they were, all dead, yet all standing tall: Engels, Lenin, Mao, Gandhi, Ho Chi Minh, Lumumba, Che, Mossadegh, Martin Luther King, Arani, Ruzbeh, Ali, Hussain, Aram, Zaman, Abbas, Hamid Ashraf, Reza, Taghi.

Then the Professor watched as a huge flatbed truck drove into the parking lot. Nixon, Carter and Agnew were in the front seat. The Shah, Somoza, Pinochet, Batista, King Khalid, Marcos, Stroessner, Mobutu, Botha, General Park, Zia, and a whole host of dictators of the "Free World"—he had forgotten some of their names—rode in back. Khalkhali, Teherani, the Barber and the Butcher were way in back, waving their hands for recognition. Carter tried to leave the car but Nixon would not let him. He told Carter, "Your human rights campaign was a coverup like my own Watergate. Face it!"

President Nixon then raised his hand the way he used to on TV. "Let me make myself perfectly clear. Pirooz can't ruin my name any more than history has. Contaminating Vietnam with Agent Orange has ruined my name in history books all over the world. We called the Agent Orange a mere defoliant, but it sure was a killer. Yes, we conducted chemical warfare all right!" Vice-president Agnew added, "Me, too." Carter said softly, "Professor Pirooz, you can't make me look any more of a failure than Reagan already did in his presidential campaign against me." The Shah said, "No MIT SOB can prove I did wrong." Somoza said defiantly, "No matter what you say I can't be executed—I mean assassinated—twice." Pinochet sneered, "Send another friend to Chile and she will disappear just like Helena." Marcos of the Philippines shouted, "I have befriended all of the U.S. presidents during my presidency and I have billions of dollars stashed away—I have no worries. Don't forget what happened to Senator Aquino in the Manila airport." King Khalid of Saudi Arabia said, "Take this ten million dollars and shut up." Botha offered Pirooz both outstretched hands filled with uncut South African diamonds, and winked toward a couple of black slaves, offering them on the side. "Don't mention us!" they now chanted.

A contingent of U.S. politicians, businessmen, professors, lawyers, engineers, reporters and blue-collar workers then appeared in the Professor's scenario. A man in front shouted, "There is no use dragging us into your book. Making napalm bombs or no napalm, bribes from the Shah or no bribes, training death squads or not training, supporting the U.S. government or not, we are not responsible for anything overseas, we're just doing our jobs. We have our careers to worry about. You can't criticize everybody, Pirooz; no liberal, no conservative, no communist, no American, no Persian will buy your book." Ali's voice silenced everyone, "Do not pay attention to these self-righteous professionals. They are anonymous terrorists, just as I and my comrades are unknown revolutionaries."

Then the Professor saw Chairman Brezhnev of the USSR and Premier Hua Guofeng of China and several Eastern European leaders in a Red Army truck speed into the lot. Brezhnev spoke with a heavy accent and the rest nodded as if at a plenary Party conference. "Comrade Pirooz, you are a struggling socialist, and we appreciate that, but unfortunately you are only a generic socialist with no party, no programs and no discipline. Of course, this is not Marxist-Leninist, but we will forgive you for your generic tendencies if you do not mention us in your book. As you know, we practice Marxist self-criticism regularly and you are right, Comrade Pirooz, we should never have supported that imperialist rat, the Shah, but we needed the bargain price gas for our socialist development in order to fight world Imperialism." Suddenly all the leaders behind Brezhnev began to chant, "Natural gas, gas, gas! We needed the gas." Hua Guofeng repeated in Chinese, "Me, too, but not the gas. The red carpet treatment in Peking for Princess Ashraf was no good, was no good, no good at all. Besides, China should not have urged the U.S. to intervene on behalf of the Shah. That was a poor diplomatic move, because the Shah was a loser, anyhow."

Pirooz broke his silence and addressed Brezhnev. "As I understand it once capitalism is overthrown by the proletariat and the means of production are nationalized, then socialism will ensue and exploitation of man by man will cease. But how do you explain a new privileged class in the USSR? Why have you not helped the workers to expropriate the power of the elite instead of supervising the repression of dissident workers and intellectuals? I also want to register my protest over the war between fraternal states, China and Vietnam, the injurious conflicts within and among socialist states, the USSR's hegemony over Eastern Europpe and her intervention in Afghanistan. And don't you dare blame all of these contradictions on the menace of U.S. imperialism still—decades after the Soviet October Revolution! Remember martyrdom for socialism is dying for the spirit of socialism, not just the word. Respect the martyrs' wish-look! The eyes of their souls are fixed on you, the leader of the first socialist country in the world!"

Brezhnev, irritated, answered tersely, "Here you go again, Professor Pirooz. Stop being simplistic! Instead warn President Reagan to stop selling arms to governments that make people disappear and then using the illegal profits for more wrongdoings. Ask the President to obey the International Court in The Hague, cease the undeclared war in Nicaragua, and stop all the pretentions that he is for law even outside his order!"

Pirooz shot back, "Come on, Mr. Chairman! This is not a marxist answer to my criticism of contemporary socialist practice. President Reagan is not responsible for your mess! He is America's George III—in fact most presidents are—what do you expect? Thank God that the President's men have not yet blown up the planet trying to finish off the USSR, which Reagan often calls the 'evil empire'!"

Brezhnev retorted, "Professor Pirooz, write in your book that it is capitalism, not socialism, which is causing pervasive job insecurity and unemployment, debt and bankruptcy, cut-throat competition, the litigation explosion, family breakups, teacher strikes and students committing suicide by the thousands in the U.S."

"Anything else?" Pirooz goaded Brezhnev.

"Yes, write that the death of honesty, tycoons gobbling up companies, chewing them up and spitting out the workers, bursting overcrowded jails, a halo of pollution surrounding all life, cancer lurking at every corner, FBI lie detecting and urine testing of citizens, drug abuse clawing at souls and bodies, the spread of hunger and homelessness, the growth of nuclear stockpiles and the corrosive fear of war in the U.S. are the fault of capitalism." Brezhnev then raised his voice, "Whose empire is evil anyhow? Write about the empire of evil U.S. profiteers and the army of unemployed workers! Yes sir! Truth will eventually leak out in spite of the U.S. monopoly of world information media today."

Pirooz reacted impatiently, "America is my home now; I know its shortcomings. But Mr. Chairman, your long and repressing rule was not a credit to socialism either. Yes, truth will leak out in spite of all the censorship, including yours!"

Gorbachev entered the scene and promptly interrupted, "Never mind, comrade Brezhnev. The USSR has big problems but we shall overcome! Wait and see, Pirooz."

President Reagan then appeared on horseback from the other side and whispered to his Press Secretary who ran alongside, "Announce that our temporary problems are due to individuals' aberrations—simply human nature. But make no mention of God in this announcement, since alert citizens may figure out that we are blaming God for the dark side of human nature in order to cover up the faults of free enterprise."

Pirooz shouted, "Ah, Mr. President! Blaming the big mess on the misguided or crooked individuals—not the system, not your darling—free enterprise.''

Reagan responded, ''Are you a legal alien?''

''Yes, I am legal.''

''What are you after, anyhow?''

''I am after justice.''

''Between us, you are an idealist, you are alone.''

''No, Mr. President! Most people are for justice except the greedy, the fooled, the silent, or the silenced.''

Reagan smiled triumphantly and replied, ''Your exceptions make up the majority of Americans! I am the President, I ought to know Professor.''

Pirooz, jarred by Reagan's point, managed to respond, ''Mr. President, one more thing.''

''Yes?'' said the passing leader.

''Remember you are the President of the U.S. and not the President of the world. Heal the ills of America; leave the world alone to heal itself!''

The President, ignoring Pirooz, whipped his horse into a waiting helicopter. Pirooz' last words were lost in the roar of the blades.

Then the Professor imagined he heard the Dean's voice arguing, ''It's no use, Professor Pirooz. There will be no money or promotion for you from this book. In fact to be frank, this book will count against you. That sabbatical you're hoping for will never come. Also remember, your colleagues will ridicule you, a scientist wasting his time writing stories.'' The dean uncharacteristically pointed his finger at him. ''I remind you, Pirooz, you will pay for it.''

Then Eric from way in the back waved his hand for attention, as if still in a classroom. ''And you can't write the novel in English. You're a foreigner. And even if you do write it, most publishers in the Free World will respect a CIA, an FBI or an editor's tip to reject it. You know your book would be considered worse than all the paperbacks printed in the U.S! People don't want to know about your so-called facts! The real facts are found in the President's memoirs, not yours! And, in case your book is printed, the critics will ignore it or kill it. No one will read your book or believe it!''

Nixon took up the argument. ''No! You can't do it! Your book would not be anything like my memoirs—my truth! And nobody knows you!''

Then a contingent of mullahs, serious and determined, led by Ayatollah Ardabili, Chief Justice of the Islamic Republic, waved a portrait of the Imam and mounted the car roofs. Chief Justice Ardabili warned, ''If you write that the Islamic Republic is the counterrevolution, we will curse you and send guards to beat you up. If you return home we will execute you.''

The Professor noticed Shamil and Kamil in the branches of a tall tree, like monkeys watching and pointing at different groups. By now the forms of thousands of people, only some of whom Pirooz recognized, had gathered and were standing on top of thousands of cars. Some chanted, "Tell the world! Keep your promise," while others said, "Don't waste your time. Don't endanger what you have."

Then millions of Iranians poured over the horizon. They had lost legs, arms, shoulders, chins, eyes, ears and skin, and some had faces with a hole left where mouths used to be. The lame were assisted by the others. A leaden gloom plated all their faces, all interest in life stamped out. Some cried, some shouted, "Tell the Imam to stop the war with Iraq! We have had enough!" Then they chanted, "We despair, we are lost. The whole nation is lost!"

Then Imam Khomeini, reclining in his bed, appeared from nowhere and declared, "The Islamic Republic forbids crying! I know the State Treasury is empty, I know shelter, food and petroleum are scarce and rationed, I know only a few planes, tanks and explosives are left, I know most of our youth are dead, maimed, dodging the draft or escaping the country, but I will not stop the war—I will not even consider it! My good Muslims, if you want peace without victory pray to God to take me away!"

Pirooz, agitated, saw himself outside pointing at him, "Be committed to human rights, to the survival of the nation and of the truth! Write the book! What are you waiting for?"

The Professor turned away from the panorama outside his window and covered his face. He banged his desk repeatedly with his fist, so hard that the secretary knocked at the door. "Are you okay, Professor Pirooz?" "Yes, yes." Pain rushed up and down his soul. The thoughts flew out of his mind as he decided, "I will not read Ali's poem anymore. His nightmares and his life have become my hallucinations. I can't bear it! I can't live with this knowledge in my head. I must dig it out, write it down. This is the best I can do for my life. I will do it no matter what. I couldn't help fight for the revolution or against the counterrevolution, but writing this book is part of the story—it is my revolution!" Then he mumbled to himself, "In the U.S. I will live like a dissident lives in the USSR. If not here in the U.S., I will publish the book in another country, maybe in another language."

He rushed downstairs to his car. The parking lot was empty except for the silent cars. Two squirrels sat where Shamil and Kamil had been.

Pirooz drove home recklessly, anxious to start work. The unwritten book had waited too long. He poured a glass of iced tea to calm himself down as many thoughts pressed him for recognition at the same time.

Pirooz put a white sheet of paper on the desk. He felt its silent but persuasive demand. Suddenly the sheet stretched, in his imagination, into a vast flat desert land. On the sandy surface he recognized a thousand footprints, fingerprints, faceprints, heartprints and soul prints like on a battlefield which had just been cleared of the corpses. There, further up he noticed a huge clef followed by music notes. Upon deciphering them, he heard the first four notes of Beethoveen's number five in his mind, those powerful awakening sounds—the fate knocking at the door, at his door. "What is, or what ought to be my fate at this juncture?" he asked. He thought of the impossibility of one person ever filling the vast zones of darkness and ambiguity between cause and effect, between biography and history, between justice and injustice, between truth and falsehood. "Can all people thinking together find the answers?" he asked then wondered, "How should I, even imperfectly, transform the souls, the society, the history, the subconscious into black scribbles—a series of meaningful words on a white page? Does this vast desert of history need my prints too, would words left by me be worth the effort?" Then he heard the fate knocking at his will, urging him on, and so he began to write.

The Professor's thoughts, old reruns, flowed like water down a hill, with no resistance on his part. "No single force in the universe is in command. There is no beginning, no end; everything is beginning, everything ending. Man struggles alone and uncertain, but his dreams remain at a distance. The individual is glued to the crowd and, with clouds, is held by gravity. Each man's destiny depends on all the others, as others' destinies depend on him. The individual is alone, yet he is carried away by the collective surge. Man makes choices, yet he is not free. He is responsible for his motions and emotions, yet he cannot turn them on and off.

"Each man's perception is unique and his thoughts are fuzzy. They are not black, not white, not even grey. Motivations are confused; clarity is in the fifth dimension, neither here nor there. Worse still are the conflicting thoughts that fill my head. Can they ever resolve themselves into a whole, just as they arise from a single brain? Oh, that would be the day that all the confusion ends." Then he began to find some answers; isolated ideas gathering force like flood water broke the dam of his resistance.

"In the beginning the world is full of beginnings."

"There is no history, no man, no cannibal, no slaveowner, no feudal landlord, no capitalist, no commissar to fight over possessions."

"How can anyone ever know where he is being taken at any one time?"

"True, I have had plans for my life, but I have learned that plans once made have their own minds!"

"Damn it, the Shah kept the nation in the dark, so now we have a darkened revolution which the mullahs can control. The revolution must happen in the souls and minds of the multitudes or else it can go astray."

In front of the firing squad Ali, the unknown revolutionary, shouted, "I will come back, Iran."

"The mourning will begin after the recognition, when the unknown revolutionary—dead and forgotten—is resurrected in history. This book must do that," Pirooz told himself.

Why is love being shoved aside by conflicts in hearts and minds in America? When will the people demand honesty from themselves as they do from others? How long will the leaders lie, half lie, or be allowed to lie to protect greed and violence—two faces of the same demon? How long will history—created by us—roam over us one by one, as insignificant seasons fly? Who but us can save us from us? Who? Pirooz read these questions he had just written, then scratched them out as wishful dreams.

The Professor stopped writing. He stood up and paced around the coffee table a few times struggling with competing thoughts. He began to pack to leave for New York.

* * * * *

A few days later Pirooz and Sara and Cyrus, resting on an aging green bench in Central Park, were gazing at a placid pond surrounded by weeping willows in spots. Ducks swam carefree as though nothing had happened or would ever happen to disturb their peace. Joggers in no hurry loped past them. Melodies of a guitar barely reached them from far afield as did the sun's gentle rays through the leisurely dancing leaves. The three, deep in their thoughts, were unaware of the sounds, colors and motion engulfing them. A tired horse dragging a carriage about with lovers inside holding hands caught Cyrus' attention—reminding him of Iran, the country he often called "home." Suddenly, Cyrus grabbed Pirooz' and Sara's hands in his, and announced in excitement a just discovered thought, "You know what?"

"What?" Sara and Pirooz responded in unison.

"When I grow up, if I have a son I will call him Ali."

Sara asked, "What if you have a daughter?"

Cyrus replied, "Well, then I will name her after Aunt Zaman."

Pirooz smiled and inquired, "What else will you do when you grow up?"

"I will go back to Iran and finish what my father started."

* * * * *

"I will come back, Iran!"

Afterword

Characters of this novel stand for themselves, but they are also symbols. Ali represents the unknown altruistic revolutionary, Sara the part of America which is sensitive and wants to learn, Eric the part that considers the U.S. always right and believes might makes right, Pirooz the concerned observer who becomes deeply and dangerously involved with his reportage. Zaman represents the awakening Iranian woman, and liberated women everywhere, her mother Fatema the passive traditional woman, her father Dr. Keshavaraz the intellectual who tries to stay on the sidelines but is swept up by the historical events, and Hussain her brother the sacrificial lamb of Islam. Helena stands for numerous persons who have disappeared struggling for freedom in the so-called "free world." Aram represents a repressed member of a minority group anywhere in the world, anytime in history.

The fictional death of Ayatollah Khomeini stands for the real death of the great hope of the Shiite Muslims embodied in the Imam. The CIA stands for the force of darkness overseeing virtually all of the "free world." Cyrus stands for the Iran that was taken hostage by the CIA and freed by Ali. He is also Ali's legacy: "I will come back, Iran."

Manoucher Parvin is a scholar and human rights activist who teaches at University of Akron in Ohio. He has taught at Columbia University and the City University of New York previously. His numerous essays in social sciences have been published in major international journals and some have been translated into other languages.

ORDER FORM

Please send _____ copy(ies) of *Cry for My Revolution, IRAN* @ $14.95 each.

My payment of $_____ is enclosed.

NAME _____

ADDRESS _____

CITY _____ STATE _____ ZIP _____

Please include $1.50 for postage and handling for the first book, and $0.75 for each additional book. California residents add 6% sales tax. All payments must be made in U.S. dollars.

Mazdâ Publishers
P.O. Box 2603
Costa Mesa, CA 92626/U.S.A.
Phone: (714) 751-5252

انتشارات مزدا

ORDER FORM

Please send _____ copy(ies) of *Cry for My Revolution, IRAN* @ $14.95 each.

My payment of $_____ is enclosed.

NAME _____

ADDRESS _____

CITY _____ STATE _____ ZIP _____

Please include $1.50 for postage and handling for the first book, and $0.75 for each additional book. California residents add 6% sales tax. All payments must be made in U.S. dollars.

Mazdâ Publishers
P.O. Box 2603
Costa Mesa, CA 92626/U.S.A.
Phone: (714) 751-5252

انتشارات مزدا

ORDER FORM

Please send _____ copy(ies) of *Cry for My Revolution, IRAN* @ $14.95 each.

My payment of $_____ is enclosed.

NAME _____

ADDRESS _____

CITY _____ STATE _____ ZIP _____

Please include $1.50 for postage and handling for the first book, and $0.75 for each additional book. California residents add 6% sales tax. All payments must be made in U.S. dollars.

Mazdâ Publishers
P.O. Box 2603
Costa Mesa, CA 92626/U.S.A.
Phone: (714) 751-5252

ORDER FORM

Please send _____ copy(ies) of *Cry for My Revolution, IRAN* @ $14.95 each.

My payment of $_____ is enclosed.

NAME _____

ADDRESS _____

CITY _____ STATE _____ ZIP _____

Please include $1.50 for postage and handling for the first book, and $0.75 for each additional book. California residents add 6% sales tax. All payments must be made in U.S. dollars.

Mazdâ Publishers
P.O. Box 2603
Costa Mesa, CA 92626/U.S.A.
Phone: (714) 751-5252